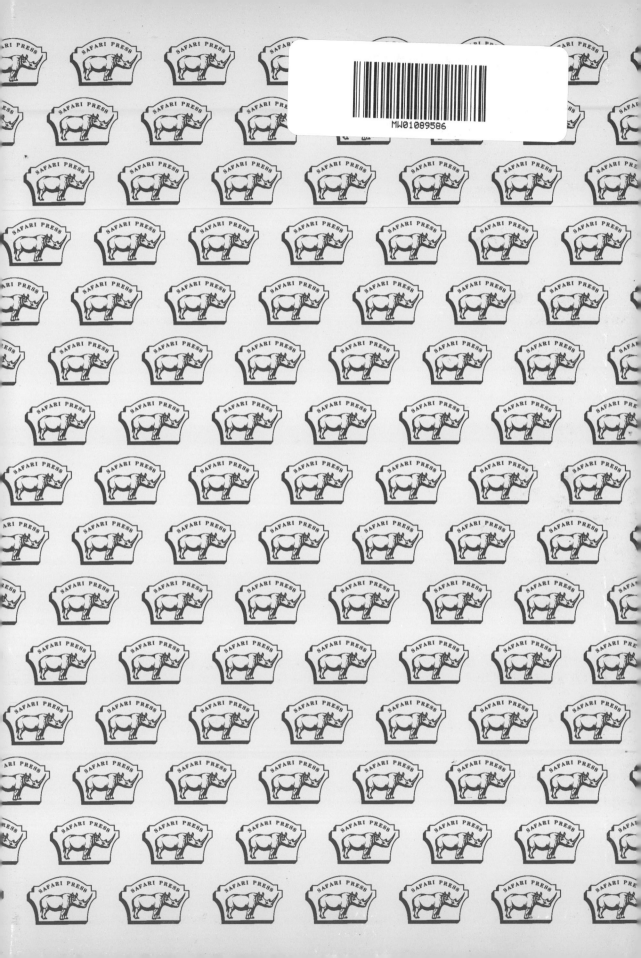

Under the African Sun

Under the African Sun

Forty-Eight Years of Hunting the African Continent

Dr. Frank C. Hibben

Safari Press Inc.

P. O. Box 3095, Long Beach, CA 90803

Under the African Sun copyright © 1999 by Dr. Frank C. Hibben; artwork copyright © Paul Bosman.   All rights reserved. No part of this publication may be used or reproduced in any form or by any means, electronic or mechanical reproduction, including photocopy, recording, or any information storage and retrieval system, without permission from the publisher.

The trademark Safari Press ® is registered with the U.S. Patent and Trademark Office and in other countries.

Hibben, Dr. Frank C.

First edition

Safari Press Inc.

1999, Long Beach, California

ISBN 1-57157-116-7

Library of Congress Catalog Card Number: 98-60902

10 9 8 7 6 5 4 3 2

Readers wishing to receive the Safari Press catalog, featuring many fine books on big-game hunting, wingshooting, and sporting firearms, should write to Safari Press Inc., P.O. Box 3095, Long Beach, CA 90803, USA. Tel: (714)894-9080 or visit our Web site at www.safaripress.com.

Table of Contents

Foreword

It has been my distinct pleasure to get to know Dr. Frank Hibben well over the past decade. Soon after we initially met, we both felt a strong kinship and common outlook on life that has evolved into an uncommon friendship. We have spent many evenings in our respective trophy rooms sharing stories of his safaris and shikars over the past fifty years. As I have come to know Frank, my respect and admiration for him as a man have grown well beyond his accomplishments in the hunting field. As a renowned archaeologist (Princeton and Harvard) and an avid hunter, he brings to the reader a unique perspective in these tales of Africa.

Frank has experienced hunting in Africa in a way that has long since disappeared. His special insight into the prehistory of the continent combined with his extensive hunting experience weaves a tapestry that connects prehistoric meat hunters to the continuing legacy of hunting in this extraordinary land.

Last year we returned to an area in northern Zimbabwe where he had hunted and done archeological work nearly thirty years ago. I had been there several times myself, and it was like a dream come true for me to return there with Frank to share a traditional African safari and get his observations on how the Chete area had changed in three decades. Except for the fact that the rhino, once so plentiful in Chete, are gone, the bush remains pretty much the same. Around a campfire overlooking Lake Kariba, we spent three glorious weeks listening intently to Frank's reminiscences of nearly fifty years of hunting in Africa. I often found myself regretting that I'd been born sixty years too late to have had similar experiences.

On this trip we shared a great buffalo hunt in the thick mopane bush and a rare daytime leopard. One day, while I chased an elusive klipspringer through the Ruzi Gorge, Frank and his beautiful wife, Marilyn, spent the day mapping a Paleolithic hunting camp on the rim. That evening he described the site so vividly and showed us the tools he had collected. Through his stories he breathed life back into those ancient hunters who had stalked the same ground 100,000 years before us.

I hope that this foreword gives you a picture of the remarkable man whose hunting life experiences are chronicled in these pages. Every time

I meet Frank I ask, "How are you doing?" and he replies, "Not as I please." It was not until our safari last year that I really understood his reply. Upon returning from a long day of walking through the thick mopane, I met him admiring the setting sun on the banks of the Ruzi. His reply to my standard greeting deviated from the norm. Basking in the fading afternoon sunlight when asked how he was doing, Frank simply replied, "Fine." It was immediately clear to me that it is when Frank is in the bush on safari that he is most at home.

I trust that through the words of my good friend and fellow hunter, Frank Hibben, you too will feel the excitement of hunting under the African sun.

Albert A. Gutierrez
11 June 1998
Albuquerque, New Mexico

Introduction

The writings of Frank C. Hibben have been entertaining, informing, and inspiring readers for more than fifty years. He is not an outdoor writer by vocation but rather a highly regarded professor emeritus at the University of New Mexico, where many believe him to be the most mesmerizing lecturer in the history of that university. He is an internationally recognized scholar who began his brilliant academic career by taking his bachelor's degree at Princeton University, his master's degree in zoology at the University of New Mexico, and his Ph.D. in archeology at Harvard University. In the course of his professional life, he became one of the world's best-known and respected archeologists. He has published numerous scholarly articles and books on archeology and anthropology, and his teaching and writings have influenced several generations of students and colleagues. He, and the students who studied under him, have led the University of New Mexico to a position of world prominence in the fields of archeology and anthropology.

Because he began hunting in Africa and other remote parts of the world more than forty years ago, Dr. Hibben's accounts of hunting and safari life offer an interesting new perspective from those of today. Although he hunted with the best of the safari companies and with outstanding white hunters, safari life in the 1950s was considerably less safe than it is now and often was difficult and uncomfortable. Even though the risks and challenges were greater, Dr. Hibben clearly thrived on high adventure, and, by constantly exploring new territory and exposing himself to hardship and danger, he has collected premium examples of nearly all of the big-game animals of Africa. He frequently combined hunting trips with archeology as he traveled to that continent's most remote and inaccessible locations.

It is as a conservationist, however, that Frank Hibben has most distinguished himself from other hunters and writers. In spite of popular opinion to the contrary, most hunters are genuinely committed to conservation. Dr. Hibben's commitment has been profound, and his life's work clearly shows that he stands in the tradition of George Bird Grinnell, Charles Sheldon, and Aldo Leopold as an extraordinary writer and a leading proponent of conservation. He served as a member of the New Mexico Fish and Game Commission for thirty years, including twenty-eight years as its chairman. Although he is best known in the academic world for his work in archeology and anthropology, he is also a wildlife biologist, doing extensive research on mountain lions while completing his master's degree in zoology. He did not simply preside over the fish and game commission during his tenure, but led the commission with the same energy and vigor that he displays as a scholar, hunter, and adventurer. During his three decades of leadership, the commission developed an outstanding program that has continued to place the state in the forefront as a model for fish and game management.

Dr. Hibben was one of the first to sound the alarm about the threats to Asian and African wildlife posed by overpopulation, the expansion of agriculture, loss of habitat, and market hunting (the poaching of rhinoceros and elephant for decorative and supposed medicinal uses of horn and ivory). He was a pioneer in the effort to convince the newly emerging independent African nations to conserve and protect game animals as a sustainable resource, and he lobbied for the continuation of a hunting industry as a very important vehicle to their future economic development as well as to the conservation of their wildlife.

He also became increasingly concerned and discouraged about the future of African and Asian game. In the 1960s, while serving as both the chairman of the fish and game commission and also as the president of the New Mexico Wildlife Conservation Association, he led the state to adopt a program entitled, Save From Extinction. It is universally agreed that the establishment of this program and its early success was the result of Frank Hibben's dedication and enthusiasm and his untiring efforts on its behalf.

Dr. Hibben had first conceived of saving some of the world's threatened and endangered species while hunting in the Atlas Mountains of Algeria after World War II. Barbary sheep, which had been so numerous there, were nearly extinct, and he believed that if they could be captured and brought to New Mexico they would fill an ecological niche and thereby serve the dual purpose of saving them as a species and establishing a new and valuable game animal in North America.

The game department was not enthusiastic to his idea, and there were many in the cattle industry who opposed introducing any new species into new Mexico regardless of the study, care, and scientific controls that night accompany the releases. He did, however, convince the commission to approve the program and to provide limited funds for the purchase of Barbary sheep. Because the funds provided by the commission were woefully inadequate, Frank Hibben helped fund the Save From Extinction program with his personal resources and convinced other hunter-conservationists to contribute more than a million dollars to the program.

He not only devoted his considerable skills as a leader, fund-raiser, and organizer to the commission's relocation program, he also agreed to serve on the Albuquerque Zoo Board and finally became the director of the Albuquerque Zoo in order to provide facilities for breeding and releasing the animals. He also used his persuasive powers to convince the governments of various African and Asian nations of the value of the project and to gain the cooperation of multiple United States government agencies whose approval was required in order to import the animals.

After he succeeded in releasing Barbary sheep in the mountains of New Mexico, Dr. Hibben and the commission then introduced ibex from Siberia and Iran and gemsbok and kudu from Southwest Africa, now known as Namibia. He traveled with friends and former students to southwest Africa to work with Walter Schultz, a rancher who shipped African species to zoos throughout the world. There, Dr. Hibben personally helped capture the kudu and gemsbok. This relocation and introduction program has been an outstanding success, and all of the introduced species are now roaming freely on the public lands of New Mexico.

It is impossible to overstate the importance of Frank Hibben's leadership in developing, promoting, and financing these new approaches to wildlife conservation and management. It was through his tireless efforts that these methods and techniques came to be accepted as the best hope of saving seriously endangered species. Dr. Frank C. Hibben will be remembered as a great hunter, prolific and prominent anthropologist and archeologist, writer, but his greatest legacy will be his efforts in the conservation of the world's wildlife.

James S. Underwood, Jr.
December, 1998

Acknowledgments

This book would never have been put together if it had not been for the encouragement and persuasion of world-class hunter and conservationist Ludo Wurfbain, also the publisher of *Under the African Sun*. In almost every episode in this volume, Ludo could apprise the situation better than any other sportsman I know because Ludo has "been there and done that."

Under the African Sun probably never would have been completed without the good offices of my wife, Marilyn. Marilyn has been with me to most of these African countries and loves Africa as I do. The only thing I ever heard her complain about in Africa was a cobra sharing her shower.

Dedication

Under the African Sun is affectionately dedicated to Ngoro, my Masai gunbearer and tracker on some twenty safaris. The Masai are not a hunting tribe but are noted for their bravery. On three occasions Ngoro undoubtedly saved my life. During one tense moment in the Northern Frontier of Kenya, Ngoro jumped in front of a charging elephant to give me the one or two seconds I badly needed. In two other encounters Ngoro attracted the charges of enraged buffalo. Most important of all, Ngoro is my friend and one of the main reasons I want to return to Africa—again and again.

Prologue

After the Boer War, a small number of sportsmen, mostly British, went to South Africa to hunt the animals of the veld. The story of the last of the South African game herds is told in such books as *A Hunter's Wanderings in South Africa* by Frederick Selous. Other hunters turned to places more difficult to reach, such as the Sudan, Abyssinia, and Somalia.

The majority of sportsmen, however, turned to East Africa, where the game herds were relatively untouched even into the twentieth century. The increase in numbers of American hunters going to Africa began with the classic hunt of Theodore Roosevelt. The beloved Teddy, following a lifelong desire to see and hunt African game, refused the nomination for another term as President of the United States in 1908. Four months later, Teddy was on his way to Africa, where he stayed a full year. He took with him a retinue of sportsmen and naturalists, for he wanted to record the flora and fauna of this last segment of unspoiled Africa, as well as to hunt, before it was too late. Following Roosevelt was the great hunter and naturalist, Carl E. Akeley. It was Akeley who created the greatest monument to the hunter Roosevelt by founding and designing the Roosevelt African Hall of the American Museum of Natural History in New York.

With the arrival of sportsmen avid to go on safari but lacking any knowledge of the country, the animals, or the dangers of both, what has come to be a typical African institution gradually came into being. This was the white hunter.

At first, the white hunters were ivory shooters or settlers who took European and American hunters on safari as a matter of convenience or personal obligation. Early in the twentieth century, however, a regular class of professional hunters developed—men who organized safaris as a business and guided sportsmen as a profession. Probably nowhere else in the world today is a professional hunter more necessary than in Africa.

In the old days of the foot safari, the white hunter acted more as a guide than in any other capacity. If the would-be sportsman did not have a resistance to malaria—and a considerable amount of common sense and an instinct for self-preservation as well—he probably did not survive. With the development of the motorized safari, however, the white hunter came into his own. Without the offices of the white hunter, the whole safari could not function and the hunt would be a dismal failure, if not a complete disaster. Realizing that hunters from Europe and the States were willing to pay fat prices to enjoy the "big league" hunting in Africa, a number of men in East Africa proclaimed themselves white hunters and began to organize safaris. Some of these—ex-elephant hunters or simply colonials who had done a bit of hunting on their own—were dismal failures in the role of white hunter. These men were capable enough hunters by themselves, but they often lacked the organizational ability to get together a complicated safari and make it work. Many of these early white hunters found that they couldn't stomach some of their clients. A few of the "sportsmen" wanted to shoot animals by the hundreds; others proved themselves cowardly when facing dangerous game.

Out of these early attempts to make safaris and African hunting a real business, there emerged a class of white hunters with the requisite qualifications for success. As one sportsman put it, his white hunter had to be a "businessman, leader, psychologist, linguist, hero, and a nice fellow, all rolled into one."

As most African safaris move cross-country with little regard for the few roads or settlements, the white hunter has to know the terrain. If a client wants a top specimen of a particular kind of game, his white hunter must know the place to get the trophy. Knowledge of where to go to get particular trophies is the stock in trade of the white hunter.

The successful white hunter has an organized band of "safari boys": gunbearers, trackers, skinners, camp boys, cook, and assistants. This crew, although they are called boys, may include veterans of sixty years or more of hunting and tracking. They answer to the white hunter; they are paid by him; and their loyalty belongs to him. They may answer to the white hunter, but without them, a safari would never be able to leave camp.

Of course, the wild animals themselves are the major reason for the presence of the white hunter. A novice, even though he might be an accomplished hunter in his home terrain, might not know what to do in the midst of a herd of rampaging buffalo. Perhaps the nimrod would be uncertain whether it is wiser to fire or to fall back when an elephant sticks out his ears or thrusts up his trunk. The white hunter, a man who has spent years among these animals, is able to admonish his client to stand firm, or to cover his retreat if it becomes necessary to retire. In the last resort, the white hunter must have nerves of iron and an excellent aim. With his double rifle, he must back up the client's play. When clients, overly nervous or careless in their shooting, wound a dangerous animal, the white hunter must go into heavy cover after the game, to see that it is killed quickly and painlessly before it becomes a menace to the next person to pass that way.

It is important for many clients that the white hunter have knowledge of trophy-sized animals. Given the tremendous amount of money spent on a safari and on the necessary licenses, the white hunter must be able to judge at a glance whether an elephant's tusks will weigh 100 pounds each or only 75. The white hunter must be able to tell, by looking through his binoculars, whether an eland has 28-inch horns and is an ordinary specimen, or 30-inch horns and an excellent trophy. All of these judgments and decisions require years of practice, and must be made under field conditions, through heat haze and at great distances. The results of these judgments make the difference between a very successful safari and a satisfied client, and a mediocre trip and a hunter who will never return.

At times, the greatest headaches for the white hunter are not the dangerous animals but the clients themselves. A man and his wife may come on safari together, and should trouble develop, the white hunter finds himself the mediator of their quarrels. Several hunting partners may organize a safari. Although these men may have hunted many years together back in the States, in Africa the situation is different. An elephant charges, and one of the partners proves himself a coward. Or one of the men bags an outstanding trophy and boasts about it. If friction develops, the white hunter must diplomatically hold the group together.

Not the least of the offices of the successful white hunter is keeping his clients healthy. The early explorers, with poor knowledge of tropical diseases and an inadequate supply of medicines, often died. Stanley lost both of his companions; most of the early explorers ultimately became victims of incurable malaria. With modern prophylactics for malaria and a medicine chest well stocked for eventualities, however, the modern safari client need have no fear. But the white hunter must be vigilant. Much of the water in Africa contains belhartzia, a nasty organism that enters the body and finally develops into flukes or worms. There are other more visible dangers, such as poisonous snakes: Cobras, puff adders, and mambas are common in the game country. A white hunter can steer his client clear of most of these snakes, and there are seldom casualties from this direction.

Sunstroke was once greatly feared by the early explorers. Even Teddy Roosevelt wore a pith helmet and a spine pad to protect himself from the dangerous rays of the African sun. Modern white hunters, however, have found that with ordinary precautions, the African sun is no more dangerous than a bright day at Coney Island.

Not the least concern of the white hunter is the food on a safari. In the early walking safaris, the hunters carried hardtack, and lived on the meat of the animals they shot as they moved. In the modern motorized cavalcade, the successful white hunter trains a native cook to make everything from filet mignon of gazelle to crêpe suzette.

Only a few white hunters of the early days had all of the qualifications for success. Those who did not soon dropped the business, or went back to ivory hunting. Those who succeeded, however, achieved fame. Such names as George Lucy, John Hunter, and George Cuninghame are remembered from the days of Teddy Roosevelt. White hunters such as Alexander Dugmore and Syd Downey earned the gratitude of hundreds of clients, who rate these men as the finest individuals they have ever met.

As increasing numbers of sportsmen poured money into the hunting safari, some of the successful white hunters formed safari companies. Perhaps the best known of these were Ker and Downey, White Hunters Limited, Safariland, Lawrence-Brown Safaris, and Selby and Holmberg. During the keenly competitive days after World War II, some of these companies were forced to close. Safariland dissolved, and the various white hunters in its company went out on their own or joined other groups. Andrew Holmberg and Harry Selby, two of the outstandingly successful white hunters of our time, dissolved their partnership, each continuing his work alone.

With the tremendous postwar increase of the safari business, it was inevitable that a number of men who were in no way qualified for the job should declare themselves white hunters. Many of these newcomers lacked some or all of the qualifications of the successful white hunter. Clients unfortunate enough to go on safari with these unqualified individuals invariably returned from their trips bitterly disappointed and without the trophies they had anticipated. Partly to guard against these upstart agents, the white hunters of East Africa organized an association to which they admitted only those who had proved themselves in the field. The East African Professional Hunters Association, consisting of some thirty members, includes most of the men who can truly call themselves white hunters.

Not all of the professional white hunters who appeared in the Congo, French Equatorial Africa, Southwest Africa, Angola, Rhodesia, Mozambique, and Somalia were of the high caliber of those of the Association. Some outside of East Africa proved to have all of the qualifications of the white hunters of East Africa. Others had much to learn and learned it the hard way. Practically none of the white hunters in the various countries of Africa were able to copy the plush safaris of Kenya. The well-trained safari boys, and the smooth-running organization of the safaris that leave Nairobi year after year, are without equal on the Dark Continent. Safari agents in other countries may charge as much, but they do not put on as good a trip.

For those on safari in various parts of Africa, there are over one hundred species of game animals from which to choose. These range all the way from the tiny dik-dik (an antelope that weighs no more than eight pounds) to the African elephant (which may weigh as much as eight tons).

All animals that are hunted are divided into various classes of big game. Many of the antelope and gazelle are classed as "plains game." These animals—such as the wildebeest, hartebeest, oryx, impala, eland, Grant gazelle, and a host of smaller gazelle—are found in herds and habitually occupy open country. The plains game of South and East Africa were the first to feel the brunt of the colonization of the open grasslands, for that is where these animals graze.

To the hunter, plains game is interesting in its variety and beauty, but seldom is it a major objective. Plains-dwelling antelope and gazelle are often a source of meat for the hunter, or are used as bait for the capture of lion or leopard. The chief interest of the modern sportsman in plains game is in the thrill of seeing them, and in bagging a large male specimen of each species carrying a trophy-sized head of horns.

Quite in another class are the rare antelope and gazelle that live in special habitats, such as swamps, deserts, arid brushland, or dense jungle. Some of these animals are fairly common in their own type of terrain, and therefore are less coveted trophies to the sportsman. The waterbuck, for example, is normally not found in open grasslands or very far from water. In cover along streams, or near lakes or marshes, waterbuck are numerous and, in some places, one of the commonest animals on the continent. The waterbuck, because of an oily secretion under his skin, is one of the very few animals in the African repertoire that makes poor eating.

Such animals as the gerenuk, or giraffe gazelle, which normally inhabits dry, brushy country like the Northern Frontier District of Kenya or the dry washes of Somalia, live in a totally different environment. In their chosen habitat, gerenuk are common. The sportsmen hunting in this kind of country may shoot gerenuk for meat supply, and they are very good eating. Usually a sportsman in gerenuk country will try conscientiously to find a very large bull carrying a set of heavy, long horns. Even more specialized are the true desert-dwelling antelope and gazelle. These animals are adapted (in some cases) to living in terrain with little or no water or cover. Some species, such as the addax of the Sahara, may never drink at all! They derive their supply of moisture from the scant vegetation of their desert home. The pursuit of such desert dwellers as the gemsbok of Southwest Africa, or the white oryx and the addax of the Sahara, challenges the sportsman who wants to add hardship to the list of difficulties of attaining a trophy. Even when the hunter has managed to get into the difficult places where these animals live, he may have to settle for any specimen of one of these animals, with no thought of trying to find a large bull of the species.

A few of the African antelope live in such difficult terrain that it is virtually impossible for the hunter, even armed with a modern rifle, to get a specimen. The lechwe and sitatunga fall into this category, and very few modern sportsmen can boast of having a specimen in their collection. Both the lechwe and sitatunga are swamp-dwelling antelope. These animals have elongated hoofs that enable them to walk on treacherous floating swamp vegetation too thick for a boat to penetrate and too thin to support the weight of a man. The lechwe, such as the red and black lechwe of Rhodesia and the Nile lechwe of the Sudan, are fairly numerous in the few places where the swamplands are to their liking. Because of their singular adaptation to these wetlands, the lechwe are one of the rarest game animals sought by the African hunter. The sitatunga, of several varieties, are equally difficult to find, and equally coveted by the sportsman looking for a really rare trophy.

Perhaps the most difficult of all are the okapi and the bongo. Both of these are forest-dwelling animals whose normal habitat is either the deep jungle of the Congo basin or one of the other spots in Africa with similar rain forest vegetation. The okapi, a relative of the giraffe and, like his cousin, possessing very short, fur-covered horns, is little sought after by sportsmen as a trophy. Generally, hunters covet horned animals, and the bigger and more spectacular the horns, the better. Furthermore, the okapi is so furtive and rare in the rain forest where it lives that even the Pygmies who occupy this same jungle terrain have difficulty catching one with their pits and snares.

More popular with sportsmen is the equally furtive and rare bongo; in this species, both the males and the females have lyrate horns that make a spectacular trophy. The bongo, more wide-spread than the okapi, lives in heavy jungle growth from Mount Kenya in East Africa westward through the Congo basin, wherever dense-growing rain forests are found. The difficulty of approaching a bongo in this type of cover, and of getting a good specimen, makes the bongo one of the most desirable sporting trophies in Africa.

Some African antelope and gazelle live in a very limited area and, because of this circumstance, make a desirable trophy. The Hunter hartebeest is not a particularly handsome animal and does not have spectacular horns, but it occupies only a very small area in northeastern Kenya and southern Somalia. Similarly, the dibatag, a smallish gazelle with forward-curving horns of no great size, is one of the great prizes of Africa because it inhabits only a limited area in northern Somalia and adjacent Ethiopia.

The nyala is another animal with limited distribution. The "common" nyala, an animal about the size of an American white-tailed deer, with lyrate horns, is found in heavy cover in southeast Africa from Zululand north to Nyasaland. The spectacular mountain nyala, or "Queen of Sheba's antelope," lives among giant heather only in one small spot on the Orusi Plateau of Ethiopia.

A few African antelope, although not particularly rare or of limited distribution, are of such beauty and carry such spectacular horns that they are favorites with African hunters. The two outstanding animals in this class are certainly the greater kudu and the sable antelope. The male greater kudu, which may weigh eight hundred pounds, carries spiraling horns that often reach a length of over sixty inches. The white face markings and the white body stripes of the gray-colored kudu, coupled with his spectacular horns, make a big bull kudu just about the most breathtaking sight in all of Africa; yet the kudu is neither rare nor of limited distribution. In earlier years, the greater kudu extended practically all over Africa. Even today the greater kudu, in a spotty distribution, extends all the way from the Sudan in the north to South Africa. Some African hunters have made safari after safari just to bag trophy-sized greater kudu.

In the same class as the greater kudu, and even surpassing it in the estimation of many hunters, is the sable antelope. Although less wide-spread than the greater kudu, sable antelope are plentiful in southern Tanganyika, Mozambique, the Rhodesias, and Angola. The beautiful sable color and the backward-sweeping, scimitar-shaped horns of the bull sable make him a spectacular animal. Even a mediocre sable makes a beautiful trophy.

Horned animals will usually achieve the greatest growth of horn in only one part of their range. This is true with most greater kudu and the sable antelope. The keen sportsman will soon determine the area in which he has the best chance of getting a record-sized bull. Greater kudu grow the finest and longest horns in the southern portion of their range, especially in Mozambique. The sable, in a very small area of eastern Angola, grow fantastic horns, half again as long as in other places. So marked is this difference that this animal has been called the "giant sable" and is rated as one of the top trophies in all Africa.

There are many antelope that fall between these various classi-fications and yet are fine game and greatly desired by the avid hunter. The lesser kudu, for example, is smaller in size and has correspond-ingly less horn development than his flamboyant cousin; he lives in arid brush country where he is keen-sighted and furtive, and very difficult to approach. Many a safari that has tried very hard to get a lesser kudu has left Africa without one. And yet the lesser kudu is widespread, and a very common animal. The roan antelope also falls into this category; it, too, is fairly common and ranges in brush and scattered forest areas from West Africa southward through Rho-desia. With a body as big as a mule, the roan antelope is obviously related to the sable, although his color, as the name would imply, is reddish. But the horns of the roan are short and stubby compared with the long, graceful scimitars of the sable.

Common and widely distributed is the eland, largest of the antelope, an animal that looks like a Jersey bull with twisted, stubby horns. The eland is a plains animal, but prefers brush and scattered trees. The common (or Cape) eland is found from Capetown north to Kenya and Angola. Far more spectacular is the Lord Derby or giant eland, found only in a small area in the Sudan extending westward into French Equatorial Africa (in the region now called Central African Republic). The giant eland, which may weigh 2,800 pounds, is, in spite of his size, shy and difficult to approach. Because of his rarity and limited range, the giant eland is rated high on the list of Africa's greatest trophies by sportsmen.

Some of the grass eaters seem to fall into no category at all. Such an animal is the giraffe. The giraffe is certainly spectacular in appearance, and there are many kinds, some of them occupying a very limited terrain. The giraffe, although easy to see, is very difficult to approach. A big bull giraffe may stand eighteen feet high. From this altitude he can see everything—his eyesight is excellent. Native hunters rate the giraffe as one of the most difficult animals to kill, and they often try, as giraffe meat is excellent eating. Most modern sportsmen, however, pass up the giraffe, possibly because of its lack of horn development. In some areas, such as Kenya, the giraffe is classed as royal game and may not be shot.

Not rated as rare or spectacular by most hunters are such animals as the hippopotamus, hyena, wild dog, and cheetah. Nonetheless, these animals are exciting in their way, and are rated by some sportsmen as trophy game. The hippo can be dangerous, especially to a man in a boat or to a hunter who gets between a feeding hippo and the water that is his natural sanctuary. Hyenas, of both the spotted and striped varieties, are usually considered scavengers and vermin, and therefore not game animals. And yet a hyena may be dangerous—and he is certainly intelligent. For his size, about one hundred pounds, the hyena has the most powerful jaws of all the African animals, and he can break the leg bones of a buffalo. The African wild dog, which looks like a canine version of a three-colored alley cat with long ears, travels in packs of a dozen or more and, in spite of his small size and benign appearance, is a vicious killer. Making peculiar cries (which sound more like a flock of owls than a pack of killers), the wild dogs will run down a gazelle until it is exhausted, and then eat it alive. African hunters in the past who encountered a pack of wild dogs usually shot all they could, in the interests of good sportsmanship; and the wild dog, never really abundant, has now become quite rare.

The cheetah, whose range extends into Mesopotamia and southern Asia, has been known since Biblical times as a courser and hunter capable of being trained to help the human hunter. The Queen of Sheba is supposed to have had trained cheetah. Perhaps the fastest animal on four legs, the cheetah displays a combination of canine and feline characteristics. The cheetah's feet have non-retractable claws and look like the paws of a dog. The cheetah's body, however, is much like a leopard's, although the cheetah has dark brown spots on a yellowish background instead of the rosettes of the leopard's hide. As the cheetah hunts by day and in the open, he is usually not difficult to see, and he is unwary of men; for these reasons most sportsmen consider the cheetah poor game. In the days between the two world wars, tens of thousands of cheetah skins were brought in by native hunters to sell on the market for pocketbooks, jackets, and novelties. Because of this slaughter, the cheetah is now rare in most parts of East and Central Africa. In many areas, such as Kenya, Tanganyika and Uganda, the cheetah is now classed as royal game and may not be shot.

In spite of the wide variety of plains antelope with spectacular horns, swamp dwellers, and jungle trophies, the greatest attractions in Africa by far are the Big Five. These are the dangerous animals, the ones that bite back. The Big Five are the elephant, rhino, buffalo, lion, and leopard.

Hunters differ as to which is the most dangerous animal. Under different conditions and at different times, each has been considered the most dangerous.

Which truly deserves that reputation depends mostly on which hunter you ask.

Although the lion is traditionally considered the king of beasts, certainly the elephant should occupy the regal position. In size, intelligence, and in the hazard he presents for the hunter, the elephant is probably the most thrilling game on earth. Elephant have certainly been hunted from the Ice Age to the present. Our earliest ancestors killed elephant for meat; later hunters killed elephant for their teeth.

In spite of the thousands of years of slaughter, African elephant are still fairly abundant. In East Africa, the Congo, Somalia, Sudan, and a few other spots on the continent, elephant herds are still large. One reason for this, certainly, is that the early ivory hunters usually shot bull elephant, as the cows carry relatively small tusks. Furthermore, the ivory hunters, if they had any choice, shot old bulls with the heaviest tusks. The old bulls past breeding age did not decrease the productiveness of an elephant herd. The period of gestation of an African elephant is thirteen months. Young elephant often stay with their mothers until they are ten years old. In spite of this slow rate of productivity, elephant herds continue to increase in certain parts of Africa, and will survive, perhaps, as long as any animal on the Dark Continent. The major reason is certainly their very great intelligence and adaptability.

The African elephant is larger than his Indian cousin, having greater bulk and longer and heavier tusks. The African elephant has a slanting forehead and very large ears. (The typical Indian, or Ceylonese, elephant possesses a domed forehead and relatively small ears.) A big African bull may weigh seven and a half tons, while a very large Indian bull might reach a weight of only five tons. The African elephant is found in several varieties that differ in size, coloring, and length and weight of ivory. The forest elephant of Africa, which lives in jungle terrain such as the Congo, is smaller, has long black hair on his body, and possesses tusks that are usually small in diameter and extend straight downward with only a slight curve.

The bush elephant of Africa lives in open, often arid, country; he is the largest of all, with a slate gray hide and practically no hair on his body. The bush elephant grows tusks that extend in front of his face, usually with a considerable curve and an upward swing. The largest ivory has been collected from the bush elephant. The world record was killed in Uganda; his tusks weighed 220 pounds each and were over ten feet long.

Another variety recognized by most sportsmen is the desert elephant, which has a very light-colored hide that is thickened and cracked, especially on his back, almost like the epidermis of a crocodile. The desert elephant may water once every several days, often going many miles to get a drink. He is somewhat smaller in size than other elephant and only occasionally carries big ivory.

All of these varieties of elephant undoubtedly will interbreed. The African elephant is undoubtedly a very dangerous antagonist for the sportsman, even though the modern hunter is equipped with the most recently developed elephant gun.

But most white hunters and sportsmen who have lost their lives in the pursuit of the Big Five have fallen before a charging buffalo. The African buffalo has also probably accounted for more deaths among native tribesmen than all of the other Big Five put together.

An African buffalo bull weighs about two thousand pounds. He is built heavily and close to the ground, and both males and females carry heavy horns that cover the whole top of the head in a "boss," sometimes attaining a spread of over fifty inches. The buffalo is intelligent. What makes him so dangerous is that buffalo are very common in most of the hunting areas. Many an African hunter, stalking some other kind of game, has suddenly been confronted by an irascible buffalo bull. As the white hunter Andrew Holmberg observed, "A buffalo would rather charge than run away." The natural inclination of a wounded buffalo, even though he is badly hurt, is to go into heavy cover, pick a good spot, and wait for his pursuers. The cemetery at Nairobi now holds the remains of a number of white hunters who died following wounded buffalo.

African buffalo are usually divided into two major varieties. In East Africa, and formerly numerous in South Africa, is the Cape buffalo. This is a dark gray or black animal with an enormous boss on his head and very widespread horns. From Uganda westward one finds the woodland buffalo, sometimes called the "bush cow." This is a smaller animal, reddish in color, and with much smaller horns. However, the bush cow's disposition is just as nasty as that of his larger cousin, the Cape buffalo.

Many hunters rate the rhinoceros as the most fascinating of the Big Five. The African rhino is found in three varieties, all of which carry two horns on the snout. (The Indian, or Asiatic, rhino is smaller and has only one horn.) The largest African rhino is the square-lipped, or "white," rhino, which formerly was distributed from South Africa north to the Sudan. The white rhino may weigh three tons or more, and occasionally carries a very large horn. The hook-lipped rhino, with two variations, is usually called the black rhino, and is by far the most common of these animals in Africa.

Variations of the black rhino were formerly found all over the Dark Continent except in truly arid regions. The black rhino of the variety called the "bush rhino" is inclined to be darker-colored; he has a short, blunt fore horn of about twenty inches in length, and usually inhabits savanna or brush country. Many hunters recognize a variety called the "mountain rhino." This animal habitually lives in mountainous terrain with very thick cover, sometimes in extremely wet and cold areas. The mountain rhino is somewhat larger in size and lighter in color than the black rhino, and usually carries a long, slender fore horn that occasionally reaches a length of fifty inches.

All three varieties of African rhino are now becoming scarce. The white rhino is preserved only in a few protected spots in Natal, South Africa, Uganda, and the Sudan. The black rhino has been almost shot out in French Africa, Somalia, Angola, Mozambique, and the Sudan, and rhino hunting is now prohibited entirely in Tanganyika. A few spots in Kenya still have plenty of rhino, but the number is diminishing yearly. Certainly the rhino will be the first of the Big Five to become extinct.

The rhinoceros has been described as "a dangerous idiot." With his two-or three-ton bulk and his horned snout, a charging rhinoceros is about as deadly and destructive a force as a hunter can imagine. But the rhino has a low saddle in the top of his head where his brain should be. No hunter would describe the rhino as intelligent or cunning, though every hunter would agree that the rhino has an evil temper. At the slightest noise, smell, or disturbance, a rhino will charge. Usually, however, if the hunter can avoid the first rush, he is safe. Natives usually have little difficulty spearing or snaring rhino. Rhino meat is tough but good. Native poachers also kill the rhino for his horn—which is not true horn at all but consolidated hair. Rhino horn is in tremendous demand in southern Asia and China as a material from which to make medicine, especially a concoction valued as an aphrodisiac.

The African lion is judged by some hunters to be the most thrilling of the Big Five. Frederick Selous, who killed more than three hundred during his hunting career, rated the lion as the most dangerous animal in Africa, and the rhino least. The African lion, larger and more sturdily built than his Asiatic cousin, formerly ranged all over the Dark Continent (except in the densest tropical rain forest and the true desert).

Several variations of the African lion are recognized, ranging from the "desert lion," which inhabits the semiarid bush country of Somalia and Ethiopia, to the "plains lion," which lives in the comparatively lush grasslands inhabited by plains game. Lion have been known to kill every other living thing in Africa, including elephant and humans. Some lion make a specialty of feeding on buffalo, and can kill a full-grown Cape bull. Other lion concentrate on the killing of giraffes, catching these ungainly animals at a disadvantage when they are drinking or resting. In any case, the African lion can kill what he can catch, and he is not above eating carrion if necessary.

The lion has been variously described by sportsmen as everything from a lazy and stupid dolt of a beast to a cunning, vicious, and dangerous adversary, depending on the circumstances. Depending upon the terrain and the kind of game the lion are feeding on, these big cats will hunt singly or in large "prides." In the open grass country, a pride of lion may consist of thirty or more, all living and hunting together. In more arid regions, lion habitually live in small family groups, or are solitary. But however he hunts, the African lion is a carnivore, and killing is his business. If a lion develops the habit of killing humans, he quickly becomes adept at it, and is as intelligent and cunning as any animal in the world. Teddy Roosevelt was very much impressed by the African lion, regarding these big cats as the most dangerous antagonists in Africa. Teddy's book, *African Game Trails*, is full of such statements as "We were shown where the settlers Messrs. Lucas and Goldfinch had been one killed and one crippled by a lion." Teddy was also very much impressed by African tribesmen like the Nandi, who speared and killed lion with no more protection than a buffalo-hide shield.

In areas where lion have been little hunted or harassed by humans, they seem to have no fear of man, and do not seem to regard a man with a gun as a natural enemy. However, where they have been hunted extensively, they become shy and nocturnal. By nature, the lion does most of his hunting and prowling in the twilight hours, lying at rest during the heat of the day. If hunted extensively, the lion will lie up in heavy cover during the day, and he is very skillful in keeping hidden. In parks or preserves where lion are not disturbed, they will lie in the open and pay little attention to humans or motorcars.

The discerning sportsman hunts for a large male lion bearing a heavy, long mane. A really good specimen will have a dark mane up to eighteen inches long, extending from the middle of the lion's back over the whole neck and shoulders down onto the forelegs. Most African male lion, however, do not have manes, or at best have only a small scruff along the back of the neck. Desert lion practically never have manes. The enthusiastic sportsman covets a very black-maned lion, but these are scarce, found only in a few areas of the game country. A few strains of lion in certain places seem to develop thick and dark-colored manes. Northern Tanganyika, southern Kenya, and certain spots in Uganda are especially famous for trophy lion.

Lion are hunted in many ways in the various parts of Africa where there are still any lion to hunt. In areas of heavy cover or high grass, such as Uganda, lion may be flushed out by a line of beaters, a method similar to the conventional type of tiger hunt in India. In Somalia and Ethiopia, where lion usually travel in small groups or singly, they are usually tracked. Tracking a soft-footed lion, especially in hard desert terrain, is difficult, but the Somalis are very good at it. In Mozambique, Rhodesia, and Angola, lion are called. A skillful caller, imitating the coughing grunt of a hunting lion, can draw the game within shooting distance. Calling is always done in the evening or at night when the lion are moving; the lion may be called close to a fire so that their eyes shine, or an artificial light may be used to give the shooter a chance to aim. Most sportsmen, however, believe that the use of a light at night to take any kind of game violates sporting principles, even though it may be legal.

In the Sudan, French Africa, and British East Africa, lion are usually baited. Typical lion prey, such as zebra or plains antelope, are killed by the hunter and then dragged behind a car, with the stomach of the carcass cut open so as to produce a maximum amount of smell. Usually the bait is dragged across a path that a pride would normally use when going to water. The bait is then hoisted by a rope into a tree. In Uganda, baits are usually left on the ground and covered with thornbrush to keep away the hyenas, jackals, and vultures. The lion, if he finds the bait by following the drag trail, can scatter this protective covering with one blow of his forepaw. The baiting of lion, because it destroys so many animals simply for use as bait, is now limited or forbidden in many parts of Africa. Even in those areas where it is still legal, it is not as easy a method as it was in years past, when the big cats were less wary. Under normal circumstances, the African lion is lazy and will appropriate a kill if he finds one. However, if the lion has been shot at or otherwise molested, he becomes extremely wary of a bait and will kill his own meat.

All white hunters will attest that following a wounded lion into heavy cover is the most dangerous task of the professional hunter. The lion, if he is not killed outright, will go into high grass or heavy brush and wait for his pursuers. The only saving grace, as the white hunter Syd Downey put it, is that "The lion is a gentleman even when wounded. He roars, and *then* charges." The reason that white hunters fear a wounded lion so much is that a charging lion, attacking with lightning speed in arching bounds, presents practically no target at all from the front. Many a hardened hunter who had shot all of the Big Five previously has frozen in terror when a wounded lion roared and came at him with mouth open and eyes blazing. Under these circumstances, even if he does not freeze, a hunter will get in only one shot. If the lion gets to the man, that man is almost surely dead. The fangs of the lion are so long and his jaws so powerful that a single bite is enough.

The leopard, rated by most sportsmen as the least dangerous of the Big Five, is so judged only because a leopard practically never attacks a human without provocation; moreover, he is small in body size. However, all white hunters agree that a wounded leopard is the most ferocious of any of the dangerous animals of Africa and, for his size, the most deadly of all.

The African leopard is almost identical with the Indian or Asiatic leopard in both size and appearance. Both of these spotted cats average from about 100 pounds for a female to 250 pounds for a very large male. The leopard, like the lion, is a carnivore and a killer. Both the lion and the leopard kill their prey by getting as close to the victim as possible and then making a dash. In this short burst of speed, the leopard is the fastest animal on four feet, not excepting the cheetah. The hunting leopard, when he makes his kill, can cover 40 or 50 yards in two seconds. When this lightning speed is directed against a human, it comes so fast that a hunter often cannot even get his gun to his shoulder before the spotted death is in the air before his face.

Leopard are normally hunted by baiting them along the stream where they water or along a game trail a hunting leopard is likely to use. Leopard habitually feed on smaller game than lion, but a hunting leopard will often kill a zebra, wildebeest, or even occasionally a buffalo. Normal leopard food consists of such animals as Grant gazelle, lesser kudu, and bushbuck. As leopard often kill baboons, a baboon carcass makes a good leopard bait. The hunter usually establishes three to six baits at a time, using the same method of killing and dragging the bait animal as in baiting a lion. However, leopard bait must be placed much more cautiously and carefully than lion bait, paying particular attention to obliterating all traces of human smell by rubbing the stomach contents of the bait animal on any spot on the ground or tree that the hunter might touch.

Normally, a leopard, when he makes a kill, will hoist his victim into a fork of a tree, where he can eat it at his leisure away from the hyenas and vultures. A leopard can drive off one or two hyenas on the ground, but four or five will rob him of his kill. A leopard weighing 150 pounds can seize a lesser kudu weighing 200 in his teeth and jump with the carcass up into a tree to cache the meat on a limb safely above the ground. The human hunter tries to place the bait exactly as a leopard would do it. The leopard is far more suspicious than the lion and, before appropriating a bait, will prowl the vicinity for several hours to see if any danger is near. Usually the leopard hunter will make an artificial blind some distance away from the bait, or will choose natural cover, in a spot that gives a clear view of the bait tree, especially in dim light.

The sportsman after leopard usually checks his various baits from a distance with binoculars to see if the meat has been eaten or the carcass shifted in the tree. If a bait has been appropriated by a leopard, the hunter must get into his blind or place of concealment with extreme care, as the leopard will lie nearby to guard his newly found kill. If he sees the human hunter, the chances are that he will leave and never come back.

The leopard is normally nocturnal and cautious. Many a hunter has had leopard in his bait trees and never seen them, as the cats would come only during complete darkness. But if the leopard is timid and retiring under normal circumstances, he is nothing of the sort when wounded. If a hunter shoots a leopard and does not make a swift kill, he or his white hunter has plenty of trouble. The leopard will always go into heavy cover, turn, and wait. Furthermore, unlike the lion, the leopard is no gentleman and does not give a warning roar just before he charges. The leopard may utter a coughing growl, but only when he is already in the air in his leap to kill. Undoubtedly, if the leopard were of the same body weight and his teeth were as long as those of the lion, there would be many a white hunter dead from the charge of a leopard. As it is, almost half of the members of the Professional White Hunters Association have been mauled by leopard. Some wounded leopard have displayed a ferocity and tenacity shown by no other animals of the Big Five. For this reason, if for no other, the leopard is a legitimate member of the select quintet rated as the most dangerous animals of Africa.

Any white hunter or veteran sportsman who judged that he could predict what each of the African animals would do in a given circumstance would be a foolish man indeed. Animals are like people. Most of them seem to conform; some of them do not. There is the timid lion that is the exception. There is the ferocious sable antelope that, instead of running, charges a man and runs him through with his saber horns. Any one of the Big Five will occasionally attack unprovoked. Human hunters have been killed by baboons, not even rated as game under most circumstances. So, in the dark world of Africa, the modern hunter is surrounded by different kinds of life. He meets the expected and the unexpected. In each instance, he must rely on his hunter's instinct. Perhaps he goes to Africa to find out just how keen that instinct is.

Chapter 1

THREE BAD BUFFS
(circa 1955)

A rumbling snort exploded in our faces. I saw the polished tips of black horns, and dark, evil eyes beneath. A glob of frothy saliva whipped away from the open mouth. As the vague gray body behind that mouth surged toward us, the widespread horns dropped suddenly and came forward.

"Shoot!" yelled Andrew Holmberg in my ear. "Shoot low!"

I held the .470 double rifle at an awkward angle. Those awful horns, only a few feet away, seemed paralyzing. My muscles would not move. The muzzle of the gun would not come up. "Don't shoot at the horn!" Andrew had told me before. "The bullet won't go through."

When we had first started this safari, I had wondered if I would stand up under the charge of one of the Big Five. A man never knows until he has actually tried it. To shoot a deer or even a bear across a canyon is one thing. To face a charging African Cape buffalo a few feet away is another.

When Andrew met my first wife Brownie and me in our room at the Norfolk Hotel in Nairobi, I could sense that he was sizing me up. He had had many clients in the past. He told me afterward that he had taken out some hunters who had nerves of steel, and others who threw their guns away and ran when a dangerous animal attacked. Professional hunters do not like to take an unreliable client close to dangerous game. This is the way white hunters get killed.

"Any one of the Big Five can kill a hunter—and often does," Andrew said in his slow, meticulous manner. "Of all these animals, the Cape buffalo is probably the worst. We'll go after buff first." With that comforting thought, Andrew got up rather abruptly and left.

Under the African Sun

As we drove out of town at sunup the next morning at the start of our sixty-day safari, I was thrilled, but somewhat apprehensive, too. Andrew's logic of starting with the Cape buffalo had not been lost upon me. Undoubtedly, he figured that if I stood up well to the buff, the elephant, rhino, and the rest would be a cinch. I had found out, too, in talking with some of Andrew's friends, that there was probably no man in all of East Africa who knew more about Cape buffalo than Andrew. He holds the world-record buffalo head, a magnificent bull with a horn spread of fifty-eight inches. When Andrew said these animals were dangerous, I was sure he knew what he was talking about.

During the trip to southwestern Kenya, where we were to begin our safari, Andrew did not elaborate on his opinion of the Big Five. I plied him with questions about the habits and characteristics of Cape buffalo in general. He summed it up by saying, "Buff are not only big and hard to knock down, they are dangerously intelligent. If a buff makes up his mind to kill you, chances are that he'll get it done."

Our safari was a comparatively small one. Our Willys safari car was followed by a single truck, which carried our tents, extra gasoline, food, and, perched on top, our twelve safari boys, representing six separate native tribes. With this light equipment and personnel, we moved by a circuitous route into an area of Kenya west of the Rift Valley, which had been hunted little since the Mau Mau uprising. As we camped that evening on the bank of a little stream that flowed out of the Ngutigushe hills to the west, Andrew pointed out the first buffalo tracks on a well-trampled trail that led down to the water. "Just across those hills there," he remarked, "is where I shot the world-record buffalo, two years ago. I think there are some bigger heads than that one in this country."

During our first two days of hunting, we found evidence of Cape buffalo on both sides of our camp. In the immediate vicinity were two herds of perhaps fifty animals each. These moved along trails far out into the open country at night to graze. Generally by early morning, however, they returned to the thick cover of junglelike scrub that grew in a solid band of vegetation on both sides of the little stream. The trick was to catch the buffalo in the open long enough to judge their horns, and to shoot a big bull.

On our third morning, we had a chance. We drove out of our camp before dawn to make a reconnaissance of a pride of lion that we had

Three Bad Buffs

heard roaring during the night. We passed close to the strip of jungle along the river. Our first tracker, Mohammed, who was riding on top of the safari car as a lookout, pounded frantically on the metal roof.

"*Mbogo*, bwana Andrew, *mbogo!*" he said, pointing toward the fringe of forest on our left.

How the devil could the man see a thing in that blackness? It was not yet dawn! Andrew seemed to read my thoughts, for he said, "Mohammed hears buffalo bawling." He stopped the car and motioned me to silence. Quietly also, Ngoro, the first gunbearer, unshackled the .470 double rifles from the rack in the safari car and handed one to me. I had borrowed this gun for the trip, and had tried it out on the first day of the safari. With its open sights it shot very well indeed. There was one difficulty, however. I found out that this particular gun had an interesting habit of firing both barrels at once, if you pulled the front trigger too enthusiastically. The resulting kick had laid me flat on my back. Anyway, I thought, if those 500-grain bullets have that much punch backward, they will knock down anything in front of them. It was comforting to feel the cold barrels of the .470 in my hand as we stepped off into the heavy cover.

In the semi-darkness of dawn we could hear and smell the buffalo herd much easier than see them. A calf bawled from time to time. Occasionally there would be a heavier-voiced grunt, as some cow hooked another with her horn. The smell was like that of a freshly used cow corral, and the droppings were those of domestic cattle. We could hear the buffalo feeding just ahead of us. As the light grew stronger, we could see trees bending down and trailing vines being jerked from beneath as the buffalo stripped the leaves away.

Andrew motioned us backward. "We'll circle them to find the herd bulls," he whispered. Ngoro led the way off to the left, through a tunnel-like path that skirted the center of the heaviest foliage. The path had been worn by generations of Cape buffalo and other animals. There were fresh buffalo tracks in the black earth beneath our feet, and the smell of buffalo was everywhere. We gripped our guns and swung around as a startled bushbuck jumped beside us and disappeared around a turn in the path. Then we heard a branch break to our right. Andrew pointed, and motioned me ahead. We bent over and, at a crouch, silently moved forward, turning into a cross trail. Ngoro pointed through the stems of the close-growing bushes. I could see a dark patch of hide move. I could make out cakes of mud and dirt on the side of the thing. Another branch broke with a splintering crack. I saw one split-edged ear, and an ugly head. I raised the double rifle. This was my first look at a Cape buffalo, and he wasn't thirty feet away. There was his ugly snout with a dark gray horn upon it. Another horn was just behind.

"Rhino," breathed Andrew in my ear. He was already pulling me backward. Ngoro and Sungura, our gunbearers, were backing up too. The rhino swiveled his frayed ears backward and raised his head. He had caught some sound. If the ugly beast whirled and charged in that narrow trail, he would flatten us all. We backed up slowly. Then, when we were out of sight behind a tree, we swiftly retreated to the main buffalo trail.

"Boy, what a beauty! Did you see that horn?" I whispered to Andrew.

"Only about eighteen inches," Andrew answered in a noncommittal way. "Very mediocre head. An old bull, but probably with a nasty temper," he added with a smile.

We traveled for several hundred yards along the buffalo trail that paralleled the stream. From time to time we could hear the grunts and bawling of the main herd off to our right. If the wind held, I saw that we could get ahead of the feeding animals and then look them over as they slowly moved past us. Just ahead of us, on one side of the stream, was a little clearing of perhaps an acre or so. The tall, dead grass that covered the place was partially burned away—by the natives, no doubt, as they always fired the grass when it dried sufficiently after the wet season of April and May. We crouched by the edge of this clearing, as the noise of the herd was now quite close. We could hear some of the animals splashing in the water and walking up the bed of the stream beyond.

Suddenly, a black head appeared from behind a bush, almost beside us. Slender black horns with shiny tips stood out on either side. The eyes were dark-colored and malevolent. The animal was not much more than a short stone's throw away.

"Cow! Don't move!" whispered Andrew out of the corner of his mouth. "If she charges us, we're dead."

Ahead I could see other black forms moving through the bushes. Another head appeared on the edge of the clearing. The horns on this one were massive, swinging low on both sides of the head and then up in a graceful sweep. I knew that this was a bull, and he looked tremendous. Ngoro prodded Andrew quietly in his side and pointed with his

Three Bad Buffs

eyes. Off to our left was another bull. He was standing stock still, looking straight at us. Still farther to the left was another dark form. I heard a shuffling noise on the trail behind us. I looked back out of the corner of my eye and saw another evil head with wide-sweeping horns. There were buffalo all around us.

"Shoot the one on the left," Andrew said quietly. "Aim for the lower third of the shoulder, and *don't miss.*"

I slowly raised the .470 double rifle. Fortunately, the gun was so heavy that it seemed comparatively steady. The open sights seemed just like those of the .22 I'd used when I was a kid. Perhaps when I touched off that shot, we would have African buffalo all over us. I squeezed the trigger gently. The heavy gun recoiled like the kick of a steer, but I didn't notice. As the bull turned, I shot the left barrel at his flank, and heard the solid *thunk* of the bullet in hard flesh.

There was trampling and bellowing all around us. Andrew stood up. Ngoro thrust the extra .470 into my hands and snatched the other from me. The buffalo in the trail behind us turned and ran. The others circled past. One old cow galloped by within fifteen feet, but she did not see us. Within a minute, the trampling of hoofs and the breaking of brush had receded down the valley.

I started forward toward the bull I had shot. Andrew pulled me by the shoulder. "Never straight for them, old boy," he said softly. "Not for a buff."

We circled widely, keeping to the middle of the little clearing before us. The place where the bull had disappeared was the mouth of one of the game trails that crisscrossed through this strip of jungle. We could see the black opening of the tunnel now. There was something bright protruding at one side. The thing shook, then moved out. It was one horn of the buffalo bull. The animal was on his feet, standing quite motionless, with only his head sticking out of the leaves. He seemed to sense that we saw him, and a bellow rumbled in his throat. He lurched forward. I saw that he came on three legs, and slowly, but his eyes were fixed upon us. I shot him once in the chest. The impact of the heavy bullet turned him half around. I fired the left barrel into his shoulder. Still he stood, shaking his massive head.

"If you had followed him close around that bush, he'd have had that horn through your belly," Andrew said. Then the bull collapsed all at once. We walked forward.

"It's not a big head, but it's stylish," said Andrew as he tilted the horns this way and that. "It will do for our first buff."

Under the African Sun

A week later, in another valley, we tried again. As no natives lived in the valley, and no safari party had ever penetrated this far, the buff seemed unafraid, and had been grazing in the open the afternoon before we first spotted them. This time we would have a chance to look them all over, and pick out the mightiest head of horns in the bunch.

Andrew, Ngoro, and I started out late in the morning to stalk the big herd. We left Brownie and the safari car in the middle of a grove of thorn trees near the stream. Mohammed and Sungura were enjoined to stay with her, as the place was full of rhino. We saw thirteen on that one day alone. After carefully testing the wind so as to keep the morning breeze in our faces, we circled perhaps half a mile to come up on the flank of the buffalo herd. They had moved during the night, but not very far. We soon located them by the bawling of the cows and calves. They were moving toward us, apparently coming down to the little stream in the middle of the valley to water.

Just before the first scattered groups of animals came into view, we hid ourselves in a thick clump of sansevieria. Instead of passing by us a hundred yards away, as we had anticipated, the lead animals of the herd turned down a game trail that led within forty or fifty feet of the sansevieria where we crouched.

Fortunately, the light breeze down the mountain slope held. The first group of animals stalked past at a walk. In the lead were some dry cows. Then there was a group of bulls, youngish and with long, gracefully up-curved horns. As group after group of the animals passed by—so close that we could see the lashes on their eyes—I began to understand why Andrew claimed that there were no two buffalo heads just alike. Some had long, sweeping horns with comparatively narrow shafts. Other horns were massive, with a solid boss of bone covering the whole top of the animals' heads. Still others had a wide gap between the two horns. There were straight horns and back-sweeping curved horns, some with perfect tips, others broken and worn.

Half-a-dozen times I whispered out of the corner of my mouth into Andrew's ear, "That one?" Each time he shook his head slightly. Then he whispered back, "These are the herd bulls. The big busters will be at the very end of the herd. The very last bull will be the one."

Even at these words, softly spoken, a huge bull on our side of the moving line stopped dead in his tracks and swung his head toward us.

Three Bad Buffs

His horns were caked with mud, and a bit of one tip was broken off. But the whole top of his head was covered with a spreading cap of scaly horn. His dark eyes looked directly into our own. If we so much as batted an eye, the whole herd would be upon us. He stood there for a long minute, looking at us steadily. Then he rumbled in his throat, and swung away. I heard Andrew let out a long breath beside me.

I had counted roughly two hundred animals that had already passed us. The last straggling bunches were coming into sight farther up the slope. There were some tremendous bulls among them. One old fellow with enormous handlebar horns looked like a sure bet. Again, Andrew shook his head, ever so slightly. "The last one," he whispered.

There, at last, was the gray-black back of the last buffalo, between the trees. He did look big in body. In a moment he would be before us. There he was! He held his head low, and was looking behind. It was a cow! Behind her, still wet from birth, was a forlorn little humpbacked calf, tottering along with faltering steps. I glanced at Andrew with withering scorn. "The last one will be the big bull," I reminded him.

When the cow buffalo and her newborn calf had finally walked slowly out of sight, we stood up and moved away down the valley. We made a wide circle of perhaps half a mile to avoid a rhino we had seen sleeping in the shade under a fever tree. Beyond was a park-like place of evenly spaced flat-topped thorn and fever trees. There Ngoro spotted three lone bulls. He stopped and pointed. Down below us in the big grassy flat, the animals looked like three black boulders.

"They have very heavy heads," Andrew said after a moment. "One—the one on the right—has a good spread. The distance between a buff's ears is about thirty-six inches. You can tell how wide the spread is by how far the horn sticks out on either side beyond the ear tips," Andrew commented, again reading my thoughts.

Although it was late in the morning, the buffalo here had not gone into heavy cover. As we walked through the waist-high grass, yellow-necked spurfowl and quail kept flushing before us. I noticed each time the birds went up that Andrew looked worried. I was thrilled. Africa certainly provides the world's best bird shooting. We had a 16-gauge shotgun back in the safari car. I determined to try some of this fabulous bird hunting as soon as we had finished with the buffalo business.

When we approached closer, we crouched to take advantage of the cover of the long, straw-colored grass. From time to time

Under the African Sun

Ngoro would cautiously thrust his head up and then whisper something to Andrew in Swahili. We moved forward until we were well within a hundred yards of the nearest of the three slate-colored forms. Still we moved in closer. We were within fifty yards now, creeping on our hands and knees. I heard one of the buffalo belch, like an old man after a heavy dinner. Ngoro, after cautiously raising his head, signaled us to the left with his hand, and again we moved forward. Then Andrew removed his terai hat and slowly looked over the top of the grass. Behind his shoulder I also took a look. One of the three buffalo had disappeared. The nearest one was still grazing. He wasn't fifty feet away. The third bull had turned away from us. Two tick birds skittered along his backbone. The tick birds had spotted us.

"One is lying down," Andrew whispered as he pressed his mouth against my ear. "They all have big heads, but I can't get a real good look. Keep ready." He touched the .470 in my hand.

We moved forward again, although this seemed foolhardy. I hunched along on both knees and one arm, so as to keep the double rifle ready. Suddenly there was a blur of motion before us. Two spurfowl spurted out of the grass almost under my hand. A black form moved out of nowhere. It was the bull that had been lying down. I could hear the two tick birds with their frantic *tchick, tchick!* I raised to my knees. The three buffalo were moving toward us. They broke into a run.

"Shoot!" said Andrew tersely. The middle bull was just before me. I covered the corner of his shoulder with the sights and jerked the trigger. Both barrels went off with a deafening blast. I was knocked backward against Ngoro, who was already pushing the spare double rifle into my hands. The first bull had gone down, and Ngoro and Andrew were on their feet now, yelling wildly. The two other bulls passed close beside us. One swerved away, stopped, and then turned.

"Get ready!" said Andrew. Ngoro took two or three steps toward the bull and sailed his hard felt hat along the top of the grass, into the buffalo's face. The bull snorted, pivoted on four legs, and ran off after his companion.

Andrew was looking down at the fallen buffalo. My two shots had entered the animal's shoulder a finger's breadth apart. I had shot too high, but the bullets had broken the beast's neck. The bull was not yet dead.

Three Bad Buffs

"A whole valley full of trophy buffs, and we had to pick this one!" commented Andrew sourly.

I saw immediately what he meant. The horns were massive, perhaps the heaviest and widest spread we had yet seen, but one of the tips was a freak. Instead of curving up, it stood out straight.

"Anyway," Andrew commented as we finished our photographs, "we'll get another chance at buff south of here in Tanganyika. I know a particular herd in the Loliondo country that produces some very exceptional heads."

Unfortunately, we could not get at that herd; we were turned back from Loliondo by a military patrol, which had a group of Mau Mau terrorists surrounded just north of us. We swerved west, to hunt along the Grumeti and Mara Rivers. We carried permits to take two buffalo in Tanganyika, but there was little point in taking another mediocre or freak head. We wanted only one, and Andrew knew a place on the Grumeti that had produced some of East Africa's biggest buffalo heads.

The country along the Grumeti and Mara Rivers is difficult to hunt. Although it is relatively open, with an abundance of game, here the buffalo have been shot at for years, and have become extremely wary. They spend all of the daylight hours securely hidden in the dense cover of brush along the watercourses. Buffalo are very plentiful in the Grumeti country, but a casual hunter would seldom see one.

In all of our buffalo hunting, I had found that the major difficulty was Andrew himself. I am sure that by this time we had looked over five hundred buffalo bulls, but on each occasion Andrew had shaken his head, and if I too eagerly raised the muzzle of the gun, he would slowly push the barrel down with a disapproving look. "You'd be ashamed to take *that* one back to Nairobi," he had said a hundred times. I had pointed out, on an equal number of occasions, that some dozens of buffalo bulls that we had passed up—and a lot of other game, too, for that matter—would look awfully big back home. Actually, I saw Andrew approve of only a very few animals during our whole trip. Most of these turned out to be world records, and he had been able to identify them as such a quarter of a mile away.

It was almost the last day of our stay on the Grumeti when Andrew suddenly became enthusiastic. We had stopped the safari car alongside a small tributary, which was overgrown with the usual tangle of vines and jungle trees. We were looking at a bushbuck standing motionless at the edge of this scrub. The animal was orange-colored. Even I could see that the horns were of mediocre length and development.

"There's the one we want," Andrew said quietly. "That head will go 45, and maybe 48 inches."

I looked at him in surprise. He was looking through the side of the windshield across a little flat toward another tangle of jungle growth. Two buffalo bulls stood motionless staring at us. The right-hand animal had a set of horns like a gendarme's hat—all boss and no points. The left one had everything.

As silently as we could, we got the double rifles out of the rack and crawled out the far side of the safari car on our hands and knees. Even this movement, however, alarmed the animals. Before we could slip down into the sheltering cover of the scrub along the river, they whirled and ran. In a single jump, they disappeared into the close-growing brush behind them.

We broke into a jogging run up the sandy course of the donga (arroyo) into which we had dropped. The place was a natural pathway, screened on both sides by the belt of vegetation that arched in a solid growth of branches and leaves overhead. I saw rhino tracks, and the cat imprints of lion that used this same tunnel-like path. We rounded a sharp corner and turned into the side wash where the buffalo had disappeared. In a few minutes we saw where the damp sand had spurted from their massive hooves as the heavy-bodied animals had jumped down into the wash and run along it. In a few yards the tracks turned up the bank on the far side and along a game trail. Ngoro pulled a pinch of down from a feathery-looking plant and dropped it between his fingers to test the wind. There was practically no current of air at all.

We crawled out of the donga and up along the game trail. Andrew cautioned me to silence as Ngoro moved ahead. I gathered that Ngoro and Andrew did not think that the two bulls had gotten our wind and were not badly frightened. We moved on a few yards to where the vegetation was thinning on the far side. Ngoro pointed ahead. I could just see a dark form with

Three Bad Buffs

the light making a vague outline from behind. Andrew motioned me to crawl past him. "It's the big one," he whispered. "Shoot him in the chest." Ngoro sank down so that I could shoot over him. I raised the gun quickly, centered the sights in the middle of the massive chest, and fired. The buffalo turned and ran. Only then could I see the great upsweep of his wide-spreading horns. He was a monster. I had no chance for a second shot.

I reloaded the empty right barrel, and we moved forward slowly and cautiously. The game trail opened out into a tiny clearing. I could see the tracks of the buffalo in the dark-colored dirt. There was a splash of blood close-by them. Ngoro knelt and examined the tracks carefully. He and Andrew held a whispered consultation in Swahili. Ngoro was pointing to several places on his own body as he talked. I could tell that he thought the shot had gone too high to be immediately fatal. Andrew looked questioningly at me. I shook my head.

We trailed the buffalo a couple of hundred yards farther. Here, the second animal had split off on another game trail, but the drops of blood continued straight on.

"We've got a wounded buffalo on our hands," Andrew said quite unnecessarily. "Ngoro will go first. We will look ahead while he does the tracking. Do not look down. If you see anything black-colored, shoot! Don't try to pick a spot—just shoot."

Ngoro went to follow the wounded buffalo. In a short distance the blood disappeared almost entirely, another indication that the wound was not lethal. Occasionally I had an opportunity to watch Ngoro cast around like a trailing hound. The game trails over which we moved were pockmarked with tracks of buffalo, rhino, eland, and a dozen of the lesser antelope. All had used these paths recently. Unerringly, Ngoro led the way. From time to time he showed Andrew a drop of blood on a stick or a blade of grass, as an indication that we had not switched trails and were not following some other bull. Andrew and I moved behind with our rifles ready. We had the attitude of those who expect a cock pheasant to flush at any second—only this wasn't going to be a pheasant. It was going to be an African Cape buffalo weighing close to a ton, and in a very nasty frame of mind as far as humans were concerned.

Under the African Sun

The worst places we passed were the spots where the game trail dipped into patches of high-growing cane and thick trees, forming complete tunnels shutting out almost all of the light. We talked in whispers, and made no other sound as we crept through these ambuscades on our hands and knees. I gathered from Ngoro's and Andrew's actions that they expected the wounded buffalo to stop and hide in just such a spot, to try to kill us. It was just a question of where he would do it. We must see him first.

A dozen times I raised my .470 and covered some dark shadow in the jungle beside us. Once it turned out to be a warthog. I noticed that even Andrew was edgy. Only Ngoro moved ahead methodically from track to track.

After about two hours of steady tracking, we found a place where the bull had lain down. It was a dark pocket beneath an overhanging tree, surrounded entirely by tall grass and brush. The ground beneath the tree had been raked and furrowed. There was a great deal of blood and phlegm. Ngoro looked the tracks over for a few seconds, then pointed to his throat. I had shot too high, hitting the bull at the base of the throat.

Hours dragged on, and the day became hotter. The tension was beginning to tell. We sweated profusely, and were taking more chances as we moved through narrow trails with blind corners ahead and behind. I noticed also that the buffalo had traveled in a giant half-circle, always keeping to the heaviest cover. We were now along the main Grumeti, skirting the edge of the heaviest jungle along the stream itself. Actually, we had covered no more than three or four miles at the most. In the middle of a small clearing, Ngoro and Andrew held another conference.

"Ngoro thinks he's headed for water at a pool down below here," Andrew whispered to me. "There's one place there with an open buffalo trail leading to it. He'll wait by the water. We'll get him there."

We turned to go. Ngoro strode along more confidently now, passing through a series of tiny glades separated by clumps of bushes and trees. Andrew and I stepped faster to keep up with Ngoro. We were still on the track of the wounded bull, but we now knew where he was going.

Three Bad Buffs

Ngoro paused by a bush. He turned a single leaf toward us; a ruby red spot of blood glittered in the sun. There was a bellowing roar. The whole bush flattened out. Ngoro rolled to the side. His rifle was knocked out of his hand. The bull came out of the bush like a jack rabbit leaving cover. His first bound carried him clear over Ngoro, still rolling on the ground. Andrew and I scattered like quail. My gun came up. I fired it like a shotgun—there was no time to aim. As in a dream, I saw the bull charge Andrew first, then turn toward me. Vaguely I heard the *thud-thud* of Andrew's double rifle as he fired both barrels at point-blank range. Before I could shoot again, the bull had hurtled between us.

The momentum of his charge carried the buffalo beyond us. Still he bounded, bellowing and grunting as he lurched. He spread his great feet and slid to a stop. As agile as a cutting horse, he whirled and faced us again. At one side, Ngoro was frantically trying to get to his rifle. Andrew was reloading. I had one barrel left.

The bull lowered his head. In a single jump he would be upon us. He seemed unwounded. I tried to center the sights on the shoulder, just past his head. As he swung his horns low, I pressed the trigger. At the blast of the shot, he went to his knees. His hind legs jerked and pushed him end over end. I jumped to the side to avoid the flailing feet. Just then, Ngoro pressed the freshly loaded rifle on me from behind. I waited there on my knees, but it was unnecessary. The bull bellowed once again, and then lay still.

Andrew was sitting down, wiping his forehead with his sleeve. "That was sticky," he said weakly, and I knew he wasn't talking about the weather. Only Ngoro seemed unmoved. He was already measuring the width of the bull's horns with the barrel of his rifle.

Andrew and I looked at our tracks in the earth where we had separated and fired at the charging buffalo. There were the gouged imprints where the bull had jumped between us. Andrew and I had been only six paces apart when we had fired. Our three shots had all gone too far back, and through the flanks of the bull. These shots might just as well have been paper wadding for the effect they produced. My first shot, the one that had caused all of the trouble, had hit the animal low in the neck and passed clear through without breaking the vertebrae.

"This was a bad buff," said Andrew as we admired the animal. "But a very good one after he is dead. A very good one indeed."

Chapter 2

THE MOST DANGEROUS
ANIMAL ON EARTH
(1956)

The question is often asked, "What is the most dangerous animal on earth?" There are as many opinions as there are people who have read a book about Darkest Africa, or have been kicked by a milk cow. To be very honest, the world's most dangerous animal is man, as a glance at any newspaper will verify.

When this question comes up at a meeting of sportsmen, there are as many ideas as there are sportsmen, depending on where they have been and what adventures they have had. Some who have been on shikar would pick the tiger as an animal built for killing, and when those terrible capabilities turn to the destruction of humans, the combination is frightening. Stalking a man-eater in India is an experience that will raise the hair on the back of anyone's neck. I have had encounters with four man-eating tigers, and I will never forget a single moment of those episodes.

Some animals are dangerous by reason of the country where they live. The polar bear is one of these. The arctic wastes, the driving blizzards, and the icy water of the Arctic seas are more deadly than the polar bear himself.

In the choosing of the most dangerous animal, the talk usually turns to Africa. In the Dark Continent, the dangerous animals are the Big Five. These are the elephant, rhino, buffalo, lion, and leopard. No novice should ever hunt any of the Big Five. In most places in Africa, it is unlawful to hunt dangerous game without the services of a professional hunter to back you up with a heavy rifle. Arguments as to which of Africa's Big Five is the most dangerous vary as widely as the number of evening patrons at the New Stanley bar in Nairobi.

Many a bronzed and weather-beaten hunter at the New Stanley will declare emphatically, as he slams his Pimms cup down on the counter, that the elephant is the king of beasts. Another will declare just as stoutly that the Cape buffalo is more dangerous and smarter than any other animal in the world. Buffalo advocates point out that there are more would-be hunters in the cemetery in Nairobi put there by charging buffalo than by all other animals combined. Hardly a hunter in such a group is unmarked by an encounter with one of the Big Five. Out of a dozen or more professional hunters whom I know personally, six of them have been mauled by leopard, and one of them, Ian Henderson, has had two very close calls with lion. In spite of all this, for my money, the African rhino is the most dangerous animal on earth, and I will tell you why.

Rhino have been around for a very long time. Our prehistoric ancestors were hunting rhino or avoiding them 50,000 years ago. On the walls of caves in southern Europe, early hunters painted pictures of the woolly rhinoceros, which they knew very well and probably to their sorrow. On the walls of remote canyons in the Sahara, ancient hunters pictured themselves facing the rhinoceros with spears. These prehistoric adventurers often showed themselves running away from the fearsome beast when he charged. I think the rhino is the most dangerous animal for the same reason that these ancient hunters did. He is big, fast, unbelievably powerful, and, worst of all, the rhino is stupid.

All modern rhino in the world are potentially dangerous. The one-horned rhino of Java, Sumatra, and Southeast Asia is now so scarce that we can virtually ignore this species. However, even the Asiatic rhino is treated with great respect by the people of those areas, and there are many true tales of unprovoked attacks where a hapless native was spitted on the horn of a charging rhino. In Africa, the white or square-nosed rhino has achieved a reputation for being relatively docile. These big fellows, weighing about three tons, are not as irascible as their cousin, the black rhino. But nonetheless, white rhino have left in their wake a long list of encounters with humans in which the humans came out second best. White rhino, rescued from oblivion in the last few years, have been so scarce

The Most Dangerous Animal on Earth

that we hear less about them. Most of the survivors are concentrated in the reserve at Hluhluwe in South Africa. White rhino, usually from Hluhluwe, are now being imported to many zoos of the world and also have been used to restock some of their former habitats such as areas of Rhodesia. In the wild, they soon revert to their natural instincts of "kill it first, and then see what you killed later."

The black rhino is the one that most visitors to Africa know best. In the national parks, or in the hunting reserves, the black rhino is the one animal that can cause the most trouble and usually does. The managers of "Treetops," a tourist mecca at the foot of the Aberdare Mountains in Kenya, regard the rhinoceros as the most dangerous animal in their business. The tree house at Treetops must be approached on foot. The tourists are led by an armed guard until they can safely climb the steps to the hotel on stilts up above. The elephant and buffalo are usually gentlemen and come to the water hole and salt grounds at night. The mountain rhino, and there are lots of them, come at any time, quarrel with the elephant and buffalo, and would rather chase a tourist than eat salt.

Perhaps the most dangerous characteristic of the rhino is his unpredictability. They are naturally suspicious, irascible, and unbelievably stupid. The rhino's head has a saddle-like depression where his brain should be. A rhino's brain is about the size of that of a man, and yet a rhino will weigh two and a half tons. The tragic part of this business is that the rhino simply cannot get along with any kind of civilization. When roads and fences and farms appear, the rhino is the first to go.

The menace of a rhino is best appreciated when you meet one face to face, especially if the encounter is sudden. Many a brave man has turned and bolted under these circumstances. Incidentally, don't try to outrun a rhino. If you have a chance, climb a tree—a big tree. Rhino have been known to keep a man up a tree for five days and to splinter a tree trunk a foot in diameter to get at a victim clinging to the swaying limbs above. The speed and ferocity of a rhino are almost unbelievable. He can pivot like a dancing master and reach thirty miles an hour in a few strides.

In the history of the Mombasa-Nairobi and Uganda railroad, there are eleven instances where rhino charged the trains. Apparently the whistle of a locomotive is a challenge to a rhino. In two of these collisions, the engine was knocked off the track. Usually the rhino was killed in the encounter. However, consequences don't seem to matter very much in the mental makeup of a rhino.

Encounters with cars are commonplace. Rhino and automobiles simply don't mix. The most recent instance occurred on the road into Amboseli Park in southern Kenya. A rhino telescoped a small foreign car with a head-on collision and then galloped off with only a bloody nose. The car was a total loss.

While on safari in 1976, we left Nairobi for Magadi in southwest Kenya. Just ahead of us a road repair gang started out with twelve men riding in the back of a heavy dump truck. A bull rhino came out of nowhere, caught the truck broadside, hooked his horn under the frame, and turned the truck over. The rhino then spitted three of the hapless workers as they raced frantically for the safety of a tree. As is often the case, this attack was unprovoked, unpredictable, and senseless. On this same safari at Magadi, I learned about rhino firsthand. I explained to Andrew Holmberg, one of the top hunters in the business, that I wanted an especially good rhino with a front horn at least thirty inches long. Although Andrew did not seem dismayed at the prospect, I did not realize what I was getting into. Andrew took us to the Magadi area because he said the rhino there generally had long horns. In the next few weeks, if my memory serves me correctly, we were charged nine times by as many rhino. On several of these exciting occasions, we trailed a bull rhino that left behind him wide and heavy tracks. Often the track led into heavy brush. When we came close, the rhino invariably whirled and charged. We dived into the bushes at the side of a game trail. The snort of a charging rhino sounds like an exploding steam boiler. As the beast hurtled past, Andrew whispered in my ear, "Poor quality horn." I glanced at Andrew in amazement. Only split-second timing had prevented us from being impaled on that horn.

On that memorable safari, several times we came close to using up our rhino license to save our lives. After a nerve-shattering week of dodging rhino, we saw a magnificent bull sticking his head out of the brush that fringed the Uaso Nyiro River in the gray light of early dawn. The ugly snout of this rhino carried a horn a yard long. This was the one we were looking for. We circled close, watching the wind. The rhino's senses of smell and hearing are acute. Their eyesight is supposed to be bad. This rhino hadn't heard this. He swung

The Most Dangerous Animal on Earth

his head and looked straight at us. We were in the open. His nostrils flared out in a snorting bellow. "Hit him under the chin," Andrew said out of the corner of his mouth. The rhino lunged forward. The heavy .470 double rifle kicked back against my shoulder. The 500-grain bullet hit the rhino at the base of the neck. He reeled backward and went down in a cloud of dust. Suddenly there he was again, charging straight at us. Again the double rifle kicked back. The bullet hit the point of his shoulder. As the cloud of dust rolled away, the rhino lay on his side kicking. Andrew was yelling in my ear, "Reload!" We walked forward together with our guns ready. There were two dead rhino in the trampled brush. The second one, a female, we had not even seen at first. Typical of a rhino, at the sound of the first shot, she had run forward. Any other animal would have turned tail and fled the field. I found out later that I was in almost as much trouble as the dead rhino. We had two dead animals but only one rhino license. I discovered that in the game laws of that country, just because an animal is about to kill you is no excuse to overshoot your license. Fortunately, Colonel Grey of the Kenya Game Department was sympathetic.

The mountain rhino is regarded by some who should know as the most dangerous of all the beasts that carry horns on their noses. Actually, the mountain rhino is not a separate species but a variation of the bush rhino. The mountain rhino usually has a long, slender horn that in some cases reaches fantastic lengths. Several mountain rhino from Mount Kenya and the Aberdares have been recorded with front horns over fifty inches in length. In my own experience, I don't think the mountain rhino is any more dangerous than his relative of the lower bush country. However, the mountain variety lives in thick jungle and bamboo stands where the average visibility is less than fifty feet.

David Ommanney and I met a mountain rhino on Mount Kenya that is typical of a dozen episodes I have heard about. David, one of the top professional hunters of East Africa, told me when we left on that safari that he would rather go after any other animal in any other place than a rhino in the bamboo belt of the upper mountains. David should know. He has come face to face with all of the Big Five during a lifetime in which hair-raising adventures have been commonplace.

Actually, we weren't hunting rhino at the time, although I had told David I would like to get one of the needle-nosed variety that live on the flanks of Mount Kenya. We were hunting bongo. As we tracked the elusive bongo through the cold and dripping game trails of the bamboo thickets, several times we encountered rhino, buffalo, and elephant. All of these animals seemed to resent our intrusion into their dimly lit domain. Practically every bongo-tracking episode ended by our dodging a herd of buffalo, a bunch of irritable forest elephant, or an irascible rhino.

It was almost a relief one evening when a native runner came to our camp at the foot of the mountain. The runner brought the news that a neighboring sawmill was making a road up a spur of the mountain to get at some choice stands of timber. A mountain rhino, which regarded the place as his own, had charged the bulldozer clearing the new road. The rhino's horn knocked one steel plate off the caterpillar track of the 'dozer. The terrified driver and his assistant climbed a tree. The runner added philosophically that as far as he knew, the two men were still up the tree and the rhino was down below plowing up the earth with his horn. The attack had taken place the day before.

Ommanney and I decided to turn the bongo hunt into a rhino hunt. At daylight the next day, we walked up the unfinished road and found the damaged bulldozer. Close-by was a fair-sized tree. Most of the roots of the tree had been torn and broken, so the trunk leaned at a crazy angle. If the rhino had kept at his vengeful work, he could have shaken out the two human victims and killed them both. As it was, he had vented his temper with two or three vicious thrusts through the radiator of the stalled 'dozer, leaving holes that looked as though they were made with a crowbar.

With our gunbearer, Emuru, shaking a small bag of wood ashes to test the drift of the wind, we followed the splayed imprints of the rhino in the wet mud of the mountain path. The animal was a big bull. As we crouched along the game trails and crawled through the thickets, we found tracks of the rhino coming and going. That animal lived right here. Less than two hundred yards from the crippled 'dozer we found him, or rather, he found us. David and I were on our hands and knees looking through the arch where down-curving bamboo stalks made a dusky tunnel. I saw the front horn and one eye of the bull. The rhino was standing facing us about thirty feet away. Before we could balance on our knees and raise our rifles,

The Most Dangerous Animal on Earth

the bull lunged forward. The bamboo crackled. I tried to swing my rifle with the movement of the animal. The barrel caught on a stalk. Inexplicably, instead of mowing us down, he charged obliquely past us, breaking the bamboo stalks like dry straws. I might have fired at the crashing noise as he passed, but I thought better of it. Why he did not charge straight at us can be explained only by another rhino.

Two days later, we were still tracking that particular bull. The rhino had left the ridge where the wrecked bulldozer still stood, and crossed a rocky chasm on the flank of the mountain where a goat would have had trouble negotiating the slippery rocks and deep mud. We crossed an ice-cold torrent in the bottom of the gorge and tracked the bull up the roof-steep slope on the far side. The muddy tracks went high on the flanks of Mount Kenya, then turned back to recross the gorge higher up. The bull's tracks were blurred by the rain of the previous night. A place where he had dropped his dung and kicked it showed that the bull had passed there hours before.

Ommanney decided we would stop and make tea, then go back to camp. For perhaps thirty minutes we sat around a guttering fire trying to boil tea with wet splinters of bamboo. We finally decided we would give up on the bulldozer rhino. We could find another one that was not so temperamental. David kicked out the fire and started down the elephant trail in the direction of camp. The big clover-shaped imprints of the rhino were in the mud of the trail. The tracks were dulled by moisture as before. Suddenly, there was an explosive snort. The elephant trail made a sharp curve. There was the crash of splintering bamboo. The rhino was running straight for us. He had been waiting within fifty yards while we made tea. He must have heard us talking and smelled our fire. This time it was for keeps.

David lunged for his gun, carried by Emuru. His regular gunbearer had been mauled by a leopard a few weeks before and was out of business. Emuru turned and fled back down the trail, carrying the rifle with him. I didn't blame him. I wished I was suddenly somewhere else. As it was, I was on one knee with my .458 leveled. When the rhino broke through the last bamboo, I fired. The bullet spun the bull sideways. I cranked in another shell and shot the rhino full in the shoulder. He turned again. He was staggering but still on his feet. I shot a third time, and he plowed forward on his chin as his forefeet crumpled. As he fell, I could touch his horn with my outstretched rifle.

Under the African Sun

In the last years, with the march of civilization, rhino are now becoming so scarce that they no longer appear on most game lists. That does not make the rhino any less dangerous. A critical rhino confrontation is occurring in eastern Kenya where several thousand refugees have been moved into an area of bush country in a rehabilitation program. The area is ill-suited for farming, and the *shambas* on which the few settlers try to eke out a precarious living are dry and pathetic. Bush rhino, still numerous in the area, resent the intrusion. The Kenya government will readily issue a rhino license to kill any of the beasts raiding the *shambas* at night and in some instances killing humans. One particular rhino was reported. This bull killed a woman carrying a jar of water. Apparently the same rhino had spitted a man walking along a bush trail and finally attacked a boy riding a bicycle. After killing the rider, the rhino had horned and trampled the bicycle into a twisted and unrecognizable mass of junk. My sympathies were with the rhino as he lived there and the people were moved in on him. However, the Kenya government took a different view. On the bulletin board at the Game Office was a card announcing that a license would be issued to anyone who would hunt this particular animal.

When we arrived at Kilnobo station on the Mombasa railroad, I found out why no hunter before had volunteered for the job. Dry, thorny brush covers the rolling hills in a dense mass higher than a man's head or a rhino's back. Out of this dense scrub the new settlers had hacked a few tiny, open *shambas* where they attempted to raise corn. The rhino love corn. Between the dry climate and the rhino, the new settlers were having a difficult time.

We picked up a couple of trackers from one of the *shambas*. These two fellows, one a wizened old man and the other a boy, assured us that they could identify the particular rhino that had killed three people. They added some gory details. The old man said the rhino was a huge bull. He had attacked the woman from the back and split her wide open with one upward thrust of his horn.

"A very big *kifaru*, bwana, and very dangerous," he said.

That particular *kifaru*, or rhino, may have been dangerous, all right, but there were a lot of other hazards as well, most of them in the form of other rhino. Bob Reitnauer, our professional hunter, who had reluctantly volunteered for this assignment, correctly described the situation. Bob

The Most Dangerous Animal on Earth

had been in the area before. "That bush country is crawling with rhino and they live in tunnels. We'll have to crawl on our hands and knees. When we see a rhino, it's him or us."

Bob had not exaggerated. We picked up the trail of the bull rhino at the smashed bicycle. The track was already over a day old. However, we found other imprints apparently made by the same bull as he came and went through wide patches of brush along a dry wash. Our local guide showed us where the rhino watered—a hole in the sand dug by elephant down to the wet sand of the water table. In the sand was the deep imprint of the bull. The tracks were wider than the outstretched fingers of a big man's hand. We followed the trail into the brush. In this dense and matted stuff, generations of rhino had tramped out tunnels. These were too low to walk in, so we had to crawl. At no time could we see more than fifty feet ahead. Several times I thought that this crawling after rhino was about the sportiest hunting I had ever experienced.

Our local guides wanted no part of crawling after a man-killing rhino in dense brush. Bob Reitnauer and I were on our own. We had no choice but to follow the rhino tunnel. Around a curve in the matted brush I saw an ear flick back and forth. Below the ear, a little brown eye regarded me steadily. I raised to my knees and leveled the heavy rifle. The thing looked too small. Into the opening in the trail moved a baby rhino not three feet high. Just beyond the calf I could see the great bulk of the baby's mother, asleep on her side. I punched Reitnauer on the head with the butt of my rifle. The calf made a mewing sound. This probably meant, in rhino language, "Mother, there are a couple of men here." The couple of men were scurrying back down the rhino tunnel. Crouching low, we broke into a run. We doubled up a side trail as the cow rhino came thundering past.

In the next two days we crawled up on three other rhino in this labyrinth of brush. During this time, the bull we were after chased another man and kept the fellow up a tree all night. The next morning at daylight we were on the track of the bull. As usual, the trail led back into the rhino tunnels along the dry wash. In the dry and trampled brush it was impossible to follow one trail. However, we knew about where the man-killer laid up during the heat of the day.

He was there, too. First I saw his snout and the curve of his horn. Tick birds uttered their *tchik, tchik* warning. The birds jumping on the rhino's back had already alerted the bull. He was on his feet. He did not know which way to charge. He moved forward one step and swung his ugly head. When he looked down the tunnel where Reitnauer and I knelt, that would be it. His ears twitched forward. The nostrils flared out in an explosive snort. I figured where his shoulder was above the forefoot and fired. The bull jerked back with the impact of the bullet and then charged. I fired again. The impact of the slug threw him off his balance. He charged but angled past us. Brush and small trees crackled before him as he crashed past ten feet away. I fired again. He slid on his side. When we walked forward to look at him, he still had some of the blue paint from the smashed bicycle on the side of his horn. Within minutes natives began to appear from all directions. In two hours the entire rhino had been cut up and carried away for stew meat.

Hunting a man-killing rhino in that brush is the most dangerous assignment I have ever taken on. But a rhino is unpredictable in any kind of country and under any conditions. In my opinion, this is the most dangerous animal on earth.

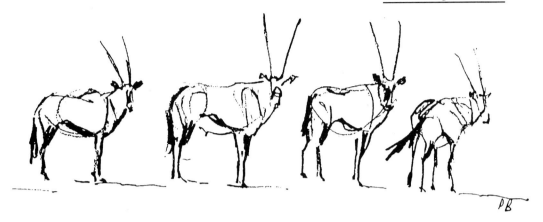

Chapter 3

WALK AROUND A RHINO
(1956)

A gray body heaved out of the brush before us. Two red-billed tick birds danced up and down on its folded skin. Their shrill *tchick, tchick, tchick*, had done the damage, warning of our approach. The rhino whirled, his little eyes glaring straight at us.

Andrew Holmberg was already pulling me backward by one shoulder. "Poor quality horn," he whispered in my ear. "Only 15 inches."

While he was speculating on the horn's length, I was thinking that both of us were likely to be impaled on that horn in the next second. Sure enough, the rhino snorted, lowered his head, and came rumbling toward us. Apparently he was charging in the general direction of our sound and scent, however, without having a good visual fix on us. At any rate, he went pounding by to one side, and kept on going.

This was a typical blind rush by a rhino, and Holmberg was no more disturbed by it than a city dweller would be by a careening taxi. It seems you're usually fairly safe from a general-direction charge if you step behind a tree or bush. Only when a rhino gets you lined up in his short-sighted eyes do you have serious trouble with which to contend.

Holmberg, who started shooting African rhino as a boy on his father's Kenya coffee plantation, almost invited the brutes to come at him. "The best way to judge the length of the horn," he blandly assured me, "is to get the rhino to look straight at you." This proved to be true, but it was obviously a difficult maneuver.

A grown African black rhinoceros will weigh two tons or more, but low mentality is precisely what makes the rhino so dangerous.

Under the African Sun

He'll charge an elephant, another rhino, a safari car, or even the sound of his own dung dropping. Rhino have tipped over trucks, spilling the people out and trampling them to death. Charging rhino have stalled trains on the Mombasa railroad, and crumpled cars on the highways.

Because of his witless willingness to charge, the African rhino has been purposely killed off as new roads and farms are established in his habitat. Kenya is practically the last area of all Africa where the black rhino can be hunted at all. Since the rhino is a slow breeder, as well as a menace to settlers, there seems little question that his days are numbered in most parts of Africa. In Kenya and northern Tanganyika, the normal range of the black rhino, it is already difficult to find one with a good head and a long front horn. The bush rhino, which lives in the low scrub country, generally has a short, stubby front horn. The long, graceful horns, so much sought after by hunters, are almost always found on animals living in mountain country, such as the slopes of Mount Kenya. One such animal met a military patrol in single file on a narrow game trail in the Mount Kenya jungles, and spitted the first two men on his horn before they could avoid him.

Mount Kenya was closed to our party, however, because bands of Mau Mau terrorists were again operating there, so we turned instead into the mountainous country to the south and west. Here, beyond the famous Rift Valley, Andrew had located a good rhino range while acting as military scout some years earlier. There were no native villages within miles. Our only difficulty was in getting a wheeled vehicle within striking distance of a particular isolated valley, in which Andrew had located several rhino with trophy-sized lengths of horn on their snouts.

Our truck, the second vehicle in our entourage, never did make the grade across the rocky escarpment that blocked the entrance to "Holmberg Valley," as we called it in honor of our white hunter. But we finally got our safari car up an old elephant trail that crossed the Rift escarpment and into the valley beyond. This valley, surrounded by thorn-tree-covered mountains and broken by lava cliffs, is as wild as any in Africa today.

We spent three weeks there and saw about fifty rhino. The first we sighted as our car topped the last rise of the trail beyond the Rift Valley. Andrew had stopped the car to look at some fresh buffalo tracks, and a pair of dik-diks suddenly skirted in front of us. These tiny antelope were frightened of something beyond a screen of bushes.

Walk around a Rhino

Sungura, our second gunbearer, pointed beyond the bush. There we saw a horn on top of an ugly snout. An ear with frayed edges tipped backward and forward, as though to catch sound. The head that showed above the brush looked like a prop from a Hollywood movie about dinosaurs.

The head swung toward us, and an explosive snort funneled through the two nostrils below the menacing horn. "If he charges the car, we've had it," Andrew whispered in my ear.

We had walked a few yards from the car, following the buffalo tracks. We bent low and sneaked back. Ngoro, our Masai gunbearer, silently handed down a pair of .470 double rifles. Then Andrew and I crawled toward the brush again, followed by our two gunbearers. We moved rapidly in a quarter circle, keeping perhaps fifty yards from the rhino. The beast snorted from time to time, swinging his head back and forth. He'd heard us but hadn't spotted us—yet.

At a break in the bushes I saw another form, standing quite close to the flank of the first.

"Calf," breathed Andrew in my ear. "I thought that first one was a cow. She has a good horn, though. About twenty-five inches." Although it is legal to shoot female rhino, most sportsmen won't do it, especially if the cow has a small calf.

Gunbearer Ngoro was now trickling dust between his fingers, watching a faint breeze drift the stuff in the direction of the animals. I heard the cow stamp her feet. Brush and branches crashed. Andrew and Ngoro stood up.

The rhino charged in our direction, but not straight at us. She pounded past us, the calf keeping pace at her flanks. A cloud of dust boiled up behind them. Then they were gone.

"Our first rhino, and a 25-inch horn," Andrew said enthusiastically. My own reactions were different. I was learning not only about rhino, but also about white hunters.

On this safari we shot elephant, buffalo, lion, and a fine leopard. In all of these encounters we moved in close. Even when it was possible to shoot from one hundred yards or so, these professionals practiced the theory that one accurate shot at close range is worth several poorly placed ones at a greater distance.

I argued that I could place my shot as well at a fair range. Then, if something should go wrong, there'd be time to form a different plan, or at least to spring for a tree. My words were lost on Andrew. I had to hunt his way—easing up within twenty or thirty yards in an effort to make the first shot count.

I also learned that a white hunter joins in the shooting only as a last resort, and Andrew's idea of a last resort was nothing like mine. It seemed to me that dangerous animals came within a hairsbreadth of doing me in a dozen times in the course of our safari. At one point, I explained to Andrew that if something had me down and was chewing on me, he should feel free to shoot.

"You'll make out all right," he shrugged.

Andrew was no doubt trying to build up my confidence, but the rhino kept tearing it down. If the brutes charged the car, as they often did, it took a wild ride through rocks and trees to get away. On one or two occasions we had a rhino huffing and puffing right at our rear wheel.

On foot the situation was even worse—especially in Holmberg Valley. Here the rhino were concentrated along a small stream that was flanked on both sides by a solid mass of junglelike vegetation. Rhino trails, worn deep, led down from the hills into the area. Apparently the rhino spent a lot of time on the mountain slopes.

Some rhino, especially cows with calves and younger bulls, stayed in the valley most of the time. We would often sneak up close to these to get a good look at their horns. Their usual response was to lower their heads and, snorting like donkey engines, come charging our way.

"You know," Andrew observed one morning, "there are a lot of rhino here that we haven't seen. I think we'll try that heavy cover right over there."

We'd already seen a dozen rhino that looked good to me, but Andrew was more particular. "Somewhere in these mountains there's a record-size rhino," he said as we started out. "He may be in that heavy cover along the stream."

We drove the car to one of the open parks near the middle of the valley. Then we took the first game trail that led toward the creek in the center. Sungura and Ngoro followed us, each carrying an extra double rifle.

The open grassland was like a sunny park. Entering the jungle growth was like going into a darkened room. Every leaf, fern, and circling vine was struggling for light. When our eyes became accustomed to the gloom, I saw great woody vines hanging like serpents about our path.

Walk around a Rhino

I noticed that Ngoro and Andrew paused at almost every step, looking intently into the shadows ahead and on both sides. At no time could we see farther than twenty or thirty feet.

We pushed along as silently as ghosts for perhaps an hour, encountering nothing larger than a flock of dark-colored partridge. Then, in a particularly dense place, Ngoro stopped—so suddenly that I bumped into him. He stared intently to the right. I'd noticed that Ngoro had seemed to be following the track of one particular rhino, turning from one trail to another as the distinctive track followed the stream's bank.

I stared in the direction he seemed to be looking, but I could see nothing. Ngoro turned and looked at Andrew. They both nodded knowingly. Andrew beckoned for me to move forward, and put his finger against his mouth.

We now redoubled our efforts at stealth. Ngoro carefully leaned over and moved small sticks from the path so that we might make no unnecessary noise, and at every step he stopped to listen. I heard the piping of a faraway bird, but that was all.

We tiptoed forward a few yards more. Ngoro pointed. Two small birds were perched on a rounded boulder in the dense shadows. They were excited, and ran back and forth calling *tchick, tchick*.

The boulder beneath the two birds quivered. Then it was still again. Andrew made motions to Sungura. Slowly, with great caution, Sungura began climbing a tree at one side of the trail. He reached the first big limb and looked intently over the screen of bushes just before us. He stared for a moment, shook his head ever so slightly, and started to ease himself down the trunk. As he dropped lithely to the ground, a twig snapped.

The gray bulk heaved up before us. As part of the same movement, it whirled to face us, and I clearly saw the snout and the curved horn. It wasn't thirty feet away. Automatically, I brought up the .470 double.

"Poor horn," muttered Andrew behind me. In that second the rhino charged, and we plunged into the brush.

The brute passed us like a truck out of control, flattening small trees and brush in its path. We could hear the thud of its feet far up the trail; then all was silent.

"The wind from that thing almost took my hat off," I said.

"Poor horn," Andrew said again. "We didn't want him."

A few minutes later and a few yards farther along the trail, Ngoro again spotted a huddled form beneath a tangle of low-growing vines. Once more we tiptoed forward. There were no tick birds here, but we saw a flick of motion.

Ngoro peered ahead, then got to his feet. There was a look of disgust on his face. Andrew stood up. "It's no rhino," Andrew said to me. "It's a bushbuck—but a good one."

Sungura silently handed me the .300 Weatherby, and I gave him the .470 double rifle. My hands were sweaty and none too steady. I stood up and saw that the bushbuck was lying flat with his back toward us. Occasionally he flicked his white-fringed tail, and that was the movement we'd seen. I shot him through the shoulder.

"Well, that shot ends the rhino hunting in here for some time," Andrew said. "It's hard to pick out a good horn in this thick stuff anyway." I readily agreed to return to open country.

For the next week we tried to catch the rhino as they came down from the hills to water. We saw perhaps ten in that time, one of them a bull with a horn about twenty-five inches long.

"That one would look awfully big where I come from," I said as we studied the bull.

Andrew wouldn't compromise. "Ngoro has seen the tracks of one particularly large bull that comes down to water at night. That's the one we want to get."

We started out before dawn to inspect the baits we had hung to attract the lion we had heard roaring every night, over on the other side of the valley. As we drove up to the first, Sungura, who was perched on top of the car as a lookout, pounded on the roof. Andrew stopped the car.

We looked ahead, expecting a lion, but Sungura was pointing behind us. There we saw the head and shoulders of a rhino looming above the brush fringing the river. Even at a distance— the rhino was about three hundred yards away—we could see that the horn was long and pointed. Andrew didn't even raise his binoculars. He just handed me the Weatherby .300.

"You're so eager to shoot something big with this," he commented. "You can try it out."

I slipped some cartridges with solid bullets into the .300, and we walked forward. Ngoro tested the wind with a piece of grass. The rhino apparently had watered at the stream and was now on his

Walk around a Rhino

way back to the hills. After a moment, he moved out of sight among the scattered bushes.

We trotted in a wide half-circle so that we might come up in front of the rhino on the downwind side. At the place where we hoped to meet the animal, there were several rhino trails with patches of brush in between. It was certainly no place to try out my long-range theories. There was enough brush to permit the rhino either to pass us unseen or to charge from a few feet away.

We stood there wondering if we'd gone too far or not far enough. Something moved in the brush to one side of us. We whirled around. The horn looked enormous, and it was pointed straight at us.

"Shoot him under the chin," Andrew said.

I raised the .300, centered the cross hairs of the scope below the chin, and squeezed the trigger. At the shot the rhino seemed to shrink backward. Then he turned sideways. Frantically I centered on a point on his shoulder and jerked the trigger. The rhino went down.

"Flattened him," said Andrew behind me. But when I started forward he pulled me back. "Never head straight for a rhino," he cautioned.

Ngoro thrust the .470 double into my hands, and impatiently I let Andrew guide me in a half-circle. Suddenly the brush shook. The brute was on his feet, the great horn aimed at us.

"Shoot!" Andrew snapped.

As if in a dream, I raised the rifle and fired at the base of the neck. The rhino swerved under the impact of the heavy bullet. I fired the left barrel into the shoulder as he swept by not six feet from the gun barrel.

The rhino lurched to a stop and stood still. Then he turned his great head toward me. I fumbled for the extra shells in the loops at my waist. Ngoro pressed another rifle on me from behind. Dropping the empty one, I snatched the loaded one and whirled around. The rhino sank forward on his face.

"That was sticky," Andrew commented. "I didn't even see this second rhino till he was right on us."

"Second rhino?" I asked, still in a daze. Andrew pointed, and I saw the great carcass of the rhino I'd shot with the .300 in the brush ahead of us. The second rhino had charged out of the same patch of brush, giving me the impression that I was still dealing with the first animal.

31

Under the African Sun

Our original rhino had a front horn measuring 30 inches. The pioneer African hunters took rhino with much longer horns, but a 30-incher is a remarkable trophy these days.

Andrew was both elated and dejected. Pleased about the trophy, he was nonetheless upset because it had been necessary to shoot two animals. The second one weighed about as much as the first, but its horn was only 18 inches long.

Later, when we explained the double kill to the game warden, he agreed that it had been necessary. "Had an experience like that myself last month," he said.

Tangling with two rhino is exciting, I'll admit, but I confess that I would never do it on purpose. I'm more loyal than ever to my notion that rhino hunters would live longer if they picked out lone bulls, and used scoped rifles to shoot from much longer ranges.

Chapter 4

RARE AFRICAN TROPHY
(1958)

The Luangwa Swamp stretched before us to the horizon. Our frail, palm-log dugout nosed along a watery trail through giant lotus leaves. Only minutes before, a bull hippo had made this swath through the swamp vegetation as he crashed away before us. But it was impossible to move in this morass without following hippo trails. Just ahead, the greenish-yellow snout of a large crocodile surfaced on the murky water. The croc looked at us with a cold eye, then sank without a ripple.

Find game in this stinking swamp? Andrew Holmberg, our white hunter, must have been crazy. More likely we'd find a watery grave. We'd come close to it already. If hippo or croc didn't get us, malaria undoubtedly would. Even the natives were unfriendly.

Holmberg had promised us a sporting chance to bag one of the rarest trophies in Africa. In fairness, I must say I'd asked him, "What game in East Africa is hardest to get, and how do we go about getting it?"

At the time, we'd been sitting on the shady veranda of the Norfolk Hotel in Nairobi, planning our two-month safari. It was to be an ordinary safari in most respects, but since I had waited twenty years for the chance to hunt in Africa, I felt I should get at least one unusual trophy.

"The bongo is considered the rarest by some," Andrew replied, having toyed with his glass for some moments before answering. "The bongo lives in the heavy forests of the Congo, and in the bamboo belt high on these East African mountains. Mighty few bongo have been taken."

Under the African Sun

"Let's try for a bongo," I said quickly.

Andrew smiled in his usual quiet way. "So far as I am concerned, I know one that will beat the bongo. Not more than ten or a dozen specimens have been taken by sportsmen in the past twenty-five years. If you're so eager, let's get a sitatunga."

So it was decided. I confess I had never even heard of a sitatunga, so I sneaked over to the library near the hotel and looked it up. "Handsome, swamp-dwelling antelope with spiral horns," the book said. Even some of the sportsmen who hang around the bar in the New Stanley Hotel in Nairobi had never heard of a sitatunga. Most of my friends there thought I was crazy, and said so frankly. They were right.

Brownie and I, with a modest-sized outfit consisting of a safari car and a truck, started off in a southwesterly direction from Nairobi. We then swung south to Tabora in western Tanganyika.

At Tabora we added another native to our group, making it a crew of twelve. This man, a Bantu, had come from the great swamp area of western Tanganyika, where the Luangwa and Mkombo Rivers unite to form a swampland of 5,000 square miles. Andrew had once hunted elephant on the fringe of this country, and he had made a few friends there. We found out from the commissioner of the Tabora District that since this was the dry season of late August, our safari car could probably make it as far as the Bantu village on the edge of the swamp.

Beyond Tabora, we passed through a tsetse fly control station, then were on our own. A fairly passable elephant trail had been partially cleared by a Hindu who hauled supplies to his small store, which ministered to the wants of the natives.

Our sitatunga search almost ended before it began. As we rounded a bend in the trail, we found ourselves in the middle of a raging forest fire. The scattered trees and the waist-high grass burned like gasoline. We quickly stopped the car and truck, and cleared a space around them. As we worked frantically to keep the fire from the vehicles, duiker, reedbuck, and other, smaller antelope rushed past us. A terrified mongoose crouched near our feet.

Eventually, the fire burned its way past us, and we resumed our trek. Farther on, elephant had blocked our progress by pulling down trees across the trail. Several times we could hear herds of the beasts, crashing and trumpeting in the distance.

Rare African Trophy

Finally, we arrived at the Bantu village, a squalid, fly-buzzing place. The Bantus raise rice along the margin of the swamp, and also fish in the deeper water. The fish are much like our black bass and weigh about two or three pounds. They will rise to a fly and are delicious eating.

For their fishing, the natives make canoes by hollowing out trunks of palm trees. They do the hollowing with the iron tools that the Bantus have made since prehistoric times. Since the palms have pithy interiors, the ends of the dugouts aren't solid, and have to be plugged with wood and resinous pitch. The plugs are constantly on the verge of coming out.

Normally the Bantus stand in these treacherous craft, and push them along with an 18-foot pole. Even when we sat down in one of the dugouts and held on with both hands, we found it about as stable as balancing on one foot on the top of a flagpole. When we actually went out for our hunt, we could man only four of these dugouts, and they were the four best ones. But the stability of the canoes became an academic matter. The Bantus weren't going to take us far out into the great swamp, they said.

"The devil people, bwana, the devil people live out there," one of the natives said, pointing a dirty finger out over the swamp.

"He means the natives who live on the island in the swamp," Andrew explained. "The Bantus are scared to death of them, since they used to raid this village and kill and eat the people."

After a day of haranguing, we finally persuaded a group of Bantu men to take the four serviceable dugouts along the edge of the swamp to a small point of land about a mile from the village. Since it was the only approximately dry ground in the vicinity, we pitched our tents there. Hippo had been accustomed to come out of the swamp at this point, and the trails they left created a mooring area for the canoes.

We devoted the next three days to careful preparations for our invasion of the swamp. We took inner tubes from the safari car's wheels and put them in each of the canoes so that if the tippy things capsized, we would at least have a fighting chance.

We prepared large pieces of canvas to use as a floor for the camp we intended to make deep in the swamp. There are islands of vegetation at many places in the swamp. They are not solid ground, but interlaced masses of papyrus, lotus, and other plants so thickly grown together that they form floating islands. We planned to use one of these as a base from which to bag a sitatunga.

The only catch was that we couldn't get native boatmen to go that far out in the swamp. Only one, Hamisi, was willing. He was the one we'd brought from Tabora. Hamisi had such confidence in us that he agreed to act as guide, although he had never been as far in the swamp as we hoped to go.

While the canoes were being prepared, we hunted near camp. The country teemed with game. In several savannas along the edge of the swamp grass, reedbuck were common. These graceful little animals normally will not stand when danger is near; they squat in the grass like crouching pheasants. We found the best way to locate them was to climb trees at the edges of open, grassy places. From such vantage points it was easy to spot bucks with good horns.

The glades were also full of warthog, duiker, bushbuck, water-buck, and greater and lesser kudu. We saw a very fine greater kudu bull just back of our camp. But our sights were set for a sitatunga, which Andrew said lived out beyond the papyrus clumps where the hippo boomed and splashed at night.

Andrew had given us a description of this rare antelope, a close relative of the bushbuck and the kudu, and also told us something of its habits. Of medium size, standing about forty inches at the withers, and weighing 200 to 250 pounds, it is especially distinguished by its ex-tremely elongated hoofs, which are well adapted to swimming and to running over spongy swamp vegetation. The animal is a powerful swim-mer. When pursued, it often will submerge itself up to the nostrils in water. The male sitatunga has spiral horns, while the females are horn-less. The record horn length for East Africa is 27 inches. The animal is covered with long, coarse hair, usually dark yellowish-brown in color, which protects it against insects.

The Bantu villagers showed us the skull and horns of a sitatunga that had been caught in one of their fishnets and drowned. It seemed likely that this was as close as we would ever get to one, for my reso-lution was weakening. In the daytime, it was the flies; at night, the mosquitoes. My wife and I had the usual mosquito bars fastened to the inside of our tent, forming something that resembled a tent within a tent. But seemingly tens of thousands of the droning insects, mov-ing in off the swamp, would get between the wall of the tent and the mosquito netting. In this confined space their humming chorus sounded like a formation of bomber planes overhead. We couldn't sleep for it. We used insect repellent constantly, and took anti-malaria pills once a day. But our safari boys were being chewed alive.

The problem raised by the refusal of the Bantu boatmen—other than Hamisi—to man our canoes was a grave one. Andrew and I visited the Bantu village and gave a pound note to the Hindu who ran the squalid little store, hoping he would wield enough influence to get boatmen for us. It was money wasted. Some natives said there were bull hippo in the swamp that would attack any canoe that came near them. Others complained that crocodiles came out on the floating islands at night, and no man would be safe there after dark. But mainly they were afraid of the inhabitants of the island.

In desperation, Andrew called for "volunteers" from our own safari group. He did it by simply pointing to four of the boys. And that was that.

Most of our boys were Masais. A few were Wakambas, and some Somalis. In their native areas, none ever got closer to water than when they stretched out on their bellies to drink from some slime-covered water hole. They were appalled at the idea of going out in a frail canoe, on a swamp so vast that they couldn't see the other side of it. Even Ngoro, our head gunbearer, who had killed a lion single-handedly with his long-bladed spear, seemed to turn pale at the prospect.

It was a sorry company that started out into the swamp early the next morning. Hamisi tried to instruct the others in poling the craft through the narrow hippo paths, between the walls of rank-growing vegetation. We were able to take very little equipment with us. I could see that Andrew was worried.

"It will be a thin camp," he muttered as he settled in the bow of one of the dugouts. "That is, if we ever get far enough to camp."

I saw what he meant. By the time we had loaded a little food and the canvas strips we intended to use as a floor for the camp, we could carry little else. No beds. No comfortable tents. I thought of what the mosquitoes would do to us as soon as the first shadows of evening stretched across the swamp, and shuddered. No wonder the sitatunga is rarely taken by sportsmen!

We clutched the inner tubes as we pushed into the first lakelike pool in the swamp. The safari boys seemed to gain a little confidence.

Under the African Sun

No one had capsized. I remember thinking that if we did, it would be almost as unpleasant having a crocodile chew off our legs as we dangled helplessly in the tubes as it would to be bitten in half immediately, *without* the tubes. Nobody could have swum more than a few strokes through that yellowish, plant-choked water.

But there were compensations. Lotus, with leaves a yard across, covered places where the water was comparatively open, and their blossoms made every patch a flowering garden. Orchidlike blossoms clung to the dark masses of entwined papyrus and feathery-topped reeds. Water birds were everywhere. In the distance, thousands of knob-nosed geese glinted their metallic gleam, and Egyptian geese circled in cackling masses over the tops of the papyrus. There were a dozen kinds of ducks. Other water birds with spiderlike feet trotted over the tops of the lotus leaves. These were jacanas, much like our rails of North America and just as good to eat.

By late afternoon Brownie had grown tired of photographing flowers and geese, and all of us were wondering how we were going to pass the night in this strange place. Long before dark, clouds of mosquitoes began to appear, all undoubtedly loaded with malaria. I'm sure each one of us wanted to turn back and give the whole thing up, but none wanted to be the first to chicken out.

Finally, Andrew signaled to Hamisi, in whose canoe I was riding, to bring the other dugouts alongside. It was no go. We were licked.

Hamisi skillfully pulled the dugout forward into a pondlike opening. Just ahead lay one of the matted islands, which had become more frequent the deeper we went into the swamp. In the comparatively open water in front of the island, we could maneuver our canoes around and turn back through the narrow hippo trail along which we'd just come. Andrew signaled Hamisi to come closer.

Hamisi was standing in the stern, using his pole to push us forward from clump to clump of vegetation. But the dugout had stopped its forward motion and was drifting slowly. We were not going toward where Andrew still beckoned us.

"Bwana," Hamisi said to me softly. "Bwana, *bunduki.*"

From my seat in the bow I turned my head cautiously to look over my shoulder. There was Hamisi standing in the stern, still as a statue, pointing with desperate urgency. I turned quickly. I could see nothing but a wall of branching papyrus stems. Two twisted sticks moved above the papyrus tops, and the late sun glinted white on their tips. Sticks? But there were no sticks here. They must be horns! Hamisi gently poled the dugout a few feet nearer, and then I saw what he was pointing at.

My first view of live sitatunga was sudden and unbelievable. There were three of them, two females and a bull. The bull stared straight at me, his head erect, and a female stood on either side, also staring.

"*Bunduki*," Hamisi whispered again. "The gun." The Weatherby .300 lay in the canoe, on top of a pile of food just behind me. I twisted around, and the dugout rocked dangerously. My feet and legs had long ago gone to sleep from being in such a cramped position in the bottom of the boat. My fingers touched the rifle, and I grabbed it, swung it around, and bolted a shell into the chamber.

One of the female sitatunga turned and trotted across the swamp on fantastically long hoofs. The other turned to run, but the bull stood and stared. I couldn't get the scope on him. The rifle stuck out at an awkward angle. Frantically, I motioned to Hamisi to twist the canoe a little since I couldn't turn my body. At that, the bull flipped his tail and whirled around, and I saw his moving shoulder in the scope. I fired. As the rifle kicked back hard, the dugout rocked and Hamisi thrust out his pole to keep us from capsizing. The sitatunga disappeared through the papyrus. I had made a clean miss, and I slumped forward against the bow in bitter disappointment.

But there was a movement beyond the papyrus stems, and through a narrow opening I saw one of the female sitatunga splashing along. She seemed to be running on the surface of the water. The other female appeared for an instant, and then the bull. I pulled the cross hairs of the sight just forward of his shoulders, and pressed the trigger. The bull disappeared in a splash of yellow water.

"*Mazuri, mazuri sana!*" yelled Hamisi in a screeching shout. He was prancing up and down the length of the canoe, brandishing his pole like a tightrope walker.

Andrew came up in his canoe. He started to get to his knees, then thought better of it.

"Hamisi says the sitatunga is dead," he said.

The jubilant Hamisi had already poled our dugout alongside the floating island. He jumped out on the matted roots, and the whole mass sank and waved beneath his weight. He moved away rapidly, but reappeared in a moment, dragging the body of the bull sitatunga over the reeds.

The animal closely fitted the descriptions I'd heard and read, except that its face was handsomer than I'd expected it to be. There were white markings on both cheeks and on the bridge of the nose; the ears were rimmed with white; and there were also two prominent white patches on the chocolate-colored throat. The bull's horns, which we measured later, were nineteen inches long—far from a record, but that didn't bother me. I was delighted with the trophy, and so was Andrew.

It was nearly dark by the time our canoes pulled up the hippo trails that led to our camp. Even the mosquitoes didn't seem quite so bad when other members of the safari crowded around to congratulate us on the sitatunga and to admire the animal.

That night, sitting by the fire, the safari boys played their home-made guitars and made up a song about the great sitatunga hunt. They sang of the bwana and brave memsahib who had dared the hippo and the crocodile to shoot the sitatunga.

As the mosquitoes closed in later that night, I didn't feel so brave. But I knew for a certainty why the sitatunga is considered to be one of Africa's rarest trophies.

Two addax taken by Governor Tom Bolack and me on the fringes of the Sahara near Chad. The addax never drink, but follow rare thunderstorms, dining on the new shoots of grass produced.

My world-record scimitar-horned oryx. This animal is probably now extinct in the wild.

I was very proud of taking this fringe-eared oryx south of Lake Magadi—it was a world record at that time.

Nick Swan and I with the elephant we shot to keep a stampede of over 500 of them from knocking down the inadequate acacia tree we clung to for precarious refuge. Swan dropped his rifle and the herd reduced it to unrecognizable junk.

The giant, or Lord Derby, eland is by far the largest of the antelope.

Following the lead of a witch doctor from Cameroon, we worked out a secret formula for bagging the elusive giant eland. It still took us thirty days of hard tracking through fly-infested country before we got a shot, however.

The lowland nyala is considered one of the most beautiful and rare of the African antelope. I took this one near the Limpopo. It was one of my best shots.

The greater kudu of Mozambique are spectacularly large animals, yet their horns seldom measure up to those of their cousins in other parts of Africa.

Abdullah, our Somali cook, was amazing: He could cook delicious pudding or roast a succulent crocodile tail using the most primitive equipment.

The northern impala is bigger bodied and has longer, wider-spreading horns than his southern cousin. I took this one in northern Kenya.

Two storks on the Chobe River, Botswana, show no fear of a feeding crocodile in spite of the fact that crocodile will eat any kind of water bird (providing they can catch them).

Tom Bolack, former governor of New Mexico, adopted my method of covering a raft with branches in order to approach wary crocodiles.

This seventeen-foot-long croc had eaten three women from a neighboring village before Tom shot him. Pieces of the women's clothing were later found in the croc's stomach.

Tom and professional croc hunter Bobby Wilmot with a week's catch from the Chobe River. Shortly after this episode Bobby stepped on a black mamba. He was found several days later in the water—a decomposing meal for his old croc enemies.

The buffalo along the Limpopo were exceptionally big. This bull with his 50-inch spread charged me while I was solo.

My very good Grant gazelle taken in the Northern Frontier of Kenya.

Chapter 5

TREK FOR A RECORD
(1958)

The valley was hard to find, and getting there was an adventure in itself. But the place teemed with game, among them an oryx with the finest head the hunter had ever seen.

The heat haze in the distance obscured the faraway animals, but on our side of the river we could see perhaps a thousand. A black mass of wildebeest and zebra drifted down the slope of the valley toward the water. A vague cloud of dust rose from the many parallel game trails in their wake. Also moving toward the river were scattered bands of Grant gazelle, their rumps and hind legs showing a brilliant white seat patch. A herd of Thomson gazelle were at rest under some widely spaced thorn trees to our left. Beyond the tommies, the red forms of several impala contrasted with the lighter brown of a straggling line of female eland. Just below us a cow rhinoceros with an enormous front horn ambled doggedly down a rutted trail worn by generations of rhino. Behind her a large calf trotted to keep up with her shambling pace.

"The game in this valley is of good quality," said Andrew Holmberg quietly as he looked through his big bell-mouthed 10X30 binoculars. "That rhino there will have a 25-inch horn or better." He shifted his glasses again. "Look at the biggest of those buffalo bulls. That one on the right has a good boss and a good spread—a 44- or 45-inch head—very good indeed."

In the fringe of dark green vegetation along the river were three slate-black spots that were feeding buffalo, all bulls. Even at that distance I could see that all had massive horns with good spreads. To one side of the buffalo was the cinnamon-red outline of a bushbuck.

This might have been in the middle of the best game preserve in all Africa. Or it might have been a scene viewed by some early explorer in the East African highlands, one of those intrepid pioneers who led a line of natives carrying bundles on their heads several hundred miles up from the coast to such a spot as this. But this place was no game preserve. And the time was not in the early 1800s, and we hadn't walked here. We had driven here in a modern safari car, which had been an adventure in itself.

It had all started in a room in the Norfolk Hotel in Nairobi, Kenya Colony, East Africa. Brownie and I had arrived there to begin a sixty-day safari. Fortunately, we had acquired the services of Andrew Holmberg, one of the top white hunters of East Africa. Holmberg had been hunting at that time with Ker & Downey Safaris, Ltd., but he was joining with another famous hunter, Harry Selby, to form Selby & Holmberg Safaris, Ltd.

Holmberg came in to see us at the Norfolk Hotel the day before our outfit was ready. Perhaps I was tired or had simply read too many books on Africa. I remarked, "I suppose we'll be following the ruts of a hundred other safari cars wherever we go." I was a little sour, I'll admit, but I hadn't been able to find a place on the maps of Kenya and Tanganyika that wasn't the subject of at least one book and a dozen articles by other hunters.

Holmberg cocked his head and stared at me as though he were weighing a decision. "You want to get a good rhino and a good lion as well as a general bag," he said slowly. "I want to get some world records to start off our new safari company. I think I know a place where we can find them all."

Naturally, I was much elated and started asking questions. But Holmberg would not elaborate. He did make some unusual preparations. First, we got permission to go through private land that belonged to a mining company. Then we spent the next morning trying to find, in the teeming crowds of Nairobi, one particular native who, it seemed, had come from the remote area of southern Kenya that Holmberg had in mind.

Our safari was nothing unusual in itself. We had one safari car fitted with special body and metal top and a truck that carried our tents, gasoline, water, icebox, and other gear. As expeditions go, this was a small outfit: two vehicles and some thirteen safari boys. My wife served as photographer, I was the single hunter, and Holmberg was the guide.

"I found this place while we were on patrol after Mau Mau," Holmberg explained. "We never managed to get a lorry near it, and I only saw it from a distance. It might be impossible to reach."

With this encouraging observation, we set out southward from Nairobi. Soon, however, we cut off at an angle from the main track and began to lurch over rough terrain. I cannot say exactly where the valley is, because the white hunters of East Africa don't reveal choice locations if they can help it. But in miles it was not very far.

Brownie and I were amazed at the amount of game we saw even on the outskirts of the modern city of Nairobi. There were scattered groups of wildebeest and zebra and occasional groups of impala. An ostrich paced along beside us with powerful strides of his big drumstick legs. Giraffe punctuated the skyline like mobile telephone poles. Then we entered the mountainous terrain on the edge of the Rift Valley. Here we made camp and I shot my first Kenya animal—a zebra.

At the foot of the escarpment that forms the side of the Rift Valley was a small and miserable village of the Sonjo tribe. Its people, like their cousins the Masai, eke out a precarious existence herding cattle and goats in this rough country. The chief of the village was a dirty individual with a pockmarked body, a scraggly skin cloak over his shoulders, and a rusty-headed spear. But his face was intelligent. Apparently, in spite of his isolation, he had observed many things and remembered them.

Yes, he had been in the valley of which the white man spoke. "The place is two days' march over the cliffs," I was told in translation. "The rhino have very large horns." He indicated the length on the haft of his spear. "There is much game." The chief of the Sonjos pointed a long, bony finger at my Weatherby rifle, which Ngoro, my Masai gunbearer, was carrying on a sling. "Never have there been guns in the valley beyond the cliffs," he said.

The chief pointed out a route that led up the side of the escarpment and across the craggy hills into the valley beyond. It looked almost impassable; so we decided to leave our truck and most of the equipment. We packed up some bedrolls, a minimum of food, our rifles, ammunition, and cameras, and stowed them in the safari car. We took three of our best boys and the old Sonjo chief as guide. I had many misgivings about him: Probably the old fellow had never ridden in a safari car before, and I wondered how he could find a route for it in the rocky country.

The cataclysm that formed the Rift Valley eons ago had torn the earth apart at this place. Rocks were everywhere, some the size of a hat, others as big as a cathedral. I'm sure that the surface of the moon would be easy going by comparison. Long before darkness fell it was obvious that we were not going to make it into the hidden valley. We tore one tire completely open on a jagged piece of lava. We rolled stones out of the way, we chopped down trees, we pushed and cajoled the safari car up impossible places where a person in his right mind wouldn't lead a horse. Finally we gave up; we couldn't go a foot farther. No wonder a safari had never reached that far valley before!

Late in the afternoon we turned back. It was dark before we followed our own tracks down the long way we had come from the Sonjo village. The old chief seemed to be the only man in the party who was not disheartened by this fruitless day.

As we drove back to our camp that night Holmberg seemed strangely preoccupied. "There's one thing that old chief said several times that may be the secret," he mused. "He said that the elephant have a path in and out of the valley, and elephant always follow an easy route. Most of the roads of this country are laid out along elephant migration paths." He was silent awhile. Then he said with determination, "By Jupiter, we'll try it again."

We did, too. But first it took us two days to mend our tires enough for a return engagement on the lava cliffs. The first part of the trip was easier; we had our old tracks to follow. What had taken us a whole day before, we now traversed in a little over three hours. But beyond that was the unknown. We spent the rest of the morning crossing an almost impossible canyon. We did it by enlarging a game trail and skirting the edge of a cliff. Dik-diks, the smallest of the African antelope, stared at us curiously from among the rocks.

Early in the afternoon we reached another deep canyon that was obviously uncrossable. We would have to turn back again. To make

Trek for a Record

matters worse, on the edge of this place was a campfire not long dead and some imprints where several men had slept in the grass. If this was a Mau Mau camp, they had been there only a few days before.

Undaunted, Holmberg sent out safari boys as scouts. In about two hours they came back, their faces cracked open in wide grins. "We have found the elephant trail, bwana," they said in Swahili. "It is an easy place to go."

Well, it turned out to be not so easy, but it was an elephant trail and it was passable. The elephant had long ago beaten out a wide trail along the slanting side of the canyon. It was an easy grade, although marked here and there by great fragments of rock from the cliffs above and by occasional gullies. But over these our safari car labored successfully.

We rounded a lava shoulder and came out on a high tableland. Here we saw our first rhino, a cow and a calf. The cow was standing asleep in the shade under a tree, her calf lying beside her. There was no way we could circle wide to avoid the inevitable. As the safari car rolled by she pricked forward her ears and her tail went up. Apparently she thought the car was another rhino—possibly a bull—invading her privacy. With a snort like a diesel truck, she came after us.

"Nice horn," Holmberg commented as he skillfully maneuvered the car among the scattered lava boulders in the high grass.

Damn the horn, I thought. *If that old cow rhino catches this safari car, it will be a piece of junk in two seconds.* But metal and gasoline triumphed. The car did not falter and we did not hit one of the awful rocks. After two or three hundred yards the rhino gave up and stood there in our dust cloud, snorting triumphantly.

In the next mile we saw four more rhino—three bulls and another female. We managed to get past them without any show of rhino temper. There were other animals as well: Impala stood in groups to watch us pass, there were occasional bands of zebra, and twice we saw oryx—my first glimpse of these splendid antelope. I had heard that the natives used their long, straight horns for swords. It was easy to see how these needle-sharp weapons would be useful.

But it was in the valley itself, beyond the tableland, that we saw the real panorama of African game, unspoiled and apparently untouched. It was dark just as we came up to the edge of the valley. We made our camp on a high shoulder, and I christened the place Holmberg Valley.

Under the African Sun

That night the lion roared and coughed in the valley. We could hear a band of eland running across the hard ground in the distance as a lion or wild dogs disturbed their nocturnal feeding.

"There must be some big male lion in this valley with manes hanging clear down to their paws," Holmberg remarked as we turned in beneath our mosquito netting.

In the morning it was a question of what to hunt first. Also, we had to get some drinkable water. As the water question was pressing, we decided to combine necessity with design. A large bull rhino had spent the night only a few hundred yards away from us on the slope of a hill; so we left two boys to keep the fire going so he'd stay out of camp. The rest of us climbed into the safari car and drove with no great difficulty down the slanting side of the valley. We headed toward a streak of deep green that stretched out across the lighter browns of the grasslands on the far side.

In the two hours that it took us to pick our way across the floor of the valley and partway up the far side, we saw eleven rhino, one with a very large horn. This was also a female with a calf, and she, too, charged our safari car on sight. Fortunately the valley floor was rather smooth at this place and we outmaneuvered her with ease, but she chased us for a quarter of a mile before she finally gave up.

We dipped our water from the stream while we kept a sharp lookout for rhino. Black-faced monkeys played in the fig trees above us, and there was the track of a python in the mud by the water. Holmberg said these big snakes were very rare and that he had seen only a few in his whole African experience.

Lower down the side of the valley we sighted an unusually large band of eland. When all our cans and bottles were filled, we stopped the safari car behind some thorn trees and stalked close enough to the eland to look them over. The females were accompanied by one large male—the herd bull. Holmberg looked him over carefully with his big binoculars.

"A very nice head," he said, "a very nice head indeed. Most safaris don't bring in one nearly as good these days. Shoot him straightaway!"

I slipped two or three solids into my .300 Weatherby rifle and slipped forward a hundred yards or so to close the range. Taking cover behind a large thorn tree, I picked out the eland bull by his dark-gray coat; the females are a reddish brown. The band had become alerted by my crawling approach—I probably looked like a lion to them.

Trek for a Record

Nervously the females began to move off. But the grayish blue bull lingered a few seconds in the rear. He turned to stare regally at me. This haughty attitude was a mistake. The solid-patch bullet struck him through the shoulders. Such a shot would have killed an ordinary animal instantly, but not an eland. He trotted perhaps a hundred yards and turned again. He was still on his feet when I came up and finished him.

After we'd photographed the eland I looked around for Holmberg. He had disappeared, but in a few minutes he returned. "Come with me," he said.

I followed his bulky form with only Ngoro behind me. Ngoro carried my .470 double rifle as rhino insurance, and I lugged the Weatherby. I had no idea what Holmberg had in mind.

"Oryx," he said.

I looked to where he pointed. We were at the edge of a natural clearing of five hundred acres or more. Along its far side straggled a line of about thirty dun-colored animals, looking like mules in the distance. But even at that range I could see the rapierlike points of their long horns towering above their heads. Both female and male oryx have almost identical horns. Indeed, it is very difficult to tell the sex of these animals at any distance.

Through the grass stems where we crouched I looked at the oryx with my binoculars. The handsome black-marked faces and the black line along the belly were clear.

"Look at that third to the last," Holmberg whispered in my ear.

I looked. The horns of that oryx stuck up like an indoor television antenna.

Holmberg and Ngoro were already circling to the left. They motioned frantically for me to follow. A group of zebra had appeared before us. Their striped faces were pricked forward. They would spook at any moment and scare the oryx, too.

"That oryx will be a record," Holmberg whispered over his shoulder as we crawled through the grass. "I have never seen a fringe-eared oryx with horns that big."

The intelligence did nothing to calm my nerves. Only once did I stick my head up above the grass tops. A Grant gazelle stood like a statue not twenty feet away. If the animal bolted, every head of game in this clearing would dash off in one grand melee. I pulled my head slowly down and continued crawling. Holmberg and Ngoro were up ahead, talking again in low tones.

"We can't get any closer," the guide whispered when I caught up. "And some of this other stuff is going to scare at any moment. Go out there and shoot the big oryx. He's the one standing this side of that tree."

I hunched forward on knees and elbows. The grass thinned and the ground dropped slightly away. Over across the clearing I could see the oryx. The animals had stopped feeding and had bunched under two or three thorn trees. It was a good three hundred yards.

My gosh, I'll miss, I thought. There was the oryx that Holmberg had pointed out. It was a heavy animal, with horns longer and wider-spreading than any of his fellows'. He still fed in a listless way, nibbling tufts of grass and shifting his position every few seconds. Slowly I rose to a sitting position. I couldn't shoot offhand; I had to get above most of the grass, or the bullet would never reach home. I had a solid in the Weatherby—perhaps this was as good a bullet as any. Those oryx looked almost as heavy-bodied as the eland.

Even as I leveled the rifle, a zebra barked like a dog close to one side. Then another and another of the animals took up the challenge. They had winded us or seen us, or both. The oryx threw up their heads. Two or three that had been lying down jumped to their feet. For a moment I lost the big one as the animals jostled and shifted.

There he was! I could just see his shoulder. I put the cross hairs a little high and squeezed off the shot.

At the report the whole clearing jumped into motion. Zebra that I hadn't even seen before galloped past. Impala and Grant gazelles bounded a few yards and then stopped to stare, turning their heads from side to side. Holmberg and Ngoro came running up. "Did you get him?" the guide asked.

"I don't know," I groaned. "I can't see a thing."

There was dust and confusion all around us. Oryx ran off through the thorn trees on the far side of the clearing. The zebra had finally decided on which direction to run, and ran that way.

"There he is," Holmberg said, leveling his finger.

Our single oryx stood alone. His long horns spread wide at the tips. He stood broadside and stared at us, apparently unhurt. Frantically I bolted another shell into the rifle, aimed quickly, and fired again. There was no visible effect. I looked in consternation at Holmberg. He was smiling at me. When I turned again to look at the oryx, the animal was down and stone-dead.

Both shots had gone through its shoulders. Each was a trifle high but certainly lethal, and yet the animal had stood there a long time. Holmberg was right when he said that these African animals had greater vitality than those in any other part of the world. Now he took out his steel tape and began measuring the horns.

"Thirty-six and a half inches—it's the world record." He jumped up to shake my hand.

When we checked with the game departments of Kenya and Tanganyika, we found that the horns of this particular oryx were an inch longer than any other fringe-eared oryx ever recorded. The Rowland Ward record book is now considerably out of date in such matters, but J. Swinnerton, head game officer of Tanganyika, maintains a current account of game heads of all sorts. His largest prior record for fringe-eared oryx is credited to Russell Douglass, who bagged one with horns measuring 35 1/2 inches.

As I stood by the beautiful-bodied antelope and looked at the graceful horns, I realized that I had at last bagged a world record. I am sure that there was a silly grin on my face, and Holmberg was talking rapidly. Suddenly the low-throated roar of a lion rumbled directly behind me. The thing was so close that I could almost feel the hot breath of the cat, and I whirled around. Ngoro was crouching there with his head thrown back, and from between his lips came the sounds of a hungry lion hunting for meat.

"Ngoro always does that when we make an important kill," Holmberg explained. "I told him he'll get shot someday, roaring like that."

He wouldn't be shot by me, I decided. He was far from a world record.

49

Chapter 6

AFRICA'S RAREST AND
MOST BEAUTIFUL ANIMAL
(1959)

A grim-faced figure stood among the close-growing papyrus stems before me, his spear arm raised. The serrated barbs on the spear point were a foot from my chest. The man himself was one of the most magnificent physical specimens I had ever seen. He was close to seven feet tall, the bulging muscles of his ebony body accentuated by his nakedness. He wore only an elephant-tusk bracelet around his upper arm, and a string of beads as a crown on top of his head.

The giant standing in the papyrus before me might have been the cannibal king in some movie extravaganza, except that his nakedness would not have passed the Hollywood censors. Certainly he would be an asset to several local basketball teams I could name. But if this was a scene from a scenario thriller, I was about to be the first victim of the plot. Curiously enough, I didn't particularly care at the moment. Fetid water reached above my waist. I couldn't possibly turn and run. To my knowledge at that time, I was surrounded by at least ten miles of unbroken swamp. I carried a .300 Weatherby by its sling on the back of my shoulder, but I made no attempt to swing the rifle into shooting position. I simply stood there in the stinking water. A flight of spurwing geese swished past over the papyrus crests above us. The dark face of the warrior before me cracked into a wide grin. He thrust forward with the barbed spear.

Why would anyone, even a dedicated hunter, get himself into a situation like this? If the mosquitoes, crocodiles, hippo, liver flukes, and belhartzia bugs didn't get you, the Dinkas certainly would. The answer to this seemingly unanswerable question is Mrs. Gray.

Hunters, at all times and in many places, have risked life and reputation in the pursuit of something rare. When that something rare is at the same time breathtakingly beautiful, the pursuit of this trophy becomes an intoxicating addiction. Such a trophy is that which is called, by both the hunters and the Dinka tribesmen who know the animal best, "Mrs. Gray's lechwe."

It was many years after the British army took over the Sudan that British sportsmen discovered this animal. Hunters from England who, in the early part of the century, had shot everything from Marco Polo sheep in central Asia to bongo in the remotest forests of Africa still did not know of the rare and beautiful animal that lived in the Nile swamps. Even sportsmen with a penchant for seeking out difficult animals in difficult places would never find Mrs. Gray in the "Sudd." The Sudd, the place where the main or White Nile spreads out into gigantic swamps covering hundreds of square miles, is the reason that the ancient Egyptians never got through to discover the sources of the Nile. Nobody—I repeat, *nobody*, hunter or desperate fugitive—would ever enter those awful swamps unless he thought there was a gold mine there.

When the British administrators managed to punch a few sketchy roads through the middle of the Anglo-Egyptian Sudan, they discovered among other things the tribe known as the Dinkas. Actually, there are several kinds of Dinkas, most of them very tall, a physical attribute they share with several cousin Nilotic tribes. Some Dinkas keep cattle, some hunt, and some live on fish. The Bahr el Ghazal Dinkas live mostly on fish, which they catch around the edge of the Sudd swamps. It was the Bahr el Ghazal Dinkas who brought in the first Nile lechwe. The British administrators, knowing that here was a new animal, sent the head and skin to London for observation. This magnificent antelope was named for the wife of Dr. Gray, then head of the British Museum Zoological Department. The Nile lechwe has been known as Mrs. Gray ever since.

But even the British hunters, who combed the Sudan from one end to the other to fill out their trophy collections, seldom bagged a Mrs. Gray. For one thing, Mrs. Gray is a lechwe, and lechwe are antelope that live in swamps. The red lechwe and black lechwe

Africa's Rarest and Most Beautiful Animal

found in Bechuanaland and Northern Rhodesia also are swamp dwellers, but these southern relatives of the lechwe clan inhabit swamps that are pocket-handkerchief in size compared to the Sudd. The red lechwe and the black lechwe had been largely killed off before the Nile lechwe was even discovered.

If any hunter was intrepid enough to push his way into the swamps to find Mrs. Gray, the chances are that still he wouldn't see one. The Sudd swamps are probably the most impenetrable in the world, in that you can't boat, swim, or walk through them. That is, no one can but a Dinka. Furthermore, even in his Nile swamp homeland, Mrs. Gray is mighty rare. The Dinkas say that the crocodiles eat the young, which reduces their number. The Dinkas themselves spear them when they can, and they are excellent spearmen. The British passed a law in the Sudan that any hunter could take but two Nile lechwe in his lifetime. Later on, they amended the law to read that a hunter could shoot only one Mrs. Gray during his entire hunting career. Few sportsmen ever had even that one chance.

Like the sitatunga and the southern lechwe tribe, the Nile lechwe has very elongated hoofs for walking or swimming in his swamp homeland. During his entire lifetime, the lechwe never comes to dry land. He escapes his enemies by running or swimming in the swamps. If necessary, he submerges all except the tip of his muzzle.

Despite all of these difficulties (and probably because I had no foggy notion of what the Sudd was like), I determined to bag a Mrs. Gray lechwe. Brownie and I were in the central Sudan for several weeks in 1959, we would be close to the Sudd swamps; the rest, I imagined, should be easy. Because a matter of actual record, nothing was easy. For one thing, the Sudan, at that time a new republic of but two years, presented physical difficulties of well-nigh insurmountable magnitude. Because a military dictatorship overlies the republic form of government, it is virtually impossible to obtain permits, and the Sudanese are "permit-happy." It is necessary, for example, to have a permit to bring a camera into the country; another is required to possess a camera; and a third permit is required for taking a picture. The procurement of hunting permits is a nightmare. Anyone less dedicated than a hunter determined to get a Mrs. Gray would chuck the whole business long before the last illegible permit was in his possession. Fortunately, the Sudanese government has since straightened out a number of these difficulties; but at the time of our junket, the situation was maddening.

Under the African Sun

Half the headache of bagging a Mrs. Gray is getting on the ground, or rather the mud, of the situation; the other half of the headache (the migraine part) is getting a look at a square inch of Mrs. Gray's hide after you get there.

Fortunately, we had the help of a Greek trader in Juba, in the southern Sudan. This man, Costi Yiaimanis, had spent most of his life in the Sudan, and had survived the changeover from the Anglo-Egyptian government of former times to the modern, hectic, and enthusiastic government of today. In those long years of ivory trading, meat hunting, and travel, Costi Yiaimanis had made friends in every tribe in the Sudan. He had learned the country, the customs, the languages, and the trails. Furthermore, Costi had a "boxcar." (In our native heath, in America, we would call this boxcar a beat-up, hand-me-down, abused, haywire, hung-together pickup truck.) In addition to the boxcar, Costi furnished us with a couple of camp beds, Sudanese camping equipment, a few cans of preserved food left over from the British army invasion of 1898, and four native boys, including one called the "driver." It must be confessed that the latter did indeed sit behind the wheel of the boxcar. Outside of this position, any resemblance to a driver was purely illusory. I have seen loco mustangs that had better sense, better timing, and a better idea of speed and direction than this Sudanese maniac. The only reason we weren't killed in the first miles of our journey after Mrs. Gray is that you simply can't go very fast on a Sudanese road. Fortunately, Costi had furnished us with a government game scout, who was a Zande. Zandes used to be cannibals, and some still are. This game scout, Rihani by name, came from the southern Sudan and previously had visited the edge of the Sudd swamps with some British, although he had never seen a Mrs. Gray lechwe. At least Rihani knew trails in that direction, although usually the driver paid little attention.

We headed northwestward from Juba, toward a fringe of the Sudd swamps called Lake Nyubor. Lake Nyubor is actually an old bed of the Nile where the annual overflow fills a vast depression. As the Nile recedes, its tributary, the Lau River, gradually dries to a trickle, which leaves Nyubor a lake of sorts, with vast stretches of papyrus swamp round about. Between Nyubor and the main Nile, the swamp never dries out, though it does recede to about waist depth in the driest season. One of the British game commissioners

Africa's Rarest and Most Beautiful Animal

had discovered that a herd of lechwe stayed in the Nyubor swamps even after the flood season. Lake Nyubor, therefore, is the best bet—if there can be any best bet—to get a glimpse of Mrs. Gray.

The British commissioner who was head of game supervision in the Sudan, Lt. Colonel Peter Molloy, spent some ten years in the area. Only twice during this time did he and his photographer wife manage to get pictures of Mrs. Gray. We had read Colonel Molloy's account of the matter and also corresponded with him, but even his admonitions of "ravenous mosquitoes" and "endless miles of waist-deep water" did not prepare us for what we found.

Frankly, we were apprehensive about the Dinka tribesmen. We met our first group of Agar Dinkas a few miles (and a whole day's travel) from Lake Nyubor. We had just been arrested by a Sudanese military patrol. We had forty permits in our possession, but it developed we should have had forty-one. It didn't restore our confidence when the native sergeant soldier held our travel permit upside down as he squinted at it with a blank expression. Several of the soldiers were Dinkas. They were the fiercest, biggest, most muscular men we had ever seen. Fortunately, we managed to get out of arrest by acting stupid, which took no great effort. I am sure that the native sergeant thought that we were Britishers who had somehow been left over from the former regime.

When we stopped at our first Dinka village, people crowded around us as though we were a new species of animal. Most of the men towered over us, and even the women were close to six feet in height. They giggled, pinched our clothes, and went through the boxcar to see what the ridiculous foreigners had with them. We found it a bit difficult to act nonchalant in the middle of a herd of male and female giants, every one of whom was stark, staring naked. It was days before we got used to it. Once we did get acquainted with the Dinkas, however, we liked them tremendously. We found them intelligent, inquisitive, proud, and with an excellent sense of humor. I might add that the jokes were mostly on us. As Rihani, our game scout, could not talk the Dinka language, we had little verbal communication. The Dinkas understood only one word. This was "Missygray," which they pronounced as one word.

As we approached the great depression that is Lake Nyubor, the brushland began to fall away and finally became open *toich*. The *toich* is the flat plain that surrounds the Sudd swamps. During the period of high water, even the *toich* is flooded, but at that time, late in February, it was dry. A few herds of Dinka cattle grazed on the *toich*. As we bounced laboriously over the dry hippo tracks that pockmarked the *toich*, we headed toward a Dinka village perched on a knoll at the very edge of the main swamps. Here, countless generations of Dinkas had built up a low mound of fish bones, garbage, and dirt so that the swamp ground was only spongy instead of being downright soupy. On this precarious hummock perched the little, round, grass-topped houses of perhaps a hundred Dinkas. There was also a somewhat larger "rest house," which had been built there years before by the intrepid British. The rest house had been taken over by the Dinkas, but they cheerfully moved out to accommodate us when we arrived. Unfortunately, a large flock of outsized bats, hanging in the thatch under the roof, stayed on. It was hard to tell, during our brief stay in the rest house, whether the noise of the mosquitoes or the noise of guano dropping from the roof was more disturbing. Colonel Molloy, who had stayed here on several occasions to observe Mrs. Grays, received our highest words of praise.

Only one of our boys could talk a bare smattering of English; the others represented four different tribes, mostly from the southernmost Sudan. Somehow, during the first evening of conviviality with the Dinkas at the village, our boys managed to get some information for us about Mrs. Gray, translated through half-a-dozen intermediate tongues. The information was not good.

The Dinkas said there were very few Mrs. Grays left in the Nyubor part of the Sudd. "Someone has killed them," they said guilelessly. As I found some lechwe horns on the stinking refuse piles at the edge of the village, I had little doubt who the killers were. After the British government left, the Dinkas had speared lechwe whenever they caught the animals at a disadvantage. As meat was hard to come by, they could not be blamed too much.

The Dinkas had a flotilla of dugout canoes pulled up in front of the village. The canoes are made of the hollowed-out trunks of the doleib palm. With them the Dinka fishermen pole up and down the semi-open water of the lake, in that part which was the old river channel. Beyond the open channel, where the papyrus begins, even the dugout canoes cannot get through.

Africa's Rarest and Most Beautiful Animal

The first day after our arrival we paid a couple of Dinka fishermen to take us in one of the treacherous dugouts to the end of the open water, where we might begin to look for lechwe. Almost immediately we regretted this plan. For one thing, if you hiccup in a palm-log dugout, you overturn it. As far as the Dinkas were concerned, this was great fun. Given that we carried a batch of cameras and a gun, I didn't think it funny at all. Furthermore, the treacherous little craft did not seem to get us to the heart of the business anyway. When we'd poled as far as we could eastward into the main swamp, the canoe could only go a short distance up the hippo paths from the open water. Then, when we stepped out of the dugout, which was an acrobatic feat in itself, we were standing up to our waists in stinking, weed-infested water. During two days of this kind of frustrating going, we got only a glimpse of a single female lechwe at the edge of the papyrus. In the same time, however, we learned a lot about Dinkas, even if our knowledge of the Nile lechwe was not increased at all.

Because of these difficulties, and also because of the bats in the belfry of the Dinka rest house, we determined to move down the edge of the *toich*, four or five miles eastward. From this vantage point I expected I would be able to walk into the swamps where the lechwe were. The major difficulty in moving camp was that our Sudanese boys didn't want to leave the Dinkas. As each of our lads possessed some remnant of store clothing, or a pair of out-at-the-heel tennis shoes, this made them city slickers in the eyes of the Dinka maidens. Kamun, the driver, was even more difficult than usual, which was mighty difficult. He thought of a thousand reasons we should stay in the bat-infested, stinking Dinka village. I drove the boxcar myself along the edge of the *toich* where the ground was dry. As soon as we got out of sight of the thatched huts of our Dinka friends, we began to pass through small herds of tiang coming down to the edge of the swamp to drink. As we jounced along over the awful pockmarks left by wallowing hippo when the *toich* was mud, herds of reedbuck and beautiful kob skittered off before us into the high grass along the edge of the water. We made camp under the last tree, which marked the periphery of what is laughingly called "dry ground" in this part of the Sudan. That evening I shot a couple of kob so we would have meat during the serious business of finding a Mrs. Gray.

The echo of the shot had not died away before fifteen Dinkas appeared to help us. They had, with commendable courtesy, dressed

Under the African Sun

themselves in suits—a process that consisted of smearing fish oil on their bodies and then sprinkling the stinking mess with cow-dung ash. Designs were smeared in the ashes with their fingertips, in the mode of the day. Three or four Dinka women insisted on helping Brownie as she skinned out the capes of a kob and a reedbuck. By this time, both of us were so inured to nakedness that we would have started up in amazement if anyone had shown up at our camp wearing so much as a bikini.

Fortunately, in the contingent of Dinkas were two stalwart fellows who, I gathered, were the hunters of the village. I never did learn their names, so I gave them a couple of titles. The shorter one, a stocky lad of about six feet two, I called "Hey You." His taller companion I gave the title of "You There." Both of my guides were very much pleased with their elegant names, and I have no doubt that they are still using them. These two guides, as well as most of the Dinka population, simply moved with us to our new encampment and stayed there. Camping arrangements were comparatively simple. At night they fell back into the dry grass and were asleep when they hit the ground. Apparently the voracious Nile mosquitoes don't like Dinka blood; but they sure do enjoy a tender American. Even with the well-constructed mosquito net Costi had loaned us, four or five of the brutes always managed to get inside somehow, and they made the night hideous with their droning and whining.

I must confess that even with all of these drawbacks, the edge of the Sudd is a thrilling place. In the early morning, scattered herds of tiang, kob, warthog, and baboon filtered past our camp to drink. Hippo, moving into the swamp from their night feeding on the *toich*, disturbed thousands of ducks and geese. The knob-nosed Nile and spurwing geese circled back and forth over the tips of the papyrus in screaming masses. Especially numerous were flocks of whistling teal, which alighted and then circled nervously over the small ponds of open water, where the tiang and kob disturbed them. Colonel Molloy had described this as the best duck and goose shooting country in Africa. But there were no such pleasures for us. I was somewhat apprehensive that the three or four rifle shots of the evening before might have driven any Mrs. Gray in the vicinity even deeper into the swamps. I need not have worried.

With my two guides, Hey You and You There, I started off at dawn into the Sudd. Rihani, the game scout, insisted upon going along, in

58

Africa's Rarest and Most Beautiful Animal

spite of the fact that I could see with half an eye that his enthusiasm for the quest was at an all-time low. Being a Zande, he had no use for swamps; but he considered that his mission was to guard me from the dangers of the Sudd, and I am sure he considered the Dinkas themselves the major hazard.

We started off down a cattle and game trail across the *toich*. For perhaps a mile we walked through grasslands with the water gradually getting deeper around our ankles. Fires started by the Dinkas had burned great patches of the dry grass above the water. In the mud I could see the tracks of tiang and hippo, but no sign of the elongated hoofprints of Mrs. Gray.

By the time we reached the papyrus, we were walking in water just above our knees. The papyrus was a sign that the ground here never dries, even in the long-enduring drought season. Papyrus is a beautiful plant. It feathers out, perhaps twelve feet tall, in a burst of fine spider-web fronds that glint in the early morning sunlight like thousands of soap bubbles throwing the spectrum of the sun in all directions. After a few hours of slogging through papyrus stems, however, the illusion of beauty is gone. The papyrus becomes a green hell of harsh, rasping stalks, tripping nodes beneath the water, and an impenetrable, endless mass of stems before the eye. I soon found why Dinkas grow so tall. They have to. The short ones quickly drown, or are eaten off above the waterline by mosquitoes. My Dinka guides, with their long legs, slipped along like storks. Rihani and I were half swimming most of the time.

Worst of all were the hippo trails. The bulky bodies of the river pigs had plowed great furrows through the papyrus. Their pudgy feet had tramped out the mud beneath to a depth of five or six feet, and crossing these hippo canals became a major feat, as I was trying to keep my rifle and camera reasonably dry. I didn't succeed. Even at that, we might have followed the hippo trails, if they had led in the right direction. The hippo moved during the day into the middle of the lake, several miles to the west, near the Dinka village. We were heading northeastward, crossing all the hippo channels at right angles. Insomuch as Hey You and You There were very purposeful about their direction, I hoped that they were taking me to some place in the heart of the Sudd where Mrs. Gray would abound.

As it was, the two Dinkas spent most of their time pulling Rihani and me out of hippo mudholes. Fortunately, they thought this was very funny. As I wiped green slime from my camera or poured water out of my gun barrel, their good humor rose to new heights.

I had been doing a good deal of walking after buffalo and other kinds of game even before we came to Lake Nyubor. I thought I was in fairly good shape. But even before noon of the first day in the swamps, I was tiring fast. We ate a romantic little picnic lunch of cold kob meat while we stood up in the water. While Rihani and I munched glumly and slapped at mosquitoes, the two Dinkas frisked around like a couple of kids. To use up part of their excess energy, they speared fish in a hippo channel just ahead. As the water is murky, the spearmen cannot see the quarry. The Dinkas pranced up and down the hippo canal, disturbing the matted papyrus roots with their feet. When they saw a swirl in the dark water, they made a stab at it with their barbed spear. Hey You soon transfixed a large tilapia, which looks like a bass. He made a sling of papyrus fiber and hung the fish over his back. Apparently this was to be their meal when we camped that night in the swamp.

Camped in the swamp! I had heard of people sleeping standing up, but never in three feet of water. The thought of my little camp bed back there on the *toich*, with only four or five voracious mosquitoes inside the netting, made me wriggle with delightful anticipation.

Early in the afternoon, we burst through the endless papyrus into an open, swampy meadow. Here the water was only a foot or so in depth, and ambatch grass stood above the water here and there in soggy hummocks. I gathered from the action of the Dinkas that this was the place where Mrs. Gray came to feed. As we walked around the edge of the swampy clearing, I saw dollops of dung on the matted grass. No other animal but a lechwe could exist in such a place.

For perhaps two hours, we circled the edge of the swamp meadow in the midst of the Sudd. Although the whole area was only half a mile across, we could see very little of it at a time. Our vantage point was so low that we could not look over even the scattered clumps of ambatch grass a hundred yards or so distant. My two Dinka friends, with their eyes a foot or so above my own, could see a lot more.

You There suddenly grabbed my arm and pointed with his spear. I could see nothing. We moved forward at a crouch. I stepped on top of a grass hummock. In the distance I could see a flick of motion. I focused the binoculars on it. It was a brownish animal with a white tail

Africa's Rarest and Most Beautiful Animal

that jerked back and forth with windshield-wiper regularity. The animal had no horns. Hey You nudged me and held up one hand with his fingers widespread. I looked again. I could see another, and then another animal. Hey You was better with his unaided eyesight than I was with a pair of 8X30 binoculars. There were indeed five Mrs. Grays. There wasn't a horn in the bunch. (The female Mrs. Gray is hornless.) But even with this disappointment, I thrilled at the movement of the animals as they walked out of the green wall of papyrus and began to feed on the tender shoots of ambatch grass. I could see in the glass, as the lechwe raised their feet, that their hoofs were elongated like sled-runners. One of the larger lechwe playfully ran forward a few steps. She looked like she was walking on the tips of the grass stems. To my certain knowledge, the water at the edge of the papyrus was two or three feet deep.

We watched the herd of female lechwe for perhaps ten minutes. I was amazed at the grace of the animals: the way they held their heads, and handled their slim feet with quick running steps as they moved out into the meadow. But Hey You and You There seemed to be down-hearted. This was unusual, as all day long they had been as happy as a couple of lobsters in mating season. Now they shook their heads sadly, and turned to go. I could only deduce that if female Mrs. Grays were in the meadow, then there would be no bulls. The only good thing I could see about the business was that my two Dinka friends had apparently given up the idea of camping in the swamp and dining in a regal manner off raw fish while we stood up all night in the water.

How we ever got out of the swamp I will never know. It was suddenly dark, with the African lack of twilight, long before we had slogged our way through the four or five miles of papyrus. I had ceased trying to keep the camera dry or my gun above water. The belt of half-rotten papyrus stems that collected in front of my thighs and waist grew bigger and bigger. I didn't even jerk it away. Somehow, by starlight, we came out on the *toich*. The pinpoint of light that was our campfire looked like a beacon of hope. I don't even remember eating or rolling onto my cot.

It was no surprise, then, in the morning, when I couldn't remember getting dressed. I found that my legs were badly swollen and my shins cut in a hundred places by the sawtooth edges of the ambatch grass. But no matter. With a hearty breakfast and a rising sun, what hunter loses hope? I gathered that my two Dinka friends had another idea for Mrs. Gray. Hey You and You There were as fresh as two daisies covered with morning dew. I gathered from their grins and their slapping each other on the back that they were reenacting for their friends' benefit the trip of the afternoon before, when the white man had gone headfirst into a hippo channel and come up blowing muddy water from every opening.

Somehow we started off. The only one less enthusiastic than myself was Rihani. (At least we knew what to expect.) We headed easterly, along the edge of the *toich*, for perhaps three or four miles and then plunged into the papyrus. We continued to head eastward, apparently to strike a spot six or eight miles distant from where we had been the day before. Long before noon I became tired, hot, and dry. I had a small canteen, and this was already empty. I noticed that the Dinkas drank water in the swamp only in the places where lotus lilies grew. Here and there, apparently, springs or seeps welled up from the bottom and kept the water comparatively fresh. I knew that the Nile and all of its tributaries are full of liver flukes, belhartzia bugs, and heaven knows what else. But the dangers of these things are notions of civilized man. Besides, you can't even see them—unless you look closely. So, at the next lotus-marked pool, I drank with the Dinkas.

Some time along in the morning, Hey You and You There dropped off to one side to spear a fish they had seen swirl. Splashing ahead, I happened to look up. There stood a giant of a man. He was motionless, facing me. He raised his right arm. He cocked his elbow. The barbed spear in his hand was level at my chest. This was it! I was going to be spitted by a Dinka, and I didn't even care.

The strange Dinka spearman apparently thought the look of woe on my face was the aspect of a confirmed coward. He thrust forward with his spear, and stuck it into the water between my feet. He broke into gales of laughter. He would have rolled on the ground, only there was no ground. So he hung onto the papyrus stems. Soon Hey You and You There joined in the general fun. It was a good joke, being in the middle of an endless swamp, dying of exhaustion, and undoubtedly being eaten from the inside by liver flukes and loathsome parasites, and being scared to death by a strange giant with a spear.

A few hundred yards farther on, we came to a muddy hummock in the swamp. Four Dinka families were perched on this hump of

Africa's Rebuilt and Most Beautiful Animal

mud, in four little grass huts. Racks of dried fish were half-obscured by the smoke of wet wood fires. Three women and half-a-dozen scraggly children stared at us in amazement. The whole village and its dozen or so occupants were on a piece of ground not fifty feet across. How the hummock came to be there in the first place, or how the Dinkas had ever found it, I'll never know.

The joker who was going to spear me apparently told Hey You and You There where Mrs. Gray lurked in the swamps beyond the little village. We soon started off again. Early in the afternoon we came out into another ambatch meadow, somewhat smaller than the one we had seen before. Again the faint trails in the grass and the dollops of dung showed that the swamp-dwelling antelope had been there. But the dung was old, the trails unused.

We waited until late evening, on the off-chance that a Mrs. Gray would appear. Even Hey You and You There seemed dispirited. They made motions above their heads, in the outline of the lyre-shaped horns of the bull lechwe. Then they looked down at their feet and made long faces. They were trying to tell me that Mrs. Gray would not come there.

So be it! The hunt was a bust. I knew that I did not have another day's hunting left in me—not in that swamp. My legs were cut to ribbons by the sawgrass, but as they were numb with weariness anyway, I didn't even notice. I moved mechanically as we turned back toward the little fishing village in the middle of the swamp. Lifting each sodden foot up and over the clods of papyrus became an impossible feat. I stumbled frequently, but no matter. Drowning would be a welcome end.

We passed the little village. Again the women and children eyed us solemnly. I scarcely noticed the clouds of mosquitoes as thick as smoke around the piles of fish guts and fish bones at the edge of the water. We splashed on. Just beyond the village, I tripped and fell into a hippo channel. Hey You had to pull me out by the seat of my pants. Had it not been for him, I think I would have floated facedown and just stayed there. Hey You grinned at me as I blew water out of my mouth. The stuff tasted like hippopotamus dung.

As I got the water out of my ears, I heard someone yelling. The voice was off in the distance. Hey You and You There whistled in reply. We splashed on. I wasn't interested. If the Dinkas wanted to meet friends in the middle of the swamp, they could meet friends and be damned. I didn't even care if I got lost. I just plain didn't care.

Under the African Sun

Running toward us was the joker I had encountered earlier, the head of the Dinka fishing village. I scarcely noticed that he was running through papyrus and water where I could scarcely move my legs. "I wonder how they bury their dead under these circumstances," I muttered to myself. "Would it be burial-at-sea technique, or a simple civil ceremony?"

The newcomer was talking in low tones to Hey You. He made the sign of horns over his head and pointed back behind him. Hey You turned to me and made the sign of horns again. He pointed to my gun. They had seen a lechwe. Well, what if they had? I couldn't get to the place if the lechwe was covered with hundred-dollar bills.

They pointed roughly in the direction of camp to the west. That was the only reason I went along with the idea. The three Dinkas frolicked along in front, as though we had not already come fifteen miles through the awfullest going in the whole of Africa. The Dinkas were obviously irked by my slow progress; even Rihani looked as though he would never make it. It appeared there was going to be a double burial somewhere in that endless papyrus.

By twilight we had made only a couple of miles. At least it was cooler. Funnyface had waltzed off into the papyrus and disappeared for ten minutes. He came back grinning broadly, again pointing behind him. I was a little excited by his infectious enthusiasm. I quickened my pace from the gait of a string-haltered sloth to a snail's gallop. The three Dinkas disappeared again, and then came back to get me. With a Dinka at each of my elbows, we somehow moved forward. The water was still waist deep. We broke through a fringe of papyrus.

There was a small opening—an ambatch meadow perhaps a hundred yards across. On the far side I saw the outline of an animal's head. At the sound of our splashing steps, the head moved upward. Two long, double-curved horns arched back over his withers. He turned and looked full at us. To both sides were other animals and other horns. Half-a-dozen Mrs. Grays stood at the edge of the papyrus. Most of the animals were half invisible. The one in the center had the longest horns. I threw the Weatherby to my shoulder. There was water on the telescopic sight. I blew off the drops. It was still dreamy, and the light was poor. The cross hairs settled on the base of the bull's throat, then jerked away to the side. My exhausted arms could not hold the rifle still. As the cross hairs moved past the bull's chest I jerked off the shot. I did not even bolt in another shell. I was done.

At the clap of the shot every lechwe disappeared as though jerked into the papyrus from behind. The Dinkas raced forward a few steps, then stood glumly. I had missed. I had seen my first and last Mrs. Gray.

I sat down heavily in the water. I heard Rihani sink down behind me. There was a splash over across the clearing. A plume of water shot up above the tips of the papyrus. Some frantic animal had made a gigantic leap there. The three Dinkas ran forward and disappeared. There was a shout, and then another. They came through the papyrus, carrying the bull on their shoulders.

It was a triumphant procession that came out of the papyrus onto the *toich* just at dark. One of the Dinkas had raced ahead to carry the news to camp. Brownie had driven the boxcar along the edge of the *toich*, to save us a walk of a mile or two. When we got back to camp, I remember only measuring the horns of the lechwe. Thirty-two-and-a-half inches.

Colonel Molloy tells me that at certain dry seasons, when the swamp water is low, Mrs. Grays come out to the edge of the *toich*, and may occasionally be seen there. Several British sportsmen have bagged a Mrs. Gray in this way. As far as I am concerned, the law which states that a hunter may take only one Mrs. Gray during his lifetime is entirely unnecessary. One Mrs. Gray is enough.

Chapter 7

HUNTING THE SAHARA OF BEAU GESTE
(1959)

Tom crawled again underneath the stalled car and lay on his belly. We had both been working there for three hours, trying to fix the shattered fuel pump. The sun burning down out of the African sky had heated the sand around us well above the 100-degree mark. We tried to keep the metal tools we were using in the shade under the car. The wrench Tom had picked up had been in the sun for only a few minutes.

"Of all the dad-blamed, double-breasted difficulties!" Tom Bolack was rolling around on the sand, flapping his arms like a trained seal. He licked his fingers where the hot metal of the wrench had branded him.

At any other time and in any other place, two full-grown men lying under a stalled car in the middle of the desert would make a funny cartoon. Under the circumstances, however, it wasn't funny and it wasn't a cartoon. Tom Bolack, lieutenant governor of New Mexico and the man who had killed the world-record polar bear, had started out into the Sahara with me to look for desert game. We did find desert game—and we also found other things. Most of these other things were several forms of death.

There is no dangerous game in the Sahara. For this reason, Tom and I had thought that our desert hunt in the northern part of French Equatorial Africa would be a country stroll. We even had brought our wives. Brownie and I had been hunting the Sudan for some time; we had arranged with Tom and Alice to meet us at the small border town of Abéché, on the eastern edge of the Sahara. The guidebook said that there was a local French airline into Abéché. It hadn't worked out that way. We had also arranged through Jacky Maeder and Company of Zurich, Switzerland, for a local French guide, one Jean Bepoix, to meet us at the Sudanese border, bringing with him a couple of vehicles and some natives as camp boys. That hadn't worked out either.

As a matter of record, Bepoix, who has spent most of his life in that country, has become almost as Arabic as the Arabs themselves. Outside of a penchant for French red wine, a copious supply of which he always had on hand, he was, in speech and manner of thinking, an Arab. We soon found that the Arabs have no words in their glossary for "close connection." There is an old Arabic saying, "Allah has given us the rest of the day, and all of tomorrow." Putting things off till the morrow makes sense in the Beau Geste country.

Abéché looks more like a stage set than a real town. The hotel, where Legionnaires drop in for cognac, and the Abéché fort look as though Hollywood directors had built them. At the camel market near the fort swarm the picturesque desert tribesmen. In the eastern Sahara, the natives are mostly Gorans. They have been covered with an overlay of Arabic culture, too; they ride swift racing camels, and carry eighteen-foot-long spears. At the markets, Gorans barter for camels, rugs, and wives. Goran crones haggle over fly-encrusted chunks of goat meat, while Goran artisans pound out wrought-iron spear points in the manner taught them by the Arab traders. It was these same spear points that were almost to cost us the hunt.

By breeding very fast racing camels, the Gorans have developed remarkable animals with speed and endurance surpassing almost anything else that moves in the desert. Given anything close to an even break, a Goran cameleer can ride down a gazelle and hamstring the fleeing animal with the razor-sharp edge of his spear. A French officer at Abéché told us that all of the desert game for a hundred miles around had been killed off by the Gorans.

Our caravan consisted of a fairly creditable truck, loaded mostly with Jean's wine, and a fossilized version of a United States Army command car. Apparently this down-at-the-wheel vehicle was left over from the campaigns against Rommel along the North African coast. The French had tied together the major parts of the weary old machine with wire, and had added a coat of paint to cover the original olive drab. From a hundred yards away, as a matter of fact, our safari car didn't look so bad. If you tried to ride in it, though,

Hunting the Sahara of Beau Geste

you had an experience worth missing. The windshield had collapsed on top of the hood long ago. There was no other vestige of a top or sides. You had the feeling you were riding on top of a disintegrating gravel crusher. I considered it a mechanical miracle that it got as far as the frontier town of Oum Chalouba.

We were amazed and dismayed when the Bolacks showed up at Oum Chalouba in an exact duplicate of "Old Decrepit." Apparently two of these vehicles of World War II had been rescued by the French. The Bolacks had been delayed by a series of airplane adventures. Plane trouble had developed over the Atlantic, and they had missed connections from Paris. The ride out into the desert from Fort Lamy, with a maniacal Arab camel driver at the wheel of their vibrating vehicle, had just about finished them. If Tom and Alice had known the Arabic for "Turn around and go back home," they would have done so.

Certainly there was game around Oum Chalouba. This far north of the general range of the Gorans, desert gazelles of several kinds were fairly common. The population of Oum Chalouba didn't bother the wildlife—mainly because there was no population. At the fort, there was a body of native troops, led by a French sergeant. Outside the fort, the one well in the bottom of the wadi, or wash, had gone dry, and most of the people had moved away. We found that this was not at all unusual in the Sahara. Water is life; where there is no water, there are no people.

As for the desert animals, most of them do not drink at all. Some of the desert gazelles get moisture from the wild melons that grow just after the infrequent rains. Other desert animals do not even seek out green grass or melons. Their bodies are so remarkably adapted to conserving moisture that the scant water contained in the dry herbage is enough.

Within sight of the fort at Oum Chalouba, Tom and I bagged Dorcas gazelles and their larger cousins, Dama gazelles. The Dorcas is very much like the East African Tommy, and about the same size; the Dama is a handsome animal, somewhat larger than our pronghorn antelope in North America but of a similar appearance. Just south of Oum Chalouba we ran into small herds of red-fronted gazelles, another of the small desert-dwelling members of the gazelle family. This was well and good, but we had not come to this far country to polish off pretty little gazelles for table meat. Our real objectives were the desert oryx and the desert addax.

69

Under the African Sun

The white oryx, or scimitar-horned oryx, is one of the handsomest members of the oryx family. Formerly common from the desert area of the Sudan westward through Libya and the French Sahara, the white oryx is now limited to a fraction of this range, and is mighty scarce even there. The oryx does not flourish when harassed by camel-riding natives with long spears or by men with guns. If humans move in, the oryx moves out. In addition to this shyness, the scimitar-horned oryx migrates at various times of the year, depending on the seasons and the occasional desert rains. At times, the oryx seems to migrate for no apparent reason at all. These migrations are not mass movements of hundreds of animals together, like some of the game treks in other parts of Africa; instead, the white oryx seems to drift in small groups of a dozen or so, or even singly. Generally, this fascinating animal lingers on the edge of the true desert. The oryx country that we saw north of Oum Chalouba as far as the Libyan border was desert enough, but not quite completely bare.

The addax, even more of a desert dweller than the white oryx, lives in the wildest solitudes of the Sahara, where there is practically no vegetation at all. We knew that we would have to go far out to the north and west to get addax, but we hoped to get oryx close to our base camp. By taking both of the disintegrating command cars, we made a sweep north and west of the fort at Oum Chalouba, as far as we could go in one day. We saw Dama gazelles, desert ostrich, and thousands of Dorcas gazelles, but no sign at all of an oryx or an addax.

Bepoix told us, on the third evening of our stay at Oum Chalouba, that he thought we should move north to the Camel Corps headquarters at Fada, and hunt from there. That same evening, a camel caravan moved through Oum Chalouba on its way south. The cameleers had just come from Fada, having made the journey in fourteen days, with one water stop on the way. In all that distance they had not seen a single oryx, or even so much as an oryx track.

This was grim news. There were no other places in the whole eastern Sahara from which we might hunt. Two of the Arabs with the caravan said they knew where oryx and addax could be found. With Jean interpreting, I asked these two men where this was. One of the fellows, a lanky, hook-nosed, wall-eyed rascal, knelt before us and smoothed the sand with one hand. On the smooth surface he made forty little depressions with the tip of his finger. Over this he made several passes with both hands. He spat between his palms and clapped his hands together. "The desert animals you seek are that way, master," he said, pointing to the northwest.

Very courteous of him, I thought, to invoke the blessings of the gods of the desert before he answered my question. The man was obviously a crossbreed, mingling in his veins the blood of some Arab slaver of years ago with that of the desert tribes. Nominally such people are Mohammedans, but they still retain much of the ancient folk magic and witchcraft of the Nilotic natives.

Jean was shaking his head. "*Ce n'est-pas bon*, that one." I didn't know whether Jean was referring to the evil-looking Arab kneeling on the sand before us or to the man's proposition that he could lead us to the country of the oryx and addax. As an afterthought I remarked to Jean, "Ask the fellow his name."

"*Ouwash*," the Arab replied. His name was also the Arabic word for white oryx. *That's a good omen*, I thought. And then aloud I said, "Let's give it a try." I was beginning to believe the desert hocus-pocus myself. Ouwash insisted on taking a friend with him as an additional guide. The other Arab's name was Jebel, which means devil. I don't know what kind of omen that was.

It was bright and cold the next morning, and we instructed our wives to stay in the main camp near the fort, where they would be comparatively safe—except from any wandering lion, leopard, scorpions, Arab bandits, or vicious desert tribesmen. (*We* did not mention the possible dangers; our wives did.) We left the truck and a driver with the women. Tom and I cranked up the two command cars and swung aboard. We took two of our retinue of camp boys and the two Arab guides, Ouwash and Jebel. Bepoix drove one car and Tom and I took turns driving the other. We rounded the Oum Chalouba fort and headed north along the faint camel track that leads to Fada. Some sixty miles north of Oum Chalouba, several hours later, we turned northwestward along the course of a large wadi. The hard-packed sand on the floor of the wadi made comparatively smooth going, which was just as well, as one of the old command cars began to cough and stutter. Late in the afternoon, it died completely.

Fortunately, Tom had worked in the oil fields when he was younger. By the light of our one lantern he dismantled certain parts of the viscera of the ailing car. "No matter what I look at, it all needs fixing," he observed philosophically.

Under the African Sun

We made a cold camp under a stunted little tree, which turned out to be the last piece of major vegetation we were to see for a long time. The next morning, Tom got the car started again and we continued west by northwest, down the floor of the big wadi. By noon we had made perhaps seventy-five miles or so. I couldn't tell for sure, as the odometer on the car I was driving had stuck at 62,000 miles some time in 1944, when the American Army had abandoned the thing.

Our noon stop was difficult, as there was absolutely no shade. The burning ball of the sun hung straight overhead. The two Mohammedans squatted and scowled at us as we sipped some of Jean's bitter red wine with our heads stuck under the running board. Bepoix was questioning the two Arabs. Again the hawk-visaged Ouwash made the forty little pits in a smooth patch of sand and then ran the tip of his finger among the depressions in a mysterious figure-eight pattern. He spat between his palms and pointed straight west down the wadi.

Tom had been standing in the back of the car for elevation. He called down to us, "What do those white oryx look like?" Tom squinted through his binoculars in the direction Ouwash pointed. "There's something jumping around down there," he commented.

Both Jean and I climbed up on the bed of the car. The shimmering heat haze made the sand dunes on either side waver and swim before our eyes. There did seem to be a light-colored animal standing on the floor of the wadi, three or four hundred yards away. It was the waves of heat over the sand that made the animal seem to jump and move. Through the moving mirage I could make out long, curving horns and a light-colored body. "*Ouwash!*" grunted Jean.

We coaxed the two vehicles into reluctant life and moved on down the wadi. As we approached, the single oryx turned and ran. Just ahead we saw two more oryx. The animals were moving across the sand dunes from our right. Just beyond was a small herd of eight or ten, also moving from right to left.

"*C'est bon, c'est bon!*" Bepoix was mumbling. In another mile we were in the midst of oryx, all moving in a southwesterly direction. We had, by the magic of the forty pits in the sand, found a migration of these desert animals. During the next two days we saw several hundred oryx.

But seeing an oryx and bagging an oryx are two different matters. We seldom got closer than three hundred yards to any of the animals, and usually it was five hundred. Toward evening, when the heat haze settled down, I jumped out of the car and ran to the top of a sand dune to try a long shot. Five or six oryx that we had been glassing immediately started off at a dead run. On the top of the sand dune I had a good prone rest. The oryx were angling away. The last one in line looked the biggest. I settled the scope of the Weatherby .300 well ahead of the animal's nose and touched it off. The bullet hit the oryx right through the middle. He dropped out of line, faltered a few steps, and then lay down. As we came up to administer the *coup de grâce*, Ouwash and Jebel turned to us, pleading and kneading their hands. Ouwash held a wicked curved knife he had jerked out of his belt. I grinned at them and shook my head.

The camp was in the middle of the oryx migration. That night, at dark, we could still see animals moving by us, always in a southerly direction. At daylight the next morning, oryx were still drifting past. By this time we were becoming very choosy about oryx. The horns of the first animal I had downed were forty inches long. This is very good for the scimitar-horned oryx, but we thought we could do better. Tom made a spectacular long shot on a single male oryx running straight away from us. The horns of Tom's oryx measured 44½ inches, about equal to the existing world record.

The next afternoon, we found a large herd of about fifteen animals moving across the wadi perhaps ten miles below camp. One of the oryx had horns that curved back and down almost to his rump. He was a monster. It was my turn to shoot. Feeling confident, I elected to try a very long one. The oryx were moving almost at right angles across our path, perhaps four hundred yards away. Settling the Weatherby very carefully, with my elbow resting on a hummock of sand on the edge of the wash, I pulled the cross hairs of the scope well ahead of the big oryx, which was running in the middle of the herd, and carefully squeezed off the shot. The oryx just behind the big one dropped as though jerked down from below. The shot had broken his neck cleanly just behind his ear. I groaned.

"Take the big one! Take the big one!" yelled Tom. I jumped back into the car. It was Tom's next shot, but he insisted that I take it. Our game licenses called for three white oryx apiece. I had not intended to shoot three, but under Tom's urging I decided to try it again. Jean was pounding the accelerator with his boot, trying to urge the car to the top of a line of dunes. We stuck in the sand with the wheels churning. I jumped out and ran forward. The herd of oryx was again four hundred yards or so away, a very long shot. The big animal with the enormous horns was running second to last. I aimed at the rump of the oryx in front of him and heard the *clunk* of the bullet hitting flesh. The big oryx dropped out of line, circled a moment, and then rolled on his side. Again Ouwash and Jebel came up with their knives in their hands pleading to *"hallel."* "Not this one," I said grimly.

The big oryx was a male, his horns measuring 51¼ inches, some six inches over the existing world record. Ouwash and Jebel were not at all pleased. Unless a true believer faces east and cuts the throat of an animal to kill him, a Mohammedan cannot eat the meat. Late that evening Tom shot a smaller male oryx and let the two Moslems *hallel* its throat just before the animal died. They made a bloody business of it, but they were happy as two clams. Now everybody had meat.

Flushed with confidence after bagging the record oryx, we did not even hesitate when Ouwash made his pits in the sand the next morning and indicated that the gods of the hunt directed us farther west to where the addax live. Farther west we went, straight into the heart of the Sahara. In that direction there was not a fort, a town, or a source of water for a thousand miles. The big wadi, which we had been following so long, gradually disappeared in a series of minor rivulets and sand dunes. Still, Ouwash directed us westward.

By the time we had gone another fifty miles from our oryx camp, the desert floor was as bare as Mother Hubbard's cupboard. I didn't understand it. Addax are animals, and animals have to eat. Still, when we asked him where the addax were, Ouwash spread his hand and pointed westward.

Our misgivings grew when both of the cars began to falter. With the increased heat around noon, vapor locks in the gas lines were a matter of course. We cooled the locks by pouring water on a rag, but the water was running low. We used Jean's red wine to cool the gas lines. Jean was not at all enthusiastic about this. Quite unnecessarily, he pointed out that if we stalled, we would have over two hundred miles to walk to the nearest French fort. No human could make it that far over this blistering desert, even if he could carry enough water for the trip. To make matters worse, the going through the sand dunes degenerated from difficult to impossible. When a car became mired in loose sand, we fed a couple of sections of perforated airstrip surfacing, which the thrifty French had taken from some desert airfield of World War II, under the churning wheels. This system worked fine, and when the car had gained momentum enough on the two strips to advance a few yards, we had no difficulty picking up the steel sections, running forward in front of the car, and placing them in position again. By noon, however, the steel strips had become so hot in the sun that we could not handle them without blistering our hands, and the pulling along in low gear had overheated the already overtaxed internals of the dying engines. The one I was driving suddenly emitted a death rattle and quit.

"It's that fuel pump," Bolack said with the air of a professional diagnostician. He was already getting out the tools. Tom dismantled the fuel pump, and we took it underneath the car, as there was no other shade. From a section of a coffee-can lid, a flattened-out brass cartridge case, and some scrap metal that we found under the seat, Tom sawed, hammered, and filed a new fuel pump into being. I did not dare to contemplate, during these preparations, what the outcome would be if Tom's makeshift contrivance didn't work. Fortunately, it did.

During the hours that Tom and I had spent underneath the car building the fuel pump, Ouwash and Jebel had squatted in the sand with their burnooses over their heads. Half-a-dozen times Ouwash had made the forty pits with his finger. After the mysterious passes with his hands, he indicated that the addax were still farther west.

The breakdown of the car had considerably diminished our enthusiasm for addax. At that time, we would have settled for any plan that would have gotten us out of the desert. When the engine of the car wheezed into life again, we motioned Ouwash and Jebel into the back, and I swung the car around to go back. Already the tracks we had made in the sand dunes were beginning to drift over from the constant wind that moved across the desert floor.

Tom, who was standing in the back of the car, pounded on the top of my hat. He was looking west, directly behind us. I stopped. As we lost momentum, the wheels sank deep in the sand dune we were crossing. It would take us an hour to dig out even if we got the engine started again.

"Addax!" yelled Tom. "Addax! A whole herd of them!" I jumped up on top of the car and focused my binoculars in the direction Tom pointed. Through the heat waves I could see moving animals. They were crossing the sand dunes perhaps a mile west of where we had stopped to rebuild the fuel pump. The crazy heat waves made the animals seem to separate so that their heads and legs moved independently.

Jean was looking too. *"Mon dieu! Beaucoup de choconas!"* I moved my glasses to the left. There were more addax to the south-west, and yet another bunch farther beyond. The whole western horizon seemed to be addax, all of them moving. Even if this mirage multiplied their numbers, there certainly were a lot of *"choconas."*

Bepoix had told us that we would be very fortunate if we found three or four addax. Half-a-dozen addax made a big herd. The mysterious addax is not a common animal by any standard, and never so easily found as the white oryx. Through the heat waves I had seen what seemed to be forty or fifty of the animals. They moved along easily over the sand, which, to my certain knowledge, was so hot that it would blister a man through the soles of his shoes.

My car was stuck, so we left it there. With the metal tracks we managed to back Bepoix's vehicle onto a hard area between two dunes, and turn in the direction of the migrating addax. I signaled Jean to drive and got my Weatherby ready. We drove between lines of dunes on hard, gravelly soil for perhaps a mile. Tom, standing in the back of the lurching command car, could no longer see the addax. We signaled Jean to stop. Tom and I ran together to the top of a crested dune. At its summit we took a second to brush aside the super-heated surface sand so that we could rest our elbows and look over.

The addax were perhaps three hundred yards away. Fifteen or twenty of the animals moved in front of us. Their bodies were white, their horns black. Their splayed-out hooves, adapted to the desert environment, scarcely sank into the sand. The addax had already seen us. They wheeled away at a dead run. Off to my right, another group of addax appeared over the top of a dune. Then another group moved into sight, and another. I stretched forward with the Weatherby and selected a heavy-horned addax in the middle of the right-hand bunch.

Just behind us, Jean ran up and began to yell. *"Le troisième!* The third one!" I didn't know which the third one was, from what end or what side, but I thought I saw the addax Jean meant. He was a magnificent animal, running in about the middle of one of the groups. I shifted the sight ahead of his nose and pulled off the shot.

"Got him!" yelled Tom and I together. Bolack and I grinned sheepishly at each other. We had both downed the same animal.

Hunting the Sahara of Beau Geste

Jean now began to yell in French and Arabic together. Apparently, he was trying to point out another trophy-sized addax. The animals now ran at all angles, one bunch cutting diagonally through another. Two more herds had appeared to add to the melee. The range had opened considerably. I quickly picked out another heavy-horned animal on the far right. I squeezed off a shot at him just as he disappeared over a sand dune. I thought I heard the *whump* of the bullet. Tom had fired at another addax somewhere on his side.

Within a few seconds there was not a living thing in that stretch of desert. Before us, in the little valley between the sand dunes, lay three dead addax. We ran forward together, shook hands all around, and thumped each other on the back. Bepoix was still exclaiming at the number of the animals. He said that in his whole lifetime he had never seen so many addax in one area. The first addax, which Tom and I had shot together, turned out to be the No. 2 addax in the world records, with a horn length of 41 3/8 inches.

As we searched for the second animal I had shot, we saw other herds of addax in the distance, always to the west. We also saw vultures beginning to appear in the late afternoon sky. My second addax had gone about half a mile before he dropped. When we got to him, the vultures had already eaten his eyes and part of his face.

On the way back to the fort, the other car conked out, and Tom built most of a new carburetor out of bits and pieces. So we brought a record oryx, a record addax, and two motorized relics out of the Sahara. If I ever go to the Beau Geste country again, I want Bolack to be the mechanic of the expedition. And someday I plan to learn how forty pits in the sand can locate game.

LEOPARD BWANA
(1959)

The open jaws were at his throat. The rifle barrel had been knocked aside. Stumbling backward, he raised his hands to fend off the cat's face. The leopard seized the hunter's pith helmet instead of his throat, and with teeth and claws the animal tore it into fragments.

In those few seconds, David Ommanney was able to raise his rifle and fire at point-blank range.

This story, and many other accounts of leopard attacks Andrew Holmberg told me around the fires of our safari camps. "A wounded leopard will always charge," Andrew had said. "Pound for pound, the leopard is the most dangerous of the Big Five of African game."

On this particular safari we had not yet bagged a leopard, though we had seen almost every other kind of game that Kenya and Tanganyika could produce. We had taken two excellent lion—one maned and one maneless—and had seen a family of cheetah make a kill. As this was in Kenya, where cheetah are considered royal game, we did not bag a cheetah. We did, however, locate and collect a serval cat, which looks like a small leopard. But we very much wanted a leopard of trophy size.

We had also learned something of the ways of white hunters. The white hunter operates by a strict code. Even with very dangerous game, the hunter does not shoot unless the situation is extremely critical. Andrew's idea of "critical" differed radically from mine. We were charged repeatedly by rhino. Two elephant tried their best to kill us. We had a very intimate experience with a nasty Cape buffalo. During all of these "sticky situations," as Andrew described them, he stood impassively behind me with his .470 double ready. But he did not shoot. It was nice to know he was there, but just the same . . .

"Andrew," I remember saying somewhat bitterly on one occasion when we were hunting lion, "if one of these friends of yours has me by the throat, please shoot."

Andrew just smiled, and pointed his gun barrel at the lion that was now trotting away. I had just shot one large male out of the pair. The remaining male had advanced threateningly from the body of his dead friend.

"Lion will hardly ever charge," Andrew said quietly. "It's different with leopard."

As far as leopard were concerned, it looked as though we were going to be skunked anyway. Leopard were indeed scarce, but we had seen two of these elusive cats. Early in our safari in southwestern Kenya, we had put out some leopard baits. Our safari boys, under Andrew's direction, had tied Grant gazelle carcasses in the trees in just the right manner. We also placed a string of four baits along a small stream that flows into the Mara River. After three days, we had two leopard on two of these baits.

We saw the first leopard just at daylight as we came to look at the string of baits. The cat was in the tree next to the gazelle and had already fed on the rotting flesh. I could see the leopard clearly against the gray morning sky. He was draped in a relaxed attitude over a couple of limbs. His tail twitched back and forth nervously. He looked straight at us.

Andrew pressed my gun barrel down. "Too small," he whispered. "Much too small. We don't want him."

The leopard looked immense to me. It certainly was far bigger than any of the mountain lion that we had bagged in our Southwestern country back home.

It was the same with the second leopard. We found this one actually feeding on the carcass, again early in the morning. Again Andrew had said, "Too small," and he added, "It's a female."

The major difficulty on our whole safari had been getting Andrew to let me shoot anything. If the animal did not seem to set a record of some kind, we didn't fire. Now, toward the end of the trip, it looked as though Andrew's particular attitude was going to cost me a leopard altogether. Many safaris do not bring back a leopard in their bag. I didn't want to be one of those.

Leopard Bwana

It was while we were after an especially large buffalo along the bank of the Mara, farther north, that we found a leopard track. Immediately, Ngoro, our gunbearer, and Andrew were on their knees in the dirt, talking in Swahili about the imprint. They gesticulated excitedly, and measured the outline of the track with their hands.

"Biggest leopard track we've ever seen," Andrew said as he rose to his feet and dusted his knees. "He came to water here last night."

The buffalo hunt was abandoned for the time being, and all our energies were turned to the baiting of the leopard. We shot a zebra and a Grant gazelle. As a leopard will seldom follow a drag mark, we had to place these two baits in a position where the cat would actually smell the carcass after we had placed it in a tree. We carefully cached the gazelle and the zebra about a mile apart, each bait placed so that the evening breeze would carry the smell of the fast-decaying flesh along the bank of the stream where the leopard would come to water. Still farther down, along a small side stream, we shot a big male baboon and placed this in the fork of a thorn tree well back from the creek, near the mouth of a side canyon where the leopard had evidently come down the night before. With these preparations completed, we carefully withdrew. We did not shoot any other game close to or between any of these baits, as such a disturbance might drive the leopard off.

The next morning, we approached the Grant gazelle cautiously. It had not been touched. As we drove our safari car toward the zebra bait, along a game trail that paralleled the river, we saw the leopard's track again. There was no mistaking that big cat's imprint. It was as big as a good-sized lion. Farther on we saw another track in the dust of the trail. The leopard was heading straight for our biggest bait.

As we approached the zebra, Andrew stopped the car so that we might investigate with our binoculars. One hind leg of the bait animal had been eaten. The heavy carcass had been hoisted higher in the tree and pulled into a different position. We crawled out of the safari car and moved forward at a low crouch to get a closer look. (We had earlier constructed a sketchy blind some fifty yards from the base of the tree that held the bait.) It was now our intention to work our way up behind this screen. The leopard should be there, guarding the meat.

Before we had crawled halfway to the tangle of vines that served as our blind, Andrew, hunching along in front, stiffened.

He motioned me up beside him. "There he is," he whispered in my ear. "It's the biggest leopard I've ever seen."

As slowly as I could, I crawled forward a few feet to the bole of a big thorn tree. Behind this, I slowly pulled myself to my knees, and looked out through the crotch where a heavy limb left the trunk. I could see nothing.

"To the right on the ground," Andrew whispered hoarsely.

There he was! I could just make out the top of the head and the erect ears in the long grass. The leopard was standing beneath the bait tree. There was no doubt that he had seen us. In a second he would whirl and go. If only I could stand erect and rest my rifle over the limb of the thorn tree just above my eyes. Such a movement, though, would certainly frighten the leopard. The largest leopard Andrew had ever seen! I must not miss.

Clumsily, I placed the gun alongside the thorn tree trunk. I flipped off the safety and rose as high on my knees as I could. Still I could make out only the upper half of the leopard's head. *I'll never hit him in the head at this distance*, I thought. *I'll try for the chest.*

I centered the cross hairs of the sight at the point where the chest of the leopard certainly would be, hoping that the thin screen of grass stems would not deflect the shot. I squeezed the trigger.

At the blast of noise, the leopard's head disappeared abruptly. Andrew scrambled to his feet, and the safari boys came running. In English or Swahili, everyone was asking the same eager question: "Did you get him?"

"I don't know," I answered tersely. "I just don't know." When I explained to Andrew that I had shot for the leopard's chest, his face took on a pained look.

"But he was standing with his tail toward us," he explained, as he might have to an imbecile child. "He was looking back over his shoulder. You shot under his chin."

That evening, Ngoro and the other safari boys would not speak to me. Andrew was more than usually courteous and cold. We had all wanted an outstanding cat trophy, but I had muffed the greatest chance on the whole safari. Andrew assured me (in a rather distant manner) that there was no chance that the leopard would come back to the bait.

"Once he's wounded, the African leopard is the fiercest thing on four legs. But otherwise the leopard is as shy as a schoolgirl. We've seen the last of the biggest leopard in all Africa."

Leopard Bwana

In spite of this, I told Andrew that I would wait by the bait tree that evening. Ngoro, who apparently felt that his own honor had been dimmed as much as mine, volunteered to wait with me. Andrew shrugged his shoulders eloquently, to indicate that if we wanted to lie there and be bitten by tsetse flies for no purpose, we richly deserved whatever awful thing might happen to us.

About four o'clock that afternoon, Ngoro and I crawled into the blind near the leopard bait tree. Andrew's prediction of tsetse flies was fulfilled. We were bitten unmercifully. There was also a species of black ant to torment us: These large insects, red underneath, had pincers on their mouths that felt like pairs of tin snips.

But the panorama of African life that moved before us was worth even this discomfort. Four hyena circled within a few yards of us as they sniffed upward toward the delicious rotting zebra in the tree. Flights of brilliant, orange-headed parakeets flew past on their way to the water in the stream behind us. A herd of lesser kudu grazed by. Two beautiful bulls in the bunch snorted and ran when they got the smell of the dead zebra. But no leopard came.

The next morning, at dawn, I persuaded Andrew to pass by the place. The bait had not been touched, and no leopard was in sight. Another leopard had appropriated the Grant gazelle, however, and a third leopard had taken over the dead baboon. This one had jerked out great mouthfuls of baboon hair and eaten about half the carcass. Ngoro and Andrew examined the tracks. These were all lesser leopards, none of them worth a real try. The whole safari company seemed dispirited. What was the use of trying for a scrawny, half-sized leopard when the big bwana had missed the king leopard of them all?

I didn't know what I could do to regain everybody's esteem. Here I was, "two *simba*" man, and I had blown my whole reputation by miscalculating where a leopard's chest ought to be. That next afternoon, I persuaded Ngoro to go back with me to the leopard bait, just to get away from the critical glances of all my companions. Brownie wanted to photograph a rhino we had seen, and Andrew said he would be glad to take her, with the inference that this, at least, was a worthwhile trip.

Ngoro and I slipped up to the leopard bait as before and lay on our stomachs behind the sketchy blind of vines. The tsetse flies were happy to see us back, and the big ants must have told all their friends about us. Even the hyena seemed to be in greater force. We watched eight of them circle the tree and sniff in a pathetic manner at the meat that they could not reach.

Just before dark the hyena drifted away. We heard a baboon chitter off in the thorn trees behind us. Ngoro, beside me, seemed half asleep. In a few minutes we would have to walk back and report another failure.

Two or three baboons barked. Ngoro tensed and raised his head slowly. He squeezed my arm and pointed with his eyes. I looked through the vine stems. There, a pair of ears were moving along above the grass tops beyond the bait tree. The leopard was returning.

Slowly, I hunched forward to my knees. I steadied the rifle against one of the vine stems. The great cat's ears moved forward, then turned from side to side. The leopard was cautious. Whatever the thunder was that had driven him away before, he was taking no chances this time.

After perhaps five minutes, he moved cautiously to the edge of the grass beneath the trees. Only then did he look up at the bait. I could see his chest now, and his two forepaws. I could also make out the tail. I moved the cross hairs of the telescopic sight to the very center of the leopard's chest. Slowly and deliberately I squeezed off the shot. This was it!

The leopard went down. Ngoro jumped up with a Masai war whoop. He thumped me on the back, and pounded on my hat. "*Mazuri, mazuri sana!*" he shouted at the top of his lungs.

The leopard was flopping on the ground like a beheaded chicken. Suddenly he seemed to regain his faculties. He pulled himself to his feet. He whirled and, in an arching bound, ran off into the high grass behind.

Ngoro and I stared numbly at each other. Another Masai shout died in Ngoro's throat. We could hear the safari car coming. Brownie and Andrew had heard the shot. The car wove crazily among the thorn trees and slid to a stop.

"Did you get him?" Andrew asked excitedly.

"I killed him. But he ran off," I said weakly.

Fortunately, Ngoro came to my assistance with a flood of Swahili. "Indeed, the big bwana, the slayer of *simbas*, had killed the monster leopard. Then the leopard, possessed of many lives, got to his feet and galloped off!"

It was almost dark. Quickly, Andrew organized us. "We've got a wounded leopard on our hands," he said tersely. "Even if he should die tonight, the hyena will eat him before morning."

Leopard Bwana

Ngoro held one .470 double rifle as a spare. Andrew carried another, and I stuck by the Weatherby .300 Magnum. As we stepped into the yellow grass, Andrew said tersely, "Shoot him as he jumps for your gun barrel."

As the three of us moved forward in a line, I thought of Andrew's description of a charging leopard. "Of all the Big Five," he had said, "the charging leopard at close quarters is the worst."

I remembered how Carl Akeley, years before, had told me of his experience with a wounded leopard. The cat had sprung at him so viciously, and from such close quarters, that he had had no time to get in a shot. The leopard seized his arm with its teeth. With one hand in the leopard's throat, Carl had wrestled the cat. The leopard's claws raked up red furrows of flesh on his thigh and stomach. Carl fell forward with the cat beneath him. With one knee, Carl had cracked the leopard's ribs one after the other. With brute strength he crushed the chest of the leopard. Carl Akeley was an extremely powerful man, but wrestling with that leopard had put him in the hospital for six months, and nearly cost him his life.

The hair on the back of my neck prickled. My hands were sweaty. Could I hit a charging leopard head on? I wasn't sure. And yet, I was the one who had set up this awful situation. What could have happened? Why wasn't the leopard dead?

A growl ripped from the grass just ahead. The rasping sound was like tearing cloth. I stiffened. Andrew had said, "When a leopard growls, he's on his way."

We stood there, the three of us, in the gathering dusk. Our rifles were pointed. Our fingers rested firmly on the triggers. The line of grass was a dark shadow. No leopard appeared.

Andrew jerked his head to motion us backward. We retreated slowly, still watching every clump of grass and fallen leaf that might suddenly become the open mouth and awful face of a charging leopard.

With Ngoro and I standing guard, Andrew maneuvered the safari car so that the lights would shine in the direction from which the growl had come. We then climbed on the metal top of the safari car. Still we could see nothing. There was no gleam of green eyes in the grass. We moved forward with the light at our backs. Suddenly Mohammed, the first tracker, darted ahead and into the brush in the full gleam of the lights.

"Come back, you fool!" Andrew yelled. Mohammed plunged into the brush like a terrier. He grasped a long black-and-yellow tail and pulled it out. The leopard was stone-dead.

Under the African Sun

It was a safari car full of wildly celebrating hunters that drove into camp that night. The safari boys wanted to carry me on their shoulders. They made up impromptu songs about the great leopard bwana. Frankly, I didn't feel so great myself. A stroke of blinding luck had pulled me out of what Andrew would have described as a "very sticky situation."

The leopard was a male, seven feet ten inches long. The bullet I had fired had entered his chest exactly in the middle and had come out behind the right foreleg, smashing straight through the lungs. And yet the leopard, with this lethal shot through him, had lived ten or twelve awful minutes before he died. This leopard is not only one of the largest ever shot in Africa, but certainly one with the most stamina. For my money, at least, it is the leopard that is the king of the cats.

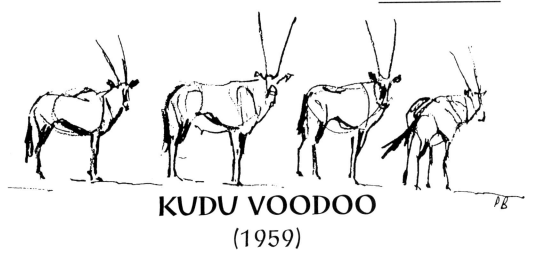

Chapter 9

KUDU VOODOO
(1959)

This whole safari had been a strange experience. Most of our difficulties stemmed from Andrew Holmberg and his uncontrollable desire to get a trophy animal of every kind and to go where no other safari has ever penetrated. Andrew Holmberg is one of the top white hunters in East Africa and very anxious to maintain his reputation as such.

We had learned many things about Andrew early in the trip. Once out of Nairobi, we had worked our safari cars, after three days of back-breaking digging and rock moving, into an unknown valley that Andrew had found during an expedition against the Mau Mau terrorists several years before. In this valley we had collected the world-record fringe-eared oryx and a trophy-sized rhino. The only major trouble on the whole trip had been in getting Andrew to let me shoot most of the varieties of game that we saw. In vain I had argued with Andrew on several occasions when we crouched behind a clump of East African vegetation within range of a good-looking specimen of some kind or other: "It will look good back in Albuquerque." But Andrew always replied, "Not big enough. We'd be ashamed to take *that* one back as far as Nairobi."

Andrew was always right, of course. With his amazing knowledge of the country and the African animals that inhabit it, he was always able to find that trophy set of horns that we were after. But when it came to greater kudu, which is considered by most sportsmen the most outstanding trophy of East Africa, we were in real trouble.

Under the African Sun

The greater kudu, perhaps the handsomest of all the African antelope, is about the size of an American elk. Formerly it ranged over almost all of the Dark Continent. In the last two centuries, however—due to disease, large-scale meat hunting, and the general spread of civilization—the greater kudu is now confined to only a few spots of its former gigantic range. These isolated areas are spread from the Sudan down through East Africa to Rhodesia and Mozambique. Even in these areas, however, the kudu is scarce in most places and concentrated in only a few. The largest sets of horns of this magnificent animal are found in the southern district. As this was the case, naturally we went south.

Most sportsmen after greater kudu hunt in the Ugalla area or farther east in the Dodoma district. Some very fine specimens of kudu in the trophy class have come from these general areas. Naturally, however, Andrew did not wish to hunt in those places. They had been hunted before!

As we traveled south from Tabora in Tanzania, Andrew as usual was vague. He would say only that he had heard from some natives that the largest kudu of all were found along the Rungwa River.

I looked at a map that I carried and saw that the Rungwa runs westward close along the border of Zambia and flows into Lake Rukwa. A road of sorts approaches the head of the Rungwa. There is no road that would give access to the river in any other place.

But Andrew spurned roads. At a place south of Tabora known apparently only to Andrew himself, we turned off into the forest. Here an elephant path led diagonally through the trees in a southerly direction. Southern Tanzania is not an open country like the grass plains farther to the north. The terrain is rolling or nearly level and covered with a close growth of deciduous trees with only small clearings in between. Much of the country looks like the more level stretches of the eastern woodlands of North America. Working our safari vehicle and the truck that carried our gear through this forest was very much like driving a car overland from Albany, New York, to Harrisburg, Pennsylvania, without using any road.

Of course, we were following an elephant trail, and the great pachyderms had cleared a path through the trees and brush. The trail led generally southward toward the Rungwa River, which was our goal. But on their way to the water, the great beasts habitually pushed over trees

Kudu Voodoo

and jerked down limbs as they fed along the trail. Every few yards we had to stop and cut out these elephant falls. Often we had to beat a path around impenetrable stretches of the elephant trail. Twice we got our truck irretrievably jammed between two heavy trees. We had to cut the things down with the small axes we carried. In two days of back-breaking work we had covered only about thirty miles.

At this point in the forest, we came across a camp of honey hunters, a small group of natives living in a palisaded enclosure—or *boma*—some fifteen feet high to protect them from the lion. Tsetse flies are so bad in this area that natives cannot raise stock of any kind, or even farm. They make their living gathering wild honey and carrying it on their backs some seventy-five miles to the nearest mission station, where they offer it for sale.

As we tasted some of the delicious wild honey they gave us, Andrew questioned them about the river. One of the men, a squat little fellow with a terribly scarred face, volunteered to show us an easy elephant path that led down to the banks of the Rungwa only a few miles away. We promised the man an East African pound note—$2.80—if he would show us the biggest kudu in the country. He couldn't collect enough wild honey in a year to be worth that much. He enthusiastically climbed up on the metal top of our car and pointed out the way.

As we approached the river, we came across a few open glades of twenty acres or more. Even these places, however, were filled with scattered trees and head-high grass. In some of the open savannas, the honey-hunting natives had fired the grass, as they usually did during the dry season of August and September. It was in these burned-over areas that the game animals collected to nibble on the short shoots of green that were just appearing above the blackened stubble. Duiker and oribi scooted off before our safari car. We saw small bunches of topi, zebra, and a few giraffe. Once, as we rounded a corner of the trail, a herd of buffalo stared at us with their dark eyes for a moment and then thundered off in a cloud of dust. But nowhere did we see the great herds of game such as we had witnessed in the open plains of northern Tanzania and Kenya. The brushy tree cover of the Rungwa region precludes a distant view in any direction. Also, there is less grass and consequently fewer animals of any kind.

Our first sight of the Rungwa River was an exciting one. As this was late August, the river was almost dry. Only a few deep pools remained. These were as full of hippo as a frog pond seething with tadpoles. As we walked along the bank to find a good camping place, we met two of the animals dusting themselves in a wallow. For a moment it seemed that they were going to gather us in. But at the last moment they turned and launched themselves off the riverbank in a perfect running dive. As long as we camped there by one of the hippo pools, some of the animals never left it.

Our honey-hunter guide had told us that some very large kudu bulls lived in the dense scrub on the south side of the river. The man also showed us a gravel bar where an elephant trail crossed the almost dry bed of the Rungwa. We easily drove our safari car down the slanting bank to make the crossing. However, as we forded the shallow water on a hard bottom, the black head of a hippo bull rose out of the pool at one side of the crossing. The animal opened his great jaws and plowed forward into the shallow water, roaring like a bass horn.

"There's a cheeky hippo for you," Andrew remarked as he manipulated the car up the far bank. "We'll have trouble with that one."

Andrew was right. The first part of our kudu hunt was interrupted by the bull hippo, which didn't like people. That evening as we drove back across the river, the bull charged at us again, opening and closing his great mouth with a noise like hitting a wet mattress with a baseball bat.

In the next two or three days, the bull became more and more aggressive each time we forded the river beside the hippo pool. It was obvious that we were going to have to shoot the hippo or someone was going to get killed.

On the third evening when we returned, we stopped the safari car some distance from the pool. Andrew and I slipped forward alone. We came up to the water behind the bole of a jungle tree with a tentlike mass of interlaced roots. Even behind this shelter the protruding eyes of the hippo spotted us. His ears wiggled rapidly. The black head rose out of the water and came toward us. I slipped a solid patch bullet into the chamber of the Weatherby .300 and steadied the rifle across one of the tree roots. I aimed for the spot just under the ear and above the eyes of the black head. The shot was good. The hippo reared backward in a swirl of yellow water and disappeared into the depths of the pool.

When we skinned out the head of the hippo, we found a large wrought-iron ball of about 50-caliber size lying against the skull between the eyes. Some native with a muzzleloading gun had tried to bag a couple of tons of hippo meat and failed. There was a good reason this particular hippo didn't like people.

The hippo hunt seemed to set the general atmosphere for our pursuit of kudu in the heart of the kudu country. We saw everything else but the great kudu bull that the honey hunter had promised us.

We did see a band of females just across the river from our camp. Even these were thrilling animals. Although the female kudu are hornless, they look like royal game. Their white-striped bodies and beautifully marked faces outlined by enormous ears are absolutely elegant.

On the third day we bagged a Lichtenstein hartebeest, and a very good one. This antelope is a cousin of the common Coke hartebeest, but is rather seldom taken by hunters as his range is limited and his numbers are few. The Lichtenstein is found only in the extreme southern edge of Tanzania and neighboring regions, and is also an animal of low and brushy terrain.

Two days later we sighted a herd of some twenty sable antelope led by a magnificent bull. Andrew was immediately interested as he looked at the bull of the herd through his 10X binoculars.

"Those horns will go forty-two, maybe forty-five inches," he said with conviction. "We'd better take him."

Andrew Holmberg so seldom enthused over any kind of game that I knew that this particular sable must be exceptional indeed. We immediately started to stalk the bull from behind the cover of the thick-growing trees. The herd had been feeding on the edge of a small glade. Some of the females had spotted us and retreated at a dead run across the open glade and into the trees on the far side. Andrew and I crawled to the edge of the opening. There was no chance of getting any closer. Most of the sable herd had disappeared into the cover. But two or three animals had stopped for a last look. The bull was standing chest toward us. I could see his long, curved horns in a gap between two trees across the clearing. He was a good three hundred yards away. I rested the rifle carefully against the trunk of a small tree in front of me. It was a long shot, but there was no help for it. Carefully I squeezed it off. The sable dropped like a stone.

Even Andrew was pleased. The horns measured 45 inches and were perfectly formed and even. Our kudu hunt was off to a good start indeed.

Under the African Sun

But as the days passed into a full week and we hunted from sunrise to sunset in the valley on both sides of the Rungwa, we had not yet sighted a single kudu bull. Several times we saw females in small groups. During this fruitless search after the elusive kudu, we found, on the far side of the valley and downstream from camp, a big herd of roan antelope. The roan is one of the larger of the antelope and a close relative of the sable. The horns of the roan are curved but less spectacular than those of his sable cousin. His body is almost the size of a mule and the color of a roan horse. The roan also has a limited range, although in places he is found north into the Sudan and west across Equatorial Africa.

With the big herd of roan antelope was a fine bull. We sighted him early in the morning. It was late afternoon by the time we made the kill. Andrew and I had crawled some hundreds of yards in the interval on our respective bellies. We had been chewed by tsetse flies in the process. The tsetse fly is one of the least attractive aspects of the Rungwa hunting area. The headquarters of these vicious little insects seemed to be in the vicinity of the roan antelope herd.

Again the shot was a long one. Although the roans had not spotted us, they kept feeding away as fast as we could crawl. But as I had plenty of time and a rest, the shot was good, although not immediately fatal. When we came up to the animal, Andrew was as pleased as a kid at the circus.

"I believe we have a record here," he said excitedly as he whipped out his steel tape. And so we did. The horns measured 32½ inches around the curve, which is the world record for an East African roan antelope.

The kudu hunt by this time obviously was progressing famously. The only difficulty was that we hadn't as yet bagged a kudu. Our time for hunting in these southern regions was running out. We had only three or four more days at the most. Then one morning, just as the sun reddened the great trees that fringed the hippo pools along the river, we saw our kudu bull. The animal was stalking along through the slanting shafts of sunlight that marked the forest floor like the light through stained-glass windows in a cathedral. Andrew and I hurriedly slipped out of the safari car on the far side and circled at a crouch to come up ahead of the animal. Screened behind a thick growth of young trees, we crawled forward. Just beyond, I could

Kudu Voodoo

make out the beautiful spiral horns of the bull. He had stopped. His white-edged ears were pricked forward. Andrew and I moved on a few more yards. We knelt down behind the bole of a slanting forest tree from which sausage-like seed pods hung on long strings.

Carefully I raised my Weatherby .300 and centered on the shoulder of the kudu. This was it. Here was the most magnificent trophy in all of Africa.

"We don't want him," said Andrew quietly. A weight was pushing down the barrel of my rifle. It was Andrew's hand.

I know my mouth dropped open. "Why, dammit, Andrew—that's what we came here for!" I stuttered.

"Too small," Andrew said firmly. "Those horns won't go 45 inches. We'd be ashamed to take *that* kudu back to Nairobi."

Confound white hunters, and confound all Nairobians, I thought. Here we had hunted ten days to find a greater kudu, and here was a magnificent kudu bull standing there politely listening to us as we argued.

But Andrew prevailed, as he always did. With a poor show of grace, I took some movies of the kudu bull as he stalked majestically off through the forest. Anyhow, in that way I really had a chance to admire the animal. So often when the gun comes up quickly, we do not have the opportunity to appreciate the beauty of our finest game.

Two days later, however, I was still bitter about the episode of the kudu bull. "That kudu would have looked big in Albuquerque," I repeated for the hundredth time.

"We'll find a really good kudu," Andrew said confidently. But his voice lacked conviction, for we had only one more day.

On the last day, we made a wider swing than usual across the valley and up the stream. Here we had heard a pride of lion roaring every evening and every morning since we had camped there. As the pride never seemed to move its location, we concluded that they must have ample game to feed upon.

Eight or ten miles from camp, our car labored through the trees and out into a series of grass-filled glades. These were larger than any we had seen before. There were some scattered groups of zebra and eight or ten giraffe in one of these savannas. We saw another herd of sable antelope with a very nice bull leading them.

Just beyond was the largest opening of all, a clearing of perhaps five hundred acres or more. In the very middle of the glade beneath a lone tree were four eland bulls. These were the first eland we had seen in the Rungwa country. The animals certainly were not common there. Several weeks ago and farther north in Kenya we had seen several hundred eland. For this reason, I scarcely remarked about the four eland bulls except to make the observation that there seemed to be no other animals in the clearing. But Andrew had out his great binoculars again.

"I think that one bull—the eland on the right—will be a world record," Andrew said quietly. "Shoot him straightaway."

Even as I climbed out of the safari car I could not quite figure why Andrew was so excited about this particular eland. We had bagged a very fair eland in Kenya. Also, we weren't hunting eland. But Andrew never seemed to be wrong. So let it be! We would shoot an eland.

I loaded some solid patch bullets into the Weatherby .300 as an eland is a very heavy-bodied animal. After circling a quarter of the way around the edge of the open glade, I had worked perhaps a hundred yards closer to the four eland bulls and had the sun almost at my back. It was an easy shot. I could pick out the one bull with the gigantic and wide-spreading set of horns easily. The twisted black spirals of his horns looked a foot longer than those of the three other bulls. Confidently I knelt and fired.

At the crack of the shot all four of the eland bulls turned and ran diagonally away. In amazement I bolted another shell into the chamber and fired again. The big eland disappeared in a cloud of dust with his long tail swinging from side to side.

Andrew drove up in the safari car. "Congratulations," he said quietly. I stared at him. "Your eland is dead over there," he said, pointing.

The eland bull had run perhaps three hundred yards with a shot through his shoulder that had pierced his lungs. My second shot had ranged from behind and also entered the lungs. I had noticed before that these African animals seemed to have more stamina and staying power than our North American breeds.

Andrew, as usual, already had out his steel tape.

"Thirty-one and five-eighths inches," he announced triumphantly. "That will be very close to the world record." And so it was.

When we returned to Nairobi some weeks later, and this eland was officially measured by Paul Zimmerman, the representative of the East African Professional Hunters Association, he found that it ranked No. 4 in the world records. The record head is $32\frac{1}{4}$ inches.

Kudu Voodoo

This was all very nice. But we had started out to bag a greater kudu. It was with mixed feelings that we broke camp on the bank of the Rungwa and packed our tents in the safari truck. We waved good-bye to a hippo friend that had made our nights hideous with his snortings and blubberings in the pool below our tent. We had bagged three trophy animals on the Rungwa, but our kudu hunt was a bust.

As we turned away from the river, I noticed that Andrew swung to the east instead of north along the elephant trail toward the road.

"We'll try one last swing for that kudu bull," he said quietly.

It was a long chance at best. We had been up this way on three or four different days and had seen no more than a few female kudu and one small bull. Also, the going was very rough for our safari truck when we left the main elephant trail. We would have to cut and hack our way through the brush as before.

It was a hot morning, and the tsetse flies were stalking us from all directions like so many enemy fighter planes. Andrew stopped the car at the crest of a low ridge a mile or two back from the river. He whipped out his big binoculars and stared through the windshield.

"Three kudu bulls," he announced with rising excitement. "One of them very nice. Fifty inches or better. Very nice indeed."

I had already snatched the Weatherby from the gun rack behind the seat. As we circled away from the safari car, I got only one glimpse of the three beautiful animals. They were standing together in a tiny clearing on the side of a low hill across from us. Even as I looked, the three bulls whirled together and ran. I could see the morning sunlight glinting on the polished tips of their spiral horns for a moment after the gray bodies had disappeared in the brush.

We stopped and leaned against a tree dejectedly. We had never had a chance to even stalk the three bulls.

"Come on," said Andrew in desperation. He started off at a trotting run around the shoulder of the hill where the kudu had disappeared.

We all knew that this was a futile gesture. The kudu, in spite of his size, is the shyest of all the antelopes. Those three bulls wouldn't stop running for a mile. We rounded the shoulder of the slope. We couldn't see more than a hundred yards or so of the brushy hillside.

There they were. Andrew pointed to the spiral horns that showed above the dry leaves. I could see the great ears fanned forward. Just beyond the hill the kudu had stopped. The animals were looking back at us over the brush.

Under the African Sun

"The one to the right," Andrew whispered. "That's the big bull."

I raised the rifle. The distance was perhaps two hundred yards. I would have to shoot offhand. The rifle barrel wavered. I could see the three heads distinctly. I could not see a square inch of the body of any one of the three animals.

"Shoot! Shoot!" hissed Andrew urgently. "That one will look good in Albuquerque."

I grinned sideways at him. It seemed to relieve the tension. In that instant the kudu broke and ran again. Through a small opening in the brush a gray body flashed past. There was the highest set of horns. I swung the cross hairs of the scope just ahead of the shoulder. At the clap of the shot, all three of the animals disappeared as though by magic.

Over there on the hillside, not a twig or a leaf moved. It was as though the kudu had never been there at all.

Andrew looked at me. I shook my head and held up both hands. We walked forward together.

Where the kudu bulls had stood there was no sign of any disturbance. No drop of blood glinted on any of the dry leaves or the brush around us. Just beyond was a small opening the size of a hotel room. On the far edge of this tiny clearing was a rounded gray boulder. Over the curve of this stone ran a series of white parallel stripes. We ran forward. It was the kudu bull lying on his side. He was stone-dead.

It was a jubilant crew that skinned out the greater kudu there on the low hill above the river. The horns of my bull measured only slightly more than 50 inches, which is no record. But even Andrew was pleased.

"This may not be the biggest kudu bull ever brought into Nairobi," Andrew observed as we made camp that night, "but we certainly broke the kudu voodoo."

"And," I added, "it surely *will* look good in Albuquerque."

Chapter 10

ELEPHANT STAMPEDE
(1960)

It started with elephant, and it ended with elephant. We had gone to the Samburu country to look for elephant, but we didn't expect three hundred of them to run over us.

Like trophy game of any kind, a really big elephant is hard to come by. A trophy-class bull elephant, ever since the old ivory trading days, is usually considered a "100-pounder." Elephant carrying tusks weighing 100 pounds or more apiece were scarce during the nineteenth century. They are a lot scarcer now, especially when one considers that a bull with that much ivory on a side is eighty years old or more. On previous trips I had found that the code of East African white hunters forbids the shooting of a bull with only one tusk, no matter how big that tusk might be. A 100-pounder, then, means a bull with two tusks, at least one of which is the specified weight. Furthermore, in only a few spots of Africa does the forage contain sufficient minerals for elephant to develop heavy ivory. Usually, the biggest tusks come from beasts of semi-arid brush country, not from those feeding on lush, tropical forage. As a rule, forest or jungle elephant have slender ivory of no great weight.

I suppose I never would have gotten the elephant hunting fever if I hadn't seen the 100-pounder on our safari in the Emboni country. I could not forget the majesty and size of the great Emboni bull. (We had seen him only after we shot his two askaris.) After this episode, the big Emboni bull disappeared from the region. The Somalis reported he had gone south across the Tana River.

Under the African Sun

Out of the hundreds of elephant shot by all of the safaris in all parts of Africa each season, only one or two of the 100-pounders are brought in each year. An elephant specialist, Don Hopkins of Spokane, Washington, has spent most of the last several years in East Africa trying to find a bull elephant carrying 150 pounds on each side. Don has spent most of his time in eastern Kenya and in northeastern Tanganyika. Any elephant hunter will tell you that the brush country near the coast, near the Tana and Galana Rivers, is the best bet to find a bull with the biggest ivory.

When I determined to bag a 100-pounder, I wrote to Don Hopkins, and to several other hunters lucky enough to have found 100-pound tusks. Most of these advised me to get Andrew Holmberg, Eric Rundren, or Stan Lawrence-Brown for a guide. Andrew Holmberg had been shot through the foot by an elephant rifle. I wrote to Stan Lawrence-Brown, one of the old-time elephant hunters of Kenya. It was Stan who shot the elephant pictured in the movie, *King Solomon's Mines*. During his lifetime he had brought in several 100-pounders, including one monster bull carrying 142 pounds in each tusk. Also, Stan knew the brush country south of the Tana. He said the natives there reported several big bulls in the 100-pound class.

But Lawrence-Brown's luck ran out at last. Before our trip started, Stan, hunting with a European client, had been cornered by two bull elephant. Stan managed to down one bull with a brain shot, but the other one picked Stan up in his trunk and crushed his back.

When Brownie and I arrived in Nairobi at the end of May, Stan met us on the porch of the Norfolk Hotel. As he limped up to us and extended his hand, he smiled wryly. "Bit of nonsense with an elephant," he apologized. "I can't go myself, but I know where to find your 100-pounder."

As we sat on the shady veranda, sipping the very good East African beer, Stan told us of his plans. He had contacted some native poachers in the Samburu country, near the Kenya coast, who had just been arrested and brought in to Mombasa. The men told of four large bull elephant in the Samburu country, along the Voi River. These bulls had been so large, and their tusks so long, that the poachers had not dared to attack them.

"The Samburu country . . . the Voi River," I said aloud. That had a familiar ring. Then I remembered: Colonel Ray Harrison, my hunting friend at home, had told me of the Voi country. He had shot two

Elephant Stampede

bulls with 100-pound ivory during his long hunting career, and he had got them both on the lower Voi River.

"There are some mighty big elephant in that Samburu country," Ray had said. "But watch out for those herds of cows and calves. The poachers torment the beasts with poisoned arrows. Those Samburu elephant will charge at the drop of a hat."

Stan Lawrence-Brown was still talking enthusiastically about the elephant hunt. "I'll have Nick Swan, my young assistant, take you down there," he said.

We had met Nick Swan, the son of a local farmer. Nick was a young, stocky lad, just starting his career as a white hunter. As Stan told us he was sending us elephant hunting with this young fellow, he must have seen the doubt in our eyes. "Nick is a good hunter," he assured us, "and he has a fine gun."

Later that day we saw the gun that Nick proposed to use. It was a .577 double rifle that he had just purchased from an old elephant hunter who had gone out of the business. The next category larger than a .577 is field artillery. If the size of Nick's double rifle was any indication, the elephant was going to be a cinch.

Our start to the Samburu country was delayed, as I had "a bit of nonsense with the fever," as Stan expressed it. I had picked up tick fever in French Equatorial Africa, and was still feeling pretty shaky the first week in June when we drove our safari car and one truck through the little railroad town of Samburu. We had a good piece of luck here, as we picked up one of the original poachers who had told Stan about the big elephant. This old fellow, Ndege by name, had been let off with a ninety-shilling fine by the magistrate in Mombasa, and was starting right back to Samburu to kill elephant again.

The Samburu country is not beautiful. It lies along the edge of the East African plateau, just back from the coast. It is both dry and wet, and looks like a semi-desert. The scattered trees are stunted and small; cactuslike plants and spiny clubs grow in thickets so dense that only an elephant can force through them. Sansevieria, which reminds me of our western yucca, grows everywhere. And yet at night across this arid country, the sea fog rolls in from the Indian Ocean. In the chilly mornings, the spine-tipped bushes are dripping with dew.

In the vast brush country of Samburu, old bulls carrying heavy tusks can live out their days and never see a hunter. Perhaps, I thought as we drove the safari car across the rolling ridges north of Samburu, I will find a 150-pounder and beat Don Hopkins at his own game.

Outside of a few scattered grass huts with small *shambas* of maize near them, there are no large villages north of Samburu for 150 miles. We camped near one of these small groups of houses, where the natives were using water that had collected in a crack in the bedrock during the rainy season now long past. Water is a problem for both humans and elephant in the Samburu area.

Both Brownie and I thought, as we sat in front of the tent that first evening, that this was not the most romantic part of Africa by any means. For one thing, there were none of the teeming herds of game that are commonplace on top of the grassland plateau farther to the west. Also, it was damp and cold as the sea air moved in from the southeast. A lion coughed in the distance. Brownie wondered how the lion would avoid freezing to death in that awful place.

But pleasant camping or not, Samburu is the land of the big elephant. The trick is to find them. We were looking for either the Emboni bull, that probably still traveled alone, or for the group of bulls that the poachers had reported. Throughout the next week, we moved through the area north and northeast, both on foot and in the safari car. Many of the Naswahilis burn the hardwood trees of the brush country into charcoal, and we followed the small trails and roads that wander everywhere through the bush, leading to these charcoal stations. (Charcoal burning is a good cover for poaching, and the illegal ivory is usually taken out in trucks under a load of charcoal bags.)

Whenever we found the huts of charcoal burners, we inquired about big bull elephant. Generally, we got very little information, as the natives thought that we were government scouts searching for poachers. However, we did learn that there was one group of five bulls feeding together, and another group of three very large bulls. Either of these might be the one we were after. Any natives who would talk at all said that there were lots of elephant, and usually added that their *shambas* were being trampled and eaten by the *"tembos,"* so they ought to be killed.

At the end of a week we had seen much fresh elephant sign but not a single square inch of elephant hide. Unfortunately, Swan had never been in the Samburu before, and we had to depend entirely upon Ndege, our poacher guide. This fellow seemed quite friendly, once he had de-

Elephant Stampede

cided we were not government game scouts. He showed us how he stalked and shot animals with his poisoned arrows. "This makes the elephant very, very angry," the man assured us.

But even the master poacher could not find the Emboni bull, or the other large bulls that had been reported. Several groups of elephant were watering at a muddy pond, which lay about eighteen miles north of our camp. Several mornings, after driving half of this distance in the darkness over the rutted charcoal trails, we got an early start in tracking the bulls from the water. The wary elephant came in and drank at night, and then walked several miles back into the bush before feeding or resting during the heat of the day. We never caught up with any of these bulls, even though we tracked some of them ten hours or more. I began to wonder if we were ever going to get a close look at one of these animals. We had planned to stay in the Samburu country for about three weeks at the most. Now it appeared that this was not going to be long enough.

We had driven to the water hole just at daylight one morning, as we had done before. After several days of tracking on foot, Nick and I were getting tired of seeing some thousands of elephant tracks but no elephant. We had picked up a charcoal burner the evening before who knew of another mud puddle about five miles to the east where elephant also drank. We decided to send Ndege and this native to the other watering place to look for signs of elephant.

While they were gone, we shot a very nice lesser kudu, which had stood on the edge of a clump of sansevieria for a few seconds before diving into the thicket. We had seen lesser kudu and oribi every day we had been elephant tracking.

About nine o'clock in the morning the two natives came back at a dead run. "Mingi, mingi!" they shouted as soon as they were in sight. "Tembo mingi!" They had found a lot of elephant.

We left Brownie with the native driver at the safari car. Nick and I snatched up our rifle, and started after the two men. They had already run three or four miles, and yet they started back toward the elephant at top speed.

We did not get so far as the second water hole before we heard the elephant. A shrill trumpet came from far ahead. (An elephant trumpet sounds like a French horn with a broken reed.) Usually trumpeting indicates a herd of cows and calves. Harrison had said to stay away from cows and calves. Well, it would do no harm to take a look.

Under the African Sun

After another half-hour of walking, we could hear elephant screaming and trumpeting to the south of us, but the thick scrub blocked the view. The elephant now sounded close. Ndege climbed up a small tree and looked out over the bush, then beckoned to us to climb up beside him.

Nick and I shinnied up the scaly trunk of the thorn tree with considerable difficulty. Even at a height of twenty feet or so we could see out over the thickest mass of thorny bush. A couple of hundred yards away, a rounded gray boulder the size of a house stuck out of the scrub. An ear flapped. A puff of dust from the dirty back drifted off in the wind. The gray mass moved a little. A trunk snaked up at one end, curled around a branch, and jerked it off. There was a crack of splitting wood.

As we shifted in the tree, we could see another elephant, and then another. Some three or four hundred yards away, a group of gray-brown backs appeared and disappeared among the stunted thorn trees. All of the elephant had recently dusted themselves. All were dirty and brown. After fifteen minutes of investigating from every angle in the tree, we could locate about thirty animals. All of them seemed to be full-grown, and some were obviously very large. From the trumpeting and squealing that came from that direction, we knew that some of the elephant were certainly cows. But off to the right were three big brown backs that could belong only to large bulls. It was impossible to see their tusks, although I did catch one glimpse of heavy ivory between the branches as an elephant moved. The thing looked as big around as my thigh.

"Those three are bulls," said Nick, swinging his binoculars as he clung to a branch of the tree. "Certainly one of them ought to carry big ivory. We'll have a look."

Nick and I dropped down from the tree and crawled forward together. As we inched through the bush, I remembered that sometimes big bulls stay around a herd of cows even though their breeding days are long past. The Samburu poachers had said that there were three very large bulls in the area. Perhaps the veterans with the big tusks were hanging on the outskirts of this bunch; or perhaps they had been attracted to the area by all the trumpeting and squealing, just as we had been.

It was fairly easy going toward the herd. From the tracks and droppings it was obvious that this group had been feeding in the area for several days. In the trails before us were large cuds of

Elephant Stampede

sansevieria where the elephants had jerked up trunk-loads of the plant and chewed it to get the moisture. We picked up several of these sansevieria cuds to see if they were wet and fresh. They were.

Nick tested the wind by shaking a little bag of wood ashes. It was steady from the southeast, as always. We had gone about two hundred yards, and figured we should be close to the first bull we had spotted from the tree. Suddenly there was a gurgling rumble, like water going down the drain of an old-fashioned bathtub. That was an elephant's intestines working. The noise was just ahead.

We could just make out a hind leg with loose folds of grayish skin. As Nick and I crawled forward on our hands and knees, the hind leg shifted back and forth in a monotonous rhythm. Apparently the bull was half asleep. He was rocking back and forth, and swatting flies with his long tail. If he would only stand there until we could crawl around to the side and have a look at his tusks!

We worked our way slowly through the brush. The bull was standing in the only available trail, so we had to crawl through the thick stuff. Nick and I were just negotiating a clump of cactus when a branch splintered off almost over our heads. There was a thunderous belch. Wood and leaves crunched, like grain going into a sorghum mill. We saw the black ear of an elephant flap forward and back. The beast was almost above us. We had not seen this second bull.

Nick and I scrambled back past the cactus. We made a lot of noise, but there was no help for it. Fortunately, the bull was breaking branches and crunching twigs so loudly that he didn't hear us.

When Nick and I got back to the tree where the natives waited, we were sweating in rivers, though it wasn't a particularly warm day.

"That was close," Nick commented. "My head was almost between that elephant's forelegs. I thought they were two trees."

We climbed our observation tree again to reorient ourselves. We could not see the bull that had given us such a bad scare. Again we picked out the larger body of the biggest bull. He had not moved. If we circled even farther downwind, we could come up on his other side and get a look at his ivory. If the tusks were a hundred pounds or better, we could polish him off then and there.

Again Nick and I made a wide circuit downwind. In the distance we could still hear the trumpeting of the cows and calves. Apparently none of the animals were really moving.

Under the African Sun

We circled a hundred yards beyond the elephant trail where we had crawled before. Within a few minutes we could again see the bulk of the largest bull through the stems of the bushes. He cleared his throat with a thunderous noise; his bowels rumbled and bubbled. The gurgling of his guts was so loud that Nick and I could not whisper to each other. The noise seemed all around us. I could see one tusk very thick at the base. I could not quite see how long the ivory was. Nick was punching my thigh from behind. I motioned him back irritably, looking over my shoulder. Nick was pointing to the other side.

About twenty feet to our right a trunk coiled among the brush like a headless serpent. Just behind, I saw elephant legs, several of them. No wonder the rumbling was so loud. I was already backing up like a startled crab. Nick had turned. Crouching low, we bolted from the brush.

Behind us, one of the elephant trumpeted. There was the noise of splintering wood. I looked over my shoulder. I could see three domed heads above the bushes. The elephant were not following. The wind still blew steadily toward us.

Personally, I had lost my enthusiasm for trying to crawl up on those particular bull elephant. Apparently, instead of three bulls, there were a dozen or more. If we tried to get up to any one of them, we would surely get stepped on.

Nick was talking Swahili to Ndege, who kept shaking his head and spreading out his hands in a flat denial. Our own tracker, Nduyai, was showing no more enthusiasm than Ndege. Nick explained his plan to me. "If these fellows circle around on the other side of the elephant," Nick said with a sweep of his arm, "the bulls will catch their wind and drift this way. As the bulls go past, we can take our pick."

The bulls might not go past, I thought. Furthermore, from all the trumpeting in the distance, the main herd seemed in no mood to be chivvied in any particular direction. However, as I couldn't think of any better plan, this one seemed worth a try. "One or two of those bulls over there certainly carry heavy ivory," Nick added as a clincher.

Nick ordered the two trackers to start circling the herd. The men were sullen and resentful. I didn't blame them especially, except that both of these fellows were elephant experts. They had spent their lives getting close to big elephant. The boy carrying the cameras we sent back a safe distance toward the safari car. We figured he might bolt in the wrong direction and ruin the whole plan.

Elephant Stampede

Nick and I sat down in the shade of a tree and waited. An hour passed. From the occasional trumpet of a cow elephant, it seemed that the herd had not shifted its location. It was, by this time, two or three o'clock in the afternoon, and the elephant were still quiet. Later on the animals would begin to move and feed.

Another hour went past. Nick began to fidget. He paced up and down an elephant trail in front of us. Twice we climbed up the tree to look at the elephant again. We could see about thirty of them. The big bulls were still almost in the same place, over to the right of the herd. Occasionally, one of these would jerk down a branch and munch it slowly. Most of the elephant were still standing, but they seemed restless. Another half-hour passed.

"Those bloody trackers have gone back to the village," Nick commented viciously. "When I get back . . ."

A shrill trumpet cut him short. A second elephant, and then a third, took up the cry. We could hear the shuffling of heavy feet. The noise increased to a rumble.

Over the brush we could see the heads of elephant. They were coming straight at us. The dark shapes rose and fell. They were running. The crash of trees and brush was lost in the thunder of jostling feet. The elephant heads seemed a solid line; dark-colored bodies appeared out of the brush as far as we could see.

"Quick! Into the tree!" yelled Nick. He had already thrust his big double rifle into my hands. He turned and leaped at the tree trunk. It was not a large tree. The first branch was perhaps twelve feet up, where the tree fanned out like an open hand. Nick shinnied up the trunk and gained the main fork. Recklessly I tossed up the rifles to him. He caught the first one, and then the other. The noise of elephant was all around me. I scrambled up the trunk. I never knew how I got to the first branches. In a second, I was there.

Choking clouds of dust billowed everywhere. The first elephant passed by us in a solid wave of indistinct bodies.

Clutching my gun, I looked out over the brush. There were elephant everywhere. Through the dust I could see cows with their trunks upraised. There were medium-sized elephant, and baby elephant. All of them were trumpeting and screaming. Just ahead a tree went down, but the crash of splintering wood could hardly be heard above the confusion of noise.

Under the African Sun

Nick was yelling something at me, although we were only three feet apart. "If they push this tree, we've had it," he shouted.

I could see what he meant. The jostling elephant were not moving along the trails. They crashed straight through the brush. Trees, thickets, and cactus were flattened before them.

As they ran, they crowded each other. Just below our tree, I saw a big cow with long, slender tusks. She reached out her trunk to protect her baby. The little fellow was no bigger than a sheep dog. The cow turned and viciously gouged the flank of another cow that had come too close. The offending elephant didn't even flinch. At full speed she rushed past. Her shoulder just grazed our refuge. The tree shook under the impact. Though I was holding onto a limb as big as my arm, I was jarred off balance and almost dropped my rifle. As I held the gun in one hand, I could have touched the back of the cow elephant with the muzzle.

I swung back into the main fork. A half-grown elephant saw the movement. He stopped. He pointed his trunk straight at us. He screamed at us. I do not remember hearing the noise at all. The end of his trunk flared out like a trumpet, and his eyes looked as big as dinner plates. The African elephant isn't reputed to have good eyesight. This one did. He stood his ground and stared straight at us. His trunk stretched out toward us like an accusing finger.

If that elephant's mother comes up, I thought, *we're cooked. A big cow could pick us out of this tree as easily as if we were apples.* A group of cows and young bulls surged from behind. Still the young elephant stood under our tree and pointed us out. "Here they are," he seemed to trumpet. The other elephant jostled against him, paying him no attention. None of the bigger bulls or cows looked up. Another cloud of yellow dust moved over us. The young elephant was gone, swept away in the stampede.

"Must be three hundred elephant!" Nick shouted again. His voice was lost in a new blast of trumpeting and squealing. What was Nick counting elephant for? It would just take one bull or one cow. At that moment, another mass of running forms rushed past. I noticed that they all seemed to be bulls. There were big bulls and little bulls. Beyond, through the dust, the elephant were now scattered. Most of the herd had already swept by. "I believe we are going to make it," I yelled over my shoulder.

Elephant Stampede

"Look at that bull!" I noticed for the first time that the noise of splintering brush and trumpeting was lessening. Nick's shout was over-loud. One of the bulls beneath us swung out his ears, and his trunk went up like the spout of a teapot. I could have touched the red tip of it with my hand. Certainly he would smell us. But he moved on. Just behind, I saw an enormous bull. He came straight at us out of the dust. His tusks were very thick.

"He's a 100-pounder!" Nick said in my ear. "He'll go a hundred pounds."

I hitched the Weatherby rifle up on top of a branch. It was going to be awkward. The big bull swung slightly to one side. A knot of other bulls came just behind him. I threw off the safety of the .460 rifle and lay at full length along a tree branch. As the big bull swept past, I could see his shoulder through the sight. There was the spot, just below the edge of his ragged ear, right on the point of his shoulder. There were branches in the way. Now! The recoil of the gun jerked my shoulder back. I saw the bull half turn and go to his knees. I lost my balance. It was difficult to bolt another shell into the chamber. Six or eight bulls were coming straight at us. The rifle shot seemed to drive them berserk.

"Shoot!" Nick yelled. "Shoot—!"

I could see the muzzle of Nick's big .577 thrust out past me. I was having trouble getting my balance in the tree for a second shot. Nick's double rifle blasted out. The end of the limb that I held dis-appeared. I half turned. Nick's gun was sailing through the air. So was Nick. Both barrels had somehow gone off at once. Nick shot out of the tree like a rocket. Thrown against a branch, he clutched desperately at it. It broke. He grabbed at another, hanging by one hand. The elephant thundered beneath us. The feet of the bulls broke Nick's double rifle into splinters. They could not miss the man hanging in the air before their faces.

I jammed my own gun between two branches and leaped out along the limb. Nick was struggling up. I reached for the back of his belt and pulled him into the tree. An elephant ran by beneath us. Nick's feet dragged on its back.

Nick lay over a limb on his stomach. "That was a bit sticky," he said with a wry grin. He looked down at his gun. We could make out some of the pieces in the trampled earth. "Getting stepped on by an elephant would be awfully messy, wouldn't it?" he commented.

Under the African Sun

We might yet be down there with Nick's shattered double rifle. At the sound of the shot, the main herd of elephant had wheeled in panic. They were coming back at us again. For another ten minutes the earth shook under their running feet and the air was filled with noise, dust, and confusion. Nick and I clung to our tree of refuge and waited. We did no talking, and we did not move around. If the elephant ever stopped running, they'd smell us or spot us in a second and jerk us down.

But the elephant did not stop running, at least for a couple of hours. The main stampede had broken up into small groups of fifteen or twenty animals. These now rushed aimlessly back and forth. Some elephant stood, raising their trunks in the air and taking the wind. Far off in the distance, we could hear broken fragments of the herd, still trumpeting and running. By sundown some of the elephant had quieted down and begun to feed. Those downwind from us moved off, still screaming.

There was no sign of our native trackers. For all we knew, they might have been caught in the middle of the stampede. Our camera boy, too, had disappeared. *If an elephant stepped on my cameras*, I thought, *they would look worse than Nick's double rifle.*

It was almost dark when Nick and I slipped down from the tree. We could still see seven or eight elephant nearby. We took no time to go and look at the bull I had shot. We had to move quickly. There were a lot of elephant downwind of us.

At a half run we moved crosswind. I still hoped to find the camera boy. Chances were that he had run when the stampede started. Nick and I rounded a clump of trampled brush at a dead run. There was a bull elephant not thirty feet from us. The bull shook his head and stuck out his ears. He turned and ran.

Brownie, at the car, had heard the trumpeting of the stampeding herd even at that distance. The two trackers had already come in, and the camera boy had shown up soon afterward. The natives had been smarter than we were.

The next day we worked our way cautiously back to our favorite tree. We had a bad moment when we saw twenty or thirty elephant not far away. Fortunately, the animals were already moving off. We waited a half-hour to make sure they were gone, and then worked our way back to the stampede grounds. The area looked as

Elephant Stampede

though the greatest of tornadoes had swept by. Trees, clumps of brush, and cactus were flattened like cobwebs. The earth itself was churned into powder. There was no square foot of that area that didn't have an elephant track on it.

My bull lay about thirty yards from our tree. He had apparently been carried part of the way by the stampede of his fellows before he dropped dead. His tusks weighed only 81 pounds, as they proved to be fairly short. He had looked awfully big coming straight at us out of the dust and confusion. Nick was picking up the parts of his double rifle, to see if anything could be salvaged. "I think," he said ruefully, "that this is the wrong way to get a big elephant."

Chapter 11

GHOST OF THE FOREST
(1960)

The Pygmies of the Bangui River country called it a *boruya*, and so it was. In the language of the Pygmy people of the Congo rain forest, *boruya* means ghost. This ghost, the Pygmies told me, lived in the Big Forest and wore horns on his head. Furthermore, the Pygmies stated with conviction, the *boruya* could not be killed.

I reasoned that if the thing had horns, it was an animal and not a ghost. In the Congo rain forest it could only be a bongo. It took me two weeks and a walk of three hundred miles to find out that I was dead wrong.

Jean Bepoix, our French guide in Equatorial Africa, had promised to show us a bongo. The forest-dwelling bongo is perhaps the most difficult animal in all of Africa for a sportsman to bag. Though the bongo is the Beau Brummell of the animal world, his dark red coloring and white stripes blend in well with the shadows of the forest places where this rare antelope lives. There are few sportsmen who can boast of having a bongo in their trophy collection. I wanted to be one of those.

Furthermore, Bepoix told me, as we drove southward from Fort Archambault in French Equatorial Africa to the Bangui River, that he had found, on his last trip into the Big Forest, a village of Pygmies who knew all the game in the area. Bepoix had not actually seen the Pygmy village, as it was a three-day walk from the nearest road, but he had talked to two of the Pygmies from the village. Pygmies are hunters and not farmers like the larger-bodied forest Negroes of the same area. The Pygmies know the rain forest and the game within it like the palms of their wizened little hands.

Under the African Sun

It sounded like a good bet for bongo, especially as two of my friends had already bagged bongo along the Ubangi River. If we could persuade the Pygmies to go with us into the country of the *boruya*, finding a bongo would be a cinch.

Jean Bepoix and I gathered what equipment we needed for a two-week walking safari. In Jean's old power wagon we headed east from the town of Bangui along the road to Aguifendi. This area, now called the Central African Republic, was, before 1960, a part of southern French Equatorial Africa. The countryside is covered with dense jungle growth very much like the Belgian Congo, which lies just across the river. The road we traveled, however, angled away from the river proper and headed easterly through the fringes of the rain forest toward the Ouarra River, where only the small side streams are flanked by belts of jungle growth. This kind of country is called "gallery forest."

We stopped at the village of Baranda, where the forest Negroes, under French supervision, had planted large banana plantations. This was as far as we could go by car. We paid a citizen of Baranda to watch our vehicle and hired fifteen other Barandians to serve as porters for a march southward into the jungle country.

This time of year, the middle of April, was, as Jean called it, "Zee dry season." It rained regularly every night and quite often during the day as well. The long, palm-thatched houses of the forest Negroes simply break up the larger drops of water and filter them in a fine, exasperating spray over the occupants within. After our first night in Baranda, we were never dry for the rest of the trip.

But wet as we were, it was exciting to start southward the next morning on a walking safari. As the line of porters with loads of equipment on their heads straggled out behind us, I felt like Livingstone penetrating the inner recesses of the Dark Continent. We followed a narrow trail through the wet grass of a big savanna between the arms of the gallery forest below Baranda. When we entered the jungle itself on the same narrow trail, the early morning sun was blotted out as though by an eclipse. We never crossed another savanna or saw the sun clearly again. Furthermore, my enthusiasm for the walking safari was considerably diminished by the time we had walked eight hours without stopping to eat or rest. As I was carrying nothing except my rifle, I could not complain. Most of our grinning porters were carrying fifty pounds or more apiece. It

Ghost of the Forest

developed that our goal for our first day's march was a new plantation of the forest Negroes some thirty-five miles within the rain forest. Here a few families from Baranda had begun to clear the trees
and plant bananas. The major attraction, if there was any attraction
in that dank and dark place, was a large grove of oil-nut palms. The
forest Negroes roast the datelike nuts of this palm to eat, and they
also collect them for the oil they contain.

As we arrived at this outpost of no civilization at all, I just had
strength enough to ask Bepoix how we were going to meet our Pygmy
guides. He had already explained that the Pygmy village was two days'
march beyond Little Baranda, as they called the clearing in the forest.
"Zey send for zee Babingas when we leave zee road," Jean explained.

I went to sleep with the rain dripping in my face, trying to figure
out how any human could go one hundred miles on foot through the
forest trails when we had just gone thirty or so. Through the roar of the
tropical rain on the thatched roof, I heard the boom of thunder; it seemed
to have a regular rhythm and cadence. "Zee drums," Jean mumbled in
the dark beside me. "Zey tell that we come safe to Little Baranda."

Talking drums! So that was the way! In the morning I examined
the telegraphic apparatus of the forest blacks. The drum, a large hollow log with a slit along its upper side, was suspended horizontally on
two sharp stones. The telegraph operator sat astride the drum and
beat it with a large stick wrapped with skin. That same morning, the
two Pygmy guides, Hota and Borgu, appeared. The message had been
relayed to them by intermediate drums when we left the road.

First the porters held a ceremony over my Weatherby rifle to
make sure that the bullet would be effective against a *boruya*. They
danced around the gun, yelling "Bump-bumpa" and pushing good
luck into the barrel so that it could not miss. As I had made a couple
of spectacular misses in the previous two-months' hunt in French
Equatorial Africa, I was all for this.

While the porters were sorting loads and eliminating every unnecessary item, Bepoix was questioning the Pygmies through an interpreter. He asked them especially about the *boruya*, the ghost of
the forest. The two Pygmies nodded solemnly as they heard the
word *boruya*, and pointed behind them toward the solid walls of trees.
"Yes, the *boruya* lives there. He has twisted horns and cannot be
killed. He has never been killed."

Under the African Sun

I saw one of the Pygmies carrying a knife suspended by a bandoleer of red hide marked with white stripes. That strip of skin could only have come from a bongo. And yet these two little fellows had just said that the ghost of the forest cannot be killed. Something was very wrong here. Perhaps the Pygmies were not telling all that they knew. Maybe they were treacherous and deceitful.

I could not have been more wrong about the two Pygmy guides, Hota and Borgu, who took us next morning into the great rain forest to the south. After several days, I found that these two diminutive men were quiet, soft-spoken, and capable. Although we could not speak a word of any mutual language, I grew to know them very well and to like them immensely. Our Pygmy guides were so thoroughly at home in the great rain forest that they seemed a part of the animal life there. Curiously enough, the six forest blacks who had somewhat reluctantly agreed to accompany us on the hunt as porters were lost once they left the clearings of their banana plantations and the trails between them.

The great rain forest is like a damp cellar. The ribbed trunks of the trees tower so far overhead that their tops are lost in the green gloom of the canopy of vegetation. Trailing lianas hang out of the semi-obscurity from the tree limbs far above. The forest floor itself is in eternal darkness. Here and there younger trees and bushes struggle for a single spot of sunlight that might give them strength enough to compete with their neighbors. The silent twilight of the great forest is marked only by the steady drip of water and the occasional cry of a hornbill in the crowns of the trees above.

One of the queerest effects of the forest is the loss of a sense of direction. The faint light that filters down through the millions of glossy leaves overhead gives little indication of the whereabouts of the sun. There are no landmarks. I was astounded to find that the forest black were as easily confused about directions as myself. But the Pygmies never were. Whether we were on elephant trails or walking through the forest with no sign of a trail, our two Pygmy guides took us unerringly and directly to any spot.

Curiously enough, one of our major problems was water in that dank forest. We were, so Bepoix told me, approximately fifty miles from the nearest stream. There were, however, shallow depressions in the forest floor that filled with water during the rainy season. As it continued to rain every night during our stay, I made a mental note that I never wanted to see the rainy season if this was their idea of a dry period. My thin bed soon was slimy with mildew. My mosquito netting fell apart in gray patches. The big brown-winged mosquitoes that appeared at nightfall could sail through without folding their wings. As usual, our two Pygmies were the only sensible ones. When we camped, they constructed a low platform of small branches on which they slept. Beneath, they put a smoldering punk log. The smoke kept the mosquitoes at bay. To keep off the rain, they pulled a covering of enormous leaves over their faces and shoulders.

From Little Baranda, we marched for two days, in a generally southward direction, to a deserted Pygmy village in the forest. As we slogged into the little clearing beneath the trees, we could still see the decaying sleeping platforms the Pygmies had built there and the framework of two domed huts they had used for more permanent shelter. Near the old Pygmy camping place was a depression in the forest floor as big as a city lot and half filled with green, slime-coated water. As we approached the spot, a number of brown tree ducks flew up and perched on the limbs of the dead trees in the middle of the pond. We brushed the scum aside and filled our canteens.

There certainly were bongo in the vicinity of the old Pygmy village. If I needed any further proof, the moldering skull and horns of a bongo bull that I found in the Pygmy camp furnished it. Our two Pygmies were armed with tiny bows and arrows and long-shafted spears. If they could get a bongo with that equipment, I certainly ought to be able to shoot one with a rifle.

It was typical of the Pygmies that they did not argue when Bepoix said that the *boruya* was a bongo. When I told the interpreter to tell our two little guides that I wanted a bongo very badly, the interpreter did not use *boruya*. He used a different word that means bongo in the Babinga language. But no one seemed to wonder about this.

The first morning of hunting we found the tracks of a bongo bull two or three miles from the deserted Pygmy village. As it had rained the night before, the tracks in the mud were obviously burning fresh. With one of the Pygmies in front of me as a tracker, I tiptoed along on the sodden forest floor straining for the first view of the quarry. Four of the forest Negroes, who had come along with us to carry water bottles and lunch, trailed behind. I was amazed at how much noise these porters made as they slogged through the mud. I finally told Bepoix to order them to hang back a hundred yards so that we would have a thin chance of getting up to the bongo bull. I had learned before how keen-eared a bongo can be. Our second Pygmy guide simply faded off into the trees at the side of the trail and was gone.

We tracked the bongo where the animal had fed early that morning. He had nibbled on some pale green shoots of a three-leafed plant that grew in little clumps on the forest floor. Hota tested the juice from the severed stems. The fluid was still fresh and sticky. The bongo was just ahead. The tracks of the bongo bull straightened from his zigzag course. The imprints in the mud led toward a moss-covered log on the forest floor. Stepping as daintily as pouter pigeons, Hota and I rounded the upturned roots of the dead forest giant. There was a sudden rush of sound in the stillness. A sapling snapped. Hoofs pounded on the mud. Then the silence closed in again. We found the bongo bed just on the other side of the log. We had been no more than fifteen feet away when the animal jumped up and sprinted for safety. I grinned a sickly grin at Hota. He solemnly motioned me on. We would try again.

Late in the morning we stopped for a rest and an unappetizing lunch. In the last four hours of steady tracking, we had jumped the bongo three times. We had never so much as seen a patch of red hide in the gloom between the trees. I was wet and frankly discouraged. I had been through this kind of bongo hunting before.

While we ate our slimy sandwiches, the other Pygmy, Borgu, appeared among us. He came as silently as he had gone. He carried on his back a little knapsack made of leaves with carrying straps manufactured from vines. The package contained large land snails, some kind of bulb that he had dug up, and the carcass of a small squirrel-like rodent that I had never seen before. In all of the later days of the hunt, whenever one Pygmy guide was tracking for us, the other was off foraging. How the food gatherer could find us in that vast place was a continual mystery. I was constantly impressed by the differences between the Pygmies and the forest Negroes: The Pygmies were completely at home in the forest; the agricultural blacks were ill at ease as soon as they left their *shambas*.

In the afternoon we found the tracks of another lone bongo bull. We had already crossed the tracks of two or three groups of female bongo with young. There had been another single track of an animal with enormously elongated hoofs. I thought that it might be the track of the rare okapi, since I had never seen an okapi track. When Jean asked the Pygmies about this, they shook their heads and pointed southward. We decided to have one more try at a bongo, since the track looked very fresh, as if the animal had begun to feed early in the afternoon. The track led us in a few minutes into a half-open clearing. This was one of the depressions that hold water in the rainy season. Although it was now dry, we could see on the boles of the trees where the water had stood six or eight feet deep some months before. The standing water had killed a few trees so that a little sunlight filtered through. Where the pond had been, the ground was covered with the three-leafed plant that the bongo like. This bongo bull had apparently left his bed to feed in the clearing. His tracks were everywhere. Some of the pale green weeds growing in the pond bed had been nibbled off only minutes before. It took one of the Pygmies perhaps thirty minutes to find where the bongo had left the weed patch and returned to the forest. The tracks led straight to a blowdown of trees where some gale of long ago had uprooted four or five forest giants and laid them in a pile. Other trees and saplings had long since reached up to use the precious sunlight in the vacant place. Some large trees grew on the bodies of the fallen.

Hota, who was in the lead, held up his hand for me to stop. He looked at the fallen trees for five minutes. Then he cautiously moved a few steps to the side and stopped again. He held up his nose and sniffed the wind like a hunting hound. Hota was scenting like a wild animal for the body odor of the bongo. He looked back at me. I could not tell from his expression whether he had smelled the bongo or not, but he seemed confident. He crawled to the right and crouched again, testing the wind. Then he pointed with his hand held close to his body. There was a dark space between two of the fallen trees. A few ferns grew there. Behind the fallen trunks was dark shadow—nothing more. The Pygmy motioned me forward. I crawled behind him and looked over his shoulder. There was nothing.

Suddenly the shadows moved. There was a rush of motion behind the fallen trees. Frantically I threw the gun to my shoulder and shot at the movement. A bright splinter of wood jumped from the side of one of the trees. Even as the thing ran, I could not make out the form or the color of the animal. The bongo was gone.

After this bitter disappointment, it was too late to get back to our camp in the deserted Pygmy village. Bepoix and I split a can of sardines between us and slept sitting up against the bole of a tree. Our four porters were equally miserable as the big brown mosquitoes droned back and forth. The two Pygmies, as usual, dined well and slept well on their little platforms, which they constructed in a few minutes. I finally spent half the night making a sleeping platform for myself. I abandoned it after one try. Lying on those raw poles was like sleeping on a set of broken springs without any mattress.

Our first day of bongo hunting was a good sample of the week that followed. The bongo were present but elusive. Twice the Pygmies smelled or saw bongo ahead. I never so much as got a glimpse of a tail or a horn.

The continued dampness was making me sick. My skin began to feel like the epidermis of a toad. I had never heard that mildew can grow on a human, but in the rain forest I think it is possible. Even Bepoix was silent and moody. He had lived a good part of his life on the edge of the great forest, although only once before had he penetrated so far to the southeast. Furthermore, Jean had run out of cigarettes and we were both just about out of food. Three of our porters had deserted us. We wondered if these forest blacks would be able to find their way back to Baranda. At the time, we didn't much care.

Only the two Pygmies, Hota and Borgu, seemed to be undiscouraged, and well fed. The clammy gloom of the rain forest seemed to be a natural background for their taciturn dispositions. Nor were they downhearted that we had not yet bagged a bongo— or even seen one, for that matter. We would try again, Hota said in his quiet way. He knew where there was another forest pond about a five-hour walk to the southeast. We would try there in the morning. Neither Bepoix nor I was particularly enthusiastic. We were so leg-weary that a five-hour march to this new spot appalled us. And what difference did direction make? The country was the same no matter where we went.

We started out the next morning a dispirited and silent crew. As usual, Borgu disappeared into the forest at the side of the elephant trail an hour after we had started. Our three remaining porters carried what was left of our equipment; it amounted only to our moldering beds and what was left of our mildewed tent. Jean was down to his last jug of wine, and there were two cans of bully beef remaining. We were going to have a thin and hungry time getting back to the road.

The two Pygmies took us unerringly through twelve or fifteen miles of forest without ever so much as following an elephant trail. We had started off as the first dim daylight filtered down through the great trees. About noon, we saw ahead a lighter patch of shadow, which was the forest pond. The two Pygmies could not have taken us straighter to this remote spot if they had used radar. But the Pygmies and their forest ways seemed destined to failure anyhow. The pond itself was almost dry. What water there was looked like a bright green rug and was about the same size. As we stepped up to the edge, a half-dozen brown ducks spurted up from the slime-coated puddle and circled among the trees.

Around the edge of the scummy pond were a few old bongo tracks. There was nothing fresh enough to follow. A bongo bull had been nibbling on some weeds growing at the edge of the water a day or two before. We had come all of this distance for nothing.

Hota, as usual, was testing the wind with his nose. I was accustomed to the Pygmies' scenting like hunting hounds. It no longer seemed strange. This time Hota crouched and ran around the edge of the pond like a beagle. Borgu followed him closely. The two put their heads together but spoke no words—both of them testing the wind. A very faint breeze blew through the dead trees in the middle of the clearing. The brown ducks sat above us on some bare limbs and looked down stupidly. Jean motioned the three porters to sit down. They collapsed. We followed the two Pygmies in a half circuit around the pond. Hota and Borgu were standing behind the bole of a gigantic tree. They looked around the curve of the trunk and then shrank back. "*Boruya!*" Hota whispered beneath his breath and pointed. I looked where he pointed. There was nothing—only the great trunks of the trees growing thicker on the far side of the pond. There was no bongo, no life, nothing.

"Jean," I said half aloud, "these damn Pygmies can see . . ."

When over beyond the pond a brown something moved among the trees. There was another, and another. I could hear a rustling on the sodden leaves. Automatically I threw my rifle to my shoulder and followed the movement of the running forms. There was a pair of horns zigzagging through the shadows. Just behind was another set. I could see the ivory tips of the horns as they appeared and disappeared among the trees. Through the telescopic sight of the rifle I could see the brown shoulder of the biggest bull. I jerked the trigger savagely.

The clap of the shot sent the tree ducks spiraling into the air with unducklike shrieks. The two Pygmies disappeared as though an invisible force had jerked them from behind the big tree. Jean and I ran forward. He was muttering something in French and pounding me on the back. "*C'est bon, ça. Vous avez tué un bongo.*"

Under the African Sun

There on the dry leaves lay an animal. But it was not a bongo. The lyrate horns might have fit a bongo, but the brown hide with the white-spotted markings was a far cry from the red and white-striped bongo I had expected. The hoofs of this curious animal were shaped like skis and were almost as long.

"Why, it's a sitatunga!" I said incredulously. "A sitatunga in the Big Forest. It can't be!"

It was indeed a sitatunga. But not an ordinary one, if any sitatunga can be described as ordinary. The African sitatunga lives in vast swamps such as papyrus-bordered lakes or the great Sudd swamp of the Upper Nile. I had already shot a sitatunga in the swamps of western Tanganyika. So the ghost animal of the Pygmies was a forest sitatunga. We had been after a rare bongo. This animal was rarer still.

We found out later that the British, fifty years before, had described a new species of forest sitatunga that lived in the southern Sudan, but they had never been able to get a complete specimen. Certainly the one we bagged so accidentally was not an isolated animal, since there were at least six sitatunga in the group we had encountered by that remote pond.

We had some very bad moments during the rest of the day when we thought our two Pygmies had deserted us. We were extremely dubious if we could find our way out of the big forest without them. They joined us as silently as ghosts late in the afternoon. They would not touch the animal we carried, or even look at it. I noticed also that they would not look at me or come close to my gun. The ghost of the forest had been killed. This could only be done by very powerful magic. As for myself, I thought it was sheer unadulterated luck.

A big bull elephant carrying heavy ivory in the Karamojo country of northern Uganda.

A very good bull buffalo in the Karamojo country of northern Uganda.

Buffalo herd in northwestern Uganda. Some of the buffalo are reddish, showing a mixture of the red West African forest buffalo with the black Cape buffalo.

Buffalo bull in northern Uganda with mud on his face and horns.

A bunch of hippo basking on a sand bar of the White Nile in the southern Sudan.

A defassa, or common, waterbuck appears out of a euphorbia thicket on the bank of the Nile near Nimule.

A big bull elephant carrying heavy ivory spreads his ears and prepares to charge.

Bull elephant with long, narrow tusks, near the border of Uganda and the Congo.

I spy a herd of hippo in the upper Nile in northern Uganda.

Much of the country in northern and western Uganda is open savanna with bands of bush-veld. Here a lone buffalo has just finished his daily mud bath.

Two topi bulls against the backdrop of the mountains along the Uganda-Congo border.

A "whipped-out" hippo bull challenges an elephant that is about to swim across the Nile River near Juba in the Sudan.

In extreme western Uganda, this buffalo and his pals plowed through a herd of green-flanked baboons. (The baboons are, at this point, far off into the background.) Note that no two buffalo head and horns are alike.

Male kob, a close cousin of the impala, in a dense thicket along the upper Congo River.

A very old bull elephant with a broken ear feeds on the grass at the foot of Kilimanjaro in northern Tanzania. The hollows on his forehead show his extreme age, and his tusks are exceptional.

A bull elephant in the forests at the foot of Kilimanjaro in southern Kenya decides whether to charge us or not. Mr. Nice Guy let us go in peace.

Somali tribesmen trade goat and camels at the market in Wau, Sudan.

I contemplate the difficulty of fording through the papyrus swamps of the Nile near Lake Nyubor.

Several tons of elephant tusks recaptured from poachers along the edge of the Sudd (a great swamp found in the Nile, in the central Sudan).

Two Samburu warriors dig for water along the Bursiloi sand river in northern Kenya. An elephant, whose dung appears in the picture, had previously located the spot, using his sense of smell, where the water was close to the surface.

This mountain rhino (which has more slender horns and a darker color than his cousin, the bush rhino) overturned a bulldozer high up on the slopes of Mt. Kenya.

Two Dinka tribesmen assisted me in my adventure into the Sudd. As we could not communicate at all, I called one "Hey You" and the other "You There." This is Hey You with a Mrs. Gray.

Bongo and mountain elephant live the Aberdare Mountains of central Kenya, in an almost impenetrable rain forest. From this volcanic ridge we could see the red bongo bulls below come out at dusk.

My lesser kudu taken along the shores of Lake Rudolf in northern Kenya.

Ngoro, my gunbearer, and Sungura, a tracking expert, and I follow the tracks of a lone male lion over burned grass near the Chobe River in northern Botswana.

The greater kudu of Namibia have wide, beautiful horns, but they are not particularly long.

A lion along the a branch of the Okavango roars defiance at another male nearby .

Opposite: Brownie and I prepare to cut up an elephant that I took in southern Namibia. These tusks are short and thick and weighed only 72 pounds.

Eight riverine Bushmen cut a channel through the papyrus thickets of the Chobe River in northern Botswana. We improvised a raft of palm logs and empty oil drums and floated to the Caprivi Strip.

The usually rare red lechwe is found in fair-size herds along the reedbeds and lagoons of the Okavango Swamps in Botswana.

The common reedbuck, an antelope about the size of an American white-tailed deer, is also common in the grasslands along the Okavango Swamps.

Chapter 12

HOW TO BAG AN AFRICAN LION
(1960)

The Bushmen trackers, Maguga and Joseph, crouched and pointed. Ahead was a small clearing. A bushfire several weeks before had swept away the dry grass and seared the leaves from the mopane bushes. The place was empty of life except for a low termite hill. This too was bare, as the termites had abandoned the place after the last wet season.

A dry pole on the termite mound whipped into the air. The thing was tufted at one end like a tail. Part of the termite hill moved restlessly. A maned neck and head appeared like magic from the earth. The head turned. Two sleepy eyes looked at us. The eyes widened. They were sleepy no more. The mouth opened in a grunting roar. The lion was only fifty feet away.

I had been in this situation before, and so had Ian Henderson, who stood at my elbow. Only six months before, Ian and another friend of mine, Dr. Brandon Macomber of Albany, New York, had tracked a lion in exactly this way. That lion reacted precisely as lion do when they suddenly discover humans very close. The lion charged Henderson and Macomber. The two men shot the lion six times at point-blank range. That lion attacked Macomber twice and Henderson three times. Henderson, bitten through both thighs, and Macomber, bitten through the chest, were lucky to escape with their lives.

Under the African Sun

The lion is no friend of man. Actually, as human populations increase, the lion is fast disappearing from his former haunts. In the centuries before Christ, there were lion from Greece to India and southward throughout Africa. The lion disappeared from Europe during the time of the Homeric heroes. The lion was gone from the Holy Land before the time of Christ. The Romans got lion from North Africa to eat Christians. Now lion are gone from North Africa. In India, only a handful of Asiatic lion remain on one reserve.

Even in Uganda, Kenya, Tanzania, and Mozambique, in places where I had heard the roar of lion every night fifteen years ago, it is hard to find a lion now. In places the big cats are gone. In other areas they are scattered. Many lion, harassed by native tribesmen, traps, poison, and guns, have learned to keep their mouths shut. A lion now stands as one of the hard-to-get big-game animals.

Many of the African governments now limit the number of lion that may be bagged in different areas. They also limit the manner of taking them. This has slowed down the inevitable. Even among professional hunters, good lion hunters are now scarce.

A decade ago, in Kenya or Tanzania, the baiting of lion was a regular part of every safari. Usually a pride of lion revealed its presence by roaring. Both the males and the females roar. Apparently, they do it as a sign of satisfaction. Sometimes a pride will roar to terrify its victims when the big cats are hunting. When lion have made a kill, a wheeling circle of vultures in the sky above is a sure sign of what is going on below. When the meat birds are milling on outstretched wings, it is an indication to the hunter that the lion are feeding or lying close and guarding their meat. When the vultures fold their wings and drop out of the sky, the lion are leaving.

In Ethiopia, Somalia, and Mozambique, hunters often locate a pride of cats by imitating the roar of a lion. Some of the native hunters become extremely expert in this exacting art. Some callers use their cupped hands. Others cough and grunt through a piece of bark rolled like a megaphone and held close to the ground. If skillfully done, a series of roars like a male lion on the prowl will bring another male in close. The coughing of a lovesick lioness is a sure bet to bring an answer. I have seen a skillful caller in Somalia bring a whole pride of lion out of the darkness. On that occasion, the cats came so close we could see their bodies in the dim light of a half moon.

How to Bag an African Lion

Lion are essentially lazy. A meat carcass placed where they will find it will usually attract a pride. An old male past his prime has difficulty making enough kills. Such an old male is a setup for a bait. A few years ago, the baiting of lion was standard practice. Game licenses allowed a liberal number of zebra, wildebeest, hartebeest, buffalo, and such common animals for this practice. It was not unusual to hang up as many as ten baits to attract a pride or a single lion. Professional lion killers such as John Hunter often had fifty baits hung at a single time, and shot the lion that fed on them by daylight or at night with a spotlight. Obviously, the baiting method is wasteful. It also takes a lot of know-how.

If the lion hunter simply hangs a wildebeest or a zebra or, worse yet, leaves the carcass on the ground, the vultures will pick it clean in ten minutes. After dark, the hyenas and jackals will crunch the bones. By morning, only a set of horns and a trampled spot on the ground will mark where the bait has been. All cats must water at least once a day. The lion baiter usually drags the carcass past a water hole or across a route the lion must take to go to drink. Usually the paunch of the bait is punctured so that the drag is left with a liberal smear and smell as the carcass is pulled along. Cats find their prey by sight and hearing. Their sense of smell is only moderately developed. A good drag must have a lot of "stink" to attract a lion.

The carcass is then pulled across the limb of an appropriate tree and hung with a wire or rope. The place must be chosen so the lion can see the bait as they follow along the drag. There should be brush nearby where a cat can lie up after it has fed. A lion likes to nap in the shade after a full meal. Also, he wants to watch his meat to keep away the vultures.

A hyena can reach about as high as a man's face. The bait must be hung about 5½ feet from the ground so that a lion can reach it and a hyena can't. The worst danger is the vultures. Any projecting limb, even one leg of the carcass sticking out at an angle, will serve as a perch for the "meat birds." We lost a whole zebra on one occasion when we carelessly left a hind foot protruding. Twenty or thirty vultures took turns sitting on the zebra's hoof and eating out the flesh. In a single day the vultures left our zebra bait a limply hanging, hollowed-out drapery of skin and bones.

The position of the bait must be such that the hunter can see it from a considerable distance. With binoculars, the fellow with lion on his mind can tell whether the meat has been appropriated. If the vultures are sitting in the trees round about, then the lion are close and guarding the meat. Usually the hunter wants to have a look at the lion to see if there is a worthwhile male with a big mane. Often in the baiting business, it is necessary to attract two or three prides of lion and look them over before an appropriate male with an acceptable mane can be sorted out.

Some professional hunters are very fussy about leaving human scent around a bait. They rub the stomach contents of the carcass animal over the rope by which the carcass is suspended, and everywhere a human foot or hand has touched. Most of the job of placing a bait on a tree limb is done from the top of a safari car so that no human scent is left on the ground. Other hunters are less particular and contend that a lion's sense of smell is so weak that a few human footprints don't matter. Some professionals attach the bait with a small rope or wire so that a lion can break it and jerk the carcass down. If the lion can drag the bait into some nearby bushes, he feels more secure about the whole business and is less cautious about a hunter approaching with a gun.

The most successful lion hunters usually build a blind at the same time that the bait is hung on the tree. The blind should be about fifty to seventy-five yards away and in a position so that the hunter can enter without being seen. A path to the rear of the blind is cleared so that no crackle of twigs or leaves will give a warning. Even the back of the blind should be solid brush and grass. Cats have phenomenal eyesight and can easily detect the slightest movement.

Other hunters prefer to approach a prospective bait from behind a hill or cutbank.

The finely developed art of baiting a lion takes a lot of doing. For one thing, baiting is now illegal in many areas, because it is wasteful of game. Also, lion have grown wary of baits. A dozen years ago, hunters could photograph a pride of lion happily following a safari car while a bait was being dragged. Now, in these same areas, a lion will be wary of a bait or, at best, feed on the carcass only at night.

Some hunters have varied the old baiting method by leaving the carcass on the ground. A buffalo shot not too far from a water hole is excellent for this purpose. The bait is then covered with thornbrush in a solid blanket of interlacing branches so that no vul-

How to Bag an African Lion

ture can get through. Branches of thorn trees must be thrust under and around the bait in a solid wall so that the hyenas and jackals cannot tunnel beneath and hollow out the carcass. A lion, if he is attracted, can bat away the thornbrush with one blow of his paw. In my own opinion, the brush-covered lion bait on the ground is an act of desperation and usually doesn't work anyway. If lion are wary of bait, they usually will walk around a thornbrush bait, as well as the hanging type. In any event, the hyenas will usually crawl under the thorns and make a shambles of the business in a day or two.

In a few areas where game is very plentiful, lion will simply not come to a bait. In other places, the big cats have grown wary. In the Masai country and in other regions where the natives raise cattle, lion are especially cautious. Cattle raisers kill lion when they can. The big cats soon learn to be suspicious of any meat left lying around. Even when lion kill domestic cattle, which they often do, they will kill one cow or several, feed once, and never return. I have spent a good many days and nights sitting up over a half-eaten cow waiting for the killer to return. He seldom did.

The tracking of lion is the most exciting and most dangerous method. In most places, it is now the only way by which a lion can be bagged.

Good lion trackers are scarce. Cats have soft paws that leave little impression on hard ground. However, many of the native African trackers have uncanny skill in following the pug marks of a lion. Hunting tribes such as the Somalis or the Wakambas and Waliangulus in Kenya are very skillful in following cat tracks. Hunters with thousands of years of hunting tradition behind them such as the Bushmen of South Africa can follow any kind of track anywhere. On one occasion in Somalia, a tracker followed a lion over eight miles across stony and rocky ground where I could not detect the passage of an elephant. The tracker had a motive as well as the skill. This desert lion had killed his wife and daughter and eaten the daughter. I followed that tracker over five hours. Most of the time I was sure he was guessing or going by direction. Then, very occasionally, I saw a disturbed pebble or the faint imprint of a lion's three-lobed heel in a patch of sand. The Somali tracker finally pointed out the lion where he lay asleep beneath a clump of camelthorn. The tracker stepped back just as the lion woke up and charged.

Tracking lion is dangerous sport even if the lion is not a man-eater. The tracker invariably finds himself in a knee-to-knee situation with the big cat at the end of the trail. Under these circumstances, a lion would rather fight than run. He may do both.

Some of the best lion country in Africa, in my opinion, is in Botswana. Lion are still plentiful. There is also an abundance of game. Botswana lion will usually not take a bait and seem to prefer to make their own kills. We have even tried to tempt old males with a buffalo carcass. Although these senior lion were having trouble killing their own meat, they usually passed up our offerings.

I have hunted lion in Botswana on two occasions. Both times we used Bushman trackers, and both hunts were plenty exciting.

Our Bushman friends like to track a single male or, at best, a pair of males. Following up a whole pride is asking for sure trouble. The lioness is usually the killer among the group. She is also more watchful. If a lioness has cubs, she will charge at the drop of a hat. Four or five lion charging at once from a few yards away is a situation no sane hunter wants to get into. The Bushmen try to locate a single male by hearing him roar and watching for his spoor. If possible, they try to get a look at him. Many a lion with a big track has a poor mane. The Bushmen don't care about the mane. The hunter usually does. Bushmen eat lion—especially the heart and vital organs—so that they can acquire the cunning, the keenness of eyesight, and the strength of the big cats. It must work, too. For the Bushman hunters are the best I have ever accompanied.

The ideal situation is to find a lion that has just fed and just watered. With his belly full, he usually will not go far. A well-fed lion will crawl into a shady spot and sleep out the day. If the hunter-tracker can find the lion asleep, you are halfway to bagging that trophy you came so far to get. Sometimes lion are hunting or, like any cats, just prowling. Under these circumstances, the tracker usually does not catch up to the quarry. A lion can walk faster than a man.

On our first hunt in Botswana with Andrew Holmberg, we were following two big males. We had a pair of Bushman trackers, including one named Kweri, who had been in at the kill of over fifty lion. Kweri was like a coonhound on a hot scent. Even when a herd of buffalo passed across the track, Kweri unraveled the scrambled situation in a few minutes. Both of these lion had fed and watered. They should not have gone far. But they did. At noon we were still tracking. We were hot and had grown careless.

How to Bag an African Lion

The two males separated. I do not know why. Even Kweri seemed distressed. He also became careless. We looked in every shady spot for a sleeping lion. Kweri and the other trackers slouched along as the big imprints led farther and farther up a sandy ridge. Suddenly Andrew grabbed my coat collar from behind. "Shoot him!" he whispered. The two Bushmen just ahead of me had passed within fifteen feet of the lion. That mistake almost cost me my life. The lion was awake and charged instantly.

From the episode in Somalia, some close calls in Kenya and Tanzania, and the Botswana lion, I learned a couple of valuable lessons. The first is, never lose your respect for an African lion. He can move like lightning, and he is built for killing. The second is, use a very big gun. A .458 or even larger is not too big a cannon when you are shooting at a 600-pound cat thirty or forty feet away.

When Ian Henderson and I decided to try for the big Chobe lion, we learned another valuable lesson. This was, never let a lion get his claws or his teeth on you, or your chances for survival are mighty slim. In Somalia, the man-eating desert lion had jumped upon me even in the last throes of death. Ian Henderson was one up on me. He had survived the famous fracas with Dr. Brandon Macomber. Once before, Ian had been bitten through the leg by a lion that was not quite dead. "Don't ever let a lion get to you," Ian repeated.

We were hunting for an especially large sable along the Chobe River in northern Botswana. We saw the tracks of a very large single male lion. There were old tracks, medium tracks, and very fresh ones. Apparently the lion passed that way every three or four days. In two weeks of hunting in that area, we finally bagged our big sable. We saw the sign of the big lion on several occasions. The big male went past the leg of our buffalo but did not touch it. We tried a zebra. The lion ignored the bait, although he passed within a few yards. We decided to track him. Both Ian and I knew what we were getting into. The Bushman trackers, of course, were delighted.

We found the big splayed-out tracks of the lion where he had stepped on top of the imprints of our Land Rover tires. Ian had cut a track along the Savuti. We had passed over that track at dark the evening before. The lion had watered at the Savuti and turned south into the endless bush country of the northern Kalahari. We followed the tracks a few yards. The spoor slanted past half a buffalo that we had hung in the crotch of a tree three days before. The buffalo was in a satisfactorily stinking condition, but the tracks did not even swerve toward the meat. We could see where a leopard had run up the tree and eaten a chunk out of the buffalo.

"Our big lion friend has fed on his own kill and watered," Ian whispered. "We'll get him this time."

Ian was partly right and partly wrong. We followed the tracks for several hundred yards in the soft earth close to the river. In one track was the cone-shaped indentation of a lion. In another lion track was superimposed the small imprint of a genet, one of the lesser night-prowling cats. The trackers shook their heads. The lion had walked that way the evening before. We were a good seven or eight hours behind him. Ian motioned the trackers on.

To make matters worse, the land away from the river became hard, with sparse grass. We lost the track many times. Each time, the uncanny eyesight of the Bushmen found a bent-down grass blade or the faint outline of a padded paw that indicated the lion had passed that way. We startled herds of zebra, and a herd of eland galloped ahead of us, obliterating the lion spoor. The Bushmen cast out in wide circles. They soon found the track again. The big cat imprints showed where the lion's toes and claws had bitten into the hard dirt. Maguga made running motions with his hands. The lion had made a pass at one of the zebra. Apparently he had missed, for there was no dead zebra and no vultures to mark a kill nearby. Again the Bushmen shook their heads. If the lion was hunting, we would never catch up to him.

Doggedly Ian motioned the trackers to continue. The trail zigzagged and looped. Twice the lion turned and retraced his steps for several hundred yards along a game trail. He was hunting, all right, and had not yet made a kill. We scanned the sky to the south for any sign of wheeling vultures. There were no "meat birds" in the distance, but we did see columns of smoke. The Bushmen light these fires. They burn for weeks and blacken miles of bushland. All of the game leaves a burned-over area until weeks later when the first green shoots of new grass appear.

With half-mile-long detours to both sides, the lion track still led southward. Late in the morning we crossed the sharp line where the fire had burned. On the blackened ground the tracking was easier. But why had the lion gone into this scorched area? There was no game, and not even a sizable tree had escaped the fire. Fire itself holds no fear for the animals of this country. The lion had passed close-by a rotten log that still emitted a sputter of flame and a column of smoke. Two or three miles ahead we could see that the main fire still burned.

It was noon. We had used up the small canteen of water we had taken with us. Three or four times we held whispered consultations as to whether we should turn back. This lion was either crazy or he knew something that we did not. Every time I thought of giving up, I looked at those great lion imprints in the burned earth, and the hunter's urge to see the lion that made them overcame the fatigue and made me forget the soot-blackened sweat that ran down my neck.

"Let's at least see where he thinks he is going," I urged Ian. "Those are the biggest lion tracks I have ever seen."

Ian shrugged his shoulders and urged the trackers to start again. He looked around at this fire-blackened empty place. There was no spot where a jackal could hide, let alone a full-grown lion.

By midafternoon we were exhausted, hot, and utterly perplexed. The lion had swung behind the brushfire, keeping to the recent burned-over area. We had already come ten or twelve miles. Very shortly we would have to turn back to reach the safari car before dark. Ian admitted that it was the longest lion tracking he had ever done. Even at that, Ian kept looking ahead. I did, too. Each of us remembered our own experiences. Somewhere at the end of this long trail was a big African lion.

It was Maguga who saw him first. I bumped into him as he knelt and pointed. Just ahead lay a small basin perhaps a hundred yards across. Here the grass was so scanty that the fire had not scorched the place. In the middle of the basin was a small termite mound with two or three sickly trees growing around its base. These also were not burned. One of the trees had a few green leaves. Across the termite mound lay a pole as big around as a man's arm. At the end of the pole was a big tuft of hair. As I stared, fascinated, the thing moved. It was a lion's tail. He was perhaps fifty feet away. I felt the prickle of excitement at the back of my sweaty neck. Ian, at my elbow, drew in his breath sharply. Maguga and Joseph stepped behind us and held their spears ready.

Under the African Sun

The lion was lying across the termite mound with his head on the far side. Why he had picked such an uncomfortable position in this impossible spot, we will never know. In that instant, he woke up. He turned around one tree and came straight for us. There was no yawning and stretching. In one second he was fully awake, on his feet, and charging. He growled low in his throat. My first shot hit the point of his shoulder. The heavy 500-grain slug knocked the lion off his feet. He roared and bit clear through the small tree beside him. Carefully I took two steps to the side and shot him straight through the shoulders. I wanted to take no chance that those white teeth or those hooked claws could get to us. He dropped his head forward on the ground. I could see that he had a big and heavy mane. Ian seemed to read my thoughts. "It's better to admire a lion after he's dead," he remarked. Ian rubbed his thigh where another lion had bitten it through.

Lion hunting is called "the sport of kings." As far as I am concerned, it is well named, especially if you track one down and shoot him at close quarters.

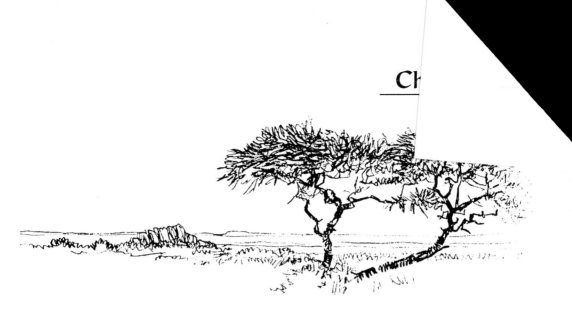

THE KILLER LEOPARD OF MANYARA
(1960)

The mouth was open, the lips were wrinkled back. Two eyes were streaks of green-yellow light. The cat head lunged forward. The open teeth were a blur of motion. The impact knocked the gun from David's hands. There was a paralyzing blow on his throat. He was thrown and pinned like a wrestler in a match to the death.

It was no accident that the leopard stood over the body of David Ommanney. David himself could have foretold that this would happen. For one thing, there were the bad omens; for another, there were the leopard themselves. Only that morning he had told his client, Baron von Boeselager, that the African leopard is the most dangerous animal in existence. "For its size and weight," David had pronounced solemnly, "the leopard is the most ferocious game on four legs. When a leopard is wounded, he *always* charges. And when he charges, he usually gets there with his teeth."

It was not that Baron von Boeselager did not believe David. Actually, the Baron had hunted twice in Africa before, and had shot all of the African Big Five, the animals that bite back. Even though the leopard is usually mentioned last in the list of the dangerous five, he is considered by many white hunters to be the deadliest of the whole quintet. Both the Baron and David Ommanney had heard, just before they started on this trip, that Eric Rundgren of the safari firm of Ker and Downey had been mauled by a leopard in the Narok district in southwestern Kenya. Dave Lunan, another white hunter, had also been badly chewed by a leopard near Lake Manyara in northern Tanganyika only a short time before.

And yet at the close of January 1959, Baron von Boeselager and his white hunter, David Ommanney, had set up camp in the very country where Lunan had almost met his death. The reason was simple. The Baron wanted a male leopard at least two and a half meters in length. Dangerous or not, some of the best leopard in all of East Africa are to be found in the Lake Manyara district. So David directed the safari boys to set up the camp on the flat plain two or three miles back from the edge of Lake Manyara itself. The country is level with scattered palm trees. Game is fairly abundant. There are many Grant gazelle, impala, and warthogs. Around the salt pans of Lake Manyara, a herd of some five hundred buffalo habitually feed. Perhaps because the smaller varieties of game are abundant, the plain around the lake is crawling with leopard. For some reason, the Manyara leopard are more aggressive than leopard elsewhere. In the last ten years, two fatal leopard attacks and a dozen maulings have occurred in the Manyara district.

David Ommanney is one of the youngest full-fledged white hunters in East Africa. Nonetheless, he felt supremely confident as he directed the safari boys to set up camp and sent the trackers out to look for leopard sign. David was born in India in 1928, and lived most of his life at Nanyuki, on the slopes of Mount Kenya in Africa. He had been hunting leopard, and every other kind of game for that matter, since he was old enough to lift the butt of a rifle. David had dealt with the forest leopard on his native Mount Kenya, and had collected on safari dozens of the beautiful spotted cats in the brush country and grasslands of both Kenya and Tanganyika. By the time he was twenty, David had personally accounted for over twenty-five leopard.

It was an old story to David as he directed the Baron to shoot some small game for leopard bait. The first evening, 20 January, the trackers brought in the information that at least four leopard were working within a mile of camp, and were watering some distance back from the edge of the lake. The next morning, the Baron shot two warthogs, a Grant gazelle, and an impala. With the cunning born of long experience, Ommanney directed his first gunbearer, Salim, and his second gunbearer, Mutia, to drag these baits, one at a time, through the grass and palmettos where the leopard would pass. Then, as each

The Killer Leopard of Manyara

leopard moved down to drink after dark, it would smell the drag and go straight to the bait. Each carcass was placed high in a tree.

That very first day, the stage was set for tragedy. Baron von Boeselager shot a hyena. Perhaps the Baron did not know that hyenas are considered very bad luck. Most of the Masai tribe (and there were several Masai among David's safari boys) regard the hyena as bad because the animal is full of evil human spirits. When a Masai dies, his relatives never bury the body. They simply place the dead on the ground outside the village. In the evening, the ever-present hyenas eat every scrap of the human body, then crack the bones and eat those, too. Hyenas often do not wait for native villagers to expose bodies, but will attack a sleeping man and bite off his arm or his face in a single snap. To the Masai, the hyena is a powerful animal, full of the evil of death.

The safari boys murmured among themselves, and rolled their eyes at the ground, when the Baron shot the hyena. None of them would touch the dead animal. When the Baron wanted the animal skinned and its head fixed for his trophy collection, not one of the skinners drew out his knife or made a move to save the carcass.

In the several days that followed, the incident of the hyena was almost forgotten, except by the most superstitious. During that time, the party found several leopard. Each one came to a bait that had been hung in one of the thorn trees on the plain. In two instances the trackers could tell by the small size of the spoor that the leopard were but half-grown cats, not worthy of further attention. However, three of the leopard that had fed on the baits provided for them were apparently large animals.

On each of three evenings, David and the Baron squatted in the high grass near one of these trees. At the first bait, they ascertained by looking with binoculars at the carcass in the tree that a leopard had appropriated the meat and was feeding upon it. From the amount of flesh eaten, they judged that the leopard was a large one, probably a male. They did not try to go near the tree from which the bait hung to get a closer look at the tracks. Such a rash action would either drive the leopard away or, worse, provoke him into charging.

When leopard appropriate a kill, they feed upon it and then lie up nearby so as to keep an eye on the remains. If they kill the animal themselves, they usually haul the carcass into a tree for safekeeping. Therefore, if the wily human places a Grant gazelle or an impala in a tree, it seems very natural to a leopard. The leopard feeds by night on his kill. He usually comes in the evening, jumps into the tree, and fills his belly. After that, he will lie in some place of concealment near the tree to guard the remains of the meat against would-be predators in the form of other leopard, hyenas, or birds of prey.

When David and the Baron slipped up to examine a leopard bait, they did so from downwind, stealthily. They squatted in the high grass among the palmettos with only the tops of their heads showing. They made no unnecessary movement. The eyesight of a leopard is extremely keen. In whispered tones Ommanney directed the Baron as to what to do. As the Baron had shot leopard before, he was steady and the hunting went well.

But Baron von Boeselager was particular. The first leopard they saw was a large male, better than seven feet in length. The animal appeared suddenly out of the grass. As it jumped up into the thorn tree, the last slanting rays of the sun lighted up the orange-yellow body marked with beautiful black rosettes. This was a trophy of which any sportsman would have been proud.

The leopard was hungry. He looked around only once, and then lay at full length on a large limb and began to feed. David had lain his hand upon the Baron's elbow so that there would be no movement that the leopard might see. When the cat began to eat, gulping down the rotten meat in great chunks, David signaled the Baron to raise his gun and fire. The Baron shook his head. "Two and a half meters," the Baron said firmly. Just behind Ommanney and the Baron, Salim, the gunbearer, swore a Moslem oath. The curse of Allah be upon this European. The misfortune of the hyena would overcome them all. Here was a fair shot in good light—and the leopard was a beauty.

But the Baron was a man of principle. He was determined to have a big leopard or none at all. On three successive evenings, the Baron shook his head firmly at three successive leopard. David himself was becoming irritated. For one thing, it was no small feat to attract five leopard in as many days. Not only had the leopard been induced to take the baits of gazelle and warthog, but each bait had been placed just right.

Each leopard had fed for two or three nights so that the hunters had had a chance to look him over. Ommanney had led the Baron through the high grass in just the right way so that the leopard would not be alarmed. Any one of the first five leopard they could have shot with ease; but still the Baron shook his head.

Perhaps it was the Baron's stubbornness; perhaps it was the evil human spirit of the hyena, as Salim said. The sixth leopard was the one.

The Killer Leopard of Manyara

David, with some show of justifiable irritation, had directed the Baron rather curtly to get another warthog, which they would hang near a dry wash or donga some two miles from camp. There were leopard tracks in the sand of this wash. Two or three cats apparently used the donga as a highway going to and from water. The warthog was appropriately placed in a thorn tree.

The next morning, as David swung the safari car within two or three hundred yards of the thorn tree, he could see that a leopard had taken the bait. The warthog had been a big boar, yet almost all of its carcass was gone. Only the head and one shoulder remained. These pathetic fragments, hanging by remnants of skin, had been hoisted higher in the tree and now hung in the fork of a branch. The rope by which Salim had tied the warthog carcass had been broken or bitten through as if it had been string. Only a very large leopard could do this. Perhaps this one would be big enough to satisfy the Baron.

It was uncertain whether the leopard would come back at all. He had fed heavily that first night. Also, there was little left for another meal—even for a hungry leopard. But it was a chance. So David and the Baron squatted behind a group of palmettos some fifty yards from the thorn tree on the edge of the wash. Salim lay on his elbow behind them. As usual, Salim shook his head and muttered under his breath. The omens were bad. As the sun sank lower, a flight of pink flamingos flew into the lake from behind: a very bad sign. A hornbill stalked up and down a branch at the top of the thorn tree. The hornbill squawked through his ridiculous overgrown beak, and to Salim the cries sounded like *mbaya, mbaya*. This means, in Swahili, "Bad, bad."

It was bad, too, when the sun lowered and the leopard did not appear. The last rays slanted over the escarpment beyond Lake Manyara. As though this were a signal, there was a rasping growl from the grass.

They saw the leopard at the edge of the donga. The end of his tail twitched back and forth in little jerks. The leopard was looking straight at them.

"He'll go eight feet, maybe more," David hissed into the Baron's ear.

The Baron was already raising his gun. He carried a European-made over-and-under, with an 8.64 rifle barrel mounted above a 16-gauge shotgun. This was not an easy shot. The leopard they had seen before were broadside, and in plain sight in a tree. This leopard was facing the hunters and looking straight at them. Any second the cat would whirl and go. The leopard's chest was a target the size of two human hands.

Under the African Sun

The Baron sighted quickly and fired. The solid ball struck too far to the right. Ommanney could see the spurt of fur as the bullet raked along the leopard's ribs. The leopard jerked sideways and leaped into the air. The squawling scream that came from between the wet teeth was a mixture of pain and rage. In an arching bound the leopard jumped sideways into the waist-high grass. Frantically, Ommanney raised his .470 double rifle and fired. The bullet was too late. It nicked the hind paw of the leopard as he sailed into the grass.

Just as the leopard leaped, he turned in midair—turned toward the three men. He had been looking at the humans before the shots. Now he was coming at them through the grass.

Ommanney grabbed the Baron by one arm. They ran sideways a few yards to where a termite hill rose out of the grass. Around the termite hill the busy little insects had cut down the vegetation for several yards. As Ommanney and the Baron scrambled up the rough knobs of the termite mound, a cobra uncoiled and slid into one of the passageways. The Baron flinched to one side. Ommanney jerked him higher on the bare dirt. Cobras usually run from humans; wounded leopard never do.

From the elevation of the termite hill, the hunters could look down into the grass. There was no sight or sound. Over across the plain of Manyara, the three rocky hills known as the pyramids were lighted by the evening sun. A lion roared in the distance down by the lake. The grass around the termite hill was empty of life.

Perhaps ten yards from the place where the leopard had stood, David hesitated. Here low-growing palmettos were mixed in the high grass. The leopard might attack from only a few feet away. He would need a second's warning to catch the charging animal on the end of his gun barrel.

David raised the shotgun and fired one barrel at the palmettos. He could still see nothing, but he listened carefully, expecting the leopard to growl at the shot and reveal his position. There was no sound. David reloaded and walked slowly forward. Again he raised the shotgun and fired, aiming at the exact spot where the leopard had disappeared. He waited tensely. Nothing. Even the birds had stopped their evening chirping.

He reloaded the empty barrel of the shotgun. Perhaps the Baron's shot had done its work after all. Ommanney stepped forward. He stood in the very grass where the leopard had jumped. With Salim peering over his shoulder, David swung slowly around. The leopard had gone.

A palmetto rustled. There was no wind. Fifteen feet away a yellow blur appeared. The thing was six feet in the air. Blindly David fired both barrels. He saw white teeth in front of his face. A paralyzing blow struck his throat. His gun flew end over end. He fell backward. Salim behind him was knocked down.

The leopard stood over him. When David looked up, he saw a white throat from beneath. Bloody saliva dripped down over the open jaws. The leopard turned to growl at Salim. The cat's face bent downward. David saw the open mouth lunge at his throat. Instinctively, he threw up his left arm. He tried to twist sideways. The weight of the leopard lay upon him. *Must keep those teeth from my throat,* he thought. The fangs closed on his shoulder as he twisted. At the first bite, his leather jacket was shredded. Muscle and bone crunched between the teeth. The leopard growled deep in his chest. The teeth shifted their grip lower, to try again for the throat. Again David twisted frantically. The teeth sank in near his elbow. David could hear tendons and muscles breaking away.

Salim sprawled on the ground. The double rifle had been knocked from his hands. The leopard lay over bwana David. As the leopard lunged forward for the kill, Salim drew his knife—the curved knife that all Mohammedans wear. With it Salim had cut the throats of animals so that orthodox Mohammedans could eat the meat.

With the knife held high, Salim took one running step. He launched himself into the air in a flying tackle. As he struck the leopard on the back, he lunged downward with his knife. He felt the blade go through skin and meat.

The leopard squawled in pain. He turned. Raking talons curved from the side. Salim rolled clear over the leopard. He still held the knife. The leopard stood there. He swung his head, first at the unconscious Ommanney, then at Salim. Which of the two men would he kill first? With a low growl, the leopard turned and jumped into the grass.

Salim stooped over David. Ommanney's eyes flickered. He raised his head weakly. Salim helped him to his knees. Blood was pumping in spurts from the severed arteries in his upper arm. He tried to hold the blood back with his right hand. The muscles and tendons of his left arm were hanging in shreds. If he had not worn a leather jacket, his arm would have been gone entirely.

Baron von Boeselager and Salim supported David on either side. Ommanney's strength was failing rapidly as blood poured down his left hand in a flood. By the time they reached the safari car, the pyramid mountains and the thorn trees were swimming before him. At camp the Baron snatched rolls of bandage from the first-aid kit and with them staunched the flow of blood. The native driver was already in the seat of the safari car. Arusha and the hospital were seventy-five miles away.

When David was on his way to help in the safari car, the faithful Salim began to wonder. Had his knife found its way between the leopard's ribs? Was the leopard dead, back there in the grass? It is the code of the hunter that a wounded and dangerous animal may not be left alone; otherwise, the next person to pass that way will surely be killed.

Salim went to the edge of the camp, where the safari boys were huddled together. They talked in low voices about the leopard that had nearly killed bwana David. Salim called to Mutia, the second gunbearer. He thrust a .30-06 rifle into Mutia's unwilling hands. Then, having loaded Ommanney's .470 double rifle, he motioned Mutia to follow.

Twilight was beginning to darken the Manyara Valley when Salim and Mutia again approached the bait tree and the edge of the donga. There was the place in the matted grass where bwana Ommanney had fallen. There, too, was the pool of blood, already growing dark and sticky. Just beyond was the place where Salim himself had rolled, after he had knifed the leopard. And just there, in the high grass, was where the leopard had gone.

Salim took a step. The grass rustled. The leopard was already in the air. Salim half raised the gun. One barrel went off. The bullet plowed into the ground. The leopard caught him full in the face. One tooth ripped through his eye. As Salim fell over backward, raking claws tore at his belly and his thigh.

Mutia threw up his rifle and fired blindly. The leopard's tail was cut by the bullet. The leopard screeched wildly. The cat turned. Darting his head downward, he bit Salim through the shoulder. Salim could feel the teeth crunch through the bone. Then he lost consciousness.

Mutia managed to get another shell into the chamber of the .30-06. Again he shot. The leopard, writhing on top of Salim, was only feet away. The shot went wild. At the noise, the leopard stood up. He growled.

The Killer Leopard of Manyara

Then he turned and leaped into the high grass. Half of the leopard's tail lay across Salim's knees.

Just after dark, Baron von Boeselager used the rest of the bandages from the first-aid kit to tie up Salim's thigh and shoulder. The teeth of the leopard had missed the jugular vein by a fraction of an inch. Salim's eye was gouged away. The Baron had the safari boys put the unconscious Salim on a mattress in the back of the truck. He drove the truck himself into Arusha. The hospital there received the second victim of the Manyara leopard a scant two hours after the first. From Mutia's story, they learned that the leopard still was not dead.

That night, over the telephone wires, the story went from Arusha to Nairobi: "A killer leopard is in the Manyara country. A safari is leaderless. We need help."

Theo Potgieter, a white hunter for the firm of Selby and Holmberg, was the only qualified hunter in Nairobi, as most white hunters were on safari. Potgieter, just in from his last hunting trip, answered the emergency.

It was Friday when the Manyara leopard had attacked David Ommanney and almost killed the brave Salim. It was Sunday before Potgieter could find his own gunbearer and drive the 150-odd miles from Nairobi to Arusha. It was Sunday afternoon, January 26, when Theo Potgieter reached the disorganized camp on the Manyara plain. That same afternoon, with Mutia and Baron von Boeselager, Theo went after the leopard.

Mutia still carried Ommanney's .30-06, but Mutia stayed well behind. From a safe distance he pointed out the trampled grass where the leopard had attacked Salim. Potgieter found the spot. The matted ground was rusty with dried blood. Jackals had carried off the leopard's tail. Of the tailless leopard himself, there was no sign.

Theo directed the Baron to take his station on the termite hill. With the double-barreled shotgun at eye level and the safety off, Potgieter walked slowly through the high grass. David had described to him, from his hospital bed, the charge of the leopard. "It was fast as light," David had said. "He was in the air before my face when I saw him."

Theo moved slowly, the shotgun ever before him. He kicked at the palmettos around the place where Ommanney and Salim had met the leopard. There was no sound. The leopard had gone. But just to make sure, Theo made a wider circle. He beat up and down the high grass on the edge of the donga for a hundred yards. He circled beyond the bait tree, back and forth. The grass was undisturbed. The wounded leopard had gone off and died.

Potgieter moved back toward the termite mound where the Baron waited tensely. Again the sun was lowering beyond the escarpment. A palmetto leaf rustled to Potgieter's left. He jerked around. The leopard was already in the air. Potgieter swung the gun. The first barrel burned fur on the leopard's neck. Frantically he pulled the second barrel. The buckshot tore into the leopard's shoulder. The momentum of the leopard's leap hurled the animal against Potgieter's chest. The gun flew from his hands. He rolled away. The leopard stood there. His left paw hung limp. The leopard was far from dead. His ears were laid back. He wrinkled his lips. On three legs he lunged forward. Theo threw up his arm before his face. In a second the leopard would be at his throat. A shot blasted out. Potgieter did not feel the tearing teeth. He raised his head. Three feet from him, the leopard twitched on the matted grass. The bloody stump of a trail thrashed back and forth in death. The Baron's shot had caught the killer leopard in the neck.

"Yes," said David Ommanney when he left the hospital with his left arm in a cast, "there are a lot of dangerous animals in Africa, but for my money, the leopard is the fastest and the worst. And," he added slowly, "I'm never going to allow a client to kill another hyena."

Chapter 14

LET SLEEPING LION LIE
(1960)

With a coughing grunt, the lion launched himself at us. All I could see was the huge head, ears laid back. The open mouth was coming straight for my face. Frantically I tried to bolt another shell into my rifle. Those teeth would be at my throat before I could raise the gun.

I hadn't set out to hunt this lion. As a matter of record, I wasn't even interested in desert lion, as they are usually maneless and make a poor trophy. The lion of Somalia on the east coast of Africa are about as maneless as they come. Furthermore, Guliano Belli, an Italian hunter, and I were busy trying to find an elephant carrying one hundred pounds of ivory in each tusk. In the Somalia desert country, it is the elephant that are big; the lion are scrawny.

Somalia became a new African country on 1 July 1960. Her transition to independence had been a peaceful one, and her new government was functioning fairly smoothly when I arrived in Somalia about six weeks later. Unlike most of the new African countries, the Somalis realize the value of their game, as they have a hunting tradition that goes back hundreds of years. With independence, they established a new game department and declared an open hunting season.

Guliano Belli del Isca remains from Benito Mussolini's day, when the Italians had hoped to form a vast African empire. When Guliano had been District Commissioner under the Italians, he had found that his district in southern Somalia was teeming with big desert elephant. After independence, Belli decided to start a new safari company. He wanted to advertise to all who might be interested that Somalia was first-class game country and contained some very intriguing specimens of a good many varieties. That's why I was there. I had come to Somalia to see just how good Guliano and his hunting area might be.

To anyone who has hunted in East Africa, especially in the Northern Frontier of Kenya, Somalia seems familiar. The country is semi-arid, but far from a complete desert. Two very large rivers flow down from the highlands of Ethiopia and through Somalia to the sea. These are the Giuba and the Uebishabelli. Guliano's best elephant country is around the Giuba, and southward toward the Kenya border.

Guliano had bought a fairly creditable Land Rover from a Kenya dealer, and had commandeered an Italian truck that was already a relic when Mussolini was a young man. Guliano met me at the airport in Mogadiscio, the picturesque capital of Somalia, and we moved southward toward the Giuba, with the truck following behind like a wounded animal. I looked under the hood of the thing once to see what made it go. Beneath the hood the engine looked even less prepossessing than the battered body outside.

With this equipment, we traveled some four hundred kilometers south over a road the Italians had built. We crossed the Giuba River on a modern bridge. Around the Giuba is a belt of plantations where several Italian farmers raise bananas to ship to Europe. Beyond the banana plantations, the country quickly becomes primitive and the road virtually disappears.

We set up our elephant camp near the small border town of Beles Cogani. It is well to camp near a town, as some Somali tribes are still a little high-spirited at times and have been known to kill travelers for their guns or other knickknacks that the Somalis covet. There is also a good deal of raiding back and forth from the Ethiopian border. When I asked what Beles Cogani might mean, I was told that it was the name of a sheik of the Galla tribe who had been eaten on the spot by a lion. I was fascinated by all of this local color, and thought that it added considerable zest to the elephant hunting.

The metropolis of Beles Cogani itself is not inspiring, in spite of the fact that it serves as the port of entry for camel caravans, and for the occasional lost and wandering automobiles that might find their way in from Kenya. The Somalis, distinctive from other Africans in physical appearance, culture, and religion, are tall and narrow-featured and dress

Let Sleeping Lion Lie

in turbans and the loose garments that they have adopted from the Arabs. The Somalis are Mohammedans and adhere rigidly to the Mohammedan principle of not eating meat unless the knife of a true believer cuts the throat of the animal in the ceremony known as *hallel*. A considerable amount of our hunting time was taken up in shooting lesser kudu and gerenuk so that our Mohammedans could cut the throats of the animals and have meat.

Just beyond Beles Cogani, toward the Kenya border, is a large depression in the desert floor filled with water from the spring rains. This place, called Tabda by the Somalis, is a favorite spot to water camels, fat-tailed sheep, goats, and cattle. Actually, the watering at Tabda takes place in a certain rhythm. At night, about three hundred elephant come in from the surrounding bush country to drop their trunks in the green, slimy water of Tabda and drink their fill. By day, hundreds of Somali herdsmen, with thousands of head of assorted stock, converge on Tabda from a dozen desert trails. Between the elephant and the humans, other animals of the region try to squeeze in a little drinking time. Among these were a dozen or so lion.

We had seen the lion tracks at Tabda on several mornings as we went there to find out what bull elephant had used the drinking hole the night before. We had heard lion roaring in the distance not far from Tabda, and I had idly wondered how the elephant, camels, cattle, sheep, goats, humans, antelope, and lion all managed to avoid each other when coming to and going from water. The answer to my speculation is that they don't avoid each other. Embarrassing meetings of domesticated and wild animals are frequent.

The third day of our hunt at Beles Cogani, a Somali herdsman, driving a small bunch of his humpbacked cattle to the Tabda pool, met a lion in the middle of the trail. The man, Gedo by name, raised his spear when the lion did not move out of the way. The bull of Gedo's small herd was in front of the line of cattle. The lion knocked Gedo's bull down with a sideways blow of his paw, and then bit the animal through the back of the neck, killing it instantly. Gedo threw his spear and missed. The lion ran off into the thickets at the side of the trail.

We did not hear about the death of Gedo's bull until the next day. We would have had no occasion to hear about it even then, except that Gedo pastured his cattle and a few camels some twenty miles north of Tabda. In that same area, he had reported seeing three gigantic bull elephant. We maneuvered our safari car along the camel trail to Gedo's grass hut in the north. When we reached his modest home, his wife and daughter talked to us shyly. Gedo himself was away. The thrifty Somali had cut up the bull that the lion had killed and packed the meat back to his wife. He had then taken his bow and quiver of poisoned arrows and set out to track the lion down and kill him. "A very sporty business," I thought as I looked at the thick desert brush of the area. Then Belli and I got on with our elephant hunt, and forgot about Gedo and his problem.

Two days later, the police sergeant in charge of the small border contingent of Beles Cogani visited our camp in the evening. He talked a little Italian, as he had been part of a military garrison under the former regime. The police sergeant told us that Gedo had not returned from tracking the lion. This was very strange, as Gedo was *arganti*. (Belli explained to me that the Somalis recognize a succession of hunters. When a Somali kills his first animal, he becomes a first-grade hunter, called *Irin*. An Irin would probably shoot a Hunter hartebeest, or one of the smaller antelope, with a poisoned arrow. The Somalis use poison made from a kind of grass called *uabahayo*, which they trade from the tribes in Kenya. If an animal is struck with this potent poison, he dies in an hour or so. The trick is to get close enough to an antelope to get an arrow into him. When a Somali hunter gets good enough to kill an elephant, rhino, buffalo, giraffe, or lion, he becomes *alghen*, or the highest grade of hunter. Anybody with audacity enough to punch a poisoned arrow into one of these animals certainly deserves the first prize, I thought. I would hate to see what a lion would do after he was hit and before he died. The giraffe is included in the list of hard-to-kill animals because it is virtually impossible for a bowman to approach a giraffe unseen. A very few Somali hunters have killed all of the dangerous animals including giraffe. Such a man is a superhunter, called an *arganti*. If any Somali survived all of these dangerous encounters and became *arganti*, he set himself up as a patron of the area in which he lived. Any hunter of lower rank who killed an animal in the *arganti*'s territory had to give the local *arganti* part of the kill—usually a brisket.)

Gedo, the *arganti*, had been a mighty hunter, but his luck had run out at last. I was sorry that I hadn't known the fellow. Belli told me that the Somali often killed lion that were attacking their camels or cattle. Gedo had killed several lion and more than ten elephant. However, he certainly had followed one lion too many. If he had not returned from his private lion hunt in three days, chances were that his wife shouldn't expect him at all.

The next evening, the police sergeant came to see us again. We were rather sorry to see him, as Belli and I had trailed five bull elephant over twenty miles that day, and we were dog-tired. But the sergeant sat at our little camp table under the thorn tree and sipped tea for twenty minutes before he came to the point of his visit. A large male lion had killed a woman and her twelve-year-old daughter just north of Tabda. Apparently the lion had killed the girl first, as she herded a little flock of sheep toward the water. The Somali woman had rushed to drive the lion away from her daughter, and the lion had killed her also. The lion had dragged the girl beneath the brush at the side of the trail and had almost completely devoured her. Her chewed and bloody clothes had been found there by other herdsmen. The woman had been killed by a blow of the lion's paw and a bite through the base of the neck, but had not been eaten. The fat-tailed sheep still grazed around the spot where the bodies lay.

"This lion is the same male lion that killed Gedo's bull, and that killed Gedo," the sergeant continued gravely.

"How can you be sure it was the same lion?" I broke in. "The track of any male lion looks the same."

"Not to a Somali," said Belli. And I took his word.

The sergeant wanted to know if we would help to kill the lion. "There is no other hunter around Beles Cogani except the one whom you have," he added as a clincher.

When Guliano translated this, I thought that the sergeant was paying a compliment to the great American hunter (myself) who was visiting their troubled village. If my fame had reached all the way to Beles Cogani, I could do nothing else but abandon my elephant hunting for a couple of days and help them out. It turned out that the police sergeant was not thinking of me as even a first-grade hunter. He was referring to a man in our camp named Kula, who had been tracking elephants for us. We had picked Kula up near the town of Afmadu, on our way south to Beles Cogani. It developed that he was the finest lion tracker in all southern Somalia, and furthermore that he was an *alghen*-grade hunter in his own right. Kula certainly was the finest elephant tracker I had ever followed, and I didn't want to lose him. We called him to the conference under the thorn tree. Kula readily agreed to track down the man-eating lion of Beles Cogani. I gathered from his enthusiastic expression that he had been planning to do just this anyway, ever since he had heard about poor Gedo.

The next morning, before daybreak, we moved past the still-sleeping town of Beles Cogani. Our headlights picked out a herd of warthogs in the very middle of the town. Being Mohammedans, the villagers never bother the pigs, which are considered religiously unclean. We swung north on a camel trail toward the spot where the two women had been killed the morning before. The place was perhaps five miles from Beles Cogani, and a little more than that distance from the water hole at Tabda. We found no lion tracks until we reached the spot itself. Here the Somalis had made one of their typical graves. The mother and daughter had been buried in an area between three thorn trees. Around the grave had been built a solid wall of heavy limbs and split pieces of wood. Outside of this was a thick *boma*, or fence, of thorn branches, to keep off any hyenas or other predators.

Outside of the trampled area where the grave had been made, Kula circled like a beagle. He soon found the track of the lion. It was, of course, twenty-four hours old. Kula started along the old track with the same assurance he had displayed on the trail of an elephant bull. I can track most elephant myself, but Somalia lion tracking is another matter. A lion, being soft-footed, does not make much impression on hard ground, and this was stony desert terrain. In the sandy spots the tracking was easy; but over the hundreds of yards of hard surface it seemed impossible. But Kula did it anyway. Without reservation, Kula is the finest tracker I have ever seen. Even at that, he was constantly losing the track and having to cast ahead. The track of the single lion had been blotted out completely where herds of camels and cattle had been driven along the trails toward Tabda. The lion had gone in a generally southwesterly direction toward Beles Cogani. By two o'clock in the afternoon we had tracked the beast about five miles and were not far from the town.

This whole lion hunt now began to seem bizarre and incongruous. In every other place in Africa, lion are hunted by hanging a bait and then shooting the beasts when they come in to chew on the meat. I had never heard of hunting lion by tracking them through thick brush. I couldn't believe it was possible.

Let Sleeping Lion Lie

But the question was academic, as late in the afternoon even Kula lost the trail. In the welter of tracks on the outskirts of Beles Cogani, the faint imprint of the paws had been blotted out. We could only tell the police sergeant that the man-eating lion had circled the outskirts of his town the evening before. We sent the truck driver back to retrieve our safari car, and we walked back to camp. The lion hunt had been a bust.

That night I slept badly. For some reason, the hyenas were especially annoying. Hyenas were always bold in the vicinity of Beles Cogani. But they had never come into our camp before. I was awakened by some of the men throwing sticks at them. Some time after this uproar, I heard a heavy panting in my tent. *Belli's going to have to do something about that asthma of his,* I thought, forgetting for the moment that Belli's tent was fifty feet away. I went back to sleep.

In the morning, the cook reported that the hyenas had jerked down a gerenuk carcass that had been hanging in the tree over his bed. The contemptible beasts had devoured the thing on the spot. Kula came up to where I was brushing my teeth with my eyes half open. He touched my elbow and pointed to the ground in front of my tent. There were the clear imprints of two big lion paws where the cat had stood and looked in. The lion had walked straight through the middle of camp, past the dining tent, and within twenty feet of a dozen sleeping men. It was the lion that had pulled down the gerenuk. He had walked off a few yards when the cook threw a piece of firewood at him. Then he had lain on his belly and had calmly eaten the gerenuk, crunching the bones within thirty feet of the entire camp.

"The same lion?" I asked.

Kula nodded. The same lion we had trailed all the day before had calmly spent most of the night in our camp. Belli was greatly perturbed. The cook was so upset that he couldn't make breakfast. Most of the camp boys got into the parked truck and stayed there, even though it was now daylight. Kula, Belli, and I started out on the track. We made a good early start. There was no breakfast, and we were anxious to track the lion before the Somalis began to move their herds and obliterate the trail.

Belli clutched a .375 Winchester, and I carried a .375 Weatherby. Usually I shoot a lighter gun, but after the lion looked in my tent, the heavier artillery seemed to be appropriate. Belli and I crouched behind

Under the African Sun

Kula with our guns ready. Several yards in the rear, Sherif, the manager of the camp, carried an extra gun and a bottle of water.

The lion had moved from our camp along the edge of the road toward Beles Cogani. Within the town are several large cisterns, or catch basins, where the inhabitants trap water in the rainy season. The Coganians put hedges of thornbrush around these to keep out the warthogs. The lion had raked away the thorns at the edge of one of these cisterns, gone through the gap, and drunk his fill. Just as the good citizens of Beles Cogani were coming out of their houses to fill their own water jars, four grim figures stalked past, crouched and ready. No one spoke to us as Kula followed the track past the customs-house station, past the corrals on the edge of town, and southward.

Somehow I expected to see the lion still lurking on the outskirts of town. Certainly a cat of that temperament would be standing somewhere out of sight, watching the people and planning his next meal. But the tracks led on.

The morning sun rose hot and high in the African sky. We followed the track of the lion in a circle almost around the town, then at a sharp angle south again. Surely the lion, with his belly full of meat and water, would lie up somewhere.

About eleven o'clock, Belli and I sat down in the shade of a wait-a-bit thorn and drank the last of the water. The lion had outwalked us. He was obviously leaving the country. In the heat of midday, Belli and I soon slumped against the bole of the tree in a half doze. Sherif also nodded. Kula slipped away and followed the track.

About one o'clock we decided to head for camp to get something to eat. As we started off, Kula slipped up behind us. He tapped me on the shoulder and grinned broadly. Sherif translated Kula's Somali: "He has found the lion asleep."

If the Somali hunters can slip up to a sleeping lion and stick a poisoned arrow in him, I thought, *I guess I can do the same with a rifle. But it certainly is an interesting way to hunt lion.*

Kula led us on tiptoe through the thickest brush I had seen in Somalia. The packed thorn bushes and stunted trees were interlaced with clumps of the thick cactus they called *galole*. As we came into the dense growing stuff, I noticed that Belli was panting hard and Sherif had fallen well to the rear. Kula kept cautioning us with his finger on his lips. In his bare feet, Kula was absolutely soundless. He grinned continuously. Obviously he was enjoying himself. I was not sure that I was.

We tiptoed to a little opening in the cactus. Kula crouched and pointed. I took one more step behind him. There was the lion.

Whatever I had expected, this was not it. All I could see was a fat stomach about fifteen feet from me. The thing rose and fell with regular breathing. The lion had made a nest underneath the cactus. I could see neither head, tail, nor feet.

Which end is the head, I wondered. I had the Weatherby to my shoulder and the safety off. Maybe it was the click of the safety. Maybe man-eating lion have guilty consciences. The lion did not wake up and look at us. He came out of his bed in one movement—with a roar like an exploding boiler. There was no doubt now which end was the head. It came straight at us. I fired as I saw the lion's chest. At that range, I couldn't miss. The lion jumped past us, tore a hole in the solid brush, and was gone. Belli and I stood dazed.

Kula beckoned us forward. He pointed to where the lion had crashed through the cactus and brush. It looked like a slaughterhouse. The softnose bullet of the Weatherby had apparently ripped away the lion's chest. I stepped forward confidently behind Kula. There was blood everywhere. The lion had torn a hole through the thick cactus like a bulldozer. We walked perhaps fifty feet. Here was an opening in the brush as big as a small room. As we stepped into the opening, the lion roared. I have heard of sounds being bloodcurdling, but this roar was congealing. It certainly was not the roar of a lion in his death agony. The roar came again, and again, from across the little clearing. Both Belli and I had our guns up. We couldn't see a thing.

Then, suddenly, there he was! I could see the curve of yellow hide through the green brush across the clearing. A tiny termite hill stood just to our left. I got up on the low mound. At the movement, the lion roared again. The sound shook the leaves around us. I pushed Kula to one side. He had been standing there grinning. I could see the outline of the lion fairly clearly now. He was crouched on his belly, facing us. His head and shoulders were behind a solid tangle of limbs and stems. He gathered his hind feet beneath him. I shot.

At the sound, the lion grunted and jumped. In one bound he cleared the brush. In the next, he was in the air before us. I heard Belli's gun go off. Frantically, I clawed at the bolt to get another shell into the chamber. I half raised the gun and fired. In the same instant, the lion hit us. I scarcely realized that the impact of the bullet had jerked his body sideways. Instead of his mouth and claws, he struck me with the back of his shoulder. Belli and I went down, with the lion on top of us. We were mashed flat by the crushing weight. The lion was still struggling. His three good paws thrashed, and his mouth opened and closed. I rolled from underneath the flailing claws in considerably less than one second. Kula was standing there laughing.

My first shot had struck to one side and broken the lion's shoulder. My second, when the lion was crouching ready to spring, had hit the same shoulder. The lion was still in good working order when he made the final leap. My last shot hit the lion in midair at the base of the neck. His momentum carried him on top of us. I found out later that I had two broken vertebrae in my back as a result.

Baiting African lion is thrilling sport. And if you crave real excitement, you should get a Somali tracker to lead you into heavy brush after a sleeping lion. But if you take my advice, you'll let a sleeping lion lie.

Chapter 15

HIPPO TROUBLE
(circa 1960)

The face before us looked like a dragon. The muzzle was shiny black, with round nose holes and loose lips. Bare rings of pinkish flesh marked the eyes. They were small eyes, too small for that wide and evil face. But it was the mouth that seemed the worst. It looked like a red cave as it opened wide. Curved teeth as big as marlinspikes jutted out from above and below. It would have been a frightening face a hundred yards away. At twenty-five feet, it was paralyzing.

Something cold pressed against my shoulder from behind. It couldn't be Andrew. He was on the other side, and pulling back on my arm.

"*Bunduki,* bwana," came a voice from behind. It was Ngoro. Good old Ngoro. None of the rest of us had thought to bring a rifle. We weren't hunting. We were looking for a place to camp.

I snatched the Weatherby .300 from Ngoro and bolted a shell into the chamber. There was no time to see if this was the softnose or solid ammunition. Any ammunition would have to do. Ngoro should have handed me the .470 double rifle. But the size of the animal close before us made any rifle a matter of small importance. How could a gun stop that great thing? Where would I shoot? The open mouth seemed to cover the whole area. The body behind was almost hidden. A great red throat and the yellow tusks were all I could see.

The mouth snapped shut. The loose lips flapped together. The two round nostrils dilated. There was a snorting roar like a bursting gasket. This was it.

Under the African Sun

Andrew Holmberg, Brownie, and I had not come to southern Tanganyika in British East Africa to hunt hippo. We hadn't even thought about hippo, although we had seen a few in the Athi River just outside Nairobi. They had looked harmless enough. "River pigs," they had been called. It seemed a good name. Usually we saw only their eyes and ears sticking up above the muddy water. Even our photographs of the Athi hippo were not particularly remarkable. I remember thinking that of all of the animals we had seen, these were the most docile looking, and the hardest to approach and photograph.

I remember saying, when Andrew asked me if I wanted to shoot a hippo, "Don't think so. It would be like killing a pig in a puddle."

"There's a hippo on your game license in case you change your mind," he remarked. "Sometimes hippo can be exciting."

But we had forgotten about such minor matters as we entered enthusiastically into the bagging of the Big Five. In addition, we wanted to round out our safari repertoire with the two coveted and beautiful trophies—the greater kudu and sable antelope. Both sable and kudu are found in the south. The best greater kudu live in southern Tanganyika and northern Mozambique. Southern sable also carry the trophy horns. We would have to move south.

"I know a place," Andrew had said in his slow manner, "where only one other safari has ever hunted. I found it last year."

We had already had some experience with Andrew's aversion to places that showed "too many safari-car ruts" or areas where, as Andrew described them, "the good game heads have been picked over." We had already taken one trip into a hidden valley he had found when he was on patrol after Mau Mau terrorists. It was a fabulous spot for game, but an impossible place to take a four-wheeled vehicle. It is no wonder that only one other safari had ever been there before us.

The long trip south to Arusha and then west to Ngorongoro, the great volcanic crater that teems with tens of thousands of head of game, was a wonderful trip in itself. But by the time we had bumped over the rough roads south to Tabora to pick up extra gasoline and supplies there, and had then moved south again to the Ugalla River, we were saddlesore and weary. We crossed the Ugalla on a built-up dike of mud and sticks, as the river in the dry season (this was in July) had degenerated into a series of pools with only swampy ground in between. Andrew had told

Hippo Trouble

us that the Ugalla country was where most safari parties went to get the greater kudu and sable antelope. I could see their point, because by that time they would be too exhausted to go any farther.

But the next day we pushed on still farther south. The road became sketchier, and finally almost disappeared altogether. Soon we turned off at an angle from even this dim track. The turnoff place was a spot just like a thousand others that we had passed in the last two days of steady driving. I could only make out a very dim trail with the marks of elephant feet upon it. We had become accustomed to seeing these round, corrugated imprints along the elephant trails that crisscrossed this country in every direction. But southern Tanganyika itself is almost flat, with few landmarks. It consists for the most part of forested country, with only here and there small glades overgrown with ten-foot-high grass. Along the Ugalla these glades are larger and, when burned over by the natives in the dry season, relatively open. I suppose this is another reason most safaris hunt the Ugalla country. South of the Ugalla the trees became thicker and the glades fewer. As we turned off through the woods, I couldn't help thinking it was like trying to drive through the Pennsylvania woods without any road.

In addition to our Willys safari car with its special body, we had a truck that carried our extra gasoline and drinking water as well as the majority of our eleven safari boys, who perched on top of the tents and other equipment. By following the old elephant trail, the safari car could usually work its way between the trees. But the truck invariably got stuck. Twice we had to cut down good-sized trees with an ax. On many occasions we made detours around close-growing groups of trees to find a path wide enough for the truck to move through. As it was, our equipment was torn and raked by the branches. Everyone was exhausted with the work of moving logs and rocks out of the way. By the end of the first day, we had made barely fifteen miles.

Not the least of the hazards of overland travel through southern Tanganyika were the elephant. During the wet season, these animals had stalked all over the landscape, pockmarking the soft, muddy soil with their huge feet. What had once been mud was now dried to flint-like consistency, but the elephant tracks in it were preserved intact. An elephant footprint is just about the size of the holes that the electric company digs to set up their wooden poles.

Under the African Sun

An elephant print also exactly fits the wheel of a car. It is the most effective automobile trap ever devised. In those places where we weren't stuck in elephant tracks, we were blocked by the trees that the elephant had pulled down or pushed over. In the areas where a herd of elephant had fed for several days, the country looked as though a tornado had passed over it.

I am not at liberty to say where we finally ended this long overland junket. (I probably wouldn't be able to describe it accurately anyway.) The white hunters of East Africa jealously guard their secret hunting places. Andrew had told us that the biggest greater kudu in all of Africa were to be found in this area. I hoped that they'd be big ones, after all this trouble.

On the second day, we found a small encampment of natives in the middle of the forest. (The place was wisely surrounded by a heavy pole *boma*, or lion fence. We had heard lion roaring on the previous three nights of our trip.) These natives made their living by gathering wild honey, packing it out on their backs over the many miles to the settlements along the Ugalla, where they would sell it to Indian traders. One of the honey hunters volunteered to accompany us and show us the best elephant trails down to the water. If the elephant trails along which this wizened little native led us were the best ones, I would hate to see the others. The country was awful. As we drew closer to the stream of water, the vegetation became thicker and there were gullies with naked rocks as well as elephant-shattered trees to block our path. It was late in the day when the little native pointed ahead and we saw the glint of water between the trees.

"I'll scout ahead and find a place to pitch camp," Andrew said.

"And I'll go with you," I answered quickly. I was glad to get out of the awful jolting seat of the safari car.

We had just rounded a thick clump of glossy-leaved bushes when it happened. There were two hippo. The one closest to us was a bull. The one behind I saw only dimly. (I thought afterward that the hippo must have been as startled as we were. They had been lying down in a small cleared area on the bank of the stream. By the dust and dried dung there it would seem that they had been taking a dust bath.) But I had few seconds to notice details, as the bull opened his mouth and came toward us. I thought we were done for.

Hippo Trouble

Andrew dragged me back by one shoulder, and we stood there, rigid, facing the bull hippo. Ngoro thrust the gun at me from behind, but it seemed useless to shoot. We stood there waiting. I held the gun ready. The bull hippo closed his mouth with the noise of a wet mattress being hit with a baseball bat. He whirled and ran. I was amazed at the agility of the animal on those short stocky legs. I was amazed, also, at the size of his body as he launched himself over the riverbank in a running dive. The yellow spray spurted up to the treetops as the two hippo hit the water together.

"That was a sticky spot," Andrew said mildly. "I thought that bull was going to take us in." And then, as an afterthought, he added, "As the hippo have mashed down all the brush here, this will be a good place for the tents."

Though I thought he was joking, Andrew proved as good as his word. He pitched our camp on the riverbank directly above the hippo pool in the place where the animals had been wallowing in the dry dirt. Fortunately, most of the hippo left that night and did not return. Only one old male remained in the morning. He was immediately dubbed "Harold the Hippo." Harold, for reasons best known to himself, refused to vacate. During the ten days that we camped there, Harold blew and bellowed just below the canvas outhouse that our safari boys had thoughtfully pitched on the very brink of the riverbank. Harold acted nasty but was apparently just bluffing, with a lot of booming and snuffling to back it up.

The case was different with another bull hippo, which lived in a pool by himself a mile down the river. One of the honey hunters had pointed out this place to us as the only spot where we could get our safari car across the river. At this one spot, a gravel bar made a solid road for our car to cross. Hippopotamus trails, worn by generations of these heavy animals as they had used this spot to climb up and down, had eroded the banks so that they formed an easy grade.

The first time we crossed the gravel bar, we were moving slowly. Andrew suddenly stopped the safari car. "Look," he said, pointing to his right and downstream. Close beside the gravel bar was a pool about the size of a city block. Beyond this was a tumble of rocks and, still farther downstream, another very large pool that seemed to extend for half a mile. In the middle of the far stretch of water was a great pile of rounded stones. A hippo bellowed in the distance, but certainly there

Under the African Sun

was nothing particularly remarkable about the scene, except perhaps for a small crocodile floating on top of the muddy water not far from our car. Suddenly one of the rounded stones moved. There was a squealing snort. Another one of the distant objects heaved up, and then another. The whole mass began moving. The pile in the distance was a solid mass of hippo! There must have been twenty-five animals, some of them lying on top of each other, three or four deep. The constant disturbance was caused by the lowermost ones, which were being squashed by the ten or fifteen tons lying on top. As we watched with the glasses, a fight broke out, apparently between two bulls. They opened their mouths wide and rushed at each other, sparring from side to side as each tried to get a grip on the muzzle of the other.

"We ought to circle around with the telephoto lens and take some movies of that mountain of hippo," Brownie said.

"Better not," Andrew answered tersely. "I think we have company." Andrew was looking not at the squirming mass of hippo in the far pool but close beside us, at the edge of the gravel bar. A hippo's head had appeared above the yellow water. He snorted and wiggled his ears. This was standard procedure, and we had seen it a hundred times in the last day or two. The hippo would come up out of the depths, blow out their nostrils like a split steam pipe, look at us a moment, and then submerge again. The hippo now close before us, however, wasn't submerging. He wasn't even moving away as most of the others had done. He was coming straight toward us, the great black head and the red-rimmed eyes moving steadily. The hippo must be walking on the bottom, I thought, but why would he come so close?

"Must think our car's another hippo come to share his pool with him," Andrew remarked. "Some of these old outcast bulls are pretty frosty."

Andrew started the car, and we climbed the far bank. When I looked back, the bull hippo was half out of the water at the edge of the gravel bar and still moving toward us.

That evening, when we returned, the bull hippo was still in his pool. As we crossed the gravel bar, he again came menacingly toward us. Ngoro and Sungura, our two gunbearers, jumped out of the car for a minute to examine the tracks of some greater kudu that had watered at this same pool sometime during the day. At the sight of the two men, the bull turned toward them and opened his mouth. Ngoro and Sungura sprinted for the safari car, which was already in motion.

156

Hippo Trouble

"Those cheeky hippo can be pretty dangerous," Andrew remarked as we drove back along the riverbank to camp.

That evening Andrew regaled us with stories of hippo he had known. "The hippo is not one of the Big Five in Africa," Andrew said as we sat around the table after dinner. "And some people think he's just a water-going clown. But I've known some nasty hippo in my time. Many of the river natives regard the hippo as the most dangerous animal in Africa. Some of my professional hunter friends have underestimated the hippo. There is the grave of one of these men in the cemetery in Nairobi. On my last safari, over toward Lake Tanganyika, we camped near a village where a native boatman had been killed the day before. He got between a hippo, feeding on the bank, and the water, which is the hippo's natural place of safety. The hippo bit the man in two with a single bite. The crocodiles had eaten the part of the fellow that fell into the water by the next morning when one of his wives came to look for him."

As Andrew talked, Harold the Hippo, not fifty feet from us, punctuated these bloody tales with bubbling roars and bellows that sounded like a waterlogged French horn. Finally, well after dark, Harold climbed out on the far side of the river and went off to feed.

During the next several days, we saw the big bull by the river crossing every time we passed his pool. The honey hunter who was acting as our guide had argued each time with Andrew that we should shoot this hippo. We hadn't paid too much attention, because the natives were always anxious for us to shoot more meat. However, we had killed a couple of impala, a Lichtenstein hartebeest, and a very large roan antelope, and still our guide argued for the shooting of the bull hippo by the river crossing.

"This man says that sooner or later that bad hippo's going to kill one of his people," Andrew said one evening as we came back from a hunt for sable antelope.

"Maybe we'd better make this river highway safe for legitimate travel," I answered lightheartedly as I viewed the wilderness around us.

"So you've changed your mind about shooting a hippo," Andrew replied, looking at me. "Get three or four of those solid patch bullets for that Weatherby of yours, and we'll see what you can do."

We stopped the safari car several hundred yards from the edge of the river so that the sound would not alarm our friend in the pool.

Under the African Sun

Andrew and I walked forward together. We moved quietly so as not to alert the bull. I don't think either of us thrilled at the possibility of shooting a bull hippo as he charged straight at us. We tiptoed along the bank, past the place where our car tracks led down to the gravel bar. At the very edge of the hippo pool was a gigantic sausage tree with half its roots sticking out over the water where some flood had washed them clear. Using the tree as cover, we slipped up behind it and lay flat along the tangle of roots.

Over across from us, a large V of ripples moved across the surface of the muddy water. I could see the snout and head of a very large crocodile.

"A big one," Andrew whispered in my ear. "Must be fifteen feet long." He pointed across the pool.

There was the bull hippo. His eyes were already fixed upon us. Perhaps he had seen the motion of Andrew's hand as he pointed. I had no time to speculate upon the strange companions that the bull hippo had in his private pool. The crocodile simply sank from sight. The hippo turned in a wide arc, and came toward us.

"The only place is the brain," said Andrew quietly. "From this angle, it's between the eye and the ear. Don't miss," he added tersely.

I steadied the Weatherby .300 over the water-worn roots of the sausage tree. Through the cross hairs of the telescopic sight, I picked out the wicked little eye of the bull. It was fixed upon us with terrible intensity. As I swung the cross hairs with his movement, his feet must have touched the shallowing bottom. The great black head began to rise. Now!

I squeezed the trigger. The blast of noise seemed to blot out the great head. A plume of yellow water spurted upward. The pool boiled with motion from beneath. In the churning eddy, leaves and sticks from the bottom rolled up. Suddenly the dirty water was stained by a spot of red. Then a great three-toed foot rolled above the surface, stood rigid for a moment straight up, and finally disappeared. Andrew clapped me on the shoulder. "*Mazuri!*" he said shortly. This was high praise indeed—the Swahili word for "well done." Andrew usually just grunted when I made a shot.

It was late in the evening. In any case, it would be necessary to wait until the carcass floated up in the pool before we could drag it onto the gravel bar.

Hippo Trouble

At sunrise the next morning, we drove the safari car out to the very edge of the pool. There was the bloated carcass, with a large crocodile sitting on top of it. The croc plopped into the water as soon as we appeared.

Volunteers to attach a rope to one of the stiff legs of the hippo bull were hard to find in our group. I didn't blame the safari boys, particularly as the crocodiles in that muddy water made the very thought of stepping into it seem like sure death. We finally rigged a crude raft of two or three empty water cans and a couple of spare tires. With this, one of the boys poled out and attached a heavy rope to the hippo. So heavy was the carcass, however, that even with the combined pull of the safari car on the hard gravel and everybody else pushing, we could not drag the carcass out onto the bar. We managed it at last by rolling the great body over and over in the shallow water. Finally, we had to skin the bull at the very edge of the water, crocodiles notwithstanding. We saved the head, as the hippo proved to be an exceptionally large bull with very fine and heavy ivory. The honey hunters were glad to have the meat. In skinning the head, we found a large iron ball, handwrought, of about 50-caliber size. The thing was embedded in the cartilage against the hippo's skull between his protruding eyes.

I had seen a few of the natives of Tanganyika with muzzleloading cap-and-ball muskets. In answer to my question, Andrew told me that there are over 25,000 cap-and-ball muskets in use in Tanganyika today. "They usually don't attempt anything as big and dangerous as a hippo with those antiquated guns. Someone tried it, though, and a long time ago. It's no wonder this bull hippo didn't like people."

This lion had killed a reticulated giraffe. We tracked him and I shot him at close range.

This luckless bush rhino had to be killed to make this area at the foot of Mt. Kenya safe to re-settle a group of Mau Mau terrorists. The woman in the center with the machete was a famous Mau Mau chief who had killed several European settlers.

Disgusted and exhausted, I brood at my bongo camp after a frustrating day high on the flanks of Mt. Kenya.

Bobby Wilmot and his gunbearer try out our sitatunga tower in the papyrus swamps of the Chobe River in northern Botswana.

Beisa oryx on banks of the Ouwash River in central Ethiopia.

Here I show a Danakil warlord my modern Weatherby rifle. The Danakils to the left have each recently killed their first man. Now they will receive tufts of ostrich feathers to wear in their hair.

This Soemmerring gazelle from Ethiopia is the northern version of the Grant gazelle. Note that the horns are turned inward rather than upward.

Our pet dik-dik, one of the smallest of all the African antelope. Later, we released "Dicky" near Olduvai, where others of his kind are common.

Don Pedro, my Portuguese-born PH and his crew pose with a Lichtenstein hartebeest that I shot for bait.

The giant baobab is perhaps the most spectacular tree in all of Africa. This one is growing on the outskirts of Dar es Salaam, the capital of Tanzania.

Male leopard track appears with the spoor of smaller nocturnal animals in the sandy Ngenge River, Selous area, Tanzania.

Don Pedro and I wearily pose with a male leopard that "came in late."

A southern impala that we bagged to use for leopard bait on the Ngenge River.

Marilyn in front of our safari camp on the banks of the Mbarangandu River, Selous area, Tanzania. To the right are numerous Paleolithic implements left by the early "man-apes" a million years ago.

Our crew of the Mbarangandu River camp view a hartebeest that had been killed by a lioness and her two cubs only minutes before.

There were two groups of African wild dogs near our camp on the Mbarangandu River. This is the "upriver" pack enjoying cool, wet sand and water on a hot afternoon.

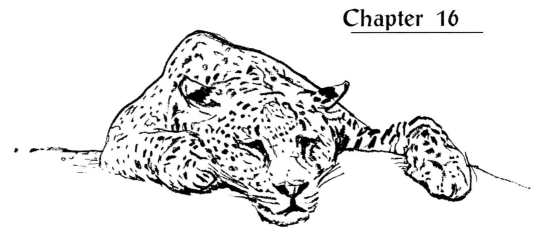

I HUNTED SOMALIA
(1961)

The dibatag streaked away on invisible legs. The long gray neck and the stiffly erect, brushy tail looked like two animals moving together through the desert brush. The horns of the dibatag arched forward above his head in a graceful curve. It was a big bull. The range was about three hundred yards—a very long shot.

I swung the Weatherby .300 to my shoulder without a second's hesitation. This was the closest I had gotten to a dibatag in five days of hunting. As I squeezed off the shot, I became the first American hunter to shoot this rare antelope officially.

On 1 July 1960, the former Italian Somaliland became an independent country called Somalia. In common with the other newly formed African states, Somalia immediately encountered almost insurmountable difficulties of taxes, administration, police, and other functions. But in spite of all this confusion, the transition to independence was made almost bloodlessly. Even in the hurly-burly of forming a new nation on the desert coast of East Africa, the Somalis formed a Department of Fish and Game and established a hunting season to begin on 15 August 1960. On 14 August I arrived on the weekly shuttle plane from Nairobi, to be greeted by Guliano Belli, who had asked me to try the hunting possibilities of the new republic. Guliano Belli is a holdover from the old Italian days when Mussolini dreamed of forming a vast African empire of Ethiopia and Somaliland. Guliano, along with about two thousand other Italians, stayed on in Somalia to make a new life. Belli was starting a brand-new safari business, and that's where I came in.

Even as we flew over the Northern Frontier of Kenya, across the Tana River, and then northward to the Giuba River and beyond, the country looked familiar. It is another version of the Tana, where I had hunted elephant with Andrew Holmberg. Instead of the blistering desert I had expected, Somalia seemed much like northern Kenya, even to the animals that are found there.

The town of Mogadiscio, capital of Somalia, with its whitewashed buildings clustered on the crest of an ancient coral reef set off by the brilliant blue of the Indian Ocean at its foot, is a tourist's gem. But few tourists ever get there, as there is no harbor in which cruise ships might stop. Unfortunately, the country of Somalia has no harbors along its more than a thousand miles of coastline. Some of the Somalia officials who took care of our gun permits and hunting licenses spoke English. A few addressed Belli in Italian. Most of the Somalis speak Arabic as well as their native Somali. They have been deeply affected by Arabic culture, which left its stain on this coast during the centuries when the slave and ivory traders came here. The Arabs have made the Somalis Mohammedans [Moslems].

After a night at a very comfortable little hotel, built in one month to celebrate the independence of the new nation, Guliano and I started south from Mogadiscio back toward the Giuba River. We had a Land Rover, and a beaten-up old Italian truck followed us, bringing extra petrol and drums of water.

There had stepped from the same shuttle plane from Nairobi two young fellows from Holdenville, Oklahoma. One of these, Bob Eckles, had hunted in Tanganyika before and was looking for new fields to conquer. John Elliston, his companion, had never hunted in Africa before but had concluded that the usual haunts of Kenya were probably overrun with hunters from the States. These two lads must have thought that they really were going off into the African blue as they also started south in an antiquated Land Rover. For their guide, Belli had gotten the two Holdenville boys a reformed crocodile hunter named Paolo Tamagnini.

Both the Holdenville contingent and myself had been lured to these regions by the promise of gigantic elephant with colossal tusks. When I had written to Belli some weeks before, he had promised to show me the biggest elephant in all of Africa. Belli himself,

I Hunted Somalia

the year before, had shot a monster bull along the Giuba. This elephant had tusks ten feet long that weighed 110 pounds apiece.

Our first camp was made near the picturesque little town of Beles Cogani, about eighty miles from the Kenya border and three hundred miles south of Mogadiscio. The area of Beles Cogani is midway between the Tana River of northern Kenya and the Giuba valley of Somalia. Not many miles to the west lies the famous Lorian Swamp, one of the favorite haunts of the early ivory hunters. To the northwest is another swamp formed by the Uebishabeli or Leopard River, which loses itself in a vast depression before it reaches the coast. I had expected Somalia to be pure desert. Most of the country is arid, all right, but in places there is plenty of water, most of which comes from the mountain snows of Ethiopia. In early September, there is so much water in the Leopard Swamp that a man on foot cannot pass through.

But the mighty elephant of southern Somalia do not normally stay in the swamps. As long as there is any water in small depressions and ponds out in the desert country, they prefer the dry areas and dry feed. For months of the year, many of the Somalia elephant do not come to water at all, but get their moisture by chewing sansevieria and other pulpy desert plants.

The southern Somalia country is a continuation of the Northern Frontier of Kenya. There are the same vast areas of barren bush and dry luggers, or washes. I am sure that many of the elephant are the same also. Small groups of old bulls and even cows and calves move from the Tana River north into the Giuba area and back again. Belli was sure that the biggest bulls came out of the Lorian Swamp and the Leopard Swamp, but only at certain times of the year. Since before World War II there have been few elephant hunters in Somalia. The Somalis themselves have a tradition of hunting elephant with poisoned arrows. But with the troubled times since Mussolini marched his legions into East Africa, even the Somali hunting had dwindled and almost died out as a tradition. Belli pointed out to me a vast area of southwestern Somalia in which he said no elephant hunter had penetrated for the last twenty-five years. As Belli had been District Commissioner in this area during the Italian regime, he ought to know.

I very much wanted to bag an elephant carrying 100-pound tusks on either side. I also wanted to get a very large gerenuk, lesser kudu, and Hunter hartebeest in the region south of the Giuba. In arid Somalia, all of these animals grow larger in size than in the Kenya country.

163

Under the African Sun

I found that these ambitious projects were mutually incompatible. It seemed that every time I was well along on the track of some mighty bull elephant, we jumped a lesser kudu whose spiral horns were obviously better than thirty inches long. Once we turned aside to bag a gerenuk that I think will be second in the world records. The shot frightened three bull elephant that we had been trailing since daylight. Guliano Belli, of course, was frantic with disappointment on each of these occasions, as any dedicated elephant hunter would be. Belli is somewhat contemptuous of what he calls the "little antelopes." But I hold to a hunting philosophy that has been formulated by many bitter experiences: If you see something you want very badly, shoot it. If you wait for a better opportunity, it never comes.

Even at that, Belli and I saw, in two weeks of hunting in southern Somalia, some thirty-five bull elephant. At least six of these were in the 85- or 90-pound class. In the Kenya country, if a safari locates an elephant carrying ninety pounds of ivory on each side, they don't hesitate a second. In Somalia, where a 100-pound elephant was our goal, we held our fire.

On our way north we stopped at the camp of the Holdenville hunters. They had tracked a whole pride of lion into thick brush and shot a charging lioness at rifle-muzzle range. They had a record Hunter hartebeest and a beautiful thirty-three-inch kudu but were still looking for a really big elephant.

North of the Uebishabeli River the country gets drier and more rocky. The low, sandy terrain of southern Somalia gives way to low ridges of jaggedly rough limestone. North of Mogadiscio some three hundred miles, the country gradually rises in a series of mesas and escarpments that look like parts of the southwestern United States. Along the low coastal plain of the Indian Ocean lies a gigantic sand-dune belt. Here in the sand dunes are the haunts of the Speke gazelle, a Somali version of the familiar Tommy gazelle of Kenya. However, the Speke has differently shaped horns and a curious profile that makes him distinctive. On top of his nose are two bumps or wrinkles of skin that make him look like a warty old man.

Farther north and inland, especially in the valleys between the limestone ridges, are the haunts of the Soemmerring gazelle. This beautiful gazelle is found no place else in the world. It is a pale dun color with a black-marked face and is about the size of the familiar Grant gazelle of

I Hunted Somalia

Kenya. The horns of the Soemmerring's arch over his head in a double graceful curve with the points approaching each other.

Still farther north and close to the border of the old British Somaliland lies the country of the famous dibatag. Few sportsmen can boast of having bagged one. For one thing, the dibatag is not numerous even in the center of his range, which is not large. The main difficulty is that the dibatag is about the shyest animal in all of Africa. Furthermore, he lives in a terrain in which most of the vegetation is less than a foot high, and very scanty at that. The dibatag is gifted with a long, slender neck very much like the gerenuk's. From this elevated position, his keen eyes can see a prospective nimrod literally a mile away. The dibatag does not stand and stare, as do many of his African cousins. When he sees a car or a hunter, he hoists his long, brushy tail straight up in the air like a warthog and is off. The dibatag never stops running until he is out of sight, and out of sight in that forlorn desert is farther than I like to contemplate.

I hunted five days for dibatag alone. During these five days we saw perhaps twenty of the animals, among them four or five very good bulls. I shot at all of these, and I am not the least ashamed to say that I fired about twelve rounds before I even hurt a dibatag's feelings, let alone bringing one to bag. I was shooting at around 350 or 400 yards at a running target that is not too big to begin with.

The only way I managed to bring one down was a freak accident. I was using a flat-shooting Weatherby .300, but I was still shooting low even with this ideal equipment for impossible ranges. After firing twice at a fleeing dibatag, I elevated a last desperate shot, centering the telescopic sight on the very tip of the dibatag's impudent raised tail. The shot went over his back and must have hit a stone beyond him. The dibatag slid to an abrupt stop in a cloud of dust. Then he reversed his direction and ran almost directly toward me. He passed a couple of hundred yards to my left. I swung with him and pinned him down. There were times in the past when I would have considered a 200-yard running shot as a long gamble. With a dibatag, such a shot is a cinch.

Also in the northern country the hunter may get the famous beira. The beira lives in the rocky hills back from the coast and is not, to my way of thinking, a spectacular animal. He looks something like a dull gray version of an oribi. Outside of the fact that a beira is very difficult to get, his little straight horns do not make much of a trophy.

In the northern deserts are also a few gerenuk of gigantic size, and large numbers of oryx. The Somali oryx belongs to the beisa oryx variety but is generally larger in body and paler in color than the oryx in Kenya. The horns of the Somali oryx are also very long. I shot a number of oryx so that our Mohammedan Somalis could cut the throat of the animals and thus have sanctified meat. Without making any special effort to pick out outstanding animals, I got a bull with 35-inch horns and a female with horns measuring 36½ inches.

Somalia is one place in Africa where cheetah are still very common and on the game list. Reticulated giraffe are very numerous, and also legal game. Our Somali trackers and camp followers liked giraffe meat more than any other kind. Unfortunately, the Somali leopard is now almost extinct, especially in the north. Leopard skins from Somalia were in such high demand by the fur buyers of Europe and America that most of the leopard have been trapped out since World War II. Crocodiles are still very common, in contrast to most of the rest of Africa, where crocodile skin hunters have converted most of these reptiles into pocketbooks and suitcases.

Whether you're hunting for big elephant, trophy horns, exotic gazelles of unusual species, or picturesque African adventure, I would recommend Somalia.

Chapter 17

GUNS ALONG THE GWAAI
(1962)

I watched the Bushman crouch and move forward in a stooping run behind the low clump of palms at the edge of the marsh. He raised his head slowly as he held his short bow at arm's length in front of him. I heard the *twang* as he released the fiber string. The arrow arched slightly and thudded into the flank of the red lechwe. The lechwe ran splashing through the marsh grass at the sting of the arrow. After a few steps, the poison began to affect the animal. The lechwe staggered and threw back his head so his horns struck his own back. He stumbled and rolled on his side. The poison-headed arrow was very near the heart.

I had witnessed an act as old as Africa itself. The Bushmen of South West Africa and Bechuanaland are perhaps the finest hunters in the Dark Continent, and perhaps also one of the oldest kinds of people.

Before I saw the Bushman kill the red lechwe, he had stalked like a hunting leopard to within thirty yards of the game before he released the poisoned arrow. As I walked forward and congratulated him, I thought that the game of Africa would be safe a long time against these primitive weapons.

The Okavango River comes out of southern Angola and spreads out into the sands of the Kalahari Desert like a six-fingered hand pointing southeastward. As the channels of water lose themselves in the thirsty sand, they form thousands of marshy lagoons and swampy pools fringed by lush vegetation. This water causes the game animals of Bechuanaland to concentrate around the Okavango swamps to crop the lush grass. One of the largest and most persistent of the Okavango channels is the Gwaai. Our old white hunter, Andrew Holmberg, looking for new pockets of unspoiled country outside of Kenya, had scouted out a track by which we might skirt the Okavango marshes to the east and then turn westward along the comparatively solid sandy banks of the Gwaai itself. In this way we could reach the very heart of the game country. We did, too, although it took a day-and-a-half of going in four-wheel drive low gear to make our way to the banks of the Gwaai. Time after time we had to build brush tracks and use the winch and the Land Rover to pull our truck through sand or mud. On the northern edge of the Gwaai, however, we could drive over comparatively solid terrain westward along the northern edge of the Okavango swamps.

As we made our first camp after an exhausting day, we heard the boom of a gun. We had seen no tracks or any sign of human habitation for many miles. We had driven past herds of sable, roan, greater kudu, lechwe, and buffalo that acted as though they had never seen a human being or a safari car before. While our boys pitched camp and maneuvered the truck through the last deep sand to a little island of dry ground where we could spend the night, Andrew and I drove the safari car along the edge of the swamp toward the sound of the gun. In a half-mile or so, we found a Bushman standing over the body of a dead impala. He still held his gun in his hand. The weapon was a smoothbore cap-and-ball musket of crude manufacture, the kind of gun that was popular in the United States during the Civil War. As I examined the weapon, Andrew was glowering at the Bushman as though he were an intruder. "I didn't know that these bloody fellows had guns," he remarked sourly.

The next day we pushed fifty miles up the Gwaai. Andrew is a white hunter who doesn't want to hunt near anyone else. The Bushman camp we had found the night before was a hundred miles from the nearest permanent village of these people. They would have had to pack all of the dried meat on the backs of their women at the end of the hunt and carry it back that far. We concluded that since there was so much game on the edge of the swamps, the Bushmen would go no farther than this up the Gwaai. But we were wrong.

We found another hunting group, and then another, even though we moved northwestward up the Gwaai as far as we could go in the safari car. Some of the Bushmen in these camps were still using bows and poisoned arrows. We found three fellows who had 1887 Enfield Martini-Henry drop-breech guns apparently from the Boer War of 1898.

Our principal purpose on the Gwaai was to get a really big-maned lion, as we had heard from the natives that the Okavango lion have the biggest manes in Africa. We visited a Bushman camp, and found a group of hunters feasting on the assorted plumbing from the insides of a lion, which they had just killed with a poisoned arrow. I had a mental picture of creeping up on a sleeping lion, punching him with a poisoned arrow, and then waiting fifteen minutes for him to die. I thought that this would probably be a very exciting fifteen minutes.

As one of our safari boys could talk a little of the peculiar "click" language of the Bushmen, we learned that they kill and eat lion regularly so that the human hunter may acquire the cunning and the power of the king of beasts. The chief of the largest Bushman camp was named Kweri. Andrew apparently figured that if we couldn't beat the Bushmen at their own game, we'd better get them to join us. He hired Kweri to show us where the lion were and to help us track them. Kweri entered enthusiastically into the job, especially when our interpreter explained that if we got one, he could eat it.

Andrew still insisted on camping as far away from the Bushman hunting groups as possible, so we took Kweri in the hunting car and moved northwestward another twenty miles or so. It was amazing how much game we saw along the Gwaai. In a single day (and we actually counted them), we saw over a thousand animals of fifteen different species. It was no wonder that the Bushman hunters came into this paradise. Our Bushman friends hadn't killed all of the lion either. The first evening in our new camp, just as the moon was coming up, we heard a series of roars. "Tao, tao," said Kweri, and nodded his head in satisfaction.

Very few people can master the click language of the Bushmen. Apparently our interpreter knew only a few words. But we had gotten across to Kweri that we wanted a very large lion with a very large mane. Kweri had indicated a particular place. We called it Crocodile Lagoon because, as we made camp, a large crocodile had galloped out through the shallow water, pushing a tidal wave in front of him like a large boat.

Andrew and I had dealt with lion before, and these back-country Gwaai lion were going to be our meat or, rather, Kweri's meat, in jig time. I shot a very nice sable with a forty-three-inch head (and then regretted it for the rest of the trip because I saw a dozen others that were better), and a waterbuck that will probably go into the records. In two days of scouting, we had found the signs of about eight lion including one tremendous male, apparently the king of the pride. The lion usually watered on the far side of Crocodile Lagoon or at another place a couple of miles up the Gwaai that we called Sable Lagoon. We hung up the sable carcass at one place and the waterbuck in another in classic safari fashion.

We hung the baits just right so that wherever the lion pride came down to drink, the easterly wind would carry the delicious scent of rotten sable or stinking waterbuck to their nostrils.

That night, as we had refreshments around the fire, we heard the pride roaring about a mile up the river. The deep-throated *oom, oom, oom, oom,* of the king of the pride was unmistakable.

In the morning we cautiously approached our baits just at daylight. There were lion tracks around both carcasses. At the waterbuck we could see where old Gwaai himself had walked right up to the bait, then reared up and raked great chunks of bark out of the trunk of the tree where the carcass hung. He hadn't touched a mouthful of the meat.

That evening, about four o'clock, Andrew, Kweri, and I secreted ourselves in a well-prepared blind 100 yards from the bait and downwind. Lion can't smell very well, but their eyesight is excellent, so we made the blind a regular hideaway and laid in it as still as three dead men. As the sun sank over the Gwaai, we heard a Bushman gun boom in the distance. Andrew cursed under his breath. At that moment, there was a stirring on the surface of the water beside us. The head of a large crocodile appeared. He raised his narrow snout toward the lion bait, then slithered out of the water toward it. I raised my Weatherby .300, but Andrew put his hand on my arm. "Too many guns along the Gwaai," he whispered. At dark the crocodile still lay beneath the carcasses looking longingly up at the stinking meat. No lion came.

Kweri had managed to convey to us, with a great deal of difficulty, that Bushman hunters always tracked the lion, found them asleep during the middle of the day, and then shot them with a poisoned arrow.

Our two gunbearers in Andrew's retinue, Sungura and Legiria, were accomplished trackers in their own right. But Kweri was the lion man. As we followed the huge imprints of old Gwaai, Kweri smacked his lips from time to time and muttered Bushman prayers to the god of all lion to let us have a look at the big cat. With a great deal of difficulty, we had persuaded Kweri to leave his muzzleloader at camp. He carried it cocked all the time, I noticed, and I figured that the hazards from his gun and a lion at close range were about equal. Sungura and Legiria also went unarmed so that they could concentrate on the tracking. I had the feeling as I followed the three men that I was hunting over three well-trained dogs. They cast ahead of me, bent over, and ranged in half-circles looking for the tracks like well-trained pointers at their favorite work. Andrew had cautioned me not to look down. I held my Weatherby .300 at the ready position and walked forward, looking at every bush and clump of dry grass as we went.

"Remember," Andrew had said for the tenth time, "when we see him, he'll either charge or run. We've got to see him first."

We didn't, though, and it was my fault. On the morning after we had successfully baited the crocodile, we heard old Gwaai roar about four in the morning. At daybreak we were on his trail. Muddy water was still seeping into the splayed imprints where the old monarch had squatted to lap up water.

I clutched my rifle tightly and stalked ahead as our three trackers followed the imprints across the open meadow at the lagoon's edge and into the brush. An hour later we were still tracking. Another hour later, we ran headlong into a herd of two or three hundred buffalo coming down to water. We had to detour a quarter of a mile to get around them. Apparently old Gwaai had done the same. It took a long time to find his tracks again on the other side of the beaten-down earth where the buffalo had passed. By this time the sun was high and many animals were coming down the game trails to drink. We lost the track again and again. Twice I found the track myself. I had tracked a lot of mountain lion back in the United States, and I felt rather proud of myself. Each time I looked down, Andrew prodded me from behind and pointed ahead. But a minute later, I looked down again. Andrew punched me from behind and pointed. In the game trail fifty feet away stood the lion. Legiria in front flattened so I could shoot over him. The lion's head looked like a haystack. His mane was blond over his eyes and black farther back. I raised the gun. Old Gwaai turned sideways. In a single leap, he was gone. I leveled my sight on his tail as it disappeared in the brush.

Under the African Sun

Andrew quickly sent Sungura up a tree. Sungura indicated that he could see the lion moving away. Then he signaled he could see six other lion. So that was the reason old Gwaai had come so far back from the lagoon! He'd come to join up with his pride. Sungura told us that he could see the lion clearly. There were three lionesses and three cubs. Sungura added that old Gwaai was the biggest-maned lion he had ever seen.

Again the next morning, we heard the lion roar and heard his females answer in the distance. We thought we could hear a strange voice in the predawn chorus. When we walked along the edge of the water above Sable Lagoon, there were old Gwaai's tracks in the mud and, on one side, the imprints of another large male. Old Gwaai had come back out of the swamps sometime during the night with either a friend or a rival.

As we stood whispering in the dawn light, old Gwaai roared just behind us. The noise seemed to tremble the deadened leaves of the palm tree beside us. I clutched the rifle and swung around. Andrew waved his arm to the three trackers, and we moved off rapidly toward the sound.

In a few hundred yards we found the imprints where the two males had walked side by side. Again we heard them roar. First, one let loose a low, rumbling cough. Then the other answered.

We moved up quickly. I held my rifle forward over the backs of the trackers as they signaled to each other as first one and then another found the track and moved ahead at a quiet trot. Just over Legiria's back, I saw a movement. I stepped forward and thrust my rifle through the brush. Just beyond was a lion. He was perhaps two feet long and spotted. As he jerked his head around with inquisitive eyes and ears, I hissed at Legiria and motioned to the others to stop. Just beyond the first cub lion was another, walking slowly, and just beyond that was a large lioness. Somehow we had bumped right into the main pride.

We crouched behind the bush and waited several minutes. Sungura went up a tree. From a low crotch he motioned that he could see the lion and that they were lying down. Sungura dropped silently to the ground and told us in whispers that old Gwaai and the other male were not with the pride.

On tiptoe, we backtracked and began a wide circle. In a few minutes we found the trails of the two males, which had apparently swung wide around the females and young and continued northward into the dry, thorny brush.

Guns along the Gwaai

It wasn't that I relaxed or forgot to keep a vigilant watch ahead. It was getting hot and we were all tired from the tension. Several times Sungura had scaled a tree to look ahead. The two lion were following an elephant trail and seemed to be going somewhere. We had already tracked them four or five miles from the water. Long ago we had expected them to stop and sleep. But as the hours wore on, the tracks continued along the same elephant trail. We fell into single file. Kweri was first. I was second with my rifle barrel still thrust forward. Sungura and Legiria were behind, and Andrew drew up the rear.

There was a movement behind me. A rifle barrel punched my shoulder. I halfturned. Andrew pointed with his gun beside us and behind. There was old Gwaai, fast asleep and not twenty feet away.

"Shoot him!" said Andrew in a hoarse whisper. Mechanically I raised the rifle. In that second old Gwaai raised up. I jerked the trigger. The bullet knocked the lion flat. With a rumbling growl, he got to his feet and lurched for us. I cranked another shell into the chamber and fired with the same movement. The shot knocked Gwaai backward. Again he reared up. I bolted the third and last shot into the chamber and fired at the base of his neck. He still stood on three feet. Andrew raised his double rifle. Old Gwaai reached forward and grasped a small tree between his teeth and bit it off and died.

It seemed only minutes after we had shot old Gwaai that a couple of strange Bushmen showed up. At the rustle of sound we whirled, thinking it was the second lion coming to help his friend. One of the Bushmen carried a comparatively modern Winchester rifle. The two new arrivals clicked happily with Kweri about the coming feast they were going to have on lion meat.

"Next safari, I'm going north to the Cevauti," Andrew muttered to no one in particular. "There are too many guns along the Gwaai."

THE QUEEN OF BEASTS
(1962)

The low-throated roar sounded almost beside us. Across the faint star shine on the surface of the water moved a shadow darker than the other shadows. I could hear the panting breathing of the animal. The shadow turned away from the edge of the water straight toward us. The lion was coming into our blind.

For three weeks we had been trying to get ourselves into this situation. Now we would have given half the remaining span of our lives to get out of it.

Brownie (expanding her role from companion to chief photographer of the expedition) and I were doing some scientific work in southern Mozambique at that time, scouting and hunting along the famous Limpopo River. I had always wanted to see the Limpopo after reading Rudyard Kipling's description of the "great grey-green greasy Limpopo River." I pictured this famous stream as slime-coated and sluggish with hippo and crocodiles sticking their snouts out of algae-covered pools. The Limpopo is interesting, but it isn't greasy and it isn't green, at least in the last several hundred miles of its length. For most months of the year it is a broad, sandy wash, innocent of any slime-covered pools and as dry as a dust bowl. Here and there the elephant have managed to dig holes in the sand deep enough to reach the water underneath. In spite of the dearth of water, a lot of game lives along the Limpopo, and a lot of other animals, too. The other animals are mostly the humped and long-horned cattle that belong to the Changane tribe. When people, cattle, and game animals mix in Africa, there usually is trouble. There was lots of trouble along the Limpopo.

The Changane manage to get along with the Limpopo elephant. The elephant drink at night, and the Changane drive their spotted cattle to the water holes during the day. Even the Limpopo buffalo have worked out a schedule that only occasionally overlaps with human usage. There are thousands of buffalo along the Limpopo. These are an especially massive and big-horned variety of the Cape buffalo. We saw Limpopo herds that numbered several hundred animals. As the dry season of August and September advanced and the water holes were reduced in size and number, the buffalo would occasionally drive the cattle and the humans away. When a bunch of determined buffalo, crazed for water, come in during the daylight hours, humans leave for other places. The Changanes tolerate the buffalo, the leopard, and the many antelope. All the animals have learned to get along with the Changanes and their cattle. That is, all of the Limpopo animals but the lion.

Lion are becoming scarce all over Africa. Regarded as the king of beasts by some, and as a clumsy buffoon by others, the maned lion is the symbol of Africa to all. The lion is one of the Big Five of African game—that is, he is one of the five most dangerous animals of Africa and one of the five top trophies sought by sportsmen. Many a hunter who baited the big cats in the early days regard the shooting of a lion as a fairly tame business. Even some professional hunters think of the lion as a lazy clown that will usually come to a bait instead of killing his own meat and getting himself shot in the process. Other hunters regard the African lion as the most dangerous of the Big Five, and they have the scars to back up their opinion. There is no doubt that under the right circumstances the African lion can be the most dangerous animal in the Dark Continent. A few years ago, a friend of mine, Joe Shaw of San Francisco, was killed by a lion. But any hunter, professional or amateur, who has ever come in contact with the African lion will tell you that the female of the species is more deadly than the male. The lioness usually does the killing.

But whether the African lion, male or female, is a dangerous villain or a fool is now becoming an academic question in most parts of Africa. As civilization advances and mankind increases, the stupid rhinoceros and the lordly lion are among the first animals to go. In many places of Africa, lion are now extinct. In large areas of Kenya and Tanzania where lion were fairly common a few years ago, the king of beasts is now scarce or gone altogether.

We first heard of the lioness in Mapai when we arrived at the station after a long and grueling drive from Lourenço Marques (now called Maputo)

The Queen of Beasts

on the coast. We drank some bitter coffee with the proprietor of the fly-buzzing Mapai cantina. The man was shaking his head slowly. He said in Portuguese, "The lioness killed six more last night."

Mapai is a little railroad station on the single-track railway line that links Zimbabwe to the sea. There is no water at the town, so the railroad company pumps the precious fluid through a pipe from a well dug into the bed of the Limpopo ten miles away. Some of the water is piped out to a puddle at the edge of town where the natives can water their cattle. The night before we arrived, a lioness, with a group of other lion, had killed six full-grown cows within sight of the light of the little cantina where we now sat.

Our guide and friend, José Ruiz, was excited at the news. As we rushed out of the cantina and the sagging and rusted screen door banged behind us, Ruiz began to tell the history of the Mapai lioness. He did not doubt for a second that this was the same diabolical female that had killed and terrorized the natives and their cattle for two years in his concession.

When we arrived at the pond on the outskirts of Mapai, the herdsmen were already skinning some of the carcasses. The lion had eaten only one of the cows. As we circled in the dust around the trampled water hole, it was clear that one female lion had killed all six of the cattle. Then the whole pride had stretched out on their bellies to eat at one carcass.

I had hunted lion in several parts of Africa before. Getting this lioness would be a cinch. This was a "natural" kill. It was not a bait that we had rigged up ourselves. The lion had killed several cows and would come back to eat again. We would fix up a blind across the little clearing. When the lion returned, we could shoot one or all of them. José Ruiz slowly shook his head as I outlined my plan. "That may work with most lion," he said in halting English, "but not on this one." He pointed as he spoke to the imprint of the paw of the lioness in the dust at our feet. "I have a permit to shoot the Mapai lioness for two years," Ruiz said sadly, "and all of her pride. Since I have tried this, she has killed over two hundred cattle and two people for sure."

José Ruiz was right. The queen of the pride did not come back to the dead cattle, or to the water hole on the edge of Mapai. We saw the tracks of the pride again, it is true. The next night, as far as we could determine, they watered at a small puddle dug by elephant in the bed of the Limpopo. Two days later the same pride led by the queen lioness killed three cows at a Changane village fifteen miles away.

José Ruiz had built a camp on the banks of the Uanetsi River, a tributary of the Limpopo on the border of South Africa. One of his duties was to protect the natives who live along the river. More than once the Changane chief had come to José to ask his help against the lion pride led by the queen lioness. As Ruiz takes hunting clients to his camp on the Uanetsi, this seemed a very happy arrangement, but it didn't turn out that way. In the previous year, in spite of constant efforts, José and his clients had bagged only one lion, and this was a lone male. José assured me that he had tried all kinds of methods to bring the lioness under his gun. "The lioness is wise like a smart man," José concluded.

In the three weeks that we hunted along the Limpopo, we saw lion tracks every day. There were perhaps twelve or fifteen lion in the area. Judging from the sign, these broke up into small groups that came together according to the kills they made. The killing was done in every instance by the lioness with big splayed-out feet, the same big feet that had made the tracks at the Mapai pond.

Some four miles from José's camp was a fast-drying puddle where a hundred buffalo and a number of nyala, kudu, and sable watered every night. In the mud by the water hole we saw the tracks of the big lioness and some of her group.

They passed by that way perhaps once a week. Well back from the edge of the water hole I shot a buffalo. We dragged the carcass to some bushes a hundred yards from the water and covered it thoroughly with the branches of thorn trees.

Vultures or hyenas cannot get through a blanket of thorns. A lion will bat the stuff aside with one stroke of a paw and eat his fill. We had had very good luck with this kind of concealed bait in Kenya and Uganda. It didn't impress the queen lion of the Limpopo. The third night after we planted the buffalo, she and seven other lion that usually ran with her watered at one end of the pond. She walked contemptuously past our stinking bait and went about her business. The buffalo bloated and disintegrated before the pride ever came back to that water again.

As the dry season advanced, there were only five water holes along the middle Limpopo, counting the one at Mapai station itself. We checked each of these daily. And yet for ten days the lion did

The Queen of Beasts

not water at any of these places. José thought that the pride probably had moved to water at a small lake on the plateau above the river valley about thirty miles to the north. As the Changane take some of their cattle out of the valley during the last of the dry season, we could get a report. We did. Changane herdsmen were losing cattle every night to a gigantic lioness and seven other lion. It could only be our killer queen and her crew.

This pond, called Benini by the natives, was the only water source on that side of the Limpopo. If the queen lion had moved there, perhaps we could outwit her at her own game.

We moved a fly camp consisting of a couple of tents, an extra barrel of gasoline, and a barrel of water and established ourselves under a lone tree about half a mile from the water hole of Benini. As we arrived, two Changane herdsmen came past driving a bullock with a wooden sled trailing behind. The lioness had killed two cows the previous night. They were trying to save some of the meat.

As I looked around our fly camp I realized that the queen lion of the Limpopo had made a mistake coming to Benini. It is the only water within thirty miles. For ten miles round about is a vast open plain with only occasional scattered trees and small clumps of bushes. If she and her pride came into the plain by daylight, we could flush them like a bunch of pheasants. When they came to water, as they must, we could get them anyway.

Lion have to water every twenty-four hours, especially when they are feeding heavily. But the queen and her pride did not come into Benini that night or the next night. The water hole at Benini is an ancient slough perhaps half a mile long. At one end is a series of puddles ringed around with papyrus and palmettos. We carefully circled every inch of the mud around the water. A herd of elephant had come in, and a group of buffalo watered at the eastern end of the pond every night. Wildebeest, zebra, and roan antelope regularly drank there, but there were no tracks of the queen lion and her tribe—that is, no fresh sign. Ruiz carefully questioned the Changane herdsmen. There was no other water within a two-day march of Benini. The Limpopo was thirty miles away in a straight line and much farther than that by trail.

This lioness had discovered, probably by bitter experience, that it was death to water at the same place every night, or to come back to a kill a second time. How she managed to maintain these evasive tactics at Benini we never discovered. Ruiz claimed that the lioness took her

Under the African Sun

pride to water back at the Limpopo as soon as she sensed our camp. Perhaps she did. It was three days before we saw her tracks again.

We tried other tactics as well. Ruiz had been a professional meat hunter years before. He had often shot lion in open country such as Benini, by flushing them out of the brush. We drove our safari car for two days around the tree-ringed glades and savannas surrounding the Benini water. In this area there were animal herds numbering several thousand, mostly wildebeest, zebra, kudu, sable, and roan. The plains antelope on the open grasslands reminded me of Kenya in the old days. Certainly there was plenty of food for a pride of lion. We found where the queen lion had killed an ostrich, apparently for an appetizer. Outside of that, the lion ate Changane cattle. If the queen lion preferred it that way, maybe we could trap her by this preference.

In our wanderings around the Benini plain, we visited the three Changane camps, each with about two hundred spotted cattle. We instructed the Changane to keep their cattle in the corrals at night and let them graze only in the full light of day when the herdsmen could watch them. Ruiz and I figured that we might starve the queen lion into making a foolish move. She didn't, but a couple of young lion of her pride did.

We had noticed that the lion had watered several days before at the end of the pond where there was a little cover from the clumps of palmettos. I shot a buffalo bull on the third evening. We dragged it behind the safari car to a spot upwind from the water. We covered the carcass with thorn branches and palmettos. If the lioness and her pride had not been able to kill cattle, perhaps they would be forced into taking the bait.

On the fifth night, the lioness and her pride came back to water. Where they had been during the interval was a mystery, but apparently they had not made a kill. The next morning we read the tracks clearly in the mud below the palmettos. Seven lion had crouched on their bellies and lapped up the water greedily. The lioness drank at one side. There were two males in the pride. As they turned from the water, the two males and one of the other smaller lion had walked up to the dead buffalo. They scattered aside some of the thornbushes and ate the belly and one haunch. Curiously enough, when we examined the bait the next morning, the thorn branches and palmettos had been pulled back over the meat to cover it again. But the tracks of the big lioness were nowhere near the carcass.

That day we made a tour of the Changane camps to tell them to keep their cattle under close watch. One of the herdsmen had heard a

180

The Queen of Beasts

lion grunt near his corral the night before. We found the tracks of the lioness where she had crouched close to the corral. Perhaps she thought of jumping in to kill a fat cow and then thought better of it.

Ruiz and I made ourselves a blind in the group of palmettos just across the last little puddle of water from the buffalo bait. From here we could see several hundred yards in all directions. We sent the safari car away to hide in the closest group of trees downwind. Ruiz had a weak flashlight with him. We intended to wait all night if necessary. His permit from the Mozambique government allowed him to kill this lioness and her pride by any means possible. But as the sun sank and the velvety blackness of an African night settled over Benini, it looked as if we were not going to get the chance.

Just at dark, a magnificent sable bull came in to the water. He was by far the best animal we had seen, with horns in the 50-inch class. I laid the Weatherby against the palmetto stems and centered the cross hairs of the telescopic sight on his shoulder. Ruiz nudged me and shook his head. We were after more important game, but I hated to pass up that sable. He was the finest I had ever seen. The sable caught the scent of the dead buffalo, snorted, and whirled away.

From the other side, a herd of about fifty eland came across the open savanna to the water. There were several massive bulls in the bunch. In the dusk I could just make out their great humped bodies and twisted horns. The eland watered and splashed along the edge of the pond as the twilight settled into complete blackness. Hyenas whooped in the distance. A zebra barked. From the noises we could tell that the eland still stood by the water, apparently resting after the hot day. There was a splash and the sound of hooves. The eland were driving the zebra away from the water. Then all was quiet. The night noises of the birds ceased. The hyenas stopped calling. There was no moon. We could see the stars reflected clearly in the still water in front of us.

We waited perhaps an hour. No suggestion of twilight remained in the western sky, and my left leg was badly cramped. We were sure that the eland and the zebra were still close to the water, but there was not a sound. Every animal was alert and listening. Then we heard it, too. A lion coughed in the distance. Ruiz nudged me. It was not a roar, but we had both heard it clearly. So had the eland. We heard them shuffling their hooves nervously. The breathing of Ruiz at my elbow sounded like he was strangling.

Perhaps twenty minutes later the lion coughed again. The sound was off to our right and only a few hundred yards away. Again Ruiz nudged me and whispered, "Male."

Under the African Sun

I shifted my cramped leg as the minutes went by. We heard faint jostling noises from the eland across the pond. Everything else was quieter than before. Suddenly a low-throated roar sounded almost beside us. The eland and zebra whirled into motion. The thunder of hooves drowned out any sound that I made as I swung my gun barrel through the palmetto leaves. The roar was not across the water by the bait. It seemed to be in our blind. Ruiz reached back for his own gun. The thudding hooves of the running eland pounded away in the distance. I could see the outline of the animal. I imagined I could see a great head. The head turned toward us. The outline was only twenty feet away. I swung the rifle barrel where I thought the shoulder was and jerked the trigger. A flash of flame jumped out into the darkness. The lion roared, then another lion roared, and another. One of the roars was behind us. I pounded Ruiz on the shoulder. He dropped the flashlight. I could hear lion running past us. One splashed through the water. Ruiz got the flashlight going. He swung the beam around. At the edge of the palmettos the sickly light picked up the shine of two enormous green eyes.

The lioness lay on her belly, crouched and ready. Behind the massive body her tail lashed from side to side. When the chips were down, she was not running. She had led the pride into our blind instead of going to the bait. She crouched lower. I fired at the massive chest. The beam of the flashlight jerked up. I spun another shell into the chamber. Ruiz got the light on the lioness again. She was moving toward us on her belly. I shot again. The bullet spun her around. I fired again as she turned sideways and went down.

The queen lion of the Limpopo turned out to be as big as any male lion I have ever seen. She was 9 ½ feet long, and we judged her weight at about 500 pounds. The Changanes came from every camp to see her and to beg a little of the lion fat to use as medicine. Some lion hunting may be tame and routine, but not this one. For my money, the lioness of the Limpopo was as intelligent and dangerous an antagonist as I have ever met.

Chapter 19

TO KILL A LEOPARD
(1963)

A leopard doesn't change his spots nor does he change his habits. Of all the dangerous animals in the world, the leopard is probably the most predictable.

The range of the leopard extends all the way from Southeast Asia across the southern portion of that continent and throughout most of Africa. The African leopard differs very little in appearance, size, or habits from his Asiatic cousin. In Asia there are variations of the leopard family such as the whitish snow leopard of the upper reaches of the Himalayan area. The cloudy leopard is a gray-mottled, short-legged cat of the Himalayan slopes. The famous black panther of Asia is simply a melanistic leopard. A regular yellowish and rosetted mother leopard may have one spotted kitten and one jet black one. The black ones may breed true if mated and produce black panther offspring. Even on a black leopard, the black rosetted spots may be seen if the light strikes his hide at just the right angle.

In India, where the population is dense and wild game is scarce, leopard may become bold, kill livestock, and even enter villages to do so. There have been many famous man-eating leopard in India, several of them with cunning and intelligence to match that of any man-eating tiger. One leopard, the famous man-eater of Kutru, piled up a total of 242 victims before he was finally finished off while attempting to stalk some women bathers.

Under the African Sun

In Africa, man-eating leopard are virtually unknown. Under the right circumstances, they will kill goats or other domestic stock. Generally they are shy and furtive in their habits and will stay away from people. However, a wounded leopard is aggressive and viciously intelligent and will charge 100 percent of the time. When you consider the unpredictability of an irascible old rhino or a cantankerous buffalo, the leopard will do just about the same thing under any set of circumstances.

In spite of its predictability, bagging a leopard takes a lot of doing. Many a hunting party that counted heavily on bringing back one of the spotted cats has failed to do so. Even a lot of professional hunters shake their heads in doubt when a client insists on getting a leopard. Curiously enough, leopard are still plentiful in most of their former habitats in Africa and southern Asia. The catch is to get your gun sights on one.

The major difficulty is obviously that leopard are mainly nocturnal. When they are harassed, or especially if the country is heavily populated, they move entirely at night and lie in heavy cover during the day. Spotlighting leopard used to be great sport in Africa. Leopard used to be suckers for a spotlight and would usually stand blinking in the glare while the gun behind the light beam picked out a vital spot and blazed away. However, spotlighting is now illegal in most parts of Africa. It is also illegal in most parts of Asia including India, except under very unusual circumstances. A man-eating leopard or a leopard killing domestic livestock may be taken at night with artificial light. As most leopard in India eat livestock when they get a chance, this leaves plenty of openings. However, when leopard are hunted extensively, they soon learn to stay away from a light and will run when they hear the noise of a car. Like most cats, leopard are smart. If they survive one ambush, it is very difficult to lure them into another.

I have hunted leopard on several occasions in India and in a dozen countries in Africa. I have been with some professional hunters who always manage to bag a leopard, and I have hunted with others who always seem to fail. From all of these men I have learned a lot about leopard. It is true, something unexpected can always go wrong. However, if you do the thing right, you have a 90 percent chance of bringing home that beautiful spotted hide.

To Kill a Leopard

Obviously, the first thing to do is to locate a leopard, or preferably several. If you look for leopard sign, usually it is obvious. Like all cats, leopard must drink every twenty-four hours. In the game trails along streams, leopard tracks show up well. The brush cover along watercourses is also the source of most of the leopard's food. Small antelope such as bushbuck and duiker are often leopard victims or, in India, the smaller deer. If a leopard family is working a vicinity, they leave kills behind them. Horns, skulls, and bones of the smaller forest animals will show where a leopard has been at work, and the condition of the kill will indicate how long ago the leopard was there. Lion usually don't bother impala, Grant gazelles, and the smaller antelope.

Leopard will often carry their kills into the fork of a tree—sometimes the very top of a tree—to protect the meat from jackals, hyenas, and other leopard. The leopard that makes the kill may stretch out on a tree branch to guard the meat from the vultures, or he may lie on the ground in heavy brush to see that nothing disturbs his meat. A festoon of loose-hanging bones and strips of skin in a tree is a sure sign of a leopard kill, and a very recent one at that.

In populated areas, leopard often make no secret of their presence. They will jump into a stock corral to kill a goat or a calf. In India a full-grown leopard will often kill a bullock or even a sizable water buffalo. On several occasions in India we were called to witness a tiger kill, only to find that a leopard had done the job.

The leopard kills in much the same way as a lion. He makes his attack from the side or the front. He bites a small animal through the back of the neck. A bigger one, he bites through the throat. From the claw marks I have seen, the leopard apparently jumps on the shoulder of his victim, sinks his hooked claws in, then swings his head down and bites the animal through the throat. There are often fang marks on the muzzle of the victim. We found a leopard in Tanzania, Africa, that had apparently jumped too far back on his victim, was shaken off, and kicked in the face to boot. His jaw was broken and his cheekbone crushed. On several occasions we have found antelope with long, raking scratches down their withers, showing where a leopard had attacked and lost his grip.

Like most cats, leopard make various sounds. The commonest is the call made when hunting. Two leopard hunting together will keep track of each other in this way. The leopard's call is a series of grunts that the novice would never recognize. It sounds most like a large saw going through a knotty board. Leopard do not call as much as lion. In places where they are hunted, they learn to keep their mouths shut and don't call at all. However, by kills, tracks, calls, or depredations, a leopard can be located if he is in the vicinity. If undisturbed, a leopard will work a comparatively limited territory, and usually drink at the same place.

The best way to kill a leopard is to find a "natural bait." This is not pure chance but does entail some luck. If a group of leopard is working the terrain around a particular water hole, the keen-eyed hunter may find a natural kill. In thirty years of hunting I have seen only four or five of these. Three were baboons. The baboon is one of the commonest food animals of leopard. The presence of a hunting leopard on a dark night is often revealed by the howling or chattering of baboons and monkeys. Baboons rest in trees at night. Apparently the hunting leopard climbs a tree and picks off a victim. But whether it's a baboon weighing 50 pounds or an antelope weighing 300, the leopard can carry his kill a prodigious distance and lift it up into a tree. All of the cats have fantastic strength, and can carry several times their own weight. On one occasion in Kenya, we found where a leopard had killed an almost full-grown zebra and hoisted the whole carcass into the crotch of a baobab tree fifty feet from the ground.

If the leopard makes his own kill and places it in a spot of his choosing, he will be much less suspicious than otherwise. The natural habit of the leopard is to lie up during the day and feed at sunset. The hunter must conceal himself near the kill with as little noise and disturbance as possible. Loud talk or the chopping of branches may drive the leopard off for good. It must be kept in mind that leopard have fantastic eyesight. A camouflage outfit or dark clothing is a must. It is a good idea to darken the face. A light-colored human face stands out like a full moon in dark foliage. If the face moves, the leopard will never come.

With a natural kill and a little caution and care, the hunter can count on getting a shot at the leopard when he jumps up into the tree to feed. However, most leopard are bagged by baiting. I have heard a lot of hunters say that in their particular area, leopard will not come to a bait. If the situation is prepared correctly, any leopard anywhere will come to a bait.

To Kill a Leopard

Different leopard in different places have varying food habits. In parts of India, leopard feed on goats or young bullocks because there is very little wild game. In other parts of India, pigs, barking deer, and the beautiful chital deer are favorite leopard food. In Africa it is the same. Leopard may regularly take impala or Grant gazelles. On Mount Kenya we found the forest leopard there feeding almost entirely on bushbuck. We offered them delectable cuts of buffalo, giant forest hog, and even a couple of domestic goats. But those leopard passed up our offerings. There they liked bushbuck and only bushbuck. Baboons or large monkeys seem to be a universal bait.

Baboons are regarded as nuisance animals, so the hunter does not feel badly about hanging up two or three. However, in places we have had leopard pass up a baboon for an impala. Recently we had a particularly fussy leopard pass up a baboon for a buffalo leg we had hung up to attract a lion. The rule seems to be, find out what the leopard are eating and then give it to them.

The placing of the bait takes a lot of doing. Usually it is dragged across the route that the leopard takes to water. However, the spotted cat usually locates the food by eyesight rather than smell. The bait should be hung from a limb so that the leopard can see it. Even in almost total darkness the fantastic eyesight of a leopard can pick out a piece of hanging meat. The bait must be placed so that the vultures cannot get at it from any adjoining limb or the hyenas from below. A slanting tree with a large overhanging limb is a good bet. Then the leopard can lie on his belly as he feeds. Some of the most successful leopard hunters hang the bait loosely and with a light rope so that the leopard can reach down and hoist the kill higher into the tree. The leopard may even break the rope and take the meat into an adjoining tree. If he picks out his own spot, it seems to make him feel more secure.

There is no doubt that a leopard bait improves with age, up to a certain point. Leopard are not a bit fussy about stinking meat full of maggots. The fact that they regularly eat carrion is one reason the bite of a leopard is so dangerous. However, there is a very hot argument as to how much a leopard can smell. Certainly the cats are short on scent when compared with a hunting hound. But there is no doubt that a leopard can smell and, under the right circumstances, very well indeed.

Under the African Sun

On our last safari I shot a big bull eland. The shot was poorly placed, and the eland took off like a bee-stung heifer. It was late evening. The eland was bleeding profusely, but African animals have tremendous stamina. At dark we gave up. The next morning we came back and picked up the blood spoor. Ahead of us on the sandy game trail was the track of a very large leopard. It had smelled the blood and was tracking the wounded eland like any other predator. When we found the eland, the leopard was already there.

Leopard can smell humans also, especially human sweat. Perhaps it depends on the wind and the moisture conditions. Under certain conditions leopard do not seem to use their noses. On one occasion a leopard came out of the bush and lay down against the front of our blind about three feet away. We could hear his panting breath plainly. We held our own. Apparently the leopard did not smell us. Soon he got up, jumped up into the bait tree, and began to feed.

Some professional hunters claim that leopard and the rest of the cats cannot smell at all. These fellows are careless about hanging a leopard bait. They allow their men to move freely about the area as they build their blind and to urinate in the vicinity. I have noticed that these hunters usually do not get a leopard.

The best rule seems to be to take for granted that the leopard can smell. He certainly can see and hear as well as any other animal. When the bait has been placed in the tree, the stomach contents of the bait animal may be rubbed on the limb to obliterate all traces of human scent. Do not cut branches or walk in the vicinity of the bait. Leave everything undisturbed and free of human smell.

When the bait is in place, then the blind should be made. Once a leopard has begun to feed, it is too late to build a blind. It is impossible for a hunter to walk up to a feeding leopard. Their eyesight and hearing are too acute. The blind itself must be a work of art. Underneath the limbs of an overhanging tree is a good place. The back of the blind should be as carefully constructed as the front so that no light leaks through. An aperture in the front as big as a grapefruit is large enough for the gun and the man who uses it. Another peg hole or two in other parts of the blind may be in order. One or two other people in the blind may help. More than three are too many. If possible, the rifle should be placed so that the man behind it sees the bait outlined against the sky.

To Kill a Leopard

Also, try to locate the blind so that the leopard comes from the front side. Twice we have had leopard come from behind us and attempt to enter the blind as a hiding place. This is not only very unnerving, but it frightens the leopard so that the blind and bait are useless.

Any rifle of average caliber is big enough to kill a leopard. The main point is that the first shot must be placed precisely and be lethal. There is very seldom an opportunity for a second chance. A leopard is as shy as a schoolgirl in approaching a bait. But once wounded, he probably is the most dangerous animal of the Big Five. The cautious leopard hunter usually has a shotgun loaded with buckshot in the blind with him.

If the leopard should be wounded, there develops what the professional hunters call "a very sticky situation." A wounded leopard will always charge—*always*. Even on three legs, or shot through the lungs or otherwise dead on his feet, the leopard will jump for the human throat and do it so fast that you can't see him coming. The worst part of it is that leopard are usually shot in the evening. A wounded leopard in the high grass or brush near the bait tree is the worst situation any hunter has to face. If you wait until morning, the leopard may die and the hyenas will eat him before you return. If you follow him immediately, someone is going to get hurt. There is hardly a professional hunter in India or Africa who has not been mauled by a leopard under these circumstances. The famous leopard of Manyara mauled David Ommanney, a very experienced hunter, David's gunbearer, and the second gunbearer on three successive days. Each of these men knew exactly where the leopard was and had his gun ready. David told me afterward that the leopard appeared before his face like an apparition. Even with the shotgun at his shoulder and the safety off, he never had a chance to fire. That leopard chewed all the muscles off his shoulder and upper arm. His gunbearer attacked the beast with a knife and drove it off. The next day the same leopard in exactly the same spot almost bit the face off the gunbearer.

Carl Akeley, the famous American naturalist, jumped by a wounded leopard, held his left hand stuffed into the leopard's mouth to keep the animal from biting through his throat. With his right arm, Akeley, a very powerful man, held the struggling leopard close against him so that the raking hind claws of the cat would not disembowel him. Akeley crushed the ribs of that leopard one by one and killed him. He himself nearly died from his wounds. Wherever hunters gather in leopard country, there are stories of hand-to-hand encounters with wounded leopard. Almost all who have been attacked marvel at the speed of the charge. Also, a leopard seems to know instinctively where a human throat is and what he can do if he can get his teeth into it.

To kill a leopard, the hunter must know a lot. Give the leopard his due. Take it for granted that he will see you or smell you or hear you if you don't take every precaution. Above all, make that first shot count.

Chapter 20

RHINO VS. BULLDOZER
(1963)

The rhino hurtled out of the bamboo like the battering ram that he was. He struck the half-raised blade of the 'dozer at one side. The machine, laboring up a steep grade, stopped dead. Ndege, the driver, frantically worked at the controls to start the engine. The rhino whirled on stubby legs and charged again. Ndege saw a trickle of blood from the flaring nostrils. The rhino came from the side. Just before he struck the bulldozer again, he lowered his head, then jerked his snout upward as he struck. The sharp-pointed horn caught the 'dozer under the top plates of the track. There was a sound like a bullet hitting hard steel. The whole bulldozer tipped precariously under the impact, and Ndege and his helper were thrown out the far side of the driver's seat. One of the plates of the track ripped away.

"A rhino charged a bulldozer and stopped it dead?" I asked incredulously. "An automobile, yes; maybe even a truck if the rhino hit it on the side; but a bulldozer. . . ."

David Ommanney, the white hunter, shook his head and stuck his pipe in his mouth at a belligerent angle. "Couldn't believe it myself till I went to look. They're repairing the bulldozer now. That driver, Ndege, is still the color of wood ashes."

Ommanney, Brownie, and I were at that moment in a wet camp well up on the slopes of Mount Kenya in East Africa. We had been there for two weeks hunting bongo, that elusive, forest-dwelling antelope considered by many sportsmen to be Africa's top trophy. As secondary prizes, I hoped to get a forest leopard and a wide-horned, forest-dwelling buffalo. During our bongo hunt we had been charged

Under the African Sun

by forest elephant and snorted at by buffalo. I had shot one buffalo bull just above our camp on a forest road. The buffalo turned out to have a very disappointing head of horns. We used the carcass for leopard baits, up and down the same road. After three nights of vigil, we finally surprised a mongoose eating the buffalo meat. While looking at the mongoose, I bagged a giant forest hog, which looks like a cross between a bacon pig and a black bear. We wanted bongo, forest leopard, or at least a good Mount Kenya buffalo. We had everything else but. All of this is to say that our hunt was not the most successful African safari in the records.

Not that Mount Kenya isn't about the most interesting country in all of East Africa. Camped as we were well up on the slope of the 17,040-foot mountain, we found ourselves in another world as far as Africa was concerned. Even in our camp the weather was wet, cold, and dark. We had pitched our tent in a small clearing formerly occupied by a sawmill. From the sawmill radiated forest roads along which the foresters had hauled in the saw logs before World War II. Farther up on the mountain, the forest roads enter the bamboo zone and most of them stop. Some of the tracks up Mount Kenya's main ridges were extended by Army bulldozers during the Mau Mau emergency so that truckloads of scouts could more easily get at the terrorists. Our white hunter, David Ommanney, was one of the scouts. He showed us where he and his men had surprised a camp of Mau Mau, killing sixteen in a hot firefight. We could still see the ashes of the old fires, and the remnants of the brush shelters where the terrorists lived.

We had spent most of our time in the bamboo, as that is where the bongo lives. We had found the bamboo forest wet and nasty, and bongoless as far as we were concerned. Finding one of the rare forest antelope in that monotonous stuff was like trying to find a flea on a hound's back when you are the size of the flea. So when David heard that the men at Keith's sawmill, some thirty miles north around the base of the mountain, had sighted a big bull mountain rhino, he took the safari car and drove around to find out.

"See a mountain rhino!" the foreman of the sawmill exploded. "We've done nothing else but see the bloody beast. He's disabled my only 'dozer, kept two of my men up a tree all night, and charges every time we go up there. The bloody thing lives there."

Next morning, David and I went to see for ourselves. Native mechanics were fitting a new plate on the broken bulldozer track.

Rhino vs. Bulldozer

Even when the machine was repaired, however, Ndege claimed that he would not again go up on the ridge where the rhino lived.

"We'll go up there and shoot him for you this afternoon," Ommanney said confidently.

Confidence is a good thing in a white hunter. As a matter of fact, I was very confident myself. Shooting a three-ton rhino was going to be a cinch, compared to the elusive bongo. But four days and a hundred miles of mountain trails later, we still had not eliminated the bulldozer rhino.

He was there all right. The foreman had said that he lived there, and we found tracks to prove it. He was a bull, too. The print of his hind foot was as wide across as my hand from outstretched thumb to extended little finger. This is a big track, even for a mountain rhino. We followed some thousand of these distinctive tracks every day, but the bulldozer rhino seemed to be as retiring as one of the rare Mount Kenya orchids that Brownie was always looking for. With a guide from the sawmill, Ommanney's gunbearer, Longolo, and a second gunbearer, Kwakai, to carry lunch and ammunition, we tracked, rested, and tracked again. As we rested, David told me about mountain rhino.

"The mountain rhino is a lot different from his lowland cousin, the bush rhino, although they both belong to the same species. The mountain variety of the black rhino, like this one here,"—David indicated one of the deep three-lobed footprints in front of us—"has a bigger body, a lighter color, and a long, slender horn compared to the short, blunt snout of the bush rhino. These mountain beasts are usually shyer than bongo," David added with a wry smile.

Apparently our mountain rhino bull had reverted to type. We hadn't even gotten a good look at him, much less a fair shot. I did have one glimpse the second morning of the hunt. I saw the rhino's eye and his front horn, about five feet from my face.

On our first reconnaissance, David and I had found tracks showing that the bull usually bedded down very close to the spot where he had effectively stopped the bulldozer from scraping a road up his home ridge. A hundred yards above the gouges in the earth where the bulldozer had been working, a thick stand of bamboo began, extending upward into the sodden clouds that always hung on the flank of the mountain. On the second morning, we went directly to this bamboo thicket, after driving our safari car as far as we could along the unfinished road. At the edge of the bamboo, where the tunnel of a game trail showed like a black doorway, was a dollop of dung fresh and wet. Longolo stuck his bare toe into the dung, and grunted in a whisper. David translated the Swahili: "Dung's warm. We'll find your rhino in there." He gestured with the barrel of his .470 double rifle.

We followed the fresh tracks and droppings into the darkness of the bamboo. I was third in line. We went a few yards, then stopped where three game trails came together. Just to my left I thought I saw a dark form. It certainly wasn't the matted stalks of several fallen bamboo. At a crouch, I moved off several yards to the left and stuck my head around a corner of the game trail. I could see a bright eye with wrinkles around it. Above was the base of a horn, brown and shredded like a coconut husk.

"Come back, you fool," Ommanney hissed behind me. The bamboos crackled as the rhino heaved to his feet and lunged. I threw up my Weatherby. The barrel caught on a bamboo. I could see nothing. The noise of breaking bamboo was deafening. Just to my left, the stalks jerked and splintered. The crashing died away.

"That was sticky," David commented as we got to our feet. "If he had charged straight at you, he would have stepped on your head." I gathered from his tone that at the moment David wished that the rhino had done just that. Longolo was taking the wind by shaking a little bag of wood ashes. He muttered something in Swahili. "That bull circled on his own trail and had our wind," David commented, shaking his head. "Can't fathom why he charged a bulldozer but didn't take on four men on foot."

Just when the bulldozer rhino lost his nerve, I do not know. The natives at the sawmill told us that as far as they could remember, the bull had lived on that ridge for the last three or four years. He had systematically charged and driven off every native who came that way, and ultimately even the bulldozer that had invaded his domain. For some reason he figured we were different. That night he left his bamboo ridge, crossed a deep canyon to the south, and disappeared. It took us a whole day of tracking to find where he went. When we did follow the sliding tracks in the mud, I could not comprehend how a three-ton beast could go down that muddy track, across the volcanic rocks in the canyon bottom, and up the other side. The terrain would have tried the ability of a mountain goat. Late on the third day, we jumped the rhino in a thick clump of bamboo, and he ran again.

Rhino vs. Bulldozer

During the fourth day of tracking, we were tired, wet, and discouraged. The belligerent bulldozer rhino had turned into a running coward. We had jumped him twice on the bamboo-covered ridges high up on the flank of Kenya. Each time, he had smelled us or heard us and galloped off through the bamboo like a frightened rabbit. Each time he ran, he circled wide and headed back to the north. Late in the afternoon, we figured he was going back to his home range, and we would all be just where we had started, which was nowhere.

We stopped in a little opening where the spreading limbs of a giant cedar had stunted the bamboo. In the sodden mess at the base of the tree, we built a fire with great difficulty (and a lot of Boy Scout lore) and ate a late lunch. The cold mountain mists were already beginning to roll down Kenya. The tree hyraxes were tuning up, as though night had already fallen. The tree hyrax, an animal about the size of an American groundhog, makes love to his mate in the next tree by screeching, a noise that sounds like a woman having her throat cut. A group of louries, with their brilliant red underwings, fluttered and settled for the night in the tree above us. Longolo and Kwakai stretched out on the wet ground with their feet to the fire. Even Ommanney seemed discouraged. "We're going to have to either get cracking and head for the car, or spend the night under this damn tree," he remarked sourly as he sucked at his dead pipe.

I nodded glumly, but added, "Let's track old bulldozer a little farther. It's almost in the direction we have to go anyway."

David shook his head, prodded the two gunbearers into life with his foot, and motioned Kwakai to carry his double rifle. While David was stamping out our sputtering fire and knocking out his pipe, I stepped along the game trail on the tracks of the bull. The tracks had never been hard to follow. In the mud of the bongo trail the rhino had sunk two inches at every stride. I saw by the splayed-out imprints that old bulldozer was still running. *Probably be clear on the other side of the mountain,* I thought glumly.

A couple of hundred feet beyond our fire, the bongo trail ended abruptly in a tangle of half-broken bamboos. This was to be expected. We had passed a hundred places like it on that day. Bushbuck, bongo, buffalo, and other animals using the forest track had made a detour around the windfall. As I stepped into the side trail, David was at my shoulder. I crouched down to crawl beneath a couple of bamboos, and then stopped on one knee. Just ahead in the open trail were four tree trunks. They didn't look natural. The closest one moved a little. A leg! A gray head moved from behind the bamboo. There was a rasping snort. A bamboo cracked. Old bulldozer charged straight through the bamboo.

Apparently the old bull had decided to run no more. Why he had taken his stand just there can be explained only by another brainless rhino. Behind that windfall in the trail, it was easily possible to hear our voices as we had stood by the fire and talked for over an hour. Certainly the old rhino could smell the smoke. But when he made up his mind, he made up his mind. He didn't take the detour around the mass of fallen bamboo, but came straight through. Bamboo stalks as big as my arm snapped like straws. David yelled something, and grabbed for his rifle. Kwakai, at the sudden appearance of the rhino's horn through the bamboos, turned and ran, carrying the double rifle with him. David matched him stride for stride, screaming like a madman. Meanwhile, it was up to me.

I was still on my knees in the mud. The rhino had apparently seen me. He came straight at me. I saw him lift his ugly head in a vicious uppercut, to toss away the bamboo stalks. Automatically I raised the Weatherby. There was no time to sight. There was no need. The rhino was twenty or thirty feet away. The solid bullet struck the rhino on the shoulder. He squealed and whirled, and ran in a complete circle. Bamboos splintered and cracked as the great body cut through them like a scythe. Here he came again. Ommanney was running up the trail. He had snatched the double rifle from Kwakai.

The rhino saw the movement and charged again. The bull was in the open trail now. I cranked in another shell and fired at his shoulder as he passed me. David, crouching and running, fired the first barrel, then the second. He and the rhino were running at each other, and only a few feet apart. David would never have a chance to reload. At the impact of the 500-grain bullets, the rhino fell to his knees and slid in the mud. I bolted in another shell and fired blindly. My gun barrel was not ten feet from the flank of the rhino as he heaved again to his feet.

Ommanney was frantically trying to reload. Usually, a hunter with a double rifle carries two extra shells between the fingers of his left hand, but David had not been carrying his own gun and was not ready. None of us were ready. Now he was trying to dig two shells

Rhino vs. Bulldozer

out of his belt loops and stuff them into the breech of his gun. I was trying to reload, too. I could not remember whether I had fired two or three times.

But old bulldozer was through. He got to his feet shakily, turned, and ran back through the swath of destruction in the bamboo that he had made seconds before. David and I reloaded and followed him with our rifles thrust forward, the safeties off. Just ahead, we heard the bamboo crash again. A heavy body rolled down a little slope. There was a gasping snort—and then silence. As we came up to the bull, he raised his head and glared at us with his little pig eyes. I shot again at the base of his neck. He quivered, and then was still. We left him there in the wet bamboo and started the long walk back to the road and the safari car.

The next morning, with cameras and extra bearers, we walked back to the spot where old bulldozer had made his last stand. In the soft ground just beyond the bamboo windfall, we found where he had fallen, gotten up, and fallen again. He had waited for us at that particular place. It was no accident. "More like a buffalo than a rhino," was David's comment. The rhino had been fifty feet from us when I had seen his four stubby legs and he had started his charge. My first bullet from the .378 Weatherby had entered at the base of his neck. We found the bullet beneath the skin of his hip on the opposite side. David's shots had struck the rhino in his chest. Any of these would have been fatal, but perhaps not quickly enough. Outside of a skinned place on one side of his flank and the broken tip of his horn, the bulldozer rhino had come off better than the bulldozer that gave him his name.

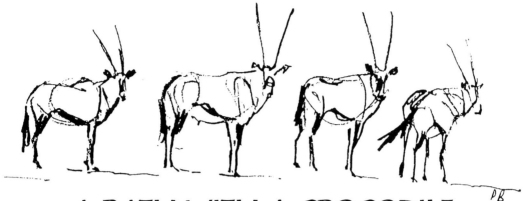

A BATH WITH A CROCODILE
(1963)

The tail hit me from behind. The pointed studs tore through my safari pants and sank deep into the flesh of my thigh. The thing was like a gigantic whip, only the whip was as big as a fire hose and as strong as the bumper on a truck. A truck could not have knocked me harder or farther. I sailed clear over the paddler in the bow of the dugout. The croc's head was just below me. I hit him with one shoulder. The yellow water of the Tana boiled as the jaws opened. Dirty water closed over my face. I felt the crocodile beneath me. He rolled on his side. The claws of one foot raked against my chest. Again the jaws opened. I could not get away.

It was my own fault. Royce Buckle had warned me: "Stay out of the water," he had said. "A croc is fast as a cobra and a killer by choice and necessity. The water is a crocodile's home ground. Stay out of that water."

Royce Buckle, a young white hunter of Kenya Colony, Africa, had been born and raised in the game country. Royce had hunted crocs for their hides before he had turned to guiding safaris. Also, like most other white hunters, Royce didn't like crocodiles. When I had suggested a crocodile hunt on the Tana River in Kenya, Royce had tried to talk me out of it.

"Those stinking crocs are the lowest form of life in my book," Royce commented. "I'd rather go on a hyena hunt."

We were in the Tana country anyway, trying to find a big bull elephant the natives had reported watering on the northern bank of

Under the African Sun

the river. We established our safari camp at the little trading post of Bura. Bura is a collection of seven little *dukas*—native stores made out of haphazard pieces of corrugated iron and parts of old coffee boxes. If I had needed any more advice about crocodiles, I could have gotten it from the Somalis who ran the *dukas* at Bura. I didn't ask them. I just watched them. When they dipped water up from the river, they let down a jug on a rope. Under no circumstances would any of the thirty or forty people of Bura go close to the Tana at night for water or any other purpose. For watering their sheep, goats, and cattle they had constructed corrals of stout logs that extended into the edge of the river. The reason was crocodiles.

In the excitement of trying to find a really big bull elephant, I had temporarily forgotten about crocodiles myself. Bura is legendary game country. The beautifully marked vulturine guinea fowl with their blue-feathered shirt fronts came right into the dusty compound in front of the *dukas*. Buffalo, waterbuck, and several varieties of monkeys lived with us along the fringe of jungle growth on both sides of the river. Farther out in the dry scrub, giraffe, lesser kudu, oryx, zebra, and the rarer Hunter hartebeest were everyday sights. Lion coughed and grunted when the sun went down.

As we ranged up and down the north bank, we checked the elephant that came in to water. About three hundred elephant were watering within twenty miles of Bura in either direction. In ten days of elephant tracking we had looked over some thirty or forty bull elephants and on the side had bagged a record-class Hunter hartebeest.

Royce and I were sitting in camp one evening congratulating ourselves on this latter achievement when the safari boys came running, chattering in Somali and Swahili together. We looked where they pointed back over their shoulders. The smooth surface of the river was marked by spouts of dirty yellow water. Something black and furry thrashed, disappeared, then came up farther downstream. Below the steep bank where our tent was pitched, the current of the Tana was swift. The thing thrashing in the middle of the river was almost past before we realized what it was. A luckless monkey had somehow dropped into the water and was drifting downstream. Two crocodiles followed the terrified monkey closely. The ugly black snout of one of them was as long as my arm. The croc himself must have been ten feet long. Below us on the steep bank, the safari boys struggled to launch a clumsy

A Bath with a Crocodile

dugout canoe. At our urging, they pushed out in the current to try to rescue the hapless monkey. The larger of the two crocodiles moved in quickly from the side. His jaws opened like a long trap with rows of teeth. I rushed into the safari tent, grabbed my .270, and jammed a cartridge in the barrel. Our crocodile hunt started at that moment.

The two crocs, seeing the dugout canoe splashing toward them, sank out of sight. The safari boys rescued the monkey. In gratitude, the monkey bit the two boatmen who hauled him out. Later on, the little fellow became tame in our camp and joined the expedition as a full-time member. Royce and I went crocodile hunting.

The native dugout canoes that the inhabitants of Bura carve out of a single tree trunk will capsize if the occupant hiccups. After one precarious crossing of the Tana in such a treacherous and unpredictable craft, I decided we needed more stability than a boat that turns over if you roll your eyes. First we lashed two dugouts together to make a sort of catamaran. Finally we lashed three of the treacherous little canoes into a fairly creditable arrangement on which a couple of crocodile hunters could feel quite confident.

In the next several days we inaugurated a surefire system for croc hunting. Royce and I, with four native paddlers to keep our croc-hunting barge going straight, drifted down the Tana eight or ten miles, hunting as we went. At a pre-arranged spot down below, the native driver met us with the safari car and brought us back to camp. The paddlers would then unleash the dugouts and poll them back along the bank. In five or six such floating trips, we saw about sixty or seventy crocs. Out of this number, I might have shot ten or fifteen, but I was after a very large one.

As the crocodile in Africa has been hunted for his valuable skin for the last fifty years, crocodiles are mighty cautious. The crocs of the Tana are no exception. The smaller ones might lie on a half-submerged mud bank as we floated by. The big boys—eight, nine, or ten feet long—never did. On our fourth day of croc drifting, we elaborately disguised our three dugouts with branches and vines to make a sort of floating duck blind out of the whole arrangement. In many places along the banks of the Tana, great tangles of jungle vines hang into the water. We looked just like one of these that had broken loose and was drifting along. It worked great. Some of the larger crocs still seemed to detect something sour in our camouflage

Under the African Sun

and slipped off into the water. Some of the others didn't. The first one of these, about a nine-footer, lay on a mud bar as we passed. As we had seen before, the croc sunned himself with his mouth held open. A little sandpiperlike bird darted in and out of the open mouth, picking pieces of decayed fish from between those awful teeth. I hoped that the little bird had adequate insurance. I steadied my .270 on a limb of our camouflage blind and shot the croc "just behind the smile" as Buckle had directed me to do. The little bronze-tipped bullet seemed to kill the saurian instantly. The jaws snapped shut. Fortunately the little bird's head was not inside at that instant. The croc never moved. We maneuvered our dugouts alongside the mud bar and hauled the croc aboard. I figure he must have weighed two hundred pounds and was fascinating in his evil ugliness.

As we drifted farther our spirits rose. It had all seemed so easy. Royce's stories of how crocodiles had been known to drag into the water and kill every animal in Africa, including man, now seemed fantastic. Only the evening before, Royce had regaled me with an eyewitness account of a tragedy that had happened right there at Bura. One of the natives had seen a rhino drinking. A large croc had seized the rhino by the snout. The croc flipped over, twisting the rhino off his feet. The weight of the croc, apparently several hundred pounds, had pulled the rhino's head underwater. When the rhino drowned, the big croc maneuvered the two-and-a-half-ton body into the deep water and cached it there so that the flesh could rot and the croc's teeth could get through the inch-thick rhino hide.

Ridiculous, I thought. Maybe such things happened in the old days. There were also stories of an 18-foot crocodile on the Tana. Such monsters might weigh over a thousand pounds. We hadn't seen anything longer than about 10 feet, and the crocs we were trying to hunt were shyer than politicians at a budget hearing. Even the stories of crocodiles knocking full-grown men from the riverbank at Bura and then dragging them under now seemed far-fetched. These things might happen very occasionally and at night, but not to us.

About two miles farther down the river one of our boatmen, crouching behind the mass of branches in the bow of our blind, hissed softly under his breath. He pointed with his chin toward the right bank. The eyes and snout of a good-sized croc showed among the bubbles and foam under a cutbank. The croc was swimming toward us. I threw up

202

A Bath with a Crocodile

the .270 and shot just between the two black bumps that were the croc's eyes. The bullet hit too low, smashing the croc's snout. He flipped his tail and rolled over. He was a big one. I didn't want to lose him. His wet belly skin flashed once above the muddy water a few yards downstream. He wasn't dead, but he was badly hit. Still farther down, the croc showed again, then caught on a mud bar just below the surface. He was moving feebly. Apparently the bullet had smashed his underwater snorkel apparatus and he couldn't submerge.

We quickly maneuvered our floating blind so as to pass near the spot where the croc was stranded. Our boat grounded on another mud bar well above the place where the crocodile still thrashed in the shallow water. Shrugging off Royce's restraining hand, I jumped into the water and raced for the bank. Fortunately the bank was low at this spot. Dodging vines and trees, I ran along the top of the bank. A couple of hundred yards downstream, I saw the croc flopping and rolling along the edge of the mud bar. The water looked about knee-deep. The swift current was already pulling him into deep water. In another second he would be gone. Howling like a Comanche, I sailed off the top of the bank. As I hit the water, I grabbed the croc's tail. I had thought the water was shallow. I was about ten feet deep. I came up blowing out muddy water like an Italian fountain, but I still had the croc. When Royce and the boatman had hauled me out, the first thing I heard when I got the water out of my ears was Royce chewing me out: ". . . and keep out of the bloody water! If you must go bathing with crocs, do it on somebody else's safari."

I pretended not to hear as I poured the water out of my gun barrel. Anyway, we had gotten the croc, and he was better than nine feet. Who can tell how deep the pea-soup Tana water is?

Buckle jerked my wet sleeve. "See if you can shoot that one without getting in the river," he whispered, pointing to a large clump of vines that hung over the steep bank. In the shadow of the vines I could see the dormer window eyes and the pointed snout of a really big crocodile.

Our clumsy craft was moving and turning in the current. I waited until we were just opposite the croc. Again his snout was straight toward us. I aimed a little high and touched off the .270. The jolt of the bronze-pointed bullet stiffened the croc. He quivered and lay still in the water. The boatmen plunged their paddles deep to swerve our barge out of the current. We approached the dead crocodile from downstream. As we nosed in under the vines, Royce directed the lead boatman to grab the forefoot of the crocodile. I leaned over and got the hind foot. One big heave and we'd have him. He was our biggest yet.

As I touched his hind foot, he came alive. In a spurt of yellow spray, the croc exploded. His head came up out of the water. The native fell backward, knocking over Buckle. The heavy tail attacked me like an independent thing. Splinters raked from the side of the dugout beside my hand. The tail hit me from behind. There was stunning pain as the sharp studs bit into the flesh of my thigh. Headfirst and on top of the croc, I fell into the water. I felt the raking claws of one foot along my chest. The croc and I were thrashing together. The croc turned to get his jaws on me. I tried to swim backward and fend him off all at once. My head was above the water for a second. I got a glimpse of his snout and teeth in front of my face. I went under again. I thought of the stories that Royce had told me—"They knock their victim into the water with their tails. Then they grab him with their jaws and drown him. They cannot chew with those jaws. They cache the body underwater somewhere until the flesh decomposes. . . ."

My head was above water again. The boat was several yards away. Close beside my shoulder, the croc opened his jaws. They snapped shut. I felt no pain. I splashed backward with both arms. I kicked my legs. I seemed to be free. The croc's belly turned up as he twisted his head. His jaws were locked on a large vine that trailed in the water. If that had been my arm. . . . I watched as the croc turned over and over to kill the vine. The tough wood wrapped around his snout, effectively closing his jaws.

Royce and the two boatmen hauled me into one of the dugouts by the back of my neck and the seat of my pants.

"Of all the bloody, blithering, blasted . . ." Royce sputtered as he rolled me into the bottom of the boat.

I held up my hand weakly and grinned. "It wasn't my own idea," I argued feebly. "And besides, I've got the croc all tied up for you."

"Bathing with crocodiles . . ." Royce began. We both laughed and slapped each other on the back. I am not going to admit this to Buckle under any circumstances, but bathing with crocodiles is no fun.

Chapter 22

MAN-EATING CROCODILE
(1963)

C. E. Clark, District Commissioner at Maun, Bechuanaland Protectorate in south-central Africa, said to come quickly. The Batawana crocodile had killed another woman, and there were two witnesses. This was the seventh person the crocodile had taken. Furthermore, E. P. Moremi O.B.E., the Queen Regent of the Batawana tribe, had requested immediate assistance with crocodiles that were destroying fishing weirs and eating the fish within them. "Indeed," Commissioner Clark said in his clipped British accent over the safariland radio, "The crocs are getting so cheeky that they'll come right into Maun next."

When it's crocodiles in Bechuanaland, or anywhere else in Africa for that matter, the expert sent for is Bobby Wilmot of Francistown. Wilmot knows more about crocodiles than anyone else in Africa and makes a business of hunting them for the market. Actually, crocs are becoming scarce in most of the rivers of Africa, chiefly due to the tremendous demand for their belly skins in Europe and America. Crocodile bellies bring about a dollar an inch for shoes and handbags. Even an average-sized croc brings three to five pounds sterling on the open market in London. With this incentive, the African crocodile has become virtually extinct in most of the continent. In the Zambezi, or the Tana, or the Upper Nile, a crocodile basking on a sand bar has become a rare sight.

It was Wilmot who discovered a crocodile concentration in the Okavango swamps of northern Bechuanaland. The Okavango, a river that rises in southern Angola and is nourished by the heavy rainfall there, flows southeastward into the arid lands of Bechuanaland, where it spreads out into a number of channels like the fingers of a gigantic hand. Before the Okavango waters are swallowed by the thirsty sand, they form a swampland roughly a hundred miles square. In the interlacing channels, lagoons, and pools of the Okavango, Wilmot has killed 18,000 crocodiles in the last seven years. The Batawana tribe who cultivate their maize fields on the southern edge of the Okavango are happy to give Bobby Wilmot the crocodile concession in the area and equally happy to see the crocodiles killed. The Batawanas, a peaceful farming people, use the damp earth on the edge of the swamps to nourish their crops and vary their diet with fish from the water. Crocodiles interfere with both of these occupations.

The British built a road from Francistown to the trading post of Maun in northern Bechuanaland. By 1963 Maun has become a civilized place with a bar and a semblance of a hotel, and is the seat of the District Commissioner's office for Ngamiland. The main Batawana village on the Thamalakane channel of the river is also now accessible by a road so that gasoline drums, tin cans, and the other debris of civilization can be brought there. Incidental to these encroachments of progress, most of the crocodiles disappeared from the Thamalakane. Only one huge croc remained in the rocky pool below the village, but the Batawanas have faced the menace of crocodiles for the last five thousand years. Bobby Wilmot, on his last crocodile hunting trips, circled the Thamalakane to the east, driving through the brush with his flat-bottomed aluminum boat on the roof of his Land Rover. He then unloaded the boat and pushed into the innermost Okavango channels, where crocodiles are still plentiful and a fortune of skins is still to be had.

It was natural, then, when Tom Bolack, formerly lieutenant governor and then governor of the state of New Mexico, wanted to get an especially large crocodile for his trophy room, that he come to the Okavango. Governor Bolack, who looks like Ernest Hemingway and has had a rags-to-riches oil career, hired for his white hunter Andrew Holmberg, who also guided Hemingway on safari in Kenya. Holmberg knows Bobby Wilmot and his specialty.

Holmberg, Wilmot, Bolack, and a retinue of safari boys set out from Maun on the first of April 1963 to shoot crocodiles and other swamp game in the Okavango swamps. Three days later they had left their safari car on the last piece of firm ground fifty miles north and east of Maun and had plunged into the swamps with Wilmot's aluminum boat powered by two outboard motors. Some twenty miles westward, in the twisting, papyrus-choked channels, they made camp on a small sand island marked by the tracks and slithering belly trails of several crocs. Bolack wanted to get a trophy-sized crocodile and a sitatunga, and the center of the Okavango certainly seemed the best bet. The sitatunga is an antelope that lives entirely in the water and has elongated hoofs like miniature skis for walking on the matted vegetation of the swamp. Sitatunga are rarely seen by ordinary hunters, and few sportsmen can boast of bagging one.

The hunting was good around the island in the swamp. Sitatunga were common in the reed beds along the channels and crocodiles even commoner. In ten days of intensive hunting, Bolack and Wilmot bagged some fifteen crocs, the largest about nine feet long. One of these had a stomach full of sitatunga hoofs. The crocodile is the deadly enemy of sitatunga, and any other animal that comes to drink or steps into the water. Governor Bolack also shot a fine bull sitatunga. They never found, however, a trophy-sized croc. Crocodiles over fifteen feet in length are rare, even in such a remote area as the Okavango swamps. Crocodiles not only eat every kind of mammal in Africa on occasion but regularly eat each other. The largest Wilmot himself had ever taken was a 16-foot leviathan, one of the largest ever recorded in Africa.

By the time the crocodile hunters had circled the swamps for two weeks, they were ready to leave. For one thing, they might be there a year before finding a really large croc. For another, they'd had several close scrapes with hippo in the swamp channels. As Wilmot does most of his croc hunting at night by shining light into the eyes of the quarry, the hippo are a major hazard. Usually the aluminum boat was close to a submerged hippo before either party was aware of the proximity. A hippo can be a very dangerous animal in a narrow channel.

On one night's hunt, a bull hippo rose out of the water beneath the boat. Feeling the impact, Wilmot turned up both the motors to outrun the hippo, but the frail craft was already lifted clear of the water. The spinning propellers of the outboards chopped away at top speed. Bolack rushed to the bow to try to shoot the hippo in the brain before he killed them all. The hippo's head was beneath the boat. At that moment, the plunging hippo found deeper water and sank beneath them. "A very sticky situation," commented Andrew Holmberg as he clicked the safety back on his .470 double rifle.

But it was not the hippo that caused them to move. It was a message over the safariland radio from District Commissioner Clark requesting Wilmot to return to Maun immediately. "A very large croc has killed a woman in front of Batawana village, and several other crocs have shown up in the fish weirs." Apparently, reasoned Wilmot, river waters rising in faraway Angola had brought a number of crocodiles down the Thamalakane with the flood. A single crocodile already lived in the pool below the village and had killed and eaten several people. Perhaps another man-eater had moved in. The Batawanas urgently requested assistance.

Commissioner Clark suggested that the man-eater was a very large crocodile. At all events, Wilmot was obliged to assist the Batawanas. Governor Bolack was intrigued by the prospect of not only a trophy-sized croc but a dangerous one. When the hunters reached the Batawana village and heard eyewitness accounts of the attacks, it was obvious that the District Commissioner had understated the situation.

Two days previously, three Batawana women had been gathering wild lily bulbs in the shallow water in front of the village. They gossiped and giggled as they bent in the knee-deep water to pull up the bulbs and put them in a wicker basket, which they trailed behind them. Suddenly, a V-shaped wake in the water moved toward them. A yellow eye and an ugly snout appeared between the women. A scaly tail whipped around, cutting one of the women down like a reed before a knife. The jaws under the snout opened and closed across the middle of the woman's body. Her scream was drowned out as the crocodile twisted her under. The other women shrieked and ran splashing to the bank. The crocodile turned and swam toward the deep water, leaving a trail of pink blood behind on the lily pads.

Five days before, another woman had been taken while she gathered lily bulbs. A month previous to that, a woman had gone to the edge of the river to dip up water and was never seen again. A man mending his fish nets just below the village had disappeared from

Man-Eating Crocodile

the upright pole in the water on which he was sitting. A companion working with him saw a splash of yellow water. In the plume of spray the white belly of the crocodile glistened as it twisted over and over to tear and drown the fisherman.

The two women, still wide-eyed with terror, who had been with the last victim described the crocodile as three times longer than themselves and of tremendous size. They said the jaws of the monster were as long as a person, and the teeth bigger than the shaft of a spear.

"I know that bloody croc," said Wilmot, "and they're not exaggerating much. He's no newcomer, either. I shot his mate in the pool below the village two years ago, and that female was a big croc in her own right. He's a sly one, and he's been taking Batawanas, goats, donkeys, cattle, or anything else he can grab a hold of for the last ten years that I know of."

The hunt for the Batawana crocodile was no ordinary hunt. For one thing, the quarry was no ordinary saurian. The crocodile, a direct descendant of the Mesozoic dinosaurs, is poorly organized as to brain matter and actually has several brains down the length of his back. But these several nervous centers in an outstanding crocodile seem to add up to stealth and cunning unmatched by any living thing except perhaps man himself. Wilmot had run into educated crocodiles before, but never one such as this one. At one moment, the Batawana crocodile was bold enough to attack and kill one woman of three in the shallow water in front of the village. When men with guns appeared, he never so much as showed an eye or a snout above the surface of the river. Commissioner Clark himself had tried to shoot the beast. The natives had tried hooks baited with goat meat and wire nooses set in the trails through the lily pads where the croc came out at night. The Batawana crocodile easily avoided all of these ordinary stratagems and stayed in the pool below the village waiting for the next human or goat to step into the water. When Wilmot, Bolack, and Holmberg stood talking to the Batawana villagers, none of them had gone close to the edge of the river since the last woman had been killed, and they were short of water.

The crocodile hunters at first reconnoitered the area by day. Wilmot was amazed to discover twelve or fifteen new crocs in the stretch of river above the village. As he had shot out all of the skins in this area two or three years before, these were obviously newcomers from upriver. The invaders had made a shambles of the nets and weirs of the fishermen. Governor Bolack photographed several crocs as they tore through the nets and swallowed the fish within. They even found a large female crocodile that had boldly made a nest on the riverbank only a mile above the village. She stood her ground over the sandy mound where she had buried her eggs and hissed a warning as the men came close. They shot her as she opened her jaws to attack. Governor Bolack killed ten others of the invading crocodiles, the largest of which was twelve feet.

But these activities were preliminary to the main business of the Batawana man-eater. In a blind the hunters waited two days for the croc to show himself. They purposely had the villagers push a group of goats toward the river to drink at the very edge of the pool where the man-eater lived. There was not so much as a ripple among the lily pads at the river's edge as the goats milled in the water and walked back up the bank.

Two nights also the hunters flashed their battery-powered spot-lights over the pool. Most crocodiles are less wary at night and can be approached in a boat and shot as a flashlight reflects their eyes. But this crocodile had seen humans and flashlights before. No red reflection appeared in the probing beams of the torches as they swept every square foot of the river below the village.

"According to Queen Moremi, this croc feeds every three or four days," mused Wilmot as he talked over the situation with his companions, "and always kills early in the morning. We'll try a trick that worked in the Zambezi once. . . ."

Wilmot's trick was to haul the aluminum boat half a mile above the village well before sunset. He also directed the villagers to go about their business as though nothing had happened. He had the men drive goats down to the river's edge. Under the guns of the hunters, several women dipped up water as they usually did at sundown.

It was after midnight when Wilmot wakened Bolack with a shake on the shoulder. The tent boy brought a cup of strong hot tea. Bolack could see by his watch that it was well after midnight. "Just the two of us," Wilmot whispered. "We don't want any unnecessary noise."

Wilmot cautioned the governor again as they stepped into the boat, not to bang the aluminum side or to cough. The slightest sound or vibration would betray them.

Man-Eating Crocodile

Like a floating log, the boat slipped through the lily pads and into the main river. The gentle current began to pull it downstream. Wilmot held his hand on the governor's shoulder and directed him by the pressure which way to turn. The boat drifted sluggishly in the current. Soon they could see the cane walls and thatched roofs of the Batawana village. There was a smell of smoke in the air from the cooking fires. Still Wilmot did not turn on his spotlight. Neither man moved.

The boat drifted slowly past the village and into the upper end of the big pool. Still Wilmot waited. The boat seemed motionless in the backwater. Judging by the angle of the tree outlines on the bank, they were in the middle of the pool. Wilmot pressed his thumb into the back of the governor's shoulder. Bolack raised his .458 rifle. Wilmot pressed the switch of the spotlight. The bright beam leaped out over the water. The illumination swept in a wide arc. At the far end of the pool the light picked out a red spot as big as a man's fist. The spot glowed like a burning coal.

"There he is!" hissed Wilmot in the governor's ear. Bolack squinted along the sights of his rifle. The distance was well over a hundred yards. At that range the light could not pick out any feature of the crocodile's head. The small brain just behind the croc's eye is a target little bigger than a golf ball.

As the two men hesitated, the glowing coal of the crocodile's eye moved steadily downstream. The drifting boat fell still farther behind.

"He'll be up and over those rocks in another minute," Wilmot whispered in Bolack's ear. "The rocks . . ."

Thrusting the electric torch into Bolack's hands, Wilmot jumped to the stern of the boat and started one of the motors with a vicious jerk of the lanyard. In a few seconds the other motor also roared into life. The boat leaped forward.

"Give me that torch and stand up," Wilmot said. Bolack passed the spotlight back and stood up as the boat spurted forward. Wilmot turned up full power on the throttles. With his other hand he held the torch high. There was a flash of bright red ahead as the croc's eye moved away. The surface of the river was marked by a ripple that deepened as the boat raced toward it. A broad snout appeared in the light. The crocodile was almost to the rocks. The water was shallow here. The croc would have to crawl over the rocks to get into the next pool.

Under the African Sun

The head of the croc rose from the water. Bolack braced his legs on either side of a boat seat. He leveled his rifle for the shot. In that instant the boat ran up on the crocodile's back. Bolack was thrown forward by the impact. The croc whipped his tail against the bow of the boat. Bolack fell heavily on one shoulder. Still holding the gun, he twisted up on one knee. He thrust the rifle barrel over the bow and fired point-blank at the ugly head beneath him. At the shot, the crocodile arched his head and tail. The boat was thrown clear out of the water. Bolack and Wilmot were thrown into the shallow water. The boat fell on its side. Both motors stopped as the propeller shafts jammed on the rocks. Instinctively the crocodile swung his tail like a battering ram. His jaws opened and closed on the gunwale of the boat. Bolack still clutched his rifle. He was half in and half out of the boat. Another blow of that awful tail and the boat would be a twisted piece of metal. Wilmot scrambled to find the spare torch. He snatched it from its clip. The light showed the boat and the crocodile side by side in a foot of water. Bolack bolted another shell into the .458. He held the muzzle where the hind legs of the crocodile came together and pulled the trigger. At the shot, the thrashing tail quivered and stopped. A brain that works the hindquarters of a crocodile lies just at this spot. Wilmot had schooled Bolack well in the way to kill a crocodile.

Next morning, when they had towed the Batawana man-eater up onto the shore with the Land Rover, the crocodile proved to be 17 feet, 6 inches long and weighed over 3,000 pounds. In the crocodile's stomach was the skirt of the woman it had killed five days before. There was a string of beads from another woman, part of a man's shirt, and human bones and teeth from two other people. As the stomach of a crocodile works somewhat like the gizzard of a bird, these things are often retained in the digestive system.

Governor Bolack had not only the most thrilling experience of his long hunting career and a trophy crocodile, but also a letter from the District Commissioner thanking him in the name of the Batawanas for "ridding the area of such a scourge."

Chapter 23

CONFESSIONS OF A MEAT HUNTER
(1968)

"The first upward hook of the bull's horn caught me in the right side just below my ribs. The horn went in deep, and stayed there. The bull shook his head. I held onto his other horn and the back of his neck. Shaking his head and roaring, the bull ran forward. I bent over his head like a broken doll. He lowered his horns to drive me into the ground."

Does this sound like the last thoughts of a famous matador in the bull ring? It could be. Actually the account was given to me by a mild-mannered, slightly built man who engaged for twenty-five years in the business of hunting dangerous animals for meat. Being gored by an African buffalo was one of the hazards of his trade.

José Ruiz was born forty-four years ago in the town of Lourenço Marques in the Portuguese Overseas Province of Mozambique. José's Spanish father was an engineer who loved to hunt. His Portuguese mother was indulgent when José, at the age of ten, first went out with his father. His first hunt was north of Lourenço Marques along the Savé River. Most lads of ten on their first hunt go after rabbits. José and his father shot a Cape buffalo that first time. The Cape buffalo of Africa may weigh two thousand pounds and has a nasty disposition to go with his size. He also carries a lot of meat on his mighty frame. The young José, who could scarcely lift the .375 H&H his father carried, was very much impressed by the fact that his father dried the meat in strips, brought it back to town, and sold it for twenty-five escudos—big money in any man's language.

Under the African Sun

How many young lads of the American frontier were lured by the same combination, the thrill of a dangerous hunt and the promise of big money? Few hunters, attracted by the romance and financial promise of hunting meat and skins, have ever made a fortune. The hide hunters who slaughtered the American buffalo by the millions ended up with peanuts for their hard work. Hunters who furnished meat for the miners of the American West almost wiped out the game of the Rocky Mountain area. Using wagons and a few helpers and loading their own ammunition, these meat hunters camped in the best game country and shot all they could skin and dress in a single day. When a wagon was loaded, it was sent back to town or to a mine. When an area was shot out, they moved on. Mountain-sheep meat brought twenty cents per pound, antelope and elk fifteen cents, and venison ten cents for the better parts. Most of the miners wouldn't eat bear. These American meat hunters came close to killing everything, but they never made much money. By the time they had paid for their horses, wagons, and camp equipment and paid off their bills, most of the professionals ended up broke.

Professional hunters in other parts of the world didn't fare much better. Hunters in South Africa who shot literally millions of head of game never could retire on their profits. Hunters of ivory and rhino horn in East Africa usually finished their careers with malaria, a lot of memories, and not much else. One notable exception was the famous Karamojo Bell, who hunted elephant for their ivory in northern Uganda, Africa. Karamojo Bell made and saved several hundred thousand pounds and went back to England a rich man. But few professional hunters go into the field for money. The financial gain, if there is any at all, is just a way of fitting out for the next hunt.

Young José Ruiz went hunting when he was fourteen years old near his native Lourenço Marques. At that time, buffalo and elephant were common on the outskirts of town. Hippo were still plentiful in the mouth of the Limpopo River. All of these animals carry a lot of meat on their carcasses. By the time he was sixteen, José left school and started his career as a meat hunter. He collected a band of twelve Shangaan tribesmen to help him butcher the carcasses and dry the meat. In a year he made enough money from the biltong (dried meat) to buy a .425 Westley Richards rifle. With this gun José Ruiz could bring down an elephant or a buffalo with a single shot. By the time he was twenty years old, he judged he had killed over a thousand animals and the barrel of the Westley Richards was worn out.

Under similar circumstances and on other continents, where commercial hunting is legal, the game rapidly disappears. So it was in Mozambique. There were a dozen other commercial meat hunters operating out of Lourenço Marques. The plantation owners and rancheros along the coast bought the cheap biltong to feed their ranch hands. The demand for dried meat increased, and the price per kilo inched upward. The animal herds disappeared from the lower Limpopo Valley. No longer could the meat hunters go out from town with a dozen packhorses and bring in a load of biltong. It was necessary by the middle 1940s to buy a truck and go a hundred miles north where the game was still plentiful. To pay for the truck and a larger crew of skinners, more and more biltong had to be bought in. With more equipment, more men, more expense, and bigger operations, it became a vicious circle.

Still, José enjoyed his work. He hunted sixteen years from the Limpopo north to the Savé River. When the buffalo, elephant, and rhino disappeared, the meat hunters killed eland, greater kudu, roan, sable, and even waterbuck. The African waterbuck tastes oily, and the meat is strong. But when mixed with other kinds, it makes a few kilos of biltong. The plantation owners didn't seem to care. They wanted more and more.

Like many a frontiersman with the surge of adventure urging him on, José decided to leave the city and competition behind him. He went to the far north of Mozambique, north of the Zambezi. Here is tsetse fly country, with few villages and thousands of head of game. The grassy savannas along the mouth of the Zambezi breed mosquitoes and malaria. Tsetse flies carry sleeping sickness. There were other diseases and, of course, always the dangerous animals. There, José organized a crew of sixty Marrais tribesmen to serve as skinners and helpers. Five of the most intelligent he taught to shoot and furnished them with rifles. José ferried a truck and a Jeep across the Zambezi and cut some crude roads north of the river into the virgin country along the Tanganyika border. He brought in ammunition by the case, always using solid rounds so as to ruin less meat. It was a big operation. Ruiz hunted the Zambezi valley for the next twenty years. At this time, probably, he was the greatest killer and trader in biltong in all of Africa. How many trophy heads and horns did José and his skinners cut off and throw away? "Hundreds of very big ones," José told me.

Like many of the explorers before him, José soon contracted malaria. Everybody did sooner or later, in spite of new kinds of prophylactics. It is impossible to take the pills regularly when out in the bush. José also got tick fever. With the Marrais, he usually slept on the ground without taking the trouble to pitch a tent. Twice he had close calls with cobras that crawled beneath his blankets to enjoy the warmth of his body. Still, it was a wonderful life—wild and free. He had reached the top of his profession. Ruiz was a good organizer. He paid for his truck and Jeep and was building up a bank account back in Lourenço Marques.

The open grasslands along the Mozambique coast were at that time, in the 1940s, teeming with game. During the dry season, his truck and Jeep could operate in the open savannas. His Marrais huntsmen would locate a herd of buffalo in the open. Driving his Jeep and truck upwind, he could approach the buffalo herd within two or three hundred yards. Even at that distance, the animals did not run. They had never seen a wheeled vehicle before. With luck, José could cut the animals off from the closest cover. Driving his Jeep like a cutting horse, he tried to pick out the leader of the herd, usually an old cow. If he found this one, he slid the Jeep to a stop, swung his rifle across the steering wheel, and shot her through the shoulder. With the leader of the herd down, the rest of the buffalo milled aimlessly. Meanwhile, the riflemen in the truck circled the confused animals and fired at point-blank range. The hunters usually picked bulls and full-grown cows, but in the melee, anything would do. In a good run, they could kill twenty or thirty animals. "Once," José told me proudly, "we laid down seventy-two buffalo. Not a one was more than a few meters from the others. In places they lay in piles. It took us three days to skin the animals and dry the meat. We almost filled our quota from the one herd."

The greatest limitation on a meat hunter was the quota imposed by the government. Each hunter could bring back eight tons of dried meat per month. For this amount he bought a permit. It takes ninety buffalo to produce eight tons of biltong. A typical bag in the early days consisted of thirty buffalo, four elephant, and four hippo. This would produce the required eight tons. Hippo were the best as they carry more meat on their bodies. However, hippo are harder to get as they come to solid ground only at night. Shooting hippo in the water makes for a miserable skinning job. As soon as the blood from the butchered carcass reddens the water around a kill, the crocodiles come. José lost four of his men in the lower Zambezi while they were trying to pull two big hippo into shallow water to butcher the carcasses.

Even with a liberal allowance of eight tons per month, no meat hunter could make money unless he cheated. Local officials usually demanded an additional fee on top of the cost of a commercial hunting permit. This fee represented precisely the profit from eight tons of biltong. Most of the hunters killed an additional four tons a month or often twice as much. The illicit meat was not weighed officially. Bags of illegal biltong were carried into Beira or Lourenço Marques at night and sold secretly. The officials winked at the practice and increased the cost of the bribe.

After a few months of hunting, every animal in the area ran at the mere sight of a truck or Jeep. Heads and horns littered the ground. Vultures were everywhere. Lion and leopard coughed and grunted through the night. Even the big cats ate carrion, entrails, and leavings. Their natural prey was either dead or so scattered and skittish that the carnivores could not catch a victim.

So the meat hunter, José Ruiz, moved on to another place where the game was plentiful and unafraid of man and his machines. Meat hunters seldom look back at the whitened bones they leave behind and the circling vultures and the hyenas. But José did. And what he saw sickened him.

But to bring back twelve or fifteen tons of biltong every month, he needed more men, more rifles, more cases of ammunition, and another truck. The hunters had to go much farther. They made camp along the Tanganyika border. They hunted the Zambezi valley clear to Rhodesia and the shores of Lake Nyasa. The hippo went first. Then the elephant, and afterward the buffalo. Actually, José and his crew shot anything that they could. In a single camp north of the Zambezi, they killed over four hundred sable antelope. Each of these yielded only a few kilos of biltong. Still the killing went on.

Across the border in Rhodesia, officials of that government were carrying on a tsetse fly campaign. The dreaded tsetse fly, which carries human diseases and is death to domestic cattle, must have blood to feed upon. Without the blood of an animal or man, the tsetse fly dies. Therefore, it was argued, if all of the animals were killed off, the tsetse would disappear. Game scouts with rifles supplied by the government killed and killed until their shoulders were sore from the recoil of heavy guns. In Rhodesia alone, this orgy of destruction removed over a million animals between 1940 and 1950. The tragedy is that the tsetse fly campaign was totally unsuccessful. Small animals such as rabbits and rodents are sufficient to nurture the fly. And then there was always human blood.

Tsetse fly must also breed on the branches of trees. Because of this, thousands of acres of acacia trees and brush were cut down in Tanganyika to rid the area of the tsetses. Needless to say, this also was a futile attempt by man to destroy his environment to no good purpose.

José Ruiz and his crew, if they felt any compunction about their own killing, were encouraged by what went on around them. After all, they dried the meat of the animals they shot and trucked it back to the coastal cities, where it provided a protein diet for thousands of undernourished people. The tsetse fly patrols shot game and let it lie to rot.

As the game became scarce and scattered, many of the professional meat hunters gave up. In accessible places, the last remnants of game disappeared. A native chief with a muzzleloading gun or a group of poachers with wire nooses caught the stragglers and sold the hides and meat. Ivory always brought a good price. Most of the tusks were sold illegally to Arab traders who carried them to India. No Hindu wedding is complete without bracelets and necklaces of ivory. Long ago, the source of native Indian ivory disappeared with the vanishing elephant herds there. African ivory made up the difference.

When does a man get tired of killing? Many professional hunters, tsetse fly operators, and officers shooting on "control" have reached this point. José cannot remember quite what it was that changed his thinking from killing to conservation. "Perhaps a man gets a bellyful, as you Americans say," José confided to me with a wry smile. "Or, it may have been the time that my boys killed a whole herd of roan antelope in one place. Every animal there was a female with a baby. But I think it was the buffalo that marked my finish as a meat hunter.

"There were about twenty buffalo in high grass along the edge of the river. The animals had smelled us. I could see several sets of heads and horns. I could not pick out the leader of the herd. Standing up in the Jeep, I could see two animals. I shot them both through the shoulder. They dropped. The grass tops swayed and twitched as the buffalo kicked out their lives and died. I saw another buffalo—a big bull. I shot him behind the shoulder. He bellowed and lunged into the higher grass. There was a splash and rumble of hooves as the rest of the herd galloped off.

"I motioned the truck to come up, and stepped out with my gunbearer. I had already killed something over 8,000 buffalo. Here were three more. A very poor day's bag. I stepped into the edge of the grass. The bull buffalo was waiting. Blood was running out of his nostrils. I turned as he bellowed. Shaking his head, he charged. The Westley Richards spun from my hand. The buffalo's horn went through my side. The hooked tip caught under my ribs. I hung over his head, gasping and fainting with the pain. The bull tried to shake me loose. He galloped forward. If he could throw me on the ground, he would drive the heavy bosses of his horns through my body and mash me like a flopping fish. I clung on desperately. i could hear my gunbearer calling "*Bassop! bassop!*" (Watch out!). Still the buffalo shook his head. Each time he bellowed and moved, his horn sank deeper. My whole body was numb. When I fainted and fell off, he would finish me.

"I heard the two gunshots only dimly, as though they were far away. Simbiri, my gunbearer, had jerked a rifle out of the truck. I felt the buffalo shudder beneath me. Blood poured out of his nostrils and down my leg. With a final bellow he pitched forward.

"That was my last hunt. Soon afterward the government made meat hunting illegal. You ask how many animals I killed in those days? I do not like to remember. I know I shot over 4,000 elephant. I am not proud of that. And the other animals? We killed them all in some places, perhaps 10,000, perhaps more, and they will never come back."

José Ruiz now runs a hunting concession along the Limpopo River. To find game herds, it is now necessary to go far from the sea and well in from the coast. Fortunately, there is plenty of game left. In spots where the meat hunters did not penetrate, the animals are much as they were twenty years ago. Sport hunting does not hurt a herd. The sportsman is usually after an old male carrying a big set of horns. José has helped dozens of visitors find trophy animals. He still carries his rifle, and he shoots occasionally when the danger is great or he needs meat for the pot. He is not afraid of a buffalo or any other animal for that matter. He now gets greater pleasure from seeing a herd of animals than he formerly did in surrounding them and killing them all. The change from destruction to conservation is a mark of maturity. José Ruiz has now learned that the game herds are a heritage not to be squandered. The next generation, and the generation after that, must have a chance to have this heritage and enjoy it.

Chapter 24

BIG AS A RHINO, FAST AS A RABBIT
(1969)

"*Voilà!*" yelled Mamadu, our tracker. A brown body the size of a Brahma bull crashed through the scrubby trees. Limbs and branches splintered and cracked as the monster plowed through the growth in a banking turn, and the black horns jerked to the side. A long tail with a mop of fur at its tip swung high. Then animal and tail disappeared together. In another two seconds, all was silent, except for the buzzing of the eye bees. The path where the brown-bodied giant had fled was marked by churned-up earth and broken trees. A berserk bulldozer with a maniac driver could not have produced more damage or moved as quickly.

"Great blue-eyed blazes!" said Tom Bolack at my elbow. "Did you see that thing go!"

"Well, no, I didn't," I remarked as calmly as I could. I realized that I had gotten my rifle only halfway to my shoulder when the quarry had bolted. I also realized that I had muffed my first chance at the giant eland of Central Africa.

Actually, it wasn't my first chance. I had already botched two weeks of giant eland hunting in the Sudan, prior to this hunt with Tom Bolack in French Equatorial Africa. I felt like the acrobat in the circus who has just missed the flying trapeze for the second time.

I first heard of the giant eland, or Lord Derby eland, from literary sources. On a safari into the Sudan in 1959, I had read carefully the account of hunting there written by Lieutenant Colonel W. Forbes, who was for many years Director of Game and Fisheries in the Sudan. Forbes, one of the old school of British sportsmen who had shot all over the world, described the giant eland as the greatest single prize of Central Africa. Forbes wrote in his account that the giant eland was the third largest land mammal of Africa, yielding rank only to the elephant and the rhino. Furthermore, Forbes stated, the giant eland is the shyest and hardest to see of all antelope.

I was intrigued by the thought of an antelope bigger than the African buffalo. I found an account by a French hunter who had weighed a giant eland and found that the carcass pushed down the scales to the 2,700-pound mark. Frankly, I couldn't believe that an animal of that size could be difficult to see. I remembered remarking to Brownie, that if any African animal is as hard to find as a Pennsylvania white-tailed deer in heavy cover, I would be happy to eat him, horn, hoof, and tail.

In the Sudan, I didn't have to eat a giant eland with his various accouterments—for the simple reason that I didn't get one to eat. I spent two weeks in the western Sudan, with a game scout furnished by the new Sudanese government. This game scout and I followed various giant eland tracks for upwards of 250 miles, as near as I could figure. We walked on tiptoe for about one hundred miles of that distance, and that's a lot of tiptoe. During all of this scientific hunting, I saw the vanishing rump of one giant eland for one second. My snap shot was a clean miss. Years ago, a certain uncomplimentary friend of mine had said that I couldn't hit a bull in the posterior with a particular variety of stringed musical instrument. *That fellow must have been right*, I now thought ruefully, *but it's a shame I had to come all the way to Africa to find out.*

The sting of failure with the giant eland in the Sudan was somewhat mollified by a correspondence that I held with Lieutenant Colonel Peter Molloy, recently Director of the National Parks of Tanganyika and formerly Commissioner of Game in the Sudan. In his six years in the Sudan, Colonel Molloy and his wife had seen giant eland on only three or four occasions. On one of these, they had managed to photograph a bull eland. This picture is the only known photograph in existence of a live giant eland.

Hunters being who they are, if something is impossible to get, they want to get it. A friend of mine, Colonel Askins, had managed to bag two giant eland in French Equatorial Africa, just across the boundary from the eland country in the Sudan. We had already arranged a hunt in French Equatorial Africa with some friends of ours, Tom Bolack and his beautiful wife.

Big as a Rhino, Fast as a Rabbit

After hunting with Jean Bepoix in the northern part of French Africa for oryx and addax, we worked our way south from the desert country into the brushlands near Fort Archambault. Bepoix had told us that while he was hunting elephant he had found one remote area in which he had seen the tracks of a very large number of giant eland, although he had not seen any of the elusive animals themselves. Jean said that the giant eland, or *tandala* (he used the Sangoan word), was "very suspicious." I knew exactly what Jean meant. Suspicious skepticism regarding the human race was an outstanding characteristic of Lord Derby eland, as I could testify at some length.

After a two-day trip through low, rolling quartzite hills covered with scraggly brush, we approached the village of Koundi. At the outskirts of its dozen or so scattered huts, we were greeted by the chief, dressed in a long blue nightgown and a white turban. The chief of Koundi, who called himself Batal, picked out eight "volunteers" from among his villagers to act as our porters and guides. He also furnished us with a game scout who was the only man within 150 miles who owned a gun. The game scout's normal duty was to kill cattle and wild animals affected by rinderpest. He also protected travelers who might be walking through the district. How he accomplished these onerous tasks with the gun he carried is beyond comprehension. His rifle was a 7mm relic with a piece of boxwood for a stock. The barrel was corroded with several years' accumulation of rust and African spiders.

But the game scout did know the country, and that, we soon discovered, was a prime recommendation in that area. There were no streams, washes, or other major landmarks within many miles of Koundi. The low, rolling ridges and the brushlike trees with their glossy green leaves were monotonously alike in all directions. Furthermore, the African sun, here almost on the equator, seemed to jump up into the sky early in the morning, hang at the zenith all day, and then plunge quickly into a twilightless sunset. With the sun acting in this peculiar manner, it was practically impossible to keep track of direction. Most of the time I could not have told within a quarter of the compass where Koundi or our camp might be. However, the game scout and Bepoix's tracker, Mamadu, seemed to carry compasses in their heads, like migrating carrier pigeons.

As we set out southwestward from Koundi on our first morning of the hunt, the country was all the same. The only source of water in that whole area was a small pond near the village, which was filled in the rainy season. A few buffalo and an elephant herd hung around here. In the low, rolling hills several miles away, however, there was no sign of an animal track. The country was lifeless. We walked across fields of grotesque termite hills, each shaped like a toadstool. There were areas of bare earth where the volcanic bedrock came so close to the surface that even the scraggly brush could not grow. But these barren patches were unmarked by the tracks of any animals.

Abruptly, some four or five miles from the village, we came upon the tracks of giant eland. We had crossed some invisible line that I suspected marked a zone close to the village and its activities, a line which the shy eland never crossed. There were the tracks of small herds of females and young bulls. There were the tracks of groups of bulls and lone bulls. Some of the signs were old, some very fresh. We found a place where a single bull had nibbled on some of the leaves of the stunted trees. The broken stalks of the leaves he had dropped still oozed sticky sap, indicating that the giant eland had been chewing there sometime during the night.

Mamadu took to the track like a hound dog after a jack rabbit. He followed the single eland's meandering course as the bull had nibbled leaves from the trees as he passed. I noticed that some of the leaves the eland had bitten off were higher than I could reach with the barrel of my rifle. "Must have walked on stilts," I mused.

Unerringly, Mamadu led us mile after mile across the tracks of other eland, some fresh and some old. Finally, the trail seemed to straighten out for a few hundred yards. Then we jumped him. He got away like a rabbit stepped on by an Airedale. There was a rush of sound and the pounding of heavy hoofs. We saw several trees jerk violently sideways. That was all. The wind was right. We had been moving like shadows over the hard ground. If we couldn't see the eland, how could he see us? "Radar!" I remarked to Tom Bolack. "These animals use radar."

Tom did not smile. Wiping the sweat out of his eyes with his loose sleeve, he signaled up the porters and took a long drink of tepid water from the cloth-covered bottle. I noticed that Tom's shirt was drenched with sweat. His pants hung at half-mast. The temperature at that time must have been well over 100 degrees.

At my insistence, Bepoix told Mamadu to get on the track of the fleeing eland again. I had been through this before. We told the gunbearers and porters to stay well behind and trail us at a distance. With our rifles ready, we crouched behind Mamadu and walked ahead.

Big as a Rhino, Fast as a Rabbit

As we moved forward, we could see where the bull had been lying beneath a small tree. His hoofs had dug deep into the gravelly ground as he jumped from his bed, and he had snapped off a tree as thick as my leg as he ran. After three or four hundred yards, the bull had slowed to a walk. About a mile farther on, he had stopped once, turned, and looked back along his track.

We stopped at this place, too, and tried to wipe the eye bees away from our faces. These contemptible little insects are undoubtedly the most irritating forms of life in all of Africa. The fact that they do not sting is beside the point. Some thousands of them were constantly crawling into our eyes to get the moisture, so our vision was continually blurred by the dancing dots of eye bees.

It was Mamadu who first sighted the bull. Late in the afternoon, Tom and I had relaxed our vigilance in spite of ourselves. The bull eland had gone on and on. The eye bees had buzzed on and on. Suddenly Mamadu crouched and pointed. A brownish body with white stripes materialized out of the green foliage. A long tail with a knot of hairs at its tip whipped high. A tree snapped off. I raised my rifle blindly and fired. Tom also shot at the same instant, leveling his gun and pulling his trigger like a shotgunner swinging at a flushing pheasant. I saw a bright splinter of wood jump into the air where Tom's bullet hit. Two black, twisted horns galloped off through the trees and were gone before I could crank in another shell.

"*Touché?*" asked Bepoix behind us. Tom and I shook our heads together and sagged down onto the ground. We called up the porters with the water. They indicated that the water was gone by turning the bottles upside down. "Maybe I can wring out my shirt and drink that," I remarked to Tom. Bolack just glared at me as we turned toward camp, eight or ten miles away.

Back at our camp near Koundi, we revived ourselves with what hunters usually revive themselves with when they come dragging back from a disastrous hunt. The next morning, in the comparative cool of the dawn, we were out in the giant eland country again, with the game scout and Mamadu.

As we crossed the mysterious line marking the edge of the giant eland country, the game scout remarked that only the month before he had discovered a giant eland that had died from rinderpest. The highly infectious rinderpest, scourge of all hoofed animals, would wipe out all the giant eland in this whole area within a year. The

225

game scout said he would take us to the dead carcass, as the animal had been a big bull.

Tom and I thought it would be nice to actually lay our hands on a giant eland, even if the thing had been dead for six months. But we never got there.

On the way to the deceased animal, we crossed a set of tracks, a very fresh set. Mamadu mumbled in Sangoan that the tracks of this eland were so fresh that the animal had been standing in them only seconds before. A limb the eland had ripped off still dripped sap from its broken end.

Again, Tom and I crouched on either side of Mamadu with our guns ready. Mamadu kept his eyes on the fresh tracks where the eland had been feeding among the trees. We inched forward slowly, like a bunch of marines about to flush a sniper. I tripped over one of the toadstool anthills. There was a movement ahead. A massive neck with a swinging dewlap beneath swung around. I could see white stripes, a white-marked face. I swung the Weatherby to my shoulder and fired blindly. The eland bellowed like a Brahma bull raked with a spur. He ran in a hacking gallop diagonally on my side. I cranked in another shell. I could see the great body flashing between the trees. I pulled just ahead of the chest and touched it off. I heard the *plunk* of the bullet. The bull bellowed and went down, sliding on his chin. We had our first eland.

My bull turned out to be a comparatively young one with wide-spreading horns measuring 43⅞ inches long, which is second or third in the record book. But no matter what the length of his horns, a giant eland is a giant in fact. For pure bulk he seems more impressive lying on the ground than a dead rhino.

Our bagging of the first giant eland had broken the spell. In the next ten days, Tom managed to get two very large old bulls to fill out his license, and I got another one, also a young bull. With all of these we found that we had to jump them and then trail them again, two, three, or four times. The shooting is about the sportiest I have ever experienced. If you want to try something as big as a rhino and fast as a rabbit, try the Lord Derby eland in Central Africa.

Chapter 25

ANTELOPE THAT
WALK ON WATER
(1969)

There is an antelope in Africa that never comes to dry land during its whole lifetime. With its long ski-like hoofs and streamlined body, this animal is built for water. Papyrus swamplands are its home. With its peculiar feet, it can walk on water with only a few reed stems and lotus pads for support. The natives call it "the swamp ghost." Some who have been to mission school call it "the animal of Christ" because the Savior also walked on water. Few sportsmen have ever seen one. Even fewer have ever bagged a specimen. This animal is the sitatunga.

In the course of animal development, certain species have adopted strange habits and habitats to escape their enemies. The sitatunga is one. Several thousand years ago it was a brush-dwelling antelope like its relative the bushbuck. Some archaeologists believe that a great many animals became extinct and a number of others radically changed their habits because of man. Even with only crude throwing spears, early human hunters became killers more deadly than the lion or leopard. Ancient man was no conservationist. He killed when he could. By the end of the Ice Age, about thirty-five major kinds of animals were extinct. Change in climate does not sufficiently explain this great die-off. About this time the sitatunga fled into the great swamps and has lived in the water ever since.

Although the water-dwelling sitatunga is found from the Sudan to South Africa, and from east Africa west to the Congo, the antelope that walks on water is almost unknown even today. Only the most

Under the African Sun

adventuresome modern sportsmen have tried for sitatunga. A few have succeeded. But even with modern boats, modern rifles, and lots of know-how, bagging the antelope is no cinch. For one thing, the wily sitatunga does not always walk on the surface of the swamp vegetation. He can slide into the water as silently as an otter and swim completely submerged with only his nostrils above the surface. Usually he simply hides in the reeds and keeps out of the way of humans with spears and guns. In the big swamps of Africa, this is easy.

Practically speaking, the sitatunga's only major enemy is the crocodile. As far as hunters are concerned, most other animals are a lot easier to get.

My first experience with the sitatunga was in western Tanzania in the Luangwa swamps. Andrew Holmberg, the famous white hunter, had suggested that we try for a sitatunga. At that time, I had scarcely heard of the animal. I had never talked to a sportsman who had ever seen one. Andrew knew some Bantu natives on the edge of the Luangwa swamps who lived by fishing and hunting. Occasionally the mysterious sitatunga became entangled in their fishnets and they managed to spear one. When we came to the Bantu village, the natives showed me the head and horns of a large male sitatunga. Immediately I got sitatunga fever. I still have it.

Our experiences in the Luangwa swamps are now a matter of history. The fly-buzzing Bantu village, the smell of fish, the clouds of man-devouring mosquitoes are all forgotten. I even remember with nostalgia the Luangwa natives' ridiculous palm-log dugout canoes. These treacherous boats capsized if you hiccuped. If you fired a gun from one, the recoil was disastrous. Since the swamp water is filled with crocodiles, hippo, and many tiny organisms that are even more deadly, the pursuit of sitatunga takes on the sinister aspect of hunting dangerous game. By some blind stroke of hunter's luck, we did get a sitatunga on the Luangwa trip. We rounded a papyrus-studded hippopotamus channel at just the right instant. Three sitatunga were walking on the water. One was a young male. I bagged him, and the dugout did not capsize—a miracle in itself. I have been hunting sitatunga ever since.

In the Congo jungles I made an extended trip with a group of Pygmies. These little fellows are the most astute and successful hunters I have ever encountered. Using their noses like a hunting hound, they can scent the body odor of a hidden animal at fifty yards, then stalk within ten yards to get one of their tiny poisoned arrows into the quarry. While I was hunting with four Babinga Pygmies south of the Uban River, my diminutive guides told me of a mystical animal they called the "Ghost

228

Antelope that Walk on Water

of the Forest." It was not an okapi or a bongo but a rare type of forest sitatunga—the only specimen of its kind. The Congo sitatunga lives only in the impossible marshy morasses of that deadly area.

A sitatunga project sounds impossible. Actually, it is not, although certainly any expedition after this remarkable animal is a major effort. Not long ago, I saw perhaps one hundred sitatunga in their natural habitat—more than I have glimpsed in half a lifetime of previous efforts. This miracle came about by reason of a tribe called the River Bushmen and a remarkable explorer named Ian Henderson.

Most of the modern Bushmen who have survived the last several thousand years of African adversity live in the Kalahari Desert of South Africa—obviously no place to look for a sitatunga. The Bushmen, like their cousins the Pygmies, are hunters. Formerly, they occupied all the dry parts of Africa from the Sahara southward. They are now confined to the inhospitable wastes of the Kalahari, where they track down the few desert animals that can survive in this almost waterless region. In the northern part of the Kalahari, the Okavango River flows out of Angola and spreads out into a series of channels that form a vast swampland. All this water finally sinks into the Kalahari sand and disappears. For generations the Bushmen hunters have moved north along the edge of the Okavango swamps to hunt the animals that gather there. When I first visited the Okavango several years ago, the River Bushmen told me of the antelope that walks on water. I knew what they meant.

Ian Henderson worked out the system. He got the idea from a crocodile hunter, Bobby Wilmot, who had penetrated the Okavango with a special aluminum boat from which he shot crocodiles for their skins. Ian Henderson improved the boat idea. I think he was searching for adventure. He certainly was little interested in crocodiles.

Ian is a pioneer; he believes that impenetrable places should be penetrated. He decided to get a look at the middle of the Okavango and, if possible, go clear to the far side. We went with him. In the process we passed through the heartland of the animal of Christ.

Bobby Wilmot said the main Okavango Swamp was full of sitatunga. It was. But it took Ian Henderson four years to get to the place.

Working out from Livingstone Falls, two other hunters, Andrew Holmberg and Eric Rundgren, with a bunch of River Bushmen, cut out a track. This they improved to the status of a rutted road over which a lorry could bring gasoline, tools, and other equipment. Working along the Chobe Channel of the Okavango system, they hacked out the road as far as the mouth of the Savuti Stream, which flows from the Chobe. The country is a game paradise. Thousands of zebra, wildebeest, and buffalo feed on the grass plains along the Chobe. Lion, leopard, and elephant are common. Sable, kudu, and roan come down to the Chobe in herds. This corner of Africa resembles the Dark Continent in the days of Stanley and Livingstone.

Ian Henderson, with a single hunter, Dan Maddox of Nashville, Tennessee, made an exploratory trip in a native dugout canoe into the Okavango. Dragging the canoe over masses of matted papyrus, Ian and Dan penetrated some ten miles into the main Okavango. They bagged an enormous sitatunga and saw several others.

In 1962, sleeping sickness broke out in the area and killed most of the native population of the Bushman village on the Chobe. It also killed two professional hunters and four clients. The Chobe country and the project to enter the heart of the Okavango Swamp was abandoned.

Ian Henderson was delayed but not defeated. After two years, the sleeping sickness had run its course. Since the disease has a human carrier, Henderson stayed away from the village on the Chobe that seemed to be the center of the epidemic. He cut another track farther south and brought in another group of natives from the Kalahari. These desert Bushmen had never lived in tsetse-fly country, and so could not be infected. Ian built a camp at the mouth of the Savuti. Here, where the Savuti and Chobe come together, the visitor can see the waving tops of the fringed papyrus plants stretching away to the north and west as far as the eye can see. Only an occasional palm, standing above the papyruses, breaks the skyline of the seemingly endless swampland. Ian was determined to get into the place.

The main Chobe channel flows swift and clear. The water is so pure that a man can drink it. It is full of bream and pike. Using spinning tackle to catch some eating fish, we might have been on the shore of some Minnesota lake except for the hippo booming in the distance and the lion grunting and roaring around the edge of the swamp.

Two miles above Henderson's camp, the Chobe channel is closed by an impenetrable mass of interlaced papyrus stems. Beyond this, the Bushmen assured us, is endless swamp with only an occasional pool kept open by the hippo, or a narrow channel where the larger crocodiles move. The main Okavango River loses itself in this vast lake basin choked with swampy growth. After the water spreads out through this morass, it re-forms on the far side in channels such as the Chobe and the Savuti. Ian Henderson set his crew of Bushmen to cutting a boat channel into the heart of the Okavango basin.

Dynamite proved ineffective. Then Ian perfected a series of special implements—long, two-handed iron hooks with cutting edges, and a special long-handled, narrow-bladed spade with a sharpened edge. One of the major hazards is the swamp vegetation itself. If a man walks on it, he sinks to his waist. If a worker stands in one place, the treacherous and spongy vegetation will suck him under. The workmen suffered several close calls—often grasping one of their fellows just as his head was disappearing. The Bushmen moved with quick and springy steps over the undulating surface. They cut masses of papyrus stalks and used them as platforms on which to work. With the new cutting tools, they gradually hacked a narrow channel into the heart of the swamp.

Ian thought a passable channel could be cut in three months. It took almost a year. He sent back for more supplies and more workmen. They established a camp on a small island in the middle of the swamp. When the treacherous swamp surface was too soft to support the weight of a man, they worked from a boat. Gradually by using such open waters as they could find, they worked the boatway some twenty miles above the Chobe camp in a serpentine course that extended northwestward toward the Caprivi strip. As the movement of the water quickened through the newly made channel, even this proved a hazard. The current pulled away whole chunks of floating papyrus roots. These lodged in narrow places and quickly piled up into a jam, which took many hours to cut away.

Ian worked out two additional ideas to see the Okavango. One was a special kind of boat. Two aluminum pontoons support a platform. An outboard motor goes on behind. On the platform he built a metal tower some fifteen feet high. Four men can sit on top of this tower. It is much like the rig that some ocean fishermen use to spot tuna and sailfish. From the tower on "Ian's Folly," as we called it, a hunter can see over the top of the papyrus.

The swamp-dwelling sitatunga can slip through the papyrus like mice through a wheat field. We caught occasional glimpses of the animals in the trails and passages that wound through the papyrus. Occasionally one would bolt and swim across the open channel. But it was the lucky hunter who got a shot at one in this uncertain fashion.

Henderson tried another trick. The River Bushmen occasionally hunt sitatunga with nets and spears. If the conditions are just right after a dry season, the papyrus will burn. After the fire, the papyrus grows up again from the blackened mass in a number of tender green buds. The sitatunga nibble at these with enthusiasm. In the burned-over areas, sitatunga are out in the open.

On the first day, Ian moved his twin-pontoon monster into a large hippo lake some fifteen miles above our camp. Brownie rode on the lower deck like a tourist. Disaster almost struck twice when we bumped into sleeping hippo. Once, an enraged bull attacked the boat.

In four selected places, we sent our Bushmen back into the papyrus to start fires. The results were frightening. As we went back to camp, the evening sky was streaked by tongues of flame with black billows of oily smoke above. Ibis, spurwinged geese, and other water birds circled terrified above the heat column that carried the feathery tufts of blackened papyrus a thousand feet into the evening sky. I was afraid our burning had destroyed the whole life of the Okavango Swamp.

An African sunrise was painting the feathery tops of the papyrus pink and orange as we prepared Ian's Folly for the trip up the mysterious Chobe Channel. Hadada ibis screamed at us as we started the motor. A flight of pygmy geese flushed from among the lotus pads as we rounded the first bend. The noise of the motor in the morning stillness seemed to anger every hippo in the whole swamp. They boomed, coughed, and complained.

Up the channel we could see the black bands where our fires had cut swaths of crumpled and burned papyrus stems. But the burning had done remarkably little damage. Only narrow strips of burned swamp vegetation showed where tongues of flame had been driven before the wind. Down these open cuts we could see animals moving in the distance. At my back, on the boat platform, stood a keen-eyed Bushman. These hunters have eyesight as good as 8X binoculars. Pointing down one of the fire swaths, he said, "*Chunga.*"

I could see a group of reddish-colored animals. Water spurted up from their hoofs as they ran across the burned area. "Red lechwe," Ian said at my elbow. "Look at that bull in the lead." He had a magnificent spread of horns. I had seen lechwe before but never one like this. I raised the .300 magnum. Ian touched my elbow. "Wait for the sitatunga."

We saw sitatunga, too. First, a female and a baby. Sitatunga walk with a hump in their backs like bushbuck. The white spots on the face give the animal the appearance of a small deer with cosmetics put on for a play. The female and her baby looked around at us with a serious but not frightened expression. Apparently, the sitatunga felt so secure in their swampland that even the fire-cleared areas did not frighten them.

As our curious craft rounded the corner of the twisting channel, we saw more. A young bull stood and watched us pass within one hundred yards. In the next fire-blackened clearing we saw four bulls together. They ran along the top of the water, then stopped and turned their heads together. Ian pressed my shoulder and shook his head. "Not big enough."

The Bushman behind me was muttering something in the curious "click" language of his race. Apparently a sitatunga was a sitatunga as far as he was concerned, and here were four.

A huge crocodile rolled off a mass of floating vegetation and disappeared in the murky water. Just ahead, our fire had burned away the vegetation across a whole bend of the Chobe. In the middle of the opening stood a magnificent sitatunga bull. He raised his head from feeding, then ran across the water for a few steps and stopped. Ian ran our floats into the edge of the papyrus at the bend of the channel. I steadied the rifle against the framework and pressed off the shot. A spurt of water flew up beneath the belly of the bull. He exploded into action and skimmed over the burned papyrus with the speed of a water skier. I swung the rifle for a second shot, but he was gone. I hung over the edge of the framework in front of me. I still had a vision of the long, lyrate horns of the sitatunga bull. Ian patted my shoulder sympathetically. He started the motor. I thought I'd never get a chance like that again.

But I did, and it wasn't fifteen minutes later. The Bushman grabbed my shoulder and pointed behind us. A sitatunga bull was lying in a small opening where a hippo had mashed down the papyrus. At the sound of our outboard, the bull jumped up and faced us. The water glistened on his long brown horns. Ian turned the boat crazily. The sitatunga bull was not fifty yards away. Desperately I tried to swing the rifle. The bull whirled on his long hoofs. As he bounced into the papyrus, I fired. It was a clean miss.

Ian tried to console me. "With the swing on top of this platform and the motion of the boat, any shot will be difficult."

"I am probably the only man in all Africa who ever missed a sitatunga bull at fifty yards," I remarked sourly. "I don't deserve another chance."

Under the African Sun

Whether I deserved it or not, I got it. We saw, in all this time, perhaps a hundred sitatungas. We made three long trips up the Chobe Channel cleared by the Bushmen. Ian wanted to establish a camp up the river on a dry-land peninsula. From this base we could hunt and explore even farther into the Okavango swamps. But we didn't see another big sitatunga bull with out-turned horns until our last trip down the channel. Most of the sitatunga had abandoned our burned-out passage. We did see a few females and young ones. Perhaps the old bulls had deduced that these open areas were dangerous. We never saw either of the big bulls I had missed.

On our last day, we were chugging down the channel, bringing our camp gear back to end the safari. Other hunters would come after me and shoot the big sitatunga. The Bushman touched me on the shoulder and pointed. A female sitatunga was running along on top of the water. She skirted the edge of the burned area where I had missed the big bull. The Bushman punched my shoulder until I winced. Then I saw it. A long pair of horns was moving through the papyrus along the edge of the clearing. The bull sitatunga was following the female. I saw the sun glint on the ivory tips of his horns. But he kept out of sight. The female skimmed over the water in a shuffling motion. Just ahead was a narrow opening where a gust of wind had blown a tongue of flame through the swamp. I stood up and swung the rifle. A brown body flashed across the narrow opening. Swaying with the motion of the boat, I swung the telescopic sight just ahead of his nose. As he dived into the wall of papyrus, I pressed off the shot. A spurt of dirty water flew up above the reeds.

The Bushman was out of the boat before we reached the edge of the channel. Swinging his legs wide, he ran over the top of the undulating swamp almost like the sitatunga ahead of him. He yelled back. Ian shouted, "He says the big bull is dead!" Ian banged me on the back.

The sitatunga is a magnificent and impossible animal. Every sportsman should have a chance to see the antelope that "walks on water."

Chapter 26

LONGONOT LEOPARD
(1970)

The hiss of steam jets sounded like the threats of angry dragons advancing along both sides of the canyon. Fumaroles and geysers blended noise and odor with the bizarre volcanic afterbirth that bubbled and belched around us. Even the colors of the rocky cliffs were psychedelic. This was a place of mystery and terror. The dying molten forces that underlie this part of Kenya were gasping to escape from every crack and crevice in the awesome valley.

And suddenly, there he was. The scenery around us belonged to some geological era millions of years in the past, but nothing was prehistoric about that leopard. He was glaring at us from behind a sulphur-streaked rock. A steam jet puffed a white plume close above his head, but he paid no heed. Apparently the monarch cat had been drinking at a small puddle where condensing steam ran down the surface of the rock. The head of the leopard was as large as a lioness's, and his shoulders were as massive. His spotted face turned, and he disappeared. "That was the leopard of Longonot," said Rooken-Smith at my elbow. "He's been here ever since I came to the ranch. Few people have ever seen him, but I've seen him twice before, and he's made a fool of me a dozen times," he added ruefully.

Rooken-Smith is the manager of the vast Akira Ranch in central Kenya. The ranch occupies most of the great Longonot volcano, which was active during the Ice Age. The Valley of Evil Spirits, as the Masais call it, is a multicolored fissure down the side of Longonot Mountain. Steam jets, geysers, fumaroles, and hot mud springs indicate that the volcanic fires are still very hot

Under the African Sun

and close to the surface. All of this country is dry, as the volcanic ash absorbs surface water. In a search for water, a hole was driven into the floor of the Valley of Evil Spirits. The result was a gushing jet of steam, but the Akira managers turned this volcanic offering to their advantage. They rigged a series of large pipes to condense the steam and drain it into a trough where domestic cattle can water. Natives from the adjoining Masai Reserve were given permission to bring their cattle in to the stream trough. They do so, but will go no farther into the Valley of Evil Spirits.

Everyone seemed to know about the great leopard. Each morning his tracks were on the floor of the canyon, and quite often he came as far as the cattle trough. He did not have to drink there as he had a number of private puddles back in the canyon where sulphurous water collected in rocky pockets. But a leopard of his size needs a lot of meat, and on several occasions he killed Masai cattle or the big cows that belong to the Akira Ranch. Ordinarily a leopard will not attack so large an animal, but the Longonot leopard often killed a full-grown cow with ease and ate the whole belly and hindquarters at once. Furthermore, he never seemed to come back to a kill a second time. Long ago he had apparently learned that if he returned to a kill, he might be shot or speared.

The Masais have a village or *manyatta* not far from the mouth of the Valley of Evil Spirits. The old Masai chief said that since he was a boy the great leopard had lived in the canyon. I doubt if the Longonot leopard could have been there that long, but no one seemed to remember just when he'd come. We were told stories of the many times that the Masais had tried to kill him.

Often a Masai *moran* or warrior will spear a lion or a leopard to prove his manhood so he is eligible for his first wife, but it is his duty to kill a cat if it is bothering the Masai stock. The Longonot leopard several times made kills within sight of the *boma* or thornbush enclosure where the Masais protect their cattle at night. Once, the great leopard jumped the *boma* fence and killed a cow with a single bite through the back of the neck. He did not get to feed on the kill as the *morans* came swarming out of their dung-covered huts, brandishing long-bladed spears and flaming pieces of wood.

Foreign hunters did equally badly with the Longonot leopard. Ordinarily a leopard can be attracted to a bait. A Grant gazelle or a

236

Longonot Leopard

zebra is dragged with the stomach contents spilling out to leave plenty of scent. Leopard do not have a keenly developed sense of smell, but their eyesight is phenomenal. The bait must be hung in a tree in just the right manner. If hung too low, a lion or a hyena will jerk it down. The bait should be hung so that the leopard can climb a large limb, reach down, and pull up the bait to feed. The bait tree is chosen with great care, so that when the leopard is feeding, he will be outlined against the sky. Usually the leopard comes just at dusk, or after dark. A very careful leopard hunter will rub dung on the tree limb so that the cat will detect not even a faint whiff of human scent. The bait and the rope suspending it are covered with vines and branches so that everything looks natural.

Once the bait is hung, the blind is built with a roof as well as a back. If any light shines through, the leopard will detect the movement of the man inside. A path or approach leading to the back of the blind is cleared of every leaf and twig so that two men crouching low can slip into the blind just before sunset and not be seen or heard by a leopard lying near the bait.

This particular leopard had apparently read all of the books written on leopard hunting. He didn't do anything he was supposed to do. In addition to the efforts of Rooken-Smith and the Masais, nine safaris had come to the Akira Ranch specifically to bag the Longonot leopard. Only two hunters ever saw the leopard. One veteran who had a dozen lesser leopard to his credit got a shot. It was twilight and the leopard was moving. The shot went wide of the mark. If anything, the Longonot leopard grew wiser and wilder.

"That leopard is as big as a lioness," Bob Reitnauer had said. "I've never seen him, but I've seen his tracks. He has a foot the size of your hand." Several other professional hunters added stories of the huge leopard.

The first night at Akira, we pitched camp under a wild fig tree at the foot of a small lava escarpment a couple of miles from the Valley of Evil Spirits. That same night, two of the lion that we were seeking fell into camp. Apparently they were coming down a game trail over the rocks in the darkness when they suddenly saw humans and fires that were not there before. In attempting to scramble back up the cliff, two of the lions actually fell end over end into the middle of our camp. It was all very exciting.

Under the African Sun

It goes without saying that I was determined to get the Longonot leopard. Both Reitnauer, our professional hunter, and Rooken-Smith spent an entire evening trying to talk me out of it.

"The leopard fever gets them all," said Rooken-Smith as he put down his beer mug and rose to his feet. "You were lucky to get a glimpse of that leopard. And that's all you'll ever get."

We knew that the Longonot leopard had been baited by experts. We also learned that he spurned the bushbuck and reedbuck that lived in his canyon. He came out every night to hunt and prowl. The Masai chief told us that the great leopard had at least twice killed adult zebra and once an eland. In the acacia-dotted flats from the base of Longonot to Narok is a wide variety of plains game. There are Grant and Thomson gazelle by the thousand. Impala are still numerous. Normally these smaller antelope are the food of leopard, but this was no ordinary leopard. By choice he killed cattle. He did not care whether the cattle belonged to the Masai or to the Akira Ranch.

There is a Masai proverb, "Fools do not have the wisdom to stay away." Nonetheless, Bob Reitnauer and I circled on the flats to shoot a zebra. This took some hunting, as Rooken-Smith shoots every zebra he can find on the ranch. Zebra, like all horses, have to drink, and here the precious water must be saved for the cattle. I made a lucky running shot at extreme range. We carried the zebra, an old battle-scarred stallion, up into the Valley of Evil Spirits. Rooken-Smith had pointed out three or four trees where baits had been hung before. We spurned these as beneath the intelligence of the leopard. Instead, we hung the zebra in a brushy little gully near the mouth of the valley. We built a blind on top of a mound of volcanic ash so that we could approach it from behind. From this elevation, we could look over the top of the bushes without disturbing anything.

The next morning, we cautiously crawled into our hiding place. The zebra had been hoisted higher in the tree. The belly and both hind legs had been eaten. Strings of skin and ligaments still dripped red. The leopard must have eaten one hundred pounds of meat. What an animal! As there were no vultures in the trees, and no jackals or hyenas to scavenge tidbits on the ground, we knew that the leopard was lying nearby to protect his kill. Silently we withdrew, crawling on our hands and knees in spite of scratches from

Longonot Leopard

the volcanic cinders. When we got into the next gulley, Reitnauer and I hugged each other. What luck! The wily old leopard had taken our bait the very first night.

Early in the afternoon, when the sun was hot and the birds quiet, we crawled again into the blind. Reitnauer carried a double-barreled shotgun loaded with buckshot. I placed my .300 magnum across the two poles I had carefully prepared as a gun rest. Through the small hole in the grass and leaves of the blind I could look through the telescope sight. I adjusted the barrel so that it pointed just above the branch where the leopard would lie to feed. The wise old leopard would come just at dark. Any movement would alarm him. I would have to move the rifle only a little and squeeze the trigger.

I looked through the sight again. It was all yellow, and the yellow was marked with black rosettes! Automatically I shifted the cross hairs of the scope to the shoulder. Wait! This was the middle of the afternoon. I punched Reitnauer's leg. He was busy killing ants that might disturb us later on. Across the flat I could see a herd of Masai cattle coming to water. The Masais with their long-bladed spears were urging the cattle along. I could hear the shouts of the men. Bob and I stared in amazement through our peephole. There was the leopard in the tree. It was *a* leopard, but not *the* leopard.

As furtively as the first, a second leopard appeared. This was a male, but of no great size. He looked around carefully, then quickly scaled the tree. He took a position above the female, lounging along a limb as though on lookout duty.

Three more leopard appeared in quick succession. These were young but almost full-grown animals. They quickly climbed into the tree and began to feed. The afternoon sun glinted on their beautiful spotted coats. Their muzzles were wet and red. Occasionally they snarled and fought with each other on the crowded tree limb. Reitnauer was mumbling something under his breath. I knew what he was thinking. Leopard never feed in the middle of the day. A male leopard never stays with the female when she has kittens. Apparently these leopard had not heard the rules. We watched in fascination for over an hour. Five leopard in one tree! I moved cautiously to the side of the blind. I took a single picture of the male leopard on his observation post as the rest of his family jumped down and faded into the brush.

239

Under the African Sun

For three weeks we sought the Longonot leopard. During that time he killed a half-grown Masai cow and a burro. During this same period we offered him two delectable Grant gazelle and a wonderful stinking warthog in just the right state of putrefaction. If we placed these tidbits in the Valley of Evil Spirits, nothing touched them. If we hung the baits in any of the side canyons around the shoulder of Longonot, other leopard helped themselves. We saw two other leopard and two families of cheetah, but not the old man of Longonot.

Every morning, as we surveyed the situation, we saw his tracks, and we never failed to marvel at their size. Every night the big leopard made excursions out of the gorge into the surrounding terrain. We always found his spoor in the damp cattle trails around a steam vent. Every morning he returned to the canyon. There was no doubt that he laired there.

"If we could just find some pattern in his habits, so that we could get ahead of him instead of behind him," Bob said for the dozenth time, "He won't take a bait . . ."

"Wait a minute! I've got an idea. We caught a wise old leopard like this once before. He ignored everything else, but he fell for an ostrich."

It didn't seem like a very good idea to me, but at least it was a plan. There wasn't an ostrich within ten miles of the Valley of Evil Spirits. We circled out on the flats until we found an old male with dirty plumes.

"I hope he won't taste as tough as he looks," Bob commented as I made the shot.

We saved the feathers, skinned the carcass, and carried it back to the volcanic valley. Now, if we could just think like a leopard, or best of all think a little better than this leopard, we might have a chance.

After discarding a dozen schemes, we decided to be subtle. We did not drag the ostrich, or even attempt to make it easy to find. We made it hard to find. We carried the carcass through the brush at one side of the valley and placed it in the fork of a tree that grew in a gnarled mass out of a crack in the red rock. We covered the ostrich with branches to keep off the vultures, then wiped our tracks clear with ostrich fat. We even pushed back the bushes and tree limbs as though we were attempting to hide the greasy old ostrich.

Two hundred yards away, we built a small blind beneath a ledge of the cliff. We were not the first to use this shadowed little cave. There was part of an ancient stone wall, and on the rock of the

Longonot Leopard

overhang, done in red and black, were pictographs of ancient men hunting ancient animals.

Through a crack in the rocks, we could barely see the tree where the ostrich was concealed. In dim light it would be impossible. Nevertheless, we carefully scraped a tunnel along the face of the cliff so that we could crawl unseen into the house of the ancient hunters.

The next morning we looked as usual for the tracks of the Longonot leopard. They were not there. We crawled along our tunnel into the cave beneath the cliff. We saw immediately that the branches over the ostrich carcass had been batted away. With binoculars we could tell that thirty or forty pounds of meat were gouged out of the belly of the bird. Bob pounded me silently on the shoulder. The wily old leopard thought we were trying to hide the meat, so he decided to help himself.

That afternoon we were in the stone-walled cave by four o'clock. We moved every twig and leaf that might make a noise. Silently we waited the long hours until sunset. The cliffs of many colors fell into shadow. Only the steam jets hissed in the twilight. When I tried the sight on my rifle, I was dismayed to see that the canyon shadows were so dark and deceiving that I could not see the leopard if he were there. We waited till midnight, and then crawled back down the tunnel and walked the mile or so to the cattle troughs where we had left the car.

"If he feeds only at night, we are finished," Reitnauer remarked. That is exactly what the Longonot leopard did. The next morning, when we crawled into the house of the ancient hunters, we could see that another piece of meat as big as a washtub had been gouged out of the ostrich. Vultures sat high on the red cliffs above, but none were close. This meant the wily old leopard was lying somewhere among the rocks guarding his banquet. He probably was watching us contemptuously at that very moment.

I motioned Bob forward. He shrugged his shoulders and followed. It is folly to walk up to a leopard bait. Ordinarily the leopard will see you, disappear, and never return. But this old veteran didn't play by the rules, and neither would we. We walked up to the bait tree. We saw the claw marks on the bark where the leopard had jumped up. The scratches on the tree trunk were as widely spaced as I could spread my hands. At one side was a little rocky basin. From a clump of moss and ferns dripped a tiny trickle of water. There in the mud between the rocks was the imprint of the leopard's mighty paw. As he lay on his belly to drink, he had pushed down the rocks and ferns longer than the height of a tall man.

I measured the distance from the water puddle to the cliff where our blind was hidden—too low and too far away. I chose a place on the side of the cliff where a small clump of brush clung to the rocks. We could reach this place from behind.

We judged that one more meal was left on the ostrich. It was our last chance. We took with us Kinyenze, a Wakamba hunter with phenomenal eyesight. We were going to need every advantage and a fantastic amount of luck to pull this one off.

We lay on our bellies behind the brush on top of the cliff. As before, the shadows deepened early in the valley. Across from us, a wide-mouthed fumarole belched yellow smoke and steam. The last of the Masai had driven their cattle away into the distance. A bushbuck barked sharply. The leopard was moving. The shadows below us were now so deep I could barely make out the form of the ostrich in the gnarled tree. I looked at the red rock basin where the water dripped. The spotted rocks there still showed some color in the fading light.

Kinyenze was jerking at my leg. "*Chui! Chui!*" he whispered urgently. The leopard had appeared out of nowhere. He crouched at the little pool and was lapping the water. His shoulders were hunched. His tail whipped back and forth nervously. I could see the white tip clearly. The middle of his body was behind a rock. In the telescope sight of the rifle I could see the blurred form of black rosettes. Suddenly the leopard turned his head. He stood up and looked straight at us. He could not have heard any sound above the hiss of the steam jets. Perhaps he had seen a movement. It was now or never. I shifted the black dot of the sight just forward of the rock. When the dot covered the base of the leopard's neck, I squeezed off the shot. In a single arching bound the Longonot leopard was gone.

The three of us climbed down over the ledges. There was little use in going up to the water pool. The long leap had shown clearly that the leopard was unhurt. My shot had missed. Bob and I decided to cut down the remnants of the ostrich carcass.

"*Chui, bwana, chui!*" screamed Kinyenze. Reitnauer swung his double-barreled shotgun. Among the scattered bushes in the red rocks, a mottled form crouched, the wide head raised. At that distance, a wounded leopard could kill us in a second. As we stood there tense,

Longonot Leopard

with guns ready, the leopard never moved. Kinyenze jumped forward and jerked the leopard's tail. The Longonot leopard was quite dead. My shot had hit the base of his neck. That long leap had been his last.

The Longonot leopard will place among the first five in the world records of spotted cats, but this is not the main point. He was a giant of his kind, possessing the intelligence of a man. The Valley of Evil Spirits will be a different place without him.

Chapter 27

BINGO ON BONGO
(1972)

The red animal was walking on mist. He humped his back and minced forward a few steps. Still, I could see no ground below or sky above. Just behind the first bongo, another appeared. The vapors swirled around their legs, and cleared for a moment. I saw white stripes against dark, chestnut-red hide. Above were massive horns a yard long. Both animals were big bulls. I had waited two years and hunted nine weeks for this one shot.

In some things I am a hard-luck guy. If a pretty girl comes to our house, I'm the kind of fellow who ends up with the chaperone. The bongo is a mighty pretty girl. But male or female, the bongo antelope of Africa is shyer than the most blushing wallflower that ever refused a dance. I ought to know. I spent over nine weeks of hunting, on four separate African safaris, before I shot at one.

If the African bongo were as common as zebra, which it isn't, it still would be one of the favorite trophy animals in Africa. Lots of sportsmen like to go after something just because it is rare and hard to get. "Rare and hard to get" are gross understatements as far as the bongo is concerned. All hunters like to bag game that makes a good trophy. Of all the trophies anywhere in the world, the bongo qualifies as one of the most beautiful. Even with the incentive of its being rare and at the same time a spectacular prize, there are very few hunters who have a bongo head over their fireplace.

The bongo is described as a beautiful member of the bushbuck and eland tribe, which inhabits the forest of Africa from the Congo to Mount Kenya. It is a large animal; the males weigh about six hundred pounds on the hoof, and both males and females are horned. The coloring of the bongo, however, is what makes the animal so especially beautiful. The body is a chestnut red, set off by parallel white stripes. The face, also, is marked with white, as is the throat. In spite of huge, ox-like ears, the bongo certainly rates as the pinup girl of all African game. But it is the bongo's retiring habits that make him so rare in game collections. The bongo has an innate shyness, a downright mania to avoid people. If humans show up in an area, the bongo move out. Bongo are never found close to a settlement, and the smell of human scent alone seems to throw them into hysteria. Habitually an animal of deep forests or heavy bamboo growth, the bongo is virtually impossible to approach in his native element.

I knew all this before I started. And yet, like many another hunter before me, I counted on luck and the gods of chance to deliver a bongo to me. It was the only major game animal of Africa that I had not yet taken. On safari into the southern Sudan in 1959, I had counted on getting a bongo. As a matter of fact, I was naïve enough to think that it might be easy. At the very headwaters of the tributaries of the Nile, on the boundary between the Belgian Congo and the Sudan, the British, during their occupation of the country, had reported a number of bongo. Along the low divide that marks the boundary is a series of seeps, rich in minerals, that the bongo use as salt licks. The British government set aside a number of these salt licks as a bongo preserve. When the Sudan became independent in 1956, the new Sudanese government, in a move to try to establish a tourist and safari business, gave me permission to take a bongo on this preserve. What a cinch! It would be like shooting a pigeon in Central Park.

With Brownie as the photographer and a game scout furnished by the Sudanese government as guide, we set about getting to the bongo preserve—a series of adventures in itself.

Our first disappointment was to find everywhere the evidence of native poaching. Game pits had been dug on all of the trails that led into the salt licks. But even at that, there were fresh bongo tracks at the main lick. Rihani (the game scout) and I visited the major licks at dawn and at dusk for several days. We stayed at one of the licks all night, for a series of mosquito-infested vigils. On the first all-night stand, a young bull bongo stepped daintily around the freshly dug game pits and approached us. He stood and looked at us for five minutes with his ears cocked forward while I admired his beauty. I passed him up. His

246

Bingo on Bongo

horns were perhaps twenty-five inches long, and slender. I have thought about that young bull bongo a thousand times since. There is a hunting adage to the effect that if you see something you want, you'd better take it. If you wait for a bigger one, the game bag will be empty.

Three months later, in the jungles of French Equatorial Africa, I went bongo hunting again. This time I went with Jean Bepoix, who knew a strip of forest country along the Ubangi River where the bongo are as thick as politicians in Paris—but a lot harder to find. Two or three French guides, of whom Bepoix is one, found some glades in the Ubangi forest where the bongo come out at night to feed. The hunters sit on a platform in a tree and pot the bongo as they come into the open. I had killed tigers this way in India, but somehow it didn't seem like a sporting way to get a bongo. I needn't have been so puritanical in my sporting code. Before I was finished more than a year later, I was ready to use anything from poison to hand grenades. As it was, Bepoix and I, with a couple of Pygmy guides, staggered around in the semi-twilight of the Ubangi rain forest following bongo tracks. By accident I managed to collect a forest sitatunga, at that time the only example of this animal ever brought in. Of bongo I didn't see so much as a square inch of red hide.

Hunters in the Belgian Congo occasionally hunt bongo, but in British Kenya they have been doing it for years. The eastern range of the bongo extends to the Aberdare Mountains and to Mount Kenya itself. Furthermore, the eastern variety of the bongo, which lives only in these mountain hideouts, is the heaviest kind and has the largest horns in Africa. British safari companies for the past twenty years have taken a few misinformed clients up on the slopes of Mount Kenya to hunt bongo. Usually, a few days in the cold and rainy bamboo forest cured these intrepid adventurers of the bongo fever. Two weeks was the outside limit for a bongo hunt, and very few clients ever came back for a second try. An even smaller number ever managed to get a shot at a bongo. But a dozen or so bongo were brought in to Nairobi over a period of years. A real spurt was given the bongo business during the Mau Mau emergency. During this exciting time, most of the white hunters in Kenya were up on Mount Kenya chasing Mau Maus. Occasionally they saw a bongo, and quite often they saw bongo tracks. Some of these hunters came back to Mount Kenya to have a crack at the bongo after the emergency was over.

Under the African Sun

I persuaded one such ex-Mau Mau scout to have a go at bongo in June of 1959. The white hunter concerned was David Ommanney, who had combed the ridges of Mount Kenya for the best part of two years with an outfit known as the Kenya Rifles. In some hundreds of patrols in the forests of Mount Kenya, Ommanney had bumped into bongo on three or four occasions. He had found several Mau Mau hangouts furnished with bongo skins. Apparently, at least some of the terrorists had worked out ways of getting these elusive animals. David and I tiptoed through the bamboo jungles of Mount Kenya for two weeks. We followed a dozen fresh bongo tracks during this time. We bagged a rampaging mountain rhino. We avoided a herd of stampeding buffalo. But we never saw a bongo.

The bamboo belt on Mount Kenya is one of the most unpleasant places in the world to hunt. Even at midday it is as dark as a cellar and twice as damp. If it isn't raining, there is a cloying mist that hangs eternally on the flank of the mountain. The bamboo itself is monotonous. It is overhead, all around you, and underfoot. I had always thought bamboo was tropical. Not this kind. Mount Kenya bamboo was as cold as a forest of dry ice and twice as doleful. At its upper edge, where it merges into open moorland on the high flanks of the mountain, the weather freezes every night.

In spite of the forbidding country, somehow the bongo fever had me. After two weeks with David Ommanney on Mount Kenya, both of us were too tired to go out and fall into another muddy elephant track. But I determined to hunt bongo again.

The opportunity came with a trip to Somalia to check new hunting possibilities there in connection with the independence of the country on 1 July 1960. Before going to Somalia, I stopped off in Kenya to have a last go at the bongo. Andrew Holmberg had said that he knew a piece of jungle country where bongo had never been hunted before and where we ought to get bongo and also the rare yellow-backed duiker. But when Brownie and I landed at the Nairobi airport, Andrew Holmberg, hobbling along on a pair of crutches, met us with a doleful face. He had been shot through the foot with a heavy double rifle while hunting elephant. It was obvious that he could not take us bongo hunting, but he would send a young member of his safari firm in his place.

We had heard of Theo Potgieter before. It was Potgieter who had finally killed the famous leopard of Manyara, which had mauled and almost killed two men. Potgieter also had been on Mau Mau

248

Bingo on Bongo

patrol, especially in the Aberdare Mountains to the west of Mount Kenya. Backed by Andrew's bongo advice and with a small safari outfit furnished by him, we started out on what was to be my last bongo hunt. As there were three or four bongo safaris milling around Mount Kenya at the time, Theo decided to try the Aberdares. Few would-be bongo hunters have ever attempted the Aberdare area, chiefly because the jungle growth and bamboo forest there are thicker and more obscure than those on Mount Kenya. Holmberg had seen many signs of bongo in the south Aberdares while on Mau Mau patrol. Furthermore, Potgieter's brother-in-law ran a sawmill at South Kinangop at the south end of the Aberdare range. This seemed a good base of operations, especially since it was only a short eighty miles or so from Nairobi.

Holyoak's sawmill proved to be a fascinating place in itself. While a ranger for the British forty years earlier, the father of Mrs. Potgieter and her brother, Eric Holyoak, had planted some thousands of acres of forest trees. The Holyoak sawmill, under license from the Kenya government, was cutting these same trees, which had matured so soon into saw lumber in the ideal wet climate of the mountain. In their lumbering operations on the slopes of the Aberdares, the Holyoaks occasionally saw traces of bongo. Young Eric, as I found later, had been something of a one-man army against the Mau Mau during the emergency. He had been given three military decorations by the government for his activities against the terrorists. During Eric's forays on the Aberdare ridges, he had learned every elephant path and bamboo thicket in the whole area. Eric had never killed a bongo, but he knew where they were.

Potgieter established our camp on the edge of a clearing near the sawmill. Even here at the foot of the mountain it was damp and cold with constant mist and rain like Mount Kenya. I had always thought of the bongo as a tropical animal. I should have known better by this time. We had one tremendous advantage: Holyoak as a guide. Instead of searching for bongo all over the Aberdares, we went straight to them.

A steep canyon with two swift streams cuts the south end of the Aberdares. This is the Cherangani, which flows past the Holyoak sawmill. The Cherangani is an ideal trout stream and has been stocked by the British for the past several years.

In its upper headwaters the Cherangani flows through steep-sided canyons. At its very head is a high hump of bare volcanic rock called the

Under the African Sun

Elephant. On the first day, Holyoak, accompanied by one of his forest-ers, led us across the Cherangani canyon and up a grueling two-hour climb on the far side. Eric told us, as we stood panting on one of the frequent rests, that when he had surprised a bunch of Mau Mau in a cave on the side of the Elephant, he had seen bongo there. The Mau Maus had eighteen bongo skins inside their cave when he found the place.

The bamboo-covered spur just below the Elephant we dubbed "Bongo Point." The place was crawling with bongo. That first morn-ing we trailed a lone bongo bull without seeing him. We crossed the fresh tracks of half-a-dozen other bongo at the same time. But the bamboo and other growth on Bongo Point was as thick as the hairs on a dog's back. There wasn't an opening the size of a card table in the whole place. And the bongo loved it.

For a week Theo and I left camp every morning before daybreak and climbed up the slippery elephant trails to Bongo Point. We trailed bongo every day, usually trying to pick out a lone bull for our quarry. Twice we got within a few feet of a bull before he jumped and ran. We heard the bongo crashing through the bamboo, but we never got a single glimpse of red hide or white stripes. At the end of a week of tiptoeing, crawling, and sneaking, we were exhausted and the bongo were spooked off Bongo Point.

At the suggestion of Eric, we attempted a flank attack on the situ-ation. We were sure that the bongo had simply moved over to another bongo ridge, at the very head of the Cherangani. On two grueling days we attempted to circle clear around the Cherangani basin. It was a six-hour hike one way. We found bongo sign all right, but we also found a lot of other wildlife. On the second expedition around the head of the Cherangani, we ran into a herd of fifteen forest elephant. The elephant were resting quietly on the very crest of a knife-edge ridge that would have been difficult going for a Rocky Mountain goat. To avoid any unpleasantness, we circled low on the flank of the ridge to get around the elephant. In the middle of the steepest place, where even the bamboo had a hard time holding on to the vertical lava rock, we jumped a herd of buffalo. We were attempting a narrow game trail that fol-lowed a crack in the lava rock. Apparently this was the only way in or out of the place, and the buffalo were using it. Crackling bamboo stalks like jackstraws, the herd swept at and through us. We got out of the game trail by hanging on to rocky projections and swaying bamboo stems. The lead buffalo plunged down the trail ten feet from us. If a

Bingo on Bongo

certain bamboo had pulled out of its none-too-secure hold on the base of a rock, I would have fallen right on top of the stampeding herd.

After the buffalo episode, we decided to give the Cherangani a rest. But we were the ones who needed it. A ten- or twelve-hour hike day after day up and down those slippery trails will take the starch out of any bongo hunter. We took a swing north of Mount Kenya in the Northern Frontier to look for a big elephant, and to let the hot desert sun dry some of the Aberdare mist out of our soggy bones. Two weeks later we were back at the Holyoak sawmill, ready to try again. We had a plan.

It was obviously a poor idea to climb up in the morning and slide back in the evening. We gathered half-a-dozen reluctant safari boys and put loads on their heads for a walking safari. We were going to establish a camp up on Bongo Point. Furthermore, we were not going to tiptoe after anymore bongo. That stuff was for the bamboo birds. We were going to sit on a rocky spur up on the side of the Elephant and look for bongo with our binoculars, in a scientific manner. Eric had said that on several occasions during the emergency he had seen bongo come out of the bamboo just as the dawn mists began to rise. The animals fed on the edge of the moorlands for a few moments and then melted back into the bamboo.

The new system worked perfectly. Not that our siwash camp on Bongo Point was perfect. It was perhaps the steepest, most uncomfortable, sketchy, soggy, dripping camp that I have ever had the misfortune to be a part of. I have never seen a sorrier set of African natives than our safari boys in Camp Bongo. For three days nobody could talk above a whisper for fear of scaring the quarry, and nobody had a dry bed or a square meal. But it was worth it.

The first evening, after we had set up our camp by a little dripping pool right at the foot of the Elephant, we saw a single bongo over across the Cherangani. Just at dusk the animal came out of the upper fringes of the bamboo and fed for a few moments at the edge of the moorlands. He looked like a spot of dark red blood in the distance.

The next morning at daybreak, we mounted the side of the Elephant to look again. At first light ten bongo came out of the bamboo and began to graze in the open. They were about a mile away, and by the time we had stalked them, they had returned to the bamboo, and we found only fresh tracks when we arrived at the spot. However, our plan was working. The next day we saw bongo again, both morning and evening. The only catch was that the unpredictable animals did not always come out of the bamboo in the same place.

The third morning, we covered the mile or so to the shallow valleys at the head of the Cherangani before daylight. Every elephant print in the trails we followed was full of icy water. Every bamboo frond that brushed against us slapped us in the face as though with a wet towel. But we didn't even notice these discomforts. Just at daylight we climbed on top of an isolated piece of rock at the base of the Elephant, four or five hundred yards from the place where we had seen bongo twice before. The morning wind blew up out of the Cherangani, drifting trailers of mist up the face of the Elephant. The first bongo appeared before the sun.

One animal, then another, stepped timidly from the dark arches of the bamboo and walked forward into the open. The bongo trotted up the slope with curious humpbacked gait. As we focused our binoculars on them, we could plainly see the white stripes on their bodies.

"They're bulls—all bulls," Theo hissed in my ear as five and then six animals stepped from the bamboo and began to feed. Kirimania, Theo's head tracker, was lying on his belly on the rock beside us. Kirimania had no binoculars, but he didn't need them. "*Ndume macuba, ndume macuba mingi,*" he mumbled.

Kirimania was right. All of the bongo were bulls, and big ones at that. Apparently this was the bull herd of all the bongo of the Cherangani. Two more animals appeared at the edge of the bamboo. The head of the first one, as he stopped in the mouth of the game-trail tunnel in the bamboo, looked like a beautiful trophy already mounted on somebody's wall. After looking around and fanning their ears, the last two bongo stepped forward. Theo and I stiffened together. The last two bulls were monsters.

"Those horns are over forty inches," Theo whispered. "And they're as big around as my leg." The last two bulls were bigger than any bongo I had ever seen, even in the museums. Their bodies were dark chestnut, several shades darker than the other bulls in the bunch.

But we didn't stay to admire the bongo, or to remark that we were probably the only hunters ever to see eight mature bongo bulls in broad daylight. Theo and I were already crawfishing off the wet rock. I picked up my Weatherby .300, cranked a shell up the spout, and checked the telescopic sight for drops of water. At a half run, Theo and I skirted the upper fringes of the bamboo to close the range. A few projecting and

Bingo on Bongo

stunted bushes screened us from the feeding bongo. Within five minutes we had crawled to a single bush that topped a low rise on the edge of the moorland. The bongo were just beyond.

I thrust the rifle forward and looked over. There were two bongo bulls, about 150 yards away. The mass of bamboo behind them had disappeared in white moisture. The mist was moving over the ground like fog in a horror film. The air behind was already filled with white vapor, moving up out of the canyon below. The bongo appeared for a few seconds, as though they were walking on clouds with no solid earth around them. I centered the cross hairs of the sight on the first bongo. He was a mature bull, but not one of the two dark-colored giants that trailed the herd. We waited tensely. A third bongo appeared in the swirling mist. Already the first streamers of vapor had reached us and passed over us. It was this way every morning. As the sun heated the air, the updrafts pulled the fog out of the canyons. Soon it would cover us.

Still I waited. A fourth bongo fed slowly forward with hesitant steps. He was perhaps the biggest bull yet, but still not one of the trophy heads of the herd. If only we hadn't seen those two giants, I would have taken this one in a second. It was an easy shot.

The lead bull circled in his feeding and turned down the slope. They were going back to the bamboo, as we had seen them do before. The timid animals never stayed in the open more than ten minutes at the most. Silently and swiftly, a mass of white fog swept up the slope. The bongo were gone.

I grabbed Theo by one shoulder and jerked him to his feet. We moved forward in a crouching run. The bongo would be lingering for a few nibbles at the very edge of the bamboo. I could get one of the bulls there, as the mist was not yet solid. As we topped the low rise where the bongo had gone, an opening appeared in the fog. I saw the outline of a back and wide, hooked horns. A black ear waved forward and back. A rift opened in the fog. There he was! I raised the rifle. Fifty feet away stood a buffalo. The white closed in again. For the first time I was grateful. Theo and I hastily backed up, and circled to the right. We had not seen the buffalo bull before. We had to get to the edge of the bamboo before the bongo disappeared completely. A few yards away we found a shallow swale in the moor grass, leading downward. We followed it at a half run. In the swale the mist was thinner. As we trotted forward, the wind carried the fog above our heads, as though a white blanket had been raised. In the grass a few feet from us was another buffalo bull, this one lying down. He was facing away from us downhill and was chewing his cud contentedly. Theo and I retreated back up the swale and circled again. We'd have to get around to the right farther to get a look at the bongo down below.

Suddenly we heard a snort and a rush of sound behind us. One of the contemptible buffalo had caught our wind or had smelled where we had been crawling. The second buffalo jumped up out of his bed. We heard the two gallop down the slope with a pounding of hoofs. There was the sound of other hoofs in the white mist.

The bongo! We had spilled the whole business.

Through the white mists Theo and I followed the retreating herd. We entered the bamboo tunnel. Perhaps the bongo would linger for a moment, once they reached the sanctuary of the bamboo. We trailed them downhill, but after fifteen minutes of silent advance we had not seen them. The tracks on the trail were confused. Some hoofprints seemed to lead off to the left. We turned that way and went perhaps another hundred yards. Theo and I stopped together. Through the bamboo stems was a red outline. I could see the curve of a dark, rounded back. There were horns above the head. The animal turned toward us. There were the white markings of the face. Between the bamboo stems was the dark red outline of the bongo's chest. I raised the Weatherby and fired in the same instant. The bongo staggered back and fell sideways against the bamboo stalks. We had him!

Theo and I ran forward. Even before we put our hands on the beautiful animal, Theo cursed.

"It's a female," he spat out. "An old female! How in the name of all the gods of bongo and man did we manage to stagger into a female?"

As for me, I was both delighted and disappointed. It was indeed an old female, so dark in color that we had mistaken her for a bull. But her horns were long and massive.

Have I got the bongo fever out of my bones? Not at all. Next year I'm going back to the Elephant, and watch for one of those two giant bulls that got away.

Chapter 28

TWO OUT OF THREE
(circa 1975)

Death comes in many sizes. This one was as big as life itself. The great head moved over us like a gray cloud. The two tusks seemed to shut off escape at either side.

No one knows just what he will do when faced by death. Will he react quickly and do the right thing? Or will his muscles freeze? This can be a pleasant question to debate in front of an open fire back home. If a man sees a big deer and reacts with buck fever, what will he do when a fighting-mad bull elephant is charging from forty feet away?

I hadn't wanted to shoot an African elephant in the first place. "I sort of like elephant," I had told our white hunter, Andrew Holmberg, when he first asked me the question. "I like the peanut-eating variety of elephant, anyway."

"The African elephant is a totally different beast from his Indian cousin," Andrew had replied. "The African will weigh two tons more, and he has tusks four or five times the size of the Indian variety. And," added Andrew, as though clinching the argument, "these African beasts have a nasty disposition to go with their bulk."

"I still like elephant," I remember answering.

"You'll change your mind," replied Andrew decisively.

I did, too, although it wasn't Andrew who changed it. It was the elephant themselves. For one thing, as our two-month safari progressed, we saw quite a lot of elephant. As we hunted in southern Kenya for lion, leopard, buffalo, and rhino, and farther south in Tanganyika for hippo and the spectacular antelope such as the greater kudu, sable, and roan, we came across herds of elephant.

Under the African Sun

Andrew, one of the foremost elephant hunters in East Africa, had carefully explained to my wife and me that the elephant in the southern Tanganyika country seldom, if ever, carried big tusks. I just as carefully explained to Andrew on a dozen such occasions that I *still* didn't want to shoot an elephant, whether he had big tusks or little ones. I could get awfully mad at a rhino; I had no love at all for Cape buffalo, one of which had come very near to killing us. But when it came to elephant, the answer was "No."

What changed my mind occurred one night at the foot of the Eyasi Escarpment. It was dark when we made camp. The place we picked out was not a particularly good spot, but we had little choice. The narrow band of junglelike country between Lake Eyasi and the foot of the escarpment was veined with rhino and elephant trails. We pitched one tent in a cleared space where two of these animal avenues crossed. Andrew directed the safari boys to light a big fire and to keep it going all night so that the animals would know we were there. We wearily turned in, listening to the cries of thousands of flamingos on the lake, and the sound of a herd of baboons settling down in a fringe of fig trees above us.

A few hours later we were suddenly wakened by the crash of a great tree, which splintered the ground right at the edge of camp. To our dismay, we saw that the fire had gone out. Somewhere an elephant squealed, and as though in answer, others trumpeted all around us. A whole herd had apparently marched into our camp before they realized anyone was there. The safari boys rolled out from under the truck where they had been sleeping. The beam of a flashlight cut through the noisy darkness. A vague gray body dragging the remnant of a tent behind it thundered by in the shadows. The earth trembled, as though a dozen freight trains were roaring past.

In a moment the stampede was over. Nobody had been stepped on, which was a miracle; in the morning the elephant tracks seemed to be through us, around us, and on top of us. A chocolate pudding that Abdullah, our cook, had set by the fire the evening before had received a direct hit. When an elephant steps on a chocolate pudding, that's it!

"Pretty good herd bull with that bunch," Andrew commented quietly at the breakfast table next morning. "Looked like his ivory might go sixty pounds or more." He seemed to be watching me as he talked.

"I was willing to leave the elephant alone," I answered shortly. "But I was looking forward to that chocolate pudding. How big did you say that bull elephant was?"

Two out of Three

And so it was decided—as all along Andrew had known it would, I suppose. On our return through Kenya, we got an elephant license at Nairobi and headed for the Northern Frontier.

We went north for two reasons. In the first place, safari parties after elephant usually head in that direction because the biggest ivory is to be found in the Northern Frontier. The more pressing reason we went to the far north, though, was that Andrew knew of a particular bull elephant in that vast country that he had determined to hunt. He told the story as we drove over the dusty road to the frontier town of Garissa on the Tana River.

Two years before, Andrew had been on the lower Tana when a lion had badly mauled five Somali tribesmen who were trying to protect their herd of cattle from the big cat. Andrew had taken the five Somalis all the way back to Nairobi to have them treated. In gratitude for all of this trouble, the Somalis had told him of a big bull elephant on the edge of the Emboni country, to the east and toward the coast. Andrew had felt that, even allowing for the usual exaggeration, this would prove to be an elephant among elephant.

When we checked into the office of the district governor at Garissa, I made the mistake of asking the official in charge about elephant in the vicinity.

"Five of the bloody beasts went through my garden last night," the man answered bitterly. "Took the fruit trees and the fence with them, they did. Don't ask *me* about elephant!"

Most elephant hunters hunt along the Tana River, either above or below Garissa, or farther south along the Galana. We passed by these usual haunts, moving in a southeasterly direction past the trading post of Bura and finally to the seacoast town of Lamu. Lamu is an old Arab and Portuguese port where many thousands of pounds of poached ivory have been smuggled out in past years. We picked up some fresh vegetables and supplies at Lamu, then doubled back up the coast into the Emboni country.

The road we followed was little more than a faint pair of ruts that curved through open savannas with dom palms round about. This track, according to our maps, eventually went north into Italian Somaliland. The country was beautiful. As we slanted north away from the coast, we entered a wide belt of jungle that is called the Emboni Forest. Actually it is a forest only in spots. Magnificent tree ferns, tropical lianas, and creepers form patches of junglelike growth that are as exotic as the plants that grew in past ages to form the beds of present-day coal. As the land rose gradually to the northward, we saw more and more game in the savanna glades. Lesser kudu and topi were common. There were waterbuck and the coastal variety of oribi. Dik-dik scuttled everywhere.

As we penetrated deeper into the forest, we could see ahead the curious houses of the local tribesmen. The Embonis live in dome-shaped houses of bark, and are a hunting tribe. For many years they have made their living poaching elephant to sell to the Arab traders along the coast. The present government has had the greatest difficulty in trying to stamp out this illegal trade in stolen tusks. At the Emboni village, in the very middle of the forest, we sought out the chief.

The chief wore a fez on his head and displayed some other mannerisms of the Arab traders. Perhaps the reason he told us where the great bull elephant lived was that his own hunters, with their bows and arrows, could not go so far. The Embonis habitually kill elephant with bows and arrows. They cover themselves with elephant dung to disguise their human scent, crawl among the unsuspecting beasts, and then shoot them through the belly with iron-tipped arrows smeared with a poison made from the juice of a grass.

The big bull we sought was one of three bulls, the chief told us. These three generally stayed on the edge of the Emboni Forest near a water hole where Somali nomads sometimes camped. The spot was remote—a hundred miles from the Tana River and other usual elephant haunts.

Bulls that carry the biggest ivory are seldom breeding bulls with a herd. The big-tusked elephant are those that early in life have been whipped out of a herd of cows and young bulls, to go off by themselves. Usually such a venerable old bull has a younger bull with him as a guard or "askari." The bull we sought had two such askaris. The big elephant himself was very, very large, the Emboni chief said. He carried tusks "as big around as a man's body, and so long"—here the chief indicated on the haft of his spear that the bull's tusks must be at least ten feet long.

We left the Emboni village and proceeded in a northeasterly direction toward the border of Somaliland. Any semblance of a road soon disappeared. We began to pioneer with our laboring safari car and truck by following elephant trails that led in the desired direction.

The water hole, as it turned out, consisted of five depressions located within a few hundred yards of each other. Each of these was the center of tracks leading in to the precious water, like spokes on the hub of a wheel. Of the water itself, there was practically none. As this was well along in the dry season, toward the end of August, the little water that remained in these shallow depressions was more nearly liquid mud. But apparently even this was enough for the elephant, several hundred buffalo, innumerable gerenuk, and Hunter hartebeest, all of which hovered around the watering place. During the next two weeks in this isolated area, we saw over two hundred elephant. The only water they had during that time was the soupy, slime-coated mess in the five pools.

We had picked up four Somali trackers and one Emboni guide. Not only could they follow elephant tracks, but they could also tell which elephant they were following. Even with this help, however, we made half-a-dozen false starts. We followed one particular bull over twenty miles until we were satisfied he was not the one we were after.

It was by accident that we came across the three bulls that were our mission in this remote country. We had taken a wide swing in the safari car to the north. There were many elephant that were feeding on sansevieria, which looks like the yucca plant of the American Southwest. Apparently they were getting enough moisture from the plant so that they did not have to come in to the water holes. The trackers saw the corrugated oval imprints where three bulls had crossed a dry wash twenty miles from the water holes. As we jumped down from the safari car, we heard the crash of a splintering tree in the distance. We were close behind them. Quickly our two gun-bearers, Ngoro and Sungura, loaded the .470 double rifles. We carried three of these. Andrew carried one, I carried another, and Ngoro carried the third as a spare. Sungura brought up the rear with binoculars and cameras. When at close quarters with elephant, Andrew much preferred the old-fashioned double rifle with its 500-grain bullet to any lighter or single-action guns.

As we approached the elephant, the trackers fell back. They had done their work well. Andrew pointed to the three slate-gray hulks that moved diagonally away from us through the scattered trees. The three bulls all had about the same body size. We knew, however, that only one of them carried a mighty set of tusks. The other two were askaris with only mediocre ivory. It was one of the askaris that detected us first. The elephant whirled around and stuck his trunk up into the air. His great ears went out on both sides. The other bulls, too, turned in alarm and began moving toward us, walking slowly.

"Look at that tusk!" Andrew whispered in amazement.

The first elephant carried tusks only three or four feet long at the most. The one behind, too, I could see was nothing extraordinary. But the great bull in the middle had a tusk that reached clear to the ground. At its base it was as big around as a large man's thigh.

"There's only one," I said in amazement. "He has only one tusk."

"That's the biggest piece of ivory I've ever seen," Andrew muttered. "A hundred and fifty pounds if it's an ounce."

The three elephant stood perhaps seventy-five feet from us. I raised the heavy double rifle. Andrew had said to shoot him in the shoulder. So be it. A weight seemed to press the barrel of the gun down. It was Andrew's hand.

"Not a one-tusker, old boy," he said quietly.

"But, Andrew, you said it's the biggest piece of ivory you ever—"

"We never shoot a one-tusker," he said with quiet finality. I had run into the code of the white hunters of East Africa before, but this was a new wrinkle. It did not matter that this one tusk would weigh more than two tusks of an ordinary trophy elephant. One-tuskers are simply not shot.

We photographed the three bulls as they circled to take our wind. Finally the one-tusked monarch himself walked right up to us. He was chewing a long, trailing root, like a farm boy sucking a straw. He flapped his ears at us, trumpeted, then walked past in front of us as if daring us to shoot.

Our trackers were very apologetic. They felt that their professional honor was at stake, as they had failed to correctly identify these three bulls. We had not yet seen the three we were after. The great bull elephant of the Emboni Forest had two such tusks. He also had two askari elephant with him.

It was ten days later, after we had examined some thirty other bull elephant in the vicinity of the water holes, that we found the tracks of three lone bulls. These, at last, were the ones we were after. The great bull of the three made very large oval tracks with his hind feet; he was the one that carried the tusks that reached the ground.

The meandering tracks of the three bulls carried us in an easterly direction along the fringe of the Emboni Forest. We found the spot where the elephant had fed the night before. There were marks in the crotch of a tree some twelve feet above our heads; there the big tusker had rested his ivory for a while, to ease the strain on his neck muscles.

From early dawn to the middle of the afternoon we trailed the erratic course of the feeding bulls. The tracks on the hard ground were almost invisible, but the devastation among the scattered trees was easy to follow. It was perhaps four o'clock in the afternoon when the leading Somali tracker pointed his spear and whispered in Swahili, "There they are!"

The trackers melted into the background. Andrew and I pressed forward cautiously. Ngoro was at our heels with the extra double rifle.

"Try for a brain shot if you can," Andrew cautioned me as we moved forward. "If you're in a hurry, shoot for the shoulder."

We had talked this over a hundred times as we sat around in front of the dining tent in the evening. The brain shot is immediately lethal. But if you miss by so much as an inch, the elephant only gets a bad headache.

The bodies of the three bulls loomed out of the brush like wrinkled gray mountains. We could see the movement of the great ears, and the occasional upward curve of a trunk, as the elephant fed slowly away from us. As it was still warm, they moved lethargically. Slowly, first one and then another of the bulls would break off the top of a tree with a splintering crash. We could hear the rumbling of their great bowels.

Andrew and I were within fifty or sixty feet of the nearest of the bulls. Still, we could not be sure which was the great monarch that carried the heavy tusks. The ivory of each of the elephant was hidden in the foliage through which they walked. We caught only an occasional glimpse of a yellow-based tusk as a bull hooked over a tree or scooped out a root from beneath.

Andrew and I were crouching so that we might see beneath the bushes. Ngoro whispered something to Andrew and pointed. The nearest bull stiffened. His trunk went up like the spout on a teapot. The tip turned toward us. I could see the flaring pink inside the trunk's tip. Two great ears, like giant sails, flapped out on either side. The elephant turned and charged.

"Shoot!" hissed Andrew in my ear. "Shoot—shoulder!"

When an elephant charges, there is little to shoot at. A brain shot from the front is so difficult that even an expert with plenty of time seldom tries it. I am no expert, and there certainly was no time.

A moment earlier there had been brush and trees between the bulls and ourselves. Now there was nothing. The charging elephant had flattened all this as though the wooden tree trunks had been dry straw.

The bull swerved toward Andrew at the side. I saw the great shoulder beneath the flapping ear. The double rifle came up like a shotgun. There was the spot. The rifle bellowed. I did not feel the recoil.

The elephant stopped. He staggered back a step. He turned even more to the side. There was the whole shoulder. I shot the second barrel. Again the bull staggered back.

Ngoro pressed the second gun into my hand from behind.

"Once again," Andrew said quietly. I fired once more into the bull's shoulder. He seemed to wilt. He fell backward and onto his side with a crash like a house dropping through a grove of trees.

The two other bulls had apparently not scented us. They shuffled off among the trees. Andrew and I ran forward with our guns ready. The two tusks of the fallen bull curved out seven or eight feet in front of his lips. They were perfectly formed and big at the base.

"Man alive, look at those tusks!" I exclaimed excitedly. Andrew was standing beside me. There was a look of utter disgust on his face. "You got yourself a nice pair of knitting needles." Abruptly he turned away.

Ngoro cut off the bull's tail, which is the age-old African way of claiming ownership of a dead elephant.

Andrew would have nothing to do with the fallen elephant. "You got one of the askari bulls," was all that he would say. We found out later that the two tusks weighed eighty-four pounds apiece, which is very fair ivory. But Andrew was inconsolable. He would not even wait until the Somalis had gone to get some of the Embonis to cut up the dead elephant for meat. Instead, he walked toward where we had left the safari car several miles back. Even when we had gotten into the car and Brownie asked us if we had found the great bull, Andrew would say nothing. Instead, he started the safari car and drove along the jungle track like a madman.

It was many miles farther on that Andrew explained to us that we were on our way back to the town of Garissa where we could telegraph to Nairobi for a second elephant license to be issued to us. In vain I explained to Andrew that I was tickled to death with the first elephant, even though he was an askari. Furthermore, I could hardly afford a second elephant license. Andrew scarcely listened to these protests. We drove most of the night and the next day.

Two out of Three

At Garissa we found that the Commissioner at Nairobi was in his office. The clicking key under the hand of the native boy in the hot little room at Garissa gave us the message that a second elephant license had been issued in my name. We could start hunting.

Back we went along the dusty miles down the Tana, then off along the jungle track through the Emboni Forest. We had not had a real sleep for two nights. Andrew hadn't slept at all. He was a man possessed. He kept saying over and over, "Biggest bloody bull I ever saw."

After two days and two nights, we came to the point where we had left our safari car before. There was one of the Somali trackers, squatting on his hunkers with his tablecloth-like skirt stretched over his knees. He rose and greeted us by lowering the tip of his spear. Without a word he turned and walked into the forest behind. We loaded our double rifles and followed.

After a walk of about four miles, we came to a place where two elephant trails crossed, and there was another Somali tracker. Andrew talked to this man for a few moments in Swahili. The tracker pointed with his spear to the north. I gathered that while we had been gone to get the second elephant license, the Somali trackers had been following the two remaining bulls. How they had managed to do this and leave some of their number so that we could follow, I will never know.

We walked in single file for another three or four miles. Behind a screen of thick-growing thorn trees we picked up another Somali tracker. This man pointed ahead. We moved off again. I heard a tree crash to the ground off to our right. Then another branch broke. The Somalis moved to the rear. Andrew and I walked forward on tiptoe.

There again were the two gray backs looming out of the brush. Andrew whispered in my ear. "Careful, old boy. If these bulls make up their minds to kill us this time, they'll probably get it done."

We edged forward again. Ngoro pointed to the bull on the right. "*Makuba*," (the big one), he whispered. Andrew shook his head. "Not sure," he whispered back.

The elephant were feeding diagonally away from us. We could catch only a glimpse of the white gleam of ivory between the spiny leaves of the plants as the bulls moved their great heads from side to side. One of them was kicking out roots from the hard soil with his foot, then scooping them all up with one tusk and the end of his trunk.

We crawled alongside the bulls, perhaps forty or fifty feet away. Ngoro was ahead. He crouched behind the splintered limbs of a tree one of the elephant had just pushed over. I knelt behind the trunk of the same tree. Andrew stood in the shadow of the upturned roots. Ngoro signaled us with his hand: It was the bull on the right. I raised the double rifle. The elephant in front of us stopped. The loose folds of gray skin seemed to tighten. The ears swung out. He straightened his trunk in front of him. There was a scream. He whirled like a cutting horse and came at us.

The head and the outflung ears seemed like a gray cloud over us. Ngoro was swinging his arms to attract the charge. Andrew yelled something. The bull swung toward Ngoro. There was the gray shoulder. The double rifle kicked back once, twice. Dust flew from the hide before me. The bull's brown eyes had a look of surprise. I dropped the empty gun. Ngoro pitched me the loaded one. I swung it up. There was the right barrel—then the left. The bull had stopped. He swung his head and looked down at me. Then slowly, a step at a time, he began to walk backward.

"Reload!" yelled Andrew frantically.

Fortunately, there was no need. A foreleg crumpled first. Then the bull rolled on his side. Two trees snapped off like matchsticks. The blood bubbled in his trunk, and then he was still.

Only then did I see the great bull. He stood there facing us with his trunk outstretched. Two massive curved tusks reached clear to the ground. They were blunt and scarred and looked a foot through. We had shot the other askari elephant!

Slowly I kept repeating this over and over, as though I were drugged. "We shot the other askari."

The great bull walked forward a few steps. He turned, and with his massive tusks he attempted to lift the body of his dead friend. But the inert carcass slipped away as he prodded beneath it. With the end of his trunk, the big bull explored the hide of the dead elephant before him. He sniffed at the spots of blood on the shoulder. He straightened out his trunk toward us. The screaming trumpet was like the blast of a thousand brass horns in our faces. He flapped his ears again, then turned slowly and walked away.

All of us let out a long breath. "That was a very sticky business—a very sticky business," Andrew said quietly. "Anyway," he added slowly with a smile, "I know where there's a bloody big elephant for next year."

A track, in southern Ethiopia, left by a lioness as she accelerated to catch a Grevy zebra about thirty yards away.

A very large male lion taken near Ikoma in northwestern Tazania. The lion is young and his mane is undeveloped.

My very good buffalo taken on the delta of the Zambezi River in northern Mozambique.

A young male sitatunga looks out at us from the papyrus swamps west of Tabora in Tanzania.

This very good roan antelope (a relative of the sable) taken in eastern Tanzania is now very scarce in all parts of its former range.

Ian Henderson and I admire the regal sable that we finally bagged after a two-week hunt.

The tsassaby is a variation of the so-called bastard hartebeest.

Previous: A very good buffalo that charged us at close range near Magadi in Kenya.

My two riverine Bushmen, Get Along and Meat-Eater, and I carrying a sitatunga out of the Caprivi Strip.

This leopard raided our camp on the Gwaai River, stealing 150 pounds of meat from the cook's tent. We ambushed him in a tree the next night where he had stashed his spoils.

Spotted Death (Ian's gunbearer who had survived smallpox) helps us arrange an impala for leopard bait downriver from our camp on the Chobe.

My blesbok taken in Natal, South Africa. A century ago the blesbok and its cousin, the bontebok, ranged in herds of millions all over South Africa.

My Rhodesian friend, Ian Henderson, with a rhebok taken in South Africa.

My very nice Cape eland taken in northwest Kenya.

The Kenya Game Department issued me a special license to kill this particular rhino. It had terrorized a native village and killed several people, including a man on a blue bicycle. I was to hunt only the bull with the blue paint on his horns.

Professional hunter Theo Potgieter holds a young bull bongo. It was our first kill in the Aberdare Mountains of central Kenya.

Mkeri, Theo's gunbearer and chief guide, Theo, and I track a bongo bull in the bamboo forests high on the slopes of Mt. Kenya.

The Grant gazelle is one of the most beautiful of all the gazelles and has a wide range in East Africa. This one is from Ethiopia.

This extraordinary 8-foot-long leopard is by far the world's record, and was taken near the steam jets and fumaroles on the flanks of Mt. Longernot—an active volcano.

On one ninety-day safari in northern Kenya we used cumels to get into otherwise inaccessible terrain. These animals can carry up to six hundred pounds.

Previous: I killed this bull elephant near the Giuba River in Somalia to help feed the starving natives. The ivory I also gave to the Somalis to buy more food.

A Somali holyman prepares to hallaleh a struggling Grant gazelle to please the Muslim members of our safari.

We looked at this old bull for an hour trying to decide if his tusks would weigh 100 pounds. This is the Northern Frontier of Kenya where bulls were usually very large and carry heavy ivory.

His tusks didn't quite make it; they weighed in at 98 pounds each.

A Samburu family treks across the arid bushlands of northeast Kenya. The tall woman in the center carries her dowry on her arms and neck.

The rhino of the Northern Frontier of Kenya are big in body and carry heavy and long horns. This old bull has a forehorn almost thirty inches long.

Chapter 29

KING OF THE CATS
(circa 1975)

The face was feline and evil, the wide-set green eyes fixed intently upon us. The beast's mouth opened and closed as he panted, the canine teeth appearing and disappearing like white daggers in a sheath. A coughing grunt rumbled from the animal's throat.

Ngoro squeezed my leg from behind. *"Simba moja,"* he whispered.

I looked where he pointed with his eyes. A second lion also had risen to his feet. He, too, turned toward us. Their manes stood out around the two lion faces. Two tails moved rhythmically from side to side. They were both going to charge at once. There was no cover. Ngoro and I were as exposed as a couple of sheep on a golf green. Why had we crawled into this mess?

The whole safari had been a series of tense situations, especially as far as the cats were concerned. Andrew Holmberg wanted desperately to get an outstanding lion to enter in the annual East African Big Game Competition. East African white hunters covet the prize in this competition more than Hollywood stars want Oscars. I was as anxious as Andrew to get outstanding trophies, but I found, during the course of the safari, that bagging record trophies of the Big Five is a dangerous business—especially if you go with Holmberg.

Andrew Holmberg knows thoroughly all types of game, but he specializes in the cats. Lion are becoming very scarce in Kenya and Tanganyika. Leopard have never been easy to get. Most of the safari companies append a paragraph of fine print to their booklets, that reads, "We cannot guarantee our clients a lion or a leopard." This situation has become even worse during the last

Under the African Sun

few years. Lion have been shot out of some areas completely—very often, surprisingly enough, by control officers, who kill them because they prey on native cattle, and, for the same reason, by the natives themselves. And really big lion—the ones with heavy, dark-colored manes—have always been scarce.

For this reason it is practically impossible to bag an outstanding lion with a long and heavy body and an outstandingly good mane. I was well familiar with this general situation, as Brownie and I had planned the hunt with Andrew in Nairobi before the start of the safari.

"I know a place—" Andrew had said, after I had explained to him that I wasn't going to leave Africa without a trophy specimen of the one animal symbolic of the Dark Continent. I further explained that, as I had successfully hunted the American mountain lion, had received a college degree because of my study of lion, and had written a book on American lionine types, my interest in lion was more than transitory.

I found out later that Andrew *always* "knew a place"—especially for each of the Big Five: elephant, rhino, Cape buffalo, lion, and leopard. Not only did Andrew always know a place, but these particular spots were usually all but impossible to get to. But when we did finally arrive, we didn't find the tracks of other safari cars before us, and the game was there.

The particular lion place Andrew knew in Kenya turned out to be a wild spot that he had found when hunting Mau Mau terrorists during what East Africans call the "Emergency." I discovered also that Andrew had located, and laid by for future reference, several such places while he acted as military scout for the Kenya Rifles. As white hunters of East Africa jealously guard the secrecy of their hunting places, I will not divulge the specific location of this one. Suffice it to say that it was in southern Kenya, and a pride of eighteen lion lived there.

The process of hunting African lion is more than just knowing where they are. A hunter might be in the very middle of a nest of lion, hear them roar every night, and yet never catch a glimpse of one. In the game parks, the lion lie around in the shade of trees and stare stupidly at tourists with cameras. Wild lion, however, don't. Lion may sometimes ignore a safari car, apparently thinking it a peculiar kind of rhino or other animal, but they never ignore a hunter on foot.

Our first gunbearer was Ngoro, a Masai who had hunted with Andrew for fifteen years. Masai and lion are practically the same word. What Andrew and Ngoro don't know about lion isn't worth bothering about.

King of the Cats

On our first night in the lion country, we heard the roaring of the carnivores in the distance. As Andrew had told us, the noise sounded more like an owl with stomach cramps than the hunting cry of the king of beasts. But this was indeed noise of Africa. I had heard it on the soundtracks of Hollywood movies, and sure enough, it was the real thing.

"The pride is on the move," Andrew remarked as we turned in beneath our mosquito netting that evening. "If they don't make a kill tonight, we'll see lion soon."

Just at daylight the next morning, I shot the first zebra. Andrew chided me for shooting the animal behind the shoulder. In vain I explained to him that behind the shoulder was the way we did it back in North America. "Here you shoot them *in* the shoulder," he said with emphasis. "And remember that when you shoot a lion. He uses his front paws to gather you into his mouth. See that you place the first shot *through* the shoulder so that he can't reach for you." Andrew then showed me his own .470 double rifle. The hard steel of the barrel was deeply dented by two freshly scarred depressions above and below. "Ngoro held this gun in a lion's mouth after a client had shot the beast through the middle. It gave me time to reload. If you look at Ngoro's shoulder, you'll see where the lion's claws dug in." Andrew would say no more about the incident.

That first morning, we set up a zebra bait and another of a big wildebeest bull. I saved the wildebeest's head, as he had an exceptionally heavy set of horns. I hoped that the lion wouldn't mind the head's absence.

During the night the lion roared again, especially just before daylight. Brownie and I were disappointed that we didn't hear them, but the day's hunt had so exhausted that us we slept soundly, not only through the coughing of the lion and the throaty yipping of the hyenas, but also through a baboon fight that had broken out in the fig tree just over our tent. Andrew remarked that if the baboons stayed there and continued throwing wild figs and other ammunition down on us, we would have to move camp.

It was daylight when we drove our safari car within three or four hundred yards of the place where we had hung the wildebeest. With binoculars we could see the carcass was only half its former size. The lion had taken the bait! We checked our rifles. I was using the Weatherby .300 Magnum, with some special softpoint hard-core bullets that I hoped to try out. Andrew and Ngoro carried

Under the African Sun

two .470 double rifles, which are the standard artillery of the white hunters of Africa. Sungura, our second gunbearer, carried an extra .470 just in case.

When I asked Andrew about so many rifles, he just smiled. "It isn't the lion you're shooting at that makes the trouble," he remarked. "The others with him sometimes charge. It's the females, especially, that are cheeky. I remember a very sticky situation when we shot a big male out of a pride of twenty-five lion. Three lionesses charged us. . . ."

Ngoro interrupted, pulling quickly at his sleeve. We looked with our glasses where he pointed. A lioness had risen out of the grass. She looked at us intently. The skin on the back of my neck prickled with excitement. We crawled to a little knoll and lay on our bellies. We looked carefully over. There were two other lion close-by. Their ears and the tops of their heads were showing above the grass tops.

"A lioness and two big kittens," said Andrew shortly. "A bad dish of tea." We squirmed backward and retreated behind the knoll.

After taking some pictures from the car, we moved on to the next bait. This one also had been eaten. As we walked forward at a crouch, we saw that some twenty or thirty vultures were sitting in the top of the fever tree above the frayed carcass. No birds were on the ground. Four lion were stretched out in the shade beneath the tree itself. As we came up, one dashed out to strike at a vulture that had flapped down from the tree to pick up a scrap of meat on the ground. We crawled up to look at the lion from behind a line of high grass. One lion was a male, big, heavy-shouldered, and gray in color. Ninety percent of all African male lion are as maneless as the females. And hardly ever do they have the big bushy collars that the farm-raised Hollywood lion have. But this male looked enormous.

"Too young," said Andrew tersely. "We'll leave him to grow up for a few years." We photographed the lion from a distance and moved cautiously away.

Farther up the little valley we set out an additional bait of a hartebeest that had been fighting and had broken one horn. He seemed a straggly specimen, fit for lion bait. We also shot an ostrich that had magnificent long black and white plumes. After the four Mohammedans of our safari crew had appropriated the fat of the ostrich, which they highly prize as a medicine, we added the ostrich to our string of baits.

King of the Cats

The next morning we saw four more lion. Another young male was among them, and the rest were females. We saw the tracks of a very large male lion in a little sandy wash. Apparently he was living apart from the main pride and was making his own kills.

On the fifth morning we got a look at the big male lion of the pride. We bumped into him quite accidentally as we stopped to admire a group of impala along the riverbank. There were two magnificent impala bulls. As we looked them over, we saw that they were staring with all of their attention at something off to the right. We focused our binoculars on the spot. There he was! He stalked along like the king of beasts that he undoubtedly considered himself. Even Andrew became enthusiastic.

"A very, very big-bodied lion," he commented.

In a few seconds the lion had walked majestically into a thick tangle of head-high grass and low brush beyond the impala. It would have been foolhardy to follow him.

The next morning we caught another glimpse of the big male, but at a great distance. Apparently he had heard the noise of our safari car and already had begun to walk down a small donga into heavy cover. Two other males lay on top of a small hillock near our zebra bait. One of them would dash out from time to time whenever a foolhardy vulture dropped down toward the meat. The two lion seemed comparatively unconcerned but watched us steadily as we crawled toward them. One of the pair, a heavy-shouldered lion of a noticeably dark gray color, almost tempted us. After a long look we decided that neither of these two was as large as the one we had seen near the impala. Somehow, in our discussing the merits of the various male lion in the pride, the big male we had seen near the impala came to be called "George."

Before dawn on the following morning we laid elaborate plans to set an ambush for George, the king of the pride. We had, by this time, seen all eighteen of the cats and could speak with some authority. We had photographs of most of them. With this knowledge of the lion tribe, we were certain we could get a shot at George if we played our cards right. As it turned out, it wasn't so easy.

On approaching the string of baits just at daylight, we had a disagreement with a big bull rhino, which loomed out of the dawn darkness right beside us. We circled him, but he charged anyway. The snorts of the rhino, and the pounding of his heavy feet along the game trail, alerted the lion. We could see eleven big cats standing by the carcass baits. Just beyond the farthest carcass we could make out two big male lion, still lying down on a little bluff overlooking the stream. George was nowhere in sight.

With Ngoro in the lead, we crouched behind the high grass and made a wide circle behind the baits. We finally crawled out on a low headland beyond the farthest lion. Down below was the little valley and the belt of jungle along it. If George tried his usual tactics of slipping away into the heavy cover, we could see him before he got there. On the point across from us, we could clearly see the two other males, about two hundred yards away. Both of them stood up and advanced a few steps toward us. In the early sunlight they looked like two statues of bronze. George was gone. We crawled a few yards farther on to look over the edge of the bluff itself. At a crouching run, I moved forward. There was George, thirty or forty yards away. He was moving at a swift trot down a gully toward the cover along the stream. I fell forward. The rifle came up. The cross hairs of the scope settled on his shoulder as he moved diagonally away. The powerful leg muscles moved beneath the gray skin. I squeezed off the shot. There was no time to get excited or to wonder what the other male lion would do.

I could see the impact of the bullet. It was a little high. George jerked around and snarled. I think he meant to bite the thing that stung his shoulder, but in that instant he saw us. He gave a coughing grunt. He turned toward us. His ears were laid back. He crouched low to charge. I shot him again through the same shoulder as before. The bullet knocked him down. He fought to get on his feet, his great eyes still glaring straight at me. The roar in his throat became a gurgle, and he fell back.

"About the biggest-bodied lion I ever saw," Andrew said as we stood over George. "If he had a thick mane, we'd have a good show."

George was indeed a monster of a cat, but his mane was a farce. He had only a scruff that ran down the back of his neck like the clipped crest on a blooded horse. George was big-headed and big-footed. As a matter of fact, George was big all over. But his size alone would not win the game competition at Nairobi.

"We'll just have to try again," said Andrew as we turned George over to Matingy, our skinner. "We have a lion permit for Tanganyika. I know a place there...."

King of the Cats

It was several weeks, and many shots, later that we arrived at the spot in northern Tanganyika where Andrew knew of a pride of lion of a particular strain that usually sported big manes. As it turned out, there were two prides in this area, one of eleven lion and another of eight.

As the country was more thickly grown with vegetation and laced with small dongas fringed with heavy jungle growth, it was more difficult to get a look at these Tanganyika cats and pick a really good one. Also, this area was teeming with game. As it was then late in August, the country had become green with new grass. Scattered herds of wildebeest, hartebeest, zebra, eland, Tommy gazelle, and impala were everywhere. We found that baiting lion was extremely difficult. Several of our carefully placed baits of zebra and wildebeest were not touched at all. These lion would rather kill their own meat.

Actually, we saw most of our lion on the Tanganyika hunt by following the vultures. These keen-eyed birds hovered over the lion as they moved out to make their kills. A group of vultures circling and diving was a sure sign that fresh meat was there. If the birds kept off the ground, perched in the trees nearby, we knew that the king of beasts also was there.

In a week of intense activity we never once saw a really good-maned lion, although we got at least a glimpse of most of the cats in the area. We collected an impala that will place among the world records, a very fine warthog, and several of the lesser antelope during this time; but our lion hunting had been a bust.

Two days before we were to return to Kenya to finish our hunt there, we put out one more zebra bait along a small wash about four miles from camp, where the lion had been roaring every night we had been there. It was a forlorn hope, as the flat on both sides of this wash was teeming with zebra. The movement of the herds was so great that they trampled out most of our drag marks. If the lion were to find our bait, they would have to do it by scenting the carcass itself.

On a sultry morning we crossed the several dongas that lay between our camp and this grassy flat. As our safari car labored up out of the last wash, a big-maned lion stood before us. Sungura, who as usual was on the car roof as lookout, pounded frantically on the metal top for us to stop. The two safari boys sitting in the back seat whispered together in an awed voice, "*Simba!*" This was the one word that to us meant Africa.

The lion before us looked like a painting. His mane was a great reddish ruff around his face. Before we could get out of the safari

Under the African Sun

car to begin the stalk, however, the lion whirled and ran. Andrew followed him with his binoculars.

"That will be one of the two big males that the natives told us were running by themselves," Andrew said as we watched the lion trot into a thick mass of low-growing scrub across the flat. Ngoro pointed to the right. Under an isolated acacia tree in full sight were two more lion, both males. Again Andrew focused his glasses. I could see in my own binoculars that both lion had big manes that extended well down on their chests.

We did not stop to wonder where the first lion had come from. A glance at our zebra bait over across the flat told us it was untouched. The circling vultures just beyond the two lion beneath the thorn tree indicated that they had made their own kill, and in sight of the bait we had hung up for their benefit. Andrew quickly issued a string of orders. Ngoro and I were to advance on foot and keep the lion in view. Andrew would take the safari car back into the wash from which we had just come.

We were on the edge of the grassy flat and in plain sight. Ngoro carried the extra .470. I carefully loaded the Weatherby .300 with softnose ammunition. Ngoro and I moved forward.

We began to crawl to the left, where the grass was higher and a scattering of small thorn trees offered a little cover. We had gone a few steps when Ngoro pulled my arm and pointed to the ground before us. A brown snake moved off swiftly. It must have been six or eight feet long. I had seen my first cobra.

But even the king of snakes could not hold my attention when the king of beasts was so close. We looked once and saw that the two lion were still staring at the spot from which the safari car had disappeared. Ngoro and I hitched ourselves forward on knees and elbows. It was evident that Ngoro had no intention of waiting until Andrew caught up with us. Perhaps the two maned monarchs would whirl and disappear into the heavy cover, as the first one had.

We had moved forward perhaps three hundred yards under fairly good cover. Beyond this, the only screen was a very tiny tree, with a trunk no bigger around than my arm. Ngoro was flat on his belly now, squirming forward. I moved along behind him. I could see the two lion clearly. They were both lying down in the patch of shade beneath the acacia tree. Both of them stared fixedly at us. I noticed also, rather incongruously, that a Tommy gazelle buck was grazing within a few yards of the two carnivores. Apparently their distended bellies after a full meal were reassurance that they did not mean to kill again. I noticed, too, that the lion differed in color. One had a very blond mane, the other a distinct reddish cast. A blond and a redhead—what a vicious combination!

Ngoro looked back along his shoulder and motioned me on with a turn of his head. He signaled me to pass him. That little tree just before us was our goal.

Behind the spindly stem of the tiny tree, I cautiously gathered my knees beneath me and raised up. Undoubtedly the two lion had thought that we were skulking hyenas. Now they knew we weren't. I saw their interest quicken. A stiffness came over the two bodies. Ngoro signaled me to shoot the right-hand one. That was the blond. So be it!

I crouched behind the little tree. The palms of my hands were already sweating. The two lion were only thirty or forty yards away. With a low growl the red-maned lion got to his feet. He turned toward us. Should I shoot? We should have waited for Andrew. Ngoro had the extra .470. If both lion charged, we wouldn't have a chance.

The second lion reared up. He walked menacingly forward a few steps. I centered the cross hairs on the point of his shoulder. In another moment he would be turned straight toward me, and I would not be able to see his shoulder at all. The cross hairs of the telescopic sight danced crazily up and down. I couldn't hold the thing still. There it was! I squeezed the trigger.

Viciously I bolted another shell in. I took all the skin off the side of my thumb, but didn't even notice. I saw, as in a dream, that the first lion was down. I had shot too high and broken his back. The range was too close. The second male wrinkled back his lips. A guttural, coughing grunt came from between his teeth. He stood there, his mouth half open. This was it. He swung his head. He turned toward us. "To fight or run?" seemed to be in his eyes. Then he turned and bounded away. A few yards farther on, he stopped and looked back at us. I followed his shoulder with the cross hairs of the scope. Then he turned again and ran off into the brush along the donga, with the thick fold of skin beneath his belly swinging from side to side.

"*Mazuri, bwana, mazuri sana,*" Ngoro said, wringing my hand. I had to stop him a moment to fire another shot at the lion on the ground before us. He was still moving a little, but now his body stiffened. He stretched to full length like an athlete. Then he was still.

Ngoro and I walked forward together. Andrew came puffing up with Sungura at his side. Andrew cursed Ngoro in a stream of Swahili. We should have waited. What about the second lion? But even Andrew could not wait to see the maned lion at close range.

Eventually Andrew showed his pleasure. Our lion had a full, well-developed, 14-inch mane. When we had finished measuring the beast, and had hung him up for photographing, we found that in bodily proportions he was not the equal of maneless George, our first trophy. George had the size; this one had the mane. Andrew held his chin in his hand.

"We'll have to change heads to get it to come out right and win that competition," he commented with a wry smile.

The competition, as it turned out, was won that year by a very fine greater kudu.

Chapter 30

THE NEXT-TO-THE-LAST SAFARI
(1994)

There are basically two kinds of safaris—good ones and bad ones. The good ones need little explanation. These are the ones where everything is perfect. All the game that you have ever wished for is there. The big bulls with trophy horns come out of the thick cover and pose as though they were proud of being a part of a perfect tableau. After you have been on safari a week or so, your professional hunter remarks ecstatically, "You haven't missed a shot."

Bad safaris are another matter. The worst thing about a bum safari is that you realize you could have avoided it if you had only followed a few simple rules. Perhaps if I categorize some of the commonest ways to get into the middle of a bad safari, it might help.

First, don't go to the wrong place. A few weeks of preliminary homework, and especially a talk with professionals who are familiar with that area, can save many days of grief later on.

Nothing is more important than the professional hunter. Talk to him *before* the hunt to find out if you are congenial. The professional hunter may be one of the best in the world but a mean SOB in-between times. Especially find out if the guy who is going to guide you knows that particular area. In other words, "Don't go elephant hunting where there are no elephant."

One of the worst safaris I have ever endured comes under the heading of a "just-as-good" safari. This sort of hunt usually starts out with the professional hunter meeting you at the airport in a jollier than usual mood. He slaps you on the back and begins, "Something has come up" (translated: Another safari paying a lot more money appeared after you had booked yours). "Don't worry, old chap. I have someone who is *just as good*." If you hear that "just as good," immediately jump to your feet, get your deposit back (if you can), and head for Alaska. I speak knowingly as I have twice been dragooned into settling for a "just-as-good" safari.

On one "just-as-good" occasion the professional hunter and guide who showed up turned out to be a Boer farmer whose grand-father had left him a .600 Nitro Express double rifle. This fellow, nice enough in his own way, had hunted very little and had never been in the areas we intended to hunt. Also, he had never before fired his grandfather's gun. During our trip together, we found that this formidable double rifle had some of the properties of a V-2 rocket and, in size and recoil, was only slightly less than field artil-lery. We had some very near disastrous episodes on that safari, mostly centering around this gun.

One of the worst kinds of safari can start with a borrowed gun. I always think of Benjamin Franklin's admonition, "Neither a bor-rower nor a lender be," as applying especially to guns.

This particular safari, in 1994, started out with my breaking one of my own rules. Several of the airlines have become particularly difficult about carrying rifles. At that time, England was especially narrow-minded in passing various laws and ordinances stipulating that if you stopped over in Britain carrying a gun, the police would confiscate your rifle with the very vague provision that they *might* give it back to you at some future date (but certainly *not* in time for *that* safari). On this occasion, I had to stop over at the British Mu-seum to see some ancient things and to talk to some learned col-leagues who were almost as ancient. I thought if I dragged a couple of hunting rifles through Britain, they would probably become per-manent acquisitions of the British Museum itself.

My professional hunter in Tanzania was to be Luis Pedro de Sa'e Mello, a Portuguese hunter with whom I had had many pleasant experiences in the past. Don Pedro was born in Mozambique and had grown up on safaris run by José Ruiz, a Portuguese hunter who took me on several safaris in Mozambique in the good old days. José himself had been flattened by an African buffalo, and his safari company, Inyalaland, had disappeared in a devastating revolution

The Next-to-the-Last Safari

that ravished the country and most of its game. Don Pedro, like many another professional hunter, fled Mozambique and ended up in Tanzania in the entourage of Girard Pasinisi.

Don Pedro assured me by fax that he had a .375 rifle worthy of such a "world-renowned hunter as myself." Don Pedro, now grown from teenhood to manhood, had acquired the courtly courtesies of his family, as reflected when he addressed me as "a hunter of world renown," and I temporarily forgot that the subject was a borrowed gun.

The question of what is the best rifle for an African safari would fill (and has already) a number of fat books. For myself, I like one relatively small-caliber, flat-shooting rifle for small stuff, especially at long ranges, and a heavy "no-nonsense" big caliber for buffalo, elephant, lion, and the like. For most of my last safaris, I ended up with a .300 Weatherby Magnum with a very early serial number chambered for a .300 Winchester Magnum round. My friend Jack O'Connor had persuaded me that the Winchester cartridge does a better job than the standard Weatherby. For the heavy, I have a Winchester Model 70 .458 that I have begun to carry instead of my old beloved .470 Rigby double rifle.

Harry Selby, Andrew Holmberg, and David Ommanney all admonished me, as they did all other hunters, to take at least two rifles—a light one and a heavy one. In the event of a breakdown you would have at least one gun you were used to and had sighted in yourself.

When my current wife, Marilyn, and I arrived in Dar es Salaam and were greeted by Don Pedro and his retinue, almost my first question was, "What gun do you have for me?" It was a .375 of French make with a demountable scope. The scope was also French made and with the proportions of a funnel like one we used to put gasoline in a Model T. I noticed the demountable scope had a little play in the mountings that would vary the point of impact a degree or two out there in the game country 150 yards or so. I also met four other hunters who had just arrived to go on safari with Pasinisi, all of whom were carrying a .375 and nothing else.

All four hunters had brought two .375s each to conform to the "take two guns or you'll be sorry" advice of the old-timers. It seems that now there is a new idea spreading over Africa that the .375 is the only necessary rifle to take on any kind of safari. The .375 *will* kill a buffalo or an elephant, and you *can* shoot a klipspringer with

277

it. My own experience has been that a .375 is a little light for elephant, buffalo, or rhino, or even for lion. With an oribi or a duiker, a .375, even with a well-placed shot, will leave very little for a trophy and even less for eating. In my case the die was cast with the .375. I thanked my host graciously for the opportunity to use his rifle and a couple of handfuls of ammunition to go with it.

Fortunately, the area we were going to hunt was a good one that I had tested out before. Tanzania in the early twentieth century belonged to the Germans and was called Tanganyika. Later, during the Great War, it was taken over by the British, and still later, with the wave of colonialism that swept over Africa, the country received its independence. During the German regime a massive outbreak of encephalitis, or "sleeping sickness," broke out in the south-central part of the country. This area, about 300x300 miles, is called the Selous because it was first explored and described by Frederick Selous. Selous, it turned out (I learned this much later), was a spy for Queen Victoria to determine whether this whole area of southern Tanzania, then Tanganyika, had enough minerals or other visible wealth to make it worthwhile to add to the British Empire. The outbreak of WW I resulted in several military skirmishes in East Africa between the British and the Germans. Frederick Selous was killed in one of these.

The Germans tried to stamp out sleeping sickness by removing all the people living there and forbidding anyone else from entering or even passing through this area. Consequently, the game of this Selous region had not been hunted or harried by humans for over a half-century.

I first heard about the Selous from a man named John Nickelson, to whom I had just been introduced. A group of us were standing around the bar in the New Stanley Hotel in Nairobi, Kenya. Nickelson had just been released as the game warden of the entire Selous area. British law and the fear of sleeping sickness had kept all people out of the Selous for the past fifty years. By this time, in the early 1960s, the encephalitis had died out, so the British decided to gradually open the area to legitimate hunting. After his second Pimms cup, Nickelson told us of several elephant he had observed in the Selous that carried well over one hundred pounds of ivory in each tusk. To clinch the matter, he showed us Polaroid pictures of four of the monsters. The Polaroid camera at that time was considered a new "Wonder of the World." Even in the blurred snapshots of these tremendous elephant, we could see that

The Next-to-the-Last Safari

each of them carried ivory in the 120- to 130-pound class. All that night at the New Stanley Bar we argued and planned how we could become the first legitimate safari to hunt in the Selous. I might add, parenthetically, that more elephant have been hunted and killed in the New Stanley Bar than in any other single spot in all of Africa.

Most of the professional old-time hunters were already booked for the following season. Andrew Holmberg couldn't go as he was committed to another safari for Ernest Hemingway and, after that, another one for some of Hemingway's friends. A young man with a military bearing stepped forward from the scattered crowd in front of the New Stanley Bar and announced that he would love to have a chance at any one of those elephant with the gigantic tusks. I held up my hand and stepped forward—it was like an auction. However, unlike some of my old auction experiences, this one turned out exceedingly well—except for one minor detail.

Bill Gentry turned out to be a military man, just as he appeared. He had only recently joined the East African Professional Hunter's Association. What Bill Gentry lacked in hunting experience he made up in enthusiasm and plain old military know-how. He turned out to be one of the most pleasant and knowledgeable professional hunters that I ever accompanied.

As no safaris had been in the Selous area since the German days, there were no roads, tracks, or trails south of the Rufiji River, which generally marks the northern terminus of the Selous area. I won't weary you with all of the details of Bill Gentry's and my sorry saga after the monster elephant. I simply want to explain why I was so anxious to get back into the Selous after thirty-odd years that had passed since we first visited this fabulous area of darkest Africa.

The two largest rivers in the northern Selous are the Chirigani and the Lukuliru, both of which flow into the Rufiji, which itself empties into the Indian Ocean between the Limpopo to the south and the Zambezi to the north. As there were no passable tracks left over from the German regime, we made our own. We usually used the sand rivers. These are well-named, as for many miles there is little or no water on the surface. Our two trucks and brand-new Land Rover would roll along the salt-encrusted sand surface at 20 mph as though we were on a graded road. Suddenly, the car slowed as though Bill had put on the brakes. We stopped. Water gurgled around our wheels. Before we could turn around or struggle up one or the other of the sandy banks to safety, the car sank into the quicksand. On one occasion it required three days to dig our vehicles out and jack them up onto log runways leading to the bank of the Chirigani, only to find that this camping place was a virtual island surrounded by more quicksand.

We finally did get to a spot, near the head of the Lukuliru, where Nickelson had pinpointed a large salt lick. This mineral ground had been used by generations of elephant, buffalo, eland, and other animals to dig for salt. It consisted of a low ridge in the wide upper valley of the Lukuliru. One whole side of the ridge had been dug away by centuries of teeth and tusks gouging to get at the salt content. The animals actually eat the salt-impregnated earth. Trails into the Lukuliru Salt Licks are worn deep into the ridges and cutbanks of the surrounding country.

We built a couple of blinds just above the cutbank where we could see that whole end of the valley. We made camp a couple of miles away where the water of the Lukuliru approached the surface and where we could dig wells in the sand to get drinkable water.

Our first night we pitched a temporary camp on the first terrace of the river and dug a water hole just below the cutbank. Just as the African moon topped the tips of the acacia trees across the Lukuliru, a leopard appropriated our water hole as his own. All that night he entertained us with his growls and roars. As the water hole was less than a hundred feet away under the bank, we were able to appreciate what an African leopard sounds like at close range. The call of a male leopard, as Andrew Holmberg once remarked, sounds like a dull saw going through a pine knot.

We moved camp 100 yards higher on the river terrace. I then built a crude blind of branches interlaced with tall elephant grass on the sandbank right above our, or I should say the leopard's, water hole. After giving instructions as to where to pitch our tents under some beautiful, wide-spreading acacia trees, I returned to the leopard blind to see if all was in readiness—it was about noon. As I topped over the last sandbank on the edge of the river, there was the leopard blind with the leopard already in it. He got up from his shaded bed of grass and turned and snarled at me. I instinctively raised the .300 magnum. I lowered the rifle. If the Selous leopard were going to be this possessive, we could dig another water hole and make another blind farther down the

The Next-to-the-Last Safari

Lukuliru. Besides, as we cleared the elephant grass and low brush from around our camp to make it fireproof, I noticed a number of deeply embedded elephant tracks in the hard, sandy ground. It would not do to shoot up the place. After all, we had come to the innermost heart of the Selous to get a record elephant and not an arrogant leopard.

I had learned from old elephant hunters, such as Harry Selby and John Hunter, that if you put your own two feet toe to heel in the imprint of the hind foot of a bull elephant and the track is longer than your own two feet, it is a *big* bull. Also, Bill Gentry showed me that if the front toe marks of a bull elephant were rounded and deeply dug in as the animal was striding forward, that bull elephant was carrying very heavy ivory. Also, at several places among the acacia trees that we had chosen for our campsite, the forks of limbs twelve or fifteen feet above our heads showed skinned areas and hanging strips of bark where elephant had lain their tusks to rest their neck muscles.

Our experience with the arrogant leopard that expropriated our water hole was typical. We made a track from our camp to the big salt lick, and other tracks along the Chirigani and other neighboring sand rivers. We learned how to avoid the worst quicksand spots. As we skirted one of these, we found a rhino and her calf hopelessly stuck in the mud. The cow had tried to save her calf by tucking it under her thrashing head. The calf was already drowned and dead. I shot the cow. As a matter of fact, this was the only shot fired in this whole area. Bill Gentry and I were afraid that the lifespan of the big bull elephant that we sought might reach back seventy or eighty years into times when there were wary hunters and poachers in this wild area. The bang of a gun in the distance might mean danger to a very old elephant with a long memory.

The other animals we saw were absolutely without fear. They showed no apprehension of a vehicle or of a man with a gun. Twice we found prides of lion lying in the shade or under a cutbank where the sand underneath was damp and cool. One pride of eleven full-grown lionesses and two enormous maned males was spread out in a clearing on the riverbank. All of the lion were fast asleep even though, in some cases, the movement of the late-morning sun had left them in full sunlight. As Bill Gentry slowly maneuvered our hunting car among the scattered pride, several of the lion sleepily raised their heads, looked at our car only a few feet away, yawned, and, in a matter-of-fact way, went back to sleep. Two lionesses got out of their beds and stalked us for a few yards, to get a closer look and smell at this strange animal moving through their midst.

Suddenly, there was an ear-splitting roar right under us. A huge male lion with a reddish-colored mane reared out of the grass and bit through our front fender. One of the front wheels of our Land Rover had run over the tip of his tail. "Sorry, old chap," Bill Gentry was saying as he speeded up the Land Rover just in case the lion should gather his faculties enough to leap into the car with us.

Every place we went in this corner of the Selous, the animals obviously had never seen a vehicle or a human. Elephant, wildebeest, giraffe, and eland stood in the sand rivers staring at us as we drove past. During the first ten days we did not fire a shot to even collect an animal for table meat. I racked up only one trophy that I had hoped to get in the Selous.

The wildebeest in this region are of a different species and have a broad buff-colored stripe from side to side across their nose. We found a beautiful bull wildebeest in prime condition that had just been killed by three lionesses, which now lay in the shade belching and swatting at flies as they watched the Land Rover approach. They still stared as I got out of the car quickly, carrying my best short-bladed skinning knife. In a few minutes I had slit the wildebeest up the back of the neck, slipped off the cape, and severed the head and horns at the atlas joint. As I quickly stuffed the cape and head into the back of the Land Rover, one of the lionesses strolled forward. She stared at the wildebeest carcass and then at me, apparently trying to decide if I had taken more than my share of the meat. I now have this particular wildebeest mounted, along with several other varieties. Almost all visitors ask what that one is with the curious, distinctive strip across the face.

"That one I didn't exactly shoot. I got it in a roundabout way," I explain lamely.

We had a number of other adventures in the Selous that are worth telling, but I only wanted to explain here why this was such a fabulous place, even though our hunt there was a bust.

We developed the habit of walking from our camp to the salt licks. Every day, as we waited in the blinds, we saw elephant, buffalo, eland, rhino, and a plethora of smaller animals. We might have dispensed with the blinds, for when we were caught in the open, the animals showed absolutely no fear of us. We made a point of skirting herds of elephant, especially cows with calves, and herds of buffalo, and in each instance, they were not only unafraid, but belligerent.

Three times during the ensuing week we saw leopard in broad daylight. The country was brushy and there were few savannas or open glades, but even at that, we saw well over a hundred animals each day. Still, we did not see our monster elephant. We had been at the eerie business of threading our way through a world of animal life that did not include mankind for about three weeks when we decided that the monster elephant must be coming to the salt licks by night. We had come to recognize especially the tracks of two very large bulls. On this particular morning, we saw their tracks on the eastern end of the salt flats just at daylight. Quickly, we got into position for our day's watch. The big elephant tracks were heading back the way we had just come. Suddenly, behind us there was a sound of heavy breathing and breaking of brush.

"Elephant—*big elephant*," Abdulla gasped. "At camp!" Abdulla, with his green turban and dirty *jelava*, was the cook's assistant. We wondered what had happened to the skinners and trackers we had left in camp. In garbled Swahili, Abdulla explained that the elephant had taken over our camp. Before Abdulla had half finished his incoherent narrative, we had turned and were running back toward camp. As we approached an open place where our camp was spread out under a grove of lordly acacias, we could see one of the elephant. He stood under a wide-spreading tree with what seemed to be the remains of a tent draped over one-half of his head and one tusk. Another bull stood under the branching limbs of the central tree where our tea table and cocktail paraphernalia, now smashed to smithereens, had been laid out in formal array.

In all there were six bulls. This acacia grove had been theirs, and they had simply reappropriated it. Various members of our entourage were perched on odd acacia limbs above the elephant. The cooking crew was cowering beneath one of the trucks. We saw at a glance that the six bulls, each with fairly sizable tusks, were not the 100-pound tusk monsters we sought.

We formed a ragged line and advanced, shouting, trying to drive the intruders off. I had found a metal tray in the debris and was pounding on this with a wooden club as I tried to drive one of the

Under the African Sun

bulls out of the remains of our kitchen. Instead of fleeing in terror, he turned his head around with an aggrieved expression on his broad face, his ears spread widely out. He shifted his huge body and stepped backward, directly onto what was left of our folding metal oven, with the morning biscuits still in place. When an African bull elephant steps on your oven, it is obvious at a glance that that particular piece of sophisticated equipment has ended its service to mankind. The six bulls finally moved off in annoyance, grumbling and rumbling in their trunks. Our camp was a complete wreck.

That evening, in a council of desperation, we decided to spend the night at the salt lick. It was apt to be our last night, as we had lost a large proportion of our food supplies, two tents and their contents had been completely destroyed, and one of the elephant had stepped on our medical kit. Of less importance but of great sentimental loss was the fact that our last three bottles of Scotch whisky had become the casualties of an elephant's trunk or foot.

As we settled down on the bank above the salt lick just at full dark, we could hear elephant trumpeting and grumbling in the distance. In the next three or four hours the noises increased. All that night there were trumpetings and rumblings of what must have been a dozen or more cows and bulls. It's an "elephant wedding," I overheard two of the trackers say.

I was bone-tired after the devastating events of the day, so I finally went to sleep on the hard-packed ground. I stuffed a handful of elephant grass under my head for a pillow as I'd seen the natives do when "laying it out." Toward morning the "wedding party" moved off.

I became fully awake when I heard closer noises of huge bodies just below us. The star shine gleamed dimly on the tusks of several big elephant as they thrust and pied at the stiff mud of the mineral ground. I snatched up my rifle. There were at least eight or ten very large elephant below us. Could any of these be the enormous bulls whose tracks we'd seen right here?

Singuida, at my elbow, whispered into my ear, then shook his head. I could just feel the movement of his turban. I couldn't hear a sound he said, but it was a negative. The three trackers who accompanied us all agreed that these were lesser bulls. I "laid out" again on the hard-packed ground and found my elephant-grass "pillow" just as it was.

284

The Next-to-the-Last Safari

By the pale light of morning we could dimly see a few elephant walking away from the salt grounds where they had spent the night. On our way back to camp we encountered two leopard walking along through the brush. I didn't even think of shooting them, even though one was a large mature male.

We ate a dispirited breakfast. There was no hot bread or biscuits. There was no hot bacon or impala chops. We couldn't even find the skillet upon which the cook prepared these delicacies. One of the men claimed he had seen one of the elephant carry off the skillet, waving it triumphantly in the air. I think this account was entirely from the imagination, but I didn't even take the trouble to label it as "nonsense" as I was feeling so badly myself. By noon I had lost the hearing in my left ear completely. After some examination, Bill Gentry found that a sizable tick had crawled into my ear as I lay on the ground in the blind the night before. The loathsome bug had there gorged on my blood, and his bloated body had completely closed the ear channel. Bill Gentry picked the hateful creature out of my ear with a pair of forceps rescued from the remains of our trampled medical kit.

In an evening council, we decided to withdraw from the Lukuliru. Our time allotted for this safari had almost expired in any event. Our safari output was totally inadequate now, thanks to the devastation by our elephant friends. We loaded what was left of our gear and started back along the tracks we had made three weeks before. As we beat an ignominious retreat from this fabulous country, we were more and more impressed with the animals and their complete lack of fear. We stopped several times during our retreat to dig the trucks out of a bog or out of quicksand. In most places we found it more expedient to cut down trees and build a path around a particularly bad place than to try to skim over the top before we sank in. During these road-building times, I had several hours to examine numerous side canyons and gullies that lay along the sand rivers. Many of these tributaries terminated against a high ash- and sand-packed plateau. Eroding from levels of this plateau were thousands of stone implements, left behind by other hunters tens of thousands of years before our luckless attempt to hunt these regions. These were the tools and weapons of the "man-apes" of Africa.

Scientists had already found and identified these "man-apes" in caves and other sites both north and south of the Selous. The most

Under the African Sun

typical of these tools was the fist ax. All along our route, as we retreated out of the Chirigani, I found fist axes. Ash from the great volcano, Kilimanjaro, which lies to the north, was dispersed among the fist axes or lay in thick layers over them. It has been known for many decades that the "fist-ax men" who came out of Africa invaded Europe and were the first humans there to begin a history of hunting and making and improving their stone tools to better equip themselves to survive.

As I wandered among the evidences of these ancient humans, as we dug and pushed our trucks through the sandrivers of the Selous, my health began to take a turn for the worse. After three days of arduous going, I began to have chills, at first in the early morning, then later, followed by periods of burning fever.

"You're having a blowup of malaria, Old Chap," Bill Gentry assured me. "We all do from time to time."

I had conscientiously taken all the prophylactics for months, as I always did before we went to Africa. Equally meticulously, I had taken prophylactics *after* a safari, in case lingering vestiges of malaria had been left by the injections of mosquitoes that carry this disease.

However, by this time I was so sick I was unable to argue with Bill. By the time our dusty and elephant-ravaged entourage reached the town of Arusha, I was having such violent chills as almost to shake myself out of my cot, and the inevitable fever that followed was burning me up. Bill Gentry had been treating me for malaria with stronger and stronger concoctions of quinine from his own stores, which had escaped the demise of our medical kit. We stopped first at Arusha in Tanganyika. However, the fly-buzzing and ill-equipped hospital discouraged Bill, so we pushed on to Nairobi, Kenya, where they had better facilities. Of that long and dusty drive I remember little, as the chills and fever were getting worse. The doctors and nurses in hospitals at both Arusha and Nairobi continued to pour various mixtures for malaria down my gullet. It had been five days since the malaria had struck. I had not eaten during all of this time.

In malaria attacks of this intensity, the brain gives up. I do remember having a thought or two as to why anyone would go through all these hazards and happenings just to get a couple of elephant tusks that weighed over a hundred pounds. Unchecked malaria usually goes into Blackwater Fever. I heard afterward that I was out of my head. My incoherent remarks were filled with references to the fist-ax men not being able to find the big-footed elephant.

The Next-to-the-Last Safari

At this critical juncture, a British physician happened through the Nairobi hospital on a casual visit. He was an expert on tropical diseases.

"Show me this man who has the incurable malaria," he said when someone told him an American was dying of Blackwater Fever.

The doctor examined me quickly.

"This man doesn't have malaria. He probably has tick fever. It is curable with antibiotics."

The doctor whipped out his prescription pad and scribbled something hastily on the sheet.

"Here, give him some of this and do not waste even a minute."

By the next day my head had cleared. By the second day the chills and fever were gone and I was actually hungry. Friends in Nairobi, who had visited me during this time, said that I looked even worse than a survivor of the Dachau death camp.

By the time I had some meat back on my bones and my eyes were not so deep-sunken, I had done a lot of thinking about the Selous and our disastrous attempts to find the monstrous elephant. I decided then and there in that drab, cheerless hospital room that I would go to the Selous again. It was thirty-odd years before I did so.

So it was that I sought Don Pedro. He now had permission to hunt in the southern Selous from the Game and Fish Department of the new government in Dar es Salaam, which now called the country Tanzania.

Marilyn was with me as we got into our little chartered plane at the Dar es Salaam airport. She had not been with me during my first attempt in the northern Selous, when I was done in by a tiny tick.

Many changes had taken place in the Selous during the previous thirty years, and in all of Africa, for that matter. The new Tanzanian government wanted to make as much revenue as possible, so they declared the country open to all kinds of hunting. They sold concessions to various professional hunters who wanted to establish a territory and take in serious sportsmen who wanted to hunt really virgin country.

My old friend, Don Pedro, had teamed up with Girard Pasinisi, who had leased the whole southern end of the Selous, which joins the Mozambique border. Some years before our arrival, they had flown in equipment and established an airstrip on the Mbarangandu River at an old abandoned village called Mkuyu, which dated back to German times. From here they had bulldozed and scraped tracks that would accommodate a hunting car or a light truck from Mkuyu

sand under a cutbank. She held her head at a regal angle, her ears forward, as she glared at us with green eyes. Her enormous paws were crossed in front of her. To one side of her were three month-old kittens in a single line, each trying to look as regal as their mother. Only as we came very close did the lioness rise to her feet with dignity and call to the kittens with a command that sounded like a bird call. She shooed the kittens up the bank and into the bush while I was desperately trying to get a telescopic lens into action.

Later in the afternoon we ran into a large pride of lion consisting of lionesses and cubs of varying ages. Marilyn thought they were the most darling animals she had even seen, but her favorites were the huge lioness and the three little kittens.

Along in the late afternoon, as we neared the Kabaoni camp, the game herds dwindled, then disappeared altogether. Don Pedro pointed over the windshield, which was laid forward on the hood, to a single ivory palm tree in the distance.

"The camp lies on the terrace just behind that tree," he whispered.

Then he pointed left to the other side of the river. "There are the camp elephant," he exclaimed triumphantly. The "camp elephant," I gathered, was a small herd that stayed in this part of the valley. The bull, Don Pedro explained, carried about thirty kilos of ivory in each of his tusks (about sixty-five pounds each). This is a very fair bull by modern standards. However, I was not interested in shooting an elephant on this safari. In fact, I had already made up my mind not to shoot another elephant, no matter how big his tusks were.

In over fifty years of African hunting, I had managed to break the 100-pound barrier three times. One of these, which I shot in Botswana, just barely made the minimum requirement, with 101 pounds in one tusk and 85 pounds in the other, which had been broken off in some elephant fight of long ago. Bill Gentry and I, of course, had failed to find the monster bulls of the Lukuliru Salt Lick.

The elephant fever dies hard. I think the tick fever burned it out of me. In any event, I had not brought a heavy rifle for elephant. Heavy rifle? I hadn't brought *any* rifle! I had a *borrowed* gun!

Just then we saw the wild dogs. There were twelve of them. They stood or lay in the water a couple of hundred yards ahead of us like so many boulders—except there were no boulders in the Mbarangandu, only sand.

The Next-to-the-Last Safari

The African wild dog is smaller than a wolf, with large, rounded ears and a straight muzzle with a nasty set of canine teeth. The dogs are colored black, orangish yellow, and white, looking like a canine version of an alley cat. In spite of the unimpressive appearance of the African wild dog, they have a fearsome reputation. They hunt in packs and usually disable an animal, then eat it alive. They can kill any animal that exists in Africa, including baby elephant and an occasional human. If a human is crippled or sick, he is fair game for the benign-looking African hunting dog. When the wild dogs move in, all other animals move out.

In the old days in Kenya and Tanganyika, every hunter on safari would shoot any wild dog he saw as a matter of custom and good game management. Later on, wild dogs became so scarce they were declared "royal game" and the various game departments forbade shooting any of the dogs in spite of their vicious nature. Even today, they are scarce over most of their very wide range. Later on, we found an even larger pack of wild dogs downriver from Kabaoni Camp. Any way you figured it, these wild dogs were bad news for us.

We discussed the matter that night at supper. The table in the spacious dining "room" was elegantly laid out in the old European manner. Waiters and cooks were dressed in red vests, bow ties, and spotlessly white *jalavas*. All of them wore red fezzes in the Muslim manner. The excellent roast of impala was served with two kinds of French wine. We might have been dining in Paris. In the distance downriver, a lion roared. Another answered from across the valley. A band of baboons, perched for the night in a wild fig tree at the other end of camp, broke into a frenzy of chattering barks.

"There's a leopard that's been trying to get our chickens," Don Pedro explained. "Those apes have probably spotted him."

As we walked to our safari tent on the edge of the compound, we could hear the nightjars calling. Far up the valley, an elephant trumpeted. This was our Africa—the Selous would not let us down. Even when we walked into the shower that night with our torchlight beam before us, and found a gray cobra enjoying the drip of water on the board slats of the shower stall, we were not unduly upset—or, I should say, I was not unduly upset. My wife insisted, ever after this petty incident, that I go with her on "cobra patrol" every time she went to the shower, which was in a grass enclosure behind our tent. We never saw our cobra friend again, but we did see a hyena, either going into the shower or coming out, in the weeks that followed.

The sights were right, the sounds were right. This was going to be a good safari in spite of the wild dogs—but what about that borrowed gun?

The next morning, I tried out the .375 with the funnel-like scope at a prepared target. The shots scattered over an area bigger than my two hands. As I looked through the scope, it reminded me of the range-finder on a WW II howitzer—too big, coarse, and fuzzy in focus. I did my best to stabilize the scope mounting with a section of wire we found in the truck toolbox. Later that morning, it did nothing to bolster my confidence when, about ten miles downriver from camp, I missed a bull hartebeest.

We had had to go that far to get away from the wild dogs. Our plan was to put up four or five leopard baits, as I hoped to get a good lion and a good leopard to complete a study on the big cats that I had started several years before. I handed the .375 to Don Pedro, who made the next two shots with no difficulty. It was a strange gun to Don Pedro also, so what was wrong?

I momentarily forgot about the borrowed rifle when our trackers, Kayai and Pajero, pulled me by the shoulder and whispered the magic word *"simba."* We looked with our binoculars in the direction they pointed. Through the shimmering heat waves dancing over the sand bars, I could barely make out a female hartebeest cowering against the bank. She had no calf.

The wild dogs, I thought. On the river sand crouched a large lioness inching forward on her belly. To one side was another lioness backing her up. The hartebeest had no place to go. We watched in fascination as the two great cats closed in on the hapless hartebeest.

Apparently, the hartebeest was afraid to jump into the bush for fear of greater dangers there, and especially afraid to try to dash past the lion, which cut off escape both up and down the river. As the hartebeest quivered in terror, the lion closed in. One lioness jumped on the head of the victim: the other leaped on top of the hartebeest and bit it through the back of the neck.

The whole broad stretch of the Mbarangandu with its little sand cutbanks and rivulets of water stretched before us for miles. On this great stage we had just witnessed the cosmic play of life and death, which is the heartbeat of Africa. As we moved in closer, the two lion-esses snarled at us, then began to move away. As they went up the brushy bank, two half-grown cubs came out of the grass and moved away with them. The muscles of the hartebeest were still quivering where one of the lion had started to take a bite on the side of the belly.

"We'll use this animal for leopard baits," I remarked cheerfully. "If I can't get them with this miserable rifle, I'll get them another way."

Actually, this fortuitous kill was a help to us financially. The Tanza-nian government, in its widespread attempt to raise money from any source, had placed very stiff trophy fees of several hundred dollars on such animals as the wildebeest, hartebeest, impala, and zebra. Trophy fees on lion and leopard are in the thousands, and the trophy fee on a big elephant, if you *did* find one, was so high that it took away most of the pleasure of the hunt.

In the days that followed, we put up more than a dozen leopard baits over a stretch of twenty-odd miles along the Mbarangandu. Twice during this work, we put up a bait near a small spring about five miles from the main river in a side valley, and again where we found drag marks of a leopard kill at the edge of a meadow. We found, in each instance, that the logical place to hang a leopard bait already had one hanging. One of these, which consisted of the two hindquarters of an impala, looked fairly fresh. Don Pedro instantly commanded the trackers to cut the baits down.

"They should *never* leave old baits like this," Don Pedro growled at the trackers. Who *they* were, we could only guess. I knew other hunters had been here before us, but this was *really* a negative.

After more than a week of hunting, I began to notice another troublesome fact. We'd seen several dozen lion, and even witnessed a kill, but in all that time we had not seen a single male or the tracks of one. I had planned to get a big-maned Selous lion as part of my study of the big cats. I had planned to shoot a buffalo as bait. As we were then about midway through our safari and had not located a male leopard or a male lion, I decided to try for a buffalo. Then I would look for a good place to put it if we found any male lion tracks. The trackers had spotted an extra-large buffalo bull, one of three bulls that hung around a big herd. The herd normally fed and wa-tered about twenty miles down the Mbarangandu at a place where a donga came in from the east, making a long, open valley. Kayai, as he described the horns of the buffalo, demonstrated the width of them on the shaft of his Masai spear. I whistled in excitement.

"If that buffalo was really carrying a head like that, those horns would be more than fifty inches across."

We started early, well before daylight. It would take us more than two hours to grind through the sand and shallow waters of the Mbarangandu to the side valley where that particular bunch of buffalo would probably be just after sunup.

The buffalo did not disappoint us. Kayai spotted the main herd of about a hundred cows and calves just as they were coming out onto the sands of the Mbarangandu. The trackers had said there were three bulls that trailed the main herd. The bull with the 50-inch horns was one of these. Kayai and Pajero circled the cows and stragglers to find the three bulls. We pulled our hunting car under the shade of an overhanging tree close to where the little side valley emptied a trickle of muddy water into the clear rivulets of the Mbarangandu. An hour passed. The main herd was out in the open now, the animals occasionally drinking and switching their long tails to drive off the flies that had followed them out to this sanctuary. Don Pedro signaled to me. We climbed out the far side of the safari car and moved at a crouch up an old elephant trail cut deeply into the riverbank on this side of the valley. There was movement ahead. Three buffalo bulls trotted through the thick brush along a game trail forty or fifty yards ahead of us. Suddenly, they stopped. In the deep shadow of the thick brush, I could hardly make out their bodies. One bull turned toward us, walking a few steps and raising his muzzle.

"It's the big one. Shoot him," Don Pedro whispered, motioning me up beside him. Kayai thrust the .375 into my hand.

"There's still a lot of brush," I hissed in Don Pedro's ear. "Did you put solids in this thing?"

Don Pedro either ignored me or didn't hear me. Again, the gunbearer punched me in the shoulder and pushed the gun under my arm. I thought of jerking back the bolt to check the load, but it would make too much noise. Don Pedro bent over and indicated I should use his back as a gun rest. I didn't like this arrangement, but there was no help for it. During these tense seconds, the bulls had turned to the left and broken into a slow trot in the direction of the main herd.

"The middle one," hissed Don Pedro.

The Next-to-the-Last Safari

I swerved the cross hairs of the ridiculous scope just ahead of the bull's shoulder as he broke into a hacking run. For a fleeting second, again, this scope reminded me of field artillery. I could see the stems and sticks of brush between me and the big buffalo. I pulled off the shot. The buffalo dropped as though pulled down from below. In a second he was up and running again. There was no chance for a second shot. As I pulled open the bolt, I saw the ugly blunt tip of a softnose bullet. Where the buffalo had been, there was now only a little cloud of dust. Just beyond, I could hear the main herd break into a shambling run at the clap of the shot.

Five hours later, Kayai and Pajero came in dragging their spears in dejection. Yes, they had found the wounded buffalo. He was still on his feet. The shot was too far back, and the bullet had hit something and tumbled. Yes, you guessed it, it was *not* the bull with the big horns.

"Never shoot a buffalo with a softnose bullet," Don Pedro was saying as he turned to get into the Land Rover. "That's good for lion. Never shoot through brush at a buffalo."

I can't remember if I said anything as we turned back toward camp, but I certainly was thinking some very sour thoughts and they all centered around a certain "borrowed gun."

As we climbed back into the car, Kayai and Pajero pronounced with finality that our hunt was beset with evil spirits, and the good luck had rolled out the barrel of my gun. I thought of what Andrew Holmberg had told me many years ago: "Never use softnose bullets for a buffalo. Solids will cut through brush and break bone. From whatever angle you shoot, aim for the opposite shoulder and never, never shoot through brush if you can possibly avoid it."

"Sloppy shooting and buffalo don't mix." I can't remember who said this, but it seemed to apply perfectly to this episode.

The next day, after the buffalo debacle, was a day of news and tidings, most of them bad. The major part of the crew had gone down the river to retrieve the buffalo carcass, by now stinking and in good shape, so they could hang up the two halves for lion baits. During the tracking of the wounded buffalo, they had seen the spoor of one large male lion, apparently by himself, where he drank from a small slough near the edge of the river.

I woke up with a headache and a little fever. "Just a touch of malaria," Don Pedro announced. "You'll be fine by tomorrow." 'You'll-be-fine-by-tomorrow' didn't work out. By the next day I was vomiting copiously and seemed to be in the middle of a bout of something or other that was going to curb my activities for the next couple of days.

A runner had come in from a newly established askari camp some thirty miles away on the eastern bank of the Ngenge. It seemed that a group of poachers had crossed the Ngenge two days before and were now in our area. I could not imagine how this group of hardy fellows had come on foot the several hundred miles from the coast.

In spite of the fact that the sale of ivory had been banned several years before, poachers were still a menace. Generally, modern poachers avoid really big elephant. In any event, there are very few of these left. With their modern rifles they shoot medium or young bulls or even cows. They cut the tusks into sections and carry these on their shoulders back the hundreds of miles to the Zanzibar coast. There they sell the precious ivory to unscrupulous Arab traders who smuggle this cargo in their *dhows* past the patrols. The "white gold" is concealed in big jars of dark, wild honey or jars of dates. In India there is a ready market for ivory that can triple or quadruple the profits of the poachers.

Incidentally, we made hundreds of inquiries as to who might have finally found the monster elephant that Bill Gentry and I had hunted unsuccessfully thirty years before. Undoubtedly, these huge tuskers were dead by this time. In one romantic moment, I thought perhaps these greatest of all elephant might have found their way to the "great elephant graveyard," if there is any such place. More practically, they had probably been slaughtered by poachers and their beautiful gigantic tusks cut into billets to be carved into tourist trinkets in India or Hong Kong.

Now, anti-poaching patrols shoot all poachers on sight, and had done so on a number of occasions. The poachers, just to make things equal, shoot any askari who tries to interfere with their illegal activities. I thought the hunting in this area would become even more exciting with the presence of well-armed poachers as part of the game picture.

The runner for the Ngenge camp also asked if he could "borrow" a "nice, fat impala" so they could have some fresh meat. I balked at this. For one thing, we had no "nice, fat impala." Also, we would have to pay the trophy fee on it, which was $700. I also knew that any askari, in uniform on anti-poaching patrol, could shoot one animal per camp per week as a free meat ration. I turned to Don

The Next-to-the-Last Safari

Pedro about this. He interpreted as the pock marked runner spoke in half Swahili and half Arabic.

"The first night of this patrol," the man said, "we killed a bull waterbuck, dressed it, and hung the carcass to ripen in the middle of our camp." As we saw later, their camp consisted of a small building made of rusted sheet iron and closely set poles. This was surrounded by a sort of veranda, roofed over with thatch, where the five men slept.

"We hung the waterbuck in the building," the fellow continued in awed wonder, "yet the leopard walked among us and pulled the waterbuck down and stole it away."

The waterbuck in that area are of the *ellipsiprymnus* variety. They are marked by a white circle that looks like a target on their behinds. A fair-sized *elipseo* bull, even dressed, would weigh three hundred pounds or more. Apparently, the leopard did not consider this meat to be as unpalatable as we had, or the carcass too heavy. The leopard, a large male, had jerked the waterbuck down, carried it half a mile or so, and lifted it up into a dead tree. There the leopard had eaten his fill of the tasty part of the prize, and the vultures had finished the rest.

On the third day of their patrol, the askaris had killed a yearling hartebeest and hung it up in the midst of their crude camp. On the following night, the same male leopard entered stealthily into the camp, pulled down the hartebeest, and carried it off through the midst of the sleeping men. The next morning, as the askaris trailed the drag marks for several hundred yards to where the leopard had left the carcass on a bushy knoll, they found the same sad story. The leopard had eaten his fill, and the vultures and hyenas were just finishing the rest when the askaris came onto the scene.

"He is a very large leopard," the runner continued, "and we are all very hungry for meat." How these two facts were connected, I did not quite comprehend. However, I suggested that we give him our last leopard bait, the front quarters of a small hartebeest. This is the Lichtenstein hartebeest, which, to begin with, is not a big animal. However, the runner seemed grateful as he wrapped the meat in a dirty old rag and threw it over his shoulder. He started back toward the anti-poacher camp just at dusk. I thought he might—carrying that fresh meat through twenty-five or thirty miles of bush country in the dark—experience some very exciting incidents along the way.

297

Under the African Sun

I forgot my aching head and heaving stomach and exclaimed enthusiastically, "We'll get that leopard. At least we know where there is one big, hungry male."

At that moment, another runner came in from the north, carrying in his hand a large folded note stuck in a long, clefted stick. Don Pedro received the note and read it gravely. I noticed that the high-quality paper had a letterhead and a crest.

"His Highness has invited us to join him at dinner the night after next. We may hunt with him afterward, if we wish." A postscript added that His Highness had just bagged an elephant with 37 kilos of ivory on a side, the best of his present series.

"His Highness is hunting elephant at the fly-camp!" I fairly exploded at Don Pedro. "Who is 'His Highness'?"

"I'll tell you at dinner," he stated quietly as he turned away. I had the distinct feeling that he had dreaded this moment since we had first left Dar es Salaam.

The dinner that evening was not an outstanding success. The drinks tasted sour, and the ground nuts had weevils. The weevils may have been a figment of my malaria-disturbed mind at the time, and Don Pedro's monotone did nothing to lower my fever.

"You are one of my oldest friends," he began. "I knew you in the old days before the wars. You hunted with my father, and with José Ruiz, who was my 'second father,' but when the Prince came, what could I do? He has hunted here before. He flew in from the Persian Gulf in his own jet airplane."

I made a mental note that the next time *I* had several million dollars rattling around in the old cash box, *I* would get a Lear jet, or something comparable, and fly into Dar es Salaam in style. I wasn't going to let any "down-the-country" Arabian Prince upstage me! I, *also*, had been to the Selous before.

"The Prince has six licenses," Don Pedro continued, "and he has shot them all as he wishes to build a new trophy room in his palace."

By the time my wife and I had stumbled up the dark path to our safari tent at the far edge of the compound, I was spitting with indignation. It had turned out that the Prince had shot six big lion, six leopard, and six elephant at Kabaoni camp just before we had arrived. Figuring in the baits, that had certainly been required to get the big cats, there had been a lot of Arabian mischief in the neighborhood in the last few months.

The Next-to-the-Last Safari

The next day my malaria (or whatever it was) was worse. Don Pedro urged me to stay on my cot. I refused. Out of sheer cussedness, I determined to go and see the sign of the big leopard on the Ngenge. On the long trip over, I enlivened the conversation with sharply worded remarks and expletives concerning a game outfit that would allow *one* man to buy *six* licenses, no matter who he was. Even the trackers and safari boys felt we'd been sold out.

We arrived at the askari camp and, surprisingly, did not find the body of the man who had carried the meat along this same road the night before. As a matter of fact, as we arrived at the miserable camp, the men thanked us profusely for the fresh meat. There must have been barely enough to go around, for the shoulders and rib cage of a rather small hartebeest do not contain much meat. Apparently, the askaris were not on patrol that day, as they all trooped out to show me the leopard tracks. A couple of hundred yards down the Ngenge was an open pool of water. As we approached, there was a splashing in the pool. A plume of white water shot up. We approached cautiously along the bank. As we peeped over a fringe of papyrus, we spied a man bathing in the pool. He threw himself this way and that, tossing up jets of water in sheer exuberance. He was stark naked. The bather turned out to be Sergeant Argonti, the chief of the anti-poaching patrol. He was a magnificent specimen—light bronze in color, beautifully muscled. He approached us gravely (still naked). My wife was a little round-eyed at the informality of the occasion. She said afterward that one of the reasons she liked Africa so well was because of the ingenuousness of the African men, especially those in authority such as askari sergeants and chiefs we had met.

Sergeant Argonti showed us the track of the leopard, which had watered at the very pool where he had been bathing. It was a gigantic track, as large as that of a lioness. Under ordinary circumstances, no leopard would water at a place used regularly by humans. However, this leopard seemed to have a contempt for people, especially if they were asleep. In the northern Selous, leopard had twice occupied blinds that we had carefully prepared. If the leopard gets in the blind first, then what? This particular leopard at the askaris' camp seemed to have an even more peculiar attitude toward humans.

Ordinarily, a leopard is as shy as a schoolgirl. In places, I had found that the leopard would eat only certain kinds of meat. I'd even found some leopards that attack the bait only if it was alive, such as a tethered goat. When wounded, the leopard will attack 100 percent of the time. I had never met a professional hunter, who had been in the business very long, who had not been mauled by a leopard. Every leopard is different. This particular male, a very successful thief, considered a large piece of meat surrounded by sleeping men only a challenge to his cunning.

Frankly, I am fascinated by leopard. I have hunted the Old World leopard from Mongolia through India, Iran, and in most of the countries in Africa. In a lifetime of leopard encounters, I have faced perhaps a hundred in Africa and India, usually over a bait or a kill, and I have never found two leopard that act the same way. I consider the leopard the most intelligent of all the great cats, with the possible exception of the Bengal tiger. Someday I'm going to write a book just about leopard, but as of yet I do not have enough information.

"Let's go look farther down the river," I suggested for lack of any better idea. The Mbarangandu had no quicksand. The Ngenge had a lot of it. In the mile or so downriver from the askari camp, we found two patches of quicksand, one with a dead buffalo in it. We skirted these along the bank, following an old elephant trail. About a mile-and-a-half down the Ngenge was a large pool beneath the west bank, fringed by papyrus. In the pool was one disgruntled old hippo with fresh scars all over his shoulders where some other bull had carved hunks of skin and meat off his rival. In one place, a diamond-shaped flap of skin hung down like the dejected ear of a cringing hound. Around the pool, in the sand of the Ngenge, and all the way across to the opposite bank were hundreds of leopard tracks. This leopard, also a large male, had been back and forth to the pool, day and night for weeks or even months. Our trackers spread out over the riverbed. They argued as to whether or not this was the same male that had stolen the meat from their camp. They finally decided it was the "thief leopard."

I managed to hobble to the far side of the river (we were still afraid of quicksand). A game trail led up the brushy bank. This the leopard had used several times. I picked a lone tree that hung out over the sand. "We'll hang a full bait here," I told Don Pedro. Unfortunately, the only good place for a blind was a hundred yards away where a small stone ledge stood out from the riverbank. This

The Next-to-the-Last Safari

was a bit far from the bait, especially for shooting in poor light. But there was no other way we could arrange the blind so as to see the leopard against the setting sun.

All these uncertainties and calculations seemed to have exhausted my fever-racked body. "We'll build the finest blind we possibly can," I pronounced in a voice as authoritative as I could muster at that time. "Put it as far east as possible so there will be some light to shoot."

On the way back to the askari camp, I was deathly sick again. A runner from our own camp awaited us there. "The poachers have killed our camp elephant," he blurted out, "and chopped out the tusks. No one heard the shots."

On the way back to Kabaoni camp, across the high plateau, Don Pedro assured me that he would build the leopard blind just as I had directed. Sergeant Argonti practically demanded that we join his forces to track down the poachers. I thought at the time that this might be a little too exciting, especially as the poachers were well-armed and un-doubtedly would shoot back. After all, the most exciting game is man himself, especially if he is armed as well as you are. Too, I had my wife with me. At any event, the malaria decided the issue for me.

I was desperately sick for the next two days. My wife finally decided I should take a full course of antibiotics. Whatever my malady was, it yielded to the new drugs. By the third day, I was coherent and sitting up. Don Pedro came past in the evening to assure me that they had finished my blind just as I had planned it. They had hung a whole waterbuck from the bait tree, and on the second night, the big leopard had come to the bait tree and climbed out on the limb. The marks where his curved claws had dug into the tree were plain to see, but he did not eat. He jumped down, crossed over to the hippo pool and drank, then vanished. Don Pedro added, as an afterthought, "The askaris found the poachers' camp, but not the poachers."

"If you have time, shoot a zebra. We'll take it over to the askari camp," I directed Don Pedro. I suppose I thought that this would compensate in some measure for my not going on "poacher patrol" myself, although the trophy fee for a Burchell zebra was $800.

I was still wobbly the next day as we loaded the zebra and started out for the Ngenge. As he had twice before, Don Pedro offered to loan me one of his two guns. I noticed even then that there was a little hesitancy in his manner. In any case, if I borrowed

301

a second gun, it would only compound my own confusion and code of ethics. I would shoot the leopard with that bell-mouthed .375 as a form of self-discipline.

When we arrived at the askari camp, it was empty except for the cook. He told us excitedly that the patrol had caught up with the poachers and they had had a running sniper's battle. They had wounded one man and had recovered one tusk of the poached elephant. I left instructions for the cook to skin the zebra and save the skin for me. He thanked me profusely for the meat. The yellow fat and horselike meat of the zebra are an especial delicacy to the tribes in this area.

By the time I had settled into the blind, my head was spinning and I felt nauseated. The blind itself was a work of art. Don Pedro had done himself proud. They had prepared a folding armchair for me with an aperture for the gun barrel at just the right height. I enlarged it to accommodate the awkward bell-mouthed scope on top of my rifle. I pushed in a piece of wire to steady the mount. I had discovered that if I pushed it firmly from the back into place, the scope was on target, or as close as this miserable gun could be. I directed Kayai to lash a thick branch beneath my elbow. In this way I could turn the rifle and the scope toward the carcass of the water-buck. I noticed as I adjusted the rifle that half of the belly of this bait had been eaten—a good sign. I readjusted the rifle and the twigs and grass around it. Looking through the huge scope, the calibrated cross hairs were centered exactly where a big leopard would be as he crouched on the limb above the bait. "At least this thing gathers a lot of light," I remarked disgustedly.

During my illness I had developed a hacking cough. One cough in the middle of the silent African night would end this leopard hunt. As a substitute medicine, I'd brought three bottles of a vile orange drink that the camp boys used. I nestled these in the grass at my feet so they would not clank together. From time to time, when I felt a cough coming on I took a swig of this horrid stuff, now warm from the hot African sun. It was so vile that it tasted like the best cough syrup I had ever had.

Don Pedro crouched at my side on a cushion before his own peephole, which he had prepared carefully. He had his binoculars, but no rifle. This show of confidence did wonders for my morale.

My wife, in the safari car, drove off down the river several hundred yards to await our signal.

The Next-to-the-Last Safari

We waited. I've done this on hundreds of occasions in the past. Some of my best thinking has been done in a leopard blind. It gives you a chance to enjoy Africa. There was absolutely no wind. Over across the river, I heard some ground hornbills, thumping and bumping in their sunset ritual. A flock of green pigeons landed in the trees over our heads, then flew across to water in one of the river's pools. A lion roared in the far distance. Then absolute silence.

When the African stars come out, they are a wonder to behold. There is no smoke or smog to obscure them or to dim their beauty, as in the civilized parts of our planet. In central Africa the Deity himself hangs out every star. They were in unfamiliar patterns compared to the ones at home, and there were millions more of them. As our blind was oriented toward the west, the Southern Cross was off to my left.

Suddenly, a leopard called. The birdlike cry came from over by the hippo pool across the river. Don Pedro looked at his luminous watch. It was eight o'clock.

By 10 P.M. the leopard had not come. All vestige of the sunset had dwindled away. There was absolutely no light. My "cough syrup" was gone. My bad leg had begun to stiffen. I leaned over. "Ten more minutes," I whispered into Don Pedro's ear. Don Pedro nodded.

We were finished. I'd been on dozens of aborted leopard hunts in the past, but this one was especially bitter. It was the last day of our safari in the Mbarangandu country.

Don Pedro clutched my thigh with iron fingers. "He comes." I could hear nothing. I could see nothing. I thought Don Pedro must be pulling my leg—almost literally. Then I heard it. It was the soft call of a leopard, and it was very close. I thought maybe the old boy had got himself a female, in which case he wouldn't come to the bait at all.

There was a scratching sound. I imagined I could hear an animal panting softly. Then there was the rasping sound of curved claws digging into bark. "He's climbing," Don Pedro exclaimed. "There he is!"

I turned the rifle slightly and peered through the scope. I could see nothing. Absolutely nothing. Don Pedro clutched my shoulder. *Shoot,* he begged. I stared intently through the huge scope as though by sheer force of will I could draw forth a cat image. There was nothing—absolutely nothing. "Wait," I whispered.

I could make out the shadow of the waterbuck or what was left of it. Above that shadow was another shadow. The shadow dipped and changed shape. I could barely make out the head. The leopard was squatting above the bait, then reaching down and tearing out great hunks of the waterbuck's belly. I could just make out his shoulder as he moved again. I moved the cross hairs of the gigantic scope to just behind his shoulder. There I could see the line of his back. I put the cross hairs lower and pulled off the shot.

The noise of the .375 in that silent place sounded like a five-inch gun. I saw the shadow-leopard fall, then cling upside-down below the body of the waterbuck. Then he dropped, as cats do, onto his feet.

Don Pedro was pounding me on my back in congratulations. "I'm afraid the shot was not well-placed," I said as I got up stiffly. The thought of a wounded leopard in all that blackness made me hesitate. Both legs and my bottom had gone to sleep during that long ordeal, so I walked slowly out the rear of the blind.

At that moment my wife and the safari boys drove up. She cried out, "Did you get him? We knew you did because there was only one shot." I didn't follow this logic, but we walked hesitantly forward together with the safari crew scattered behind us. Don Pedro, more confident than I, ran forward unarmed to the clump of grass below the bait tree. He grasped a long tail with a white tip and jerked it forward. The big body of the leopard slid out of the grass. He was stone-dead.

On the way back to the Kabaoni, at the top of the plateau, the driver stopped the car. All the boys got out with their *pangas* and began to chop off slender tree limbs and small bushes. These they tucked around in various places on the safari car where they would stand upright and form a sort of moving blind. They also tied additional branches onto both sides of the hood and around the headlights. They held the leopard on their shoulders above the car as though the animal were still alive. They lighted torches, which caused grotesque shadows to dance on the road before us. Someone fired three shots in deliberate succession. Three shots answered from the camp below. In ten minutes we had wound down the track to camp, everyone chanting an ancient hunting song. As we drove into camp, all was bedlam. The cooks and the camp boys were putting on the Hunting Dance. This ritual, I found out later, was to celebrate the death of a major, dangerous animal. This dance, and the party that followed, lasted until dawn. My wife and I did not. The askaris and gunbearers lifted me bodily out of the safari car and carried me in triumph into the dining room. As I weigh a good two hundred pounds, they soon tired of this part of the ceremony. As the leopard did not weigh nearly as much as I, they soon picked him up instead and danced with him around the huge campfire that had been lighted in front of the dining "room" on the riverbank. The whole scene might have come from a tableau of a thousand years ago in this same place, except for an occasional rifle barrel that gleamed in the firelight and a cartridge belt that Kayai carried over his shoulder.

The next day, as we drove back up the river to the airfield to end our safari, we passed the carcass of the hapless elephant only a mile or so above camp. The poachers had shot the luckless bull in the middle of the river as he drank. What had been a beautiful and vibrant elephant was now a sodden and shapeless mound covered with squabbling vultures and their excrement. We stopped our safari car some distance from this heart-rending scene. The stench was almost unbearable. The gunbearer pulled my shoulder and pointed. A long file of elephant was just emerging from the forest to our left. A stately looking cow with slender tusks led the procession. She had a tiny baby before her. The elephant turned in order to avoid the stinking carcass, which now fouled the river. The baby elephant darted from between his mother's legs toward the carcass. The matriarch mother stepped forward quickly and curled her huge trunk around the baby's bottom and boosted him upriver in the opposite direction.

Would we ever come to the Selous again? "You bet. If we can manage it," I told Don Pedro by my side.

My wife remarked, as we looked at the scene before us, "This is Africa. Here are life and death together."

Yes, we will come again to the Selous.